Praise for *The Strange Career of William Ellis*

"Elegantly written . . . fascinating." —*San Francisco Chronicle*

"[Jacoby] presents Ellis' intriguing story. . . . Equally intriguing is the history of the post–Civil War Texas-Mexican borderland. Jacoby's book may well have you searching his bibliography for books on that subject." —*St. Louis Post-Dispatch*

"A work of admirable sleuthing. . . . Jacoby has assembled a portrait of a man who deliberately sought to cover his own tracks." —*The Nation*

"A masterpiece of border history. Jacoby has a biographer's eye for detail and a detective's talent for discovery, which he deftly uses to construct both the inner emotional life and the larger social world of his subject. At once a history of the United States and of Mexico, *Strange Career* offers a truly transnational history. Today, as borders are simultaneously being dissolved and hardened, Jacoby's study of Ellis's exceptional career is as timely as it is compelling."
—Greg Grandin, author of
Empire of Necessity and *Fordlandia*

"William Ellis was a chameleon, a trickster, and a man determined to shape his own identity. With enormous skill, Karl Jacoby uncovers this tremendous subject, crafting a powerful new narrative about the porous borders of class, race, and national identity in late nineteenth- and early twentieth-century American life. Jacoby demonstrates how one man's life can help us understand the past in an entirely new way."
—Martha A. Sandweiss, professor of history
at Princeton University and author of *Passing Strange:
A Gilded Age Tale of Love and Deception across the Color Line*

"*The Strange Career of William Ellis* takes an unexpected or little-known subject and, with great insight and imagination, uses it to shed new light on our larger past. [Jacoby] has excavated a life that began in obscurity and was ever being reinvented, and, in so doing, offers a deep understanding of the shifting boundaries of place, race, and social standing. An extraordinary story told with extraordinary skill."
—Steven Hahn, Pulitzer Prize–winning
author of *A Nation under Our Feet*

"Karl Jacoby is a masterful storyteller. Skillfully drawing on new technology and methods of scholarship, he recovers Ellis's elusive life and paints a rich, complex, and revelatory portrait of the fluid concept of race." —Allyson Hobbs, author of *A Chosen Exile:*
A History of Racial Passing in American Life

"Karl Jacoby is a stellar researcher. . . . [Ellis's life is] an important slice of American history." —*Dallas Morning News*

"This stranger-than-fiction biography . . . poses fascinating questions about race and class." —*Texas Monthly*

"Jacoby [is] a smart and eloquent writer." —*Literary Review*

"Jacoby's masterly writing places race and its meaning at the center of this essential work. Readers will gain fresh insight into life during Reconstruction as well as the riddle of racial identities."
—*Library Journal* (starred review)

"A cracking good story." —*Booklist*

"Vivid and lyrical. . . . Jacoby emphasizes Ellis's individual achievements as well as his adroit manipulation of Gilded Age America's confused and contradictory ideas about race." —*Publishers Weekly*

"An amazing tale that is indeed 'almost too strange to be true.'"
—*Kirkus Reviews*

THE
STRANGE CAREER
OF
WILLIAM ELLIS

THE
STRANGE CAREER
OF
WILLIAM ELLIS

THE *TEXAS SLAVE*

WHO BECAME A

MEXICAN MILLIONAIRE

KARL JACOBY

W. W. Norton & Company • NEW YORK • LONDON
INDEPENDENT PUBLISHERS SINCE 1923

For information about permission to reproduce selections from
this book, write to Permissions, W. W. Norton & Company, Inc.,
500 Fifth Avenue, New York, NY 10110

For information about special discounts for bulk
purchases, please contact W. W. Norton Special Sales at
specialsales@wwnorton.com or 800-233-4830

Manufacturing by LSC Harrisonburg
Book design by Brooke Koven
Production manager: Anna Oler

ISBN 978-0-393-35417-1 pbk.

W. W. Norton & Company, Inc.
500 Fifth Avenue, New York, N.Y. 10110
www.wwnorton.com

W. W. Norton & Company Ltd.
15 Carlisle Street, London W1D 3BS

3 4 5 6 7 8 9 0

To the memory of Christopher Ellis Alvarez

Que en paz descanses en tu propia isla

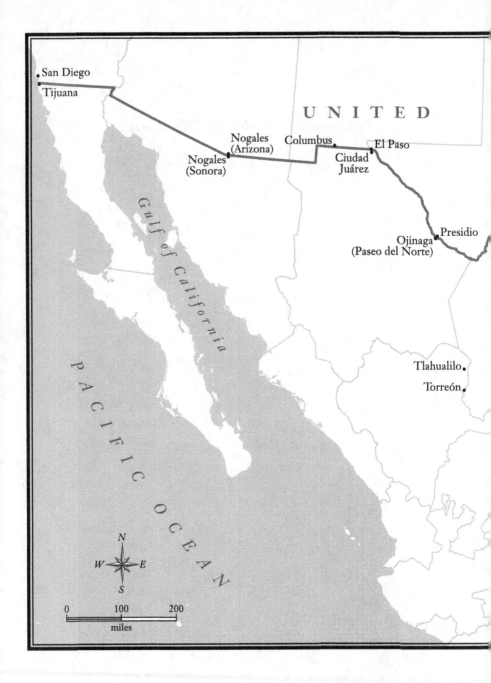

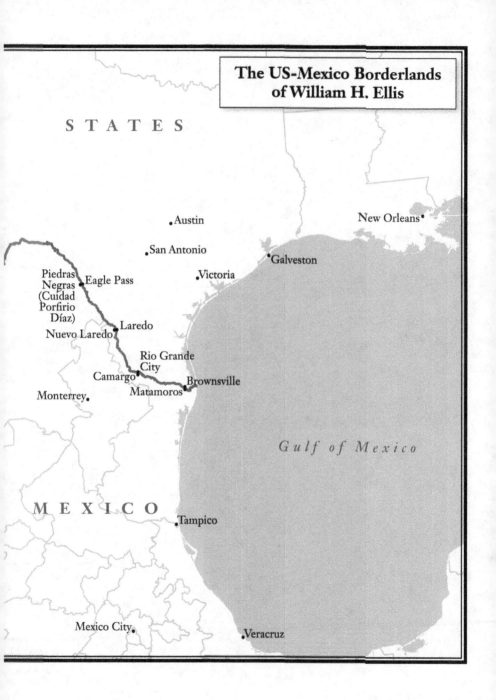

The US-Mexico Borderlands
of William H. Ellis

STATES

•Austin

•San Antonio

New Orleans•

•Galveston

Piedras Negras (Ciudad Porfirio Díaz) Eagle Pass

•Victoria

Laredo

Nuevo Laredo

Rio Grande City

Camargo

Brownsville

Monterrey•

Matamoros

Gulf of Mexico

M E X I C O   •Tampico

Mexico City•

•Veracruz

CONTENTS

Illustrations follow page 98.

Why should the world be over-wise,
In counting all our tears and sighs?
Nay, let them only see us, while
We wear the mask.

—PAUL LAURENCE DUNBAR

Uno vive durante el día una autobiografía
que escribe en las noches previas.

—PACO IGNACIO TAIBO II

To survive the Borderlands
you must live sin fronteras
be a crossroads.

—GLORIA ANZALDÚA

Prologue

THROUGH HISTORY'S CRACKS

IN 1909, the fastest way to make the three-thousand-mile journey from Mexico City to Manhattan was via the Ferrocarriles Nacionales de México's *Aztec Limited*. New York–bound passengers boarded the train in the evening at Buenavista Station, located just a short streetcar ride away from the Mexican capital's bustling central plazas. After picking their way through the vendors who thronged the station, offering everything from newspapers to tamales, ticketholders settled into all the comforts that first-class travel at the dawn of the twentieth century could provide: fully stocked library, smoking room, buffet car serving multicourse meals, and Pullman sleepers with private compartments and beds. As the train steamed its way north, and night gave way to the first light of a new day, the vista rolling by the windows slowly began to shift. In place of colonial cities with baroque cathedrals and cobblestone streets, passengers could glimpse haciendas with lowing herds of cattle and long rows of agave plants, then the dusty, far-flung villages, rugged mountains, and forbidding deserts of the Mexican North.

Near noon on their third day aboard the *Aztec Limited*, travelers reached the international borderline. Here, the twin settlements of Ciudad Porfirio Díaz and Eagle Pass faced one another across the river known alternatively as the Rio Grande and the Río Bravo del Norte, depending on whether one followed US or Mexican practice. Despite such squabbles over terminology, for much of the nineteenth century, the residents of these isolated communities had interacted more with one another than with the outside world, shuttling back and forth across the shallow, blue-green waters dividing their respective nations via a flat-bottomed ferry. With the coming of the railroad in 1882, however, this venerable ferry service found itself supplanted by the new iron bridge that enabled that marvel of the industrial age, the steam-powered engine, to complete the journey from Mexico to the United States in just a few revolutions of its piston-driven wheels. The railroad remade the geography of Eagle Pass and other border towns along the Rio Bravo del Norte such as Laredo and El Paso in other ways, too. Almost overnight, these remote outposts at the periphery of the nation were transformed, in the language of the day, to "gateways" between North America's two "sister republics."

For the passengers aboard the *Aztec Limited,* crossing the border was at once routine yet momentous. After the train journeyed across the bridge spanning the Rio Grande and pulled into the one-story depot on the eastern edge of Eagle Pass, agents of the recently created US Department of Commerce and Labor, dressed in their regulation dark blue uniforms with brass buttons, climbed aboard to inspect the passengers and their luggage. Agents evinced no interest in narcotics like heroin, marijuana, or cocaine—all legal in 1909—but sought instead imported delicacies: in an era of high tariffs and no income tax, the federal government raised the bulk of its revenue through duties on luxuries such as lace, silk, jewels, watches, and cigars.

Next, in a measure that spoke volumes as to the border's role in establishing personal identity as well as national territory, these same agents compiled a "report of inspection" on all incoming passengers, detailing each arrival's name, place of birth, occupation, and final destination. The United States would not require passports until 1914, so rather than focusing on reading one's documents, this procedure hinged instead on reading, as it were, one's person: determining the truth of an individual's stated identity through language, dress, physical traits, and other clues. On ordinary passenger trains, agents exercised particular vigilance against Chinese or Japanese laborers—

who in an effort to evade the United States' restrictions on Asians often disguised themselves as Mexicans—as well as immigrants considered "anarchists," "paupers likely to become public charges," or the possessors of "loathsome or dangerous" diseases. But on a luxury train like the *Aztec Limited*, catering to well-to-do businessmen and upper-class tourists, agents more often than not took individuals' declarations of identity at face value.

On the morning of March 14, 1909, however, a tall man with penetrating brown eyes and carefully groomed mustache, attired in the latest fashion—spats, top hat, tailored three-piece suit, gold watch chain and jeweled fob draped across a powerful barrel chest—caught the eye of authorities in Eagle Pass. Like the others on the *Aztec Limited*, the passenger had begun his journey from Mexico City in a first-class Pullman. Once he crossed the border into the United States, however, a new question arose. What race was he? For despite his elegant appearance, his skin had a somewhat swarthy tone—and, unlike Mexico, the Texas of 1909 possessed segregation laws, designed to limit contact between blacks and whites in everything from schools, restaurants, libraries, graveyards, and hotels to railroad cars.

When asked, the newcomer insisted that he was a Mexican entrepreneur, on his way back to his office on Wall Street after negotiating the purchase of several rubber plantations in his homeland. His name, he offered, was Guillermo Enrique Eliseo—which, for those who might have trouble with foreign pronunciations, could be translated into English as William Henry Ellis. Moreover, as an ethnic Mexican, he was legally white and not subject to Texas's segregation statutes.

At least a few on the train, however, had caught wind of half-whispered rumors circulating along the border that, for all his obvious wealth and sophistication, Eliseo might not be the well-to-do Mexican he claimed to be. Could it be that his olive complexion was a product not of a Hispanic background but rather of a covert African American one? Dismissing such assertions, Eliseo refused the conductors' attempts to relocate him to the "negro coach" after the *Aztec Limited* reached US soil. Only once the train crew summoned the local sheriff, charged with enforcing Texas's segregation statutes, did Eliseo grudgingly oblige—but not before vowing to all within earshot that he would spend hundreds of thousands of dollars, if necessary, to sue the railway for the humiliation of forcing him to ride in the "Jim Crow" car.

———

WHO WAS GUILLERMO Enrique Eliseo? Such was the question many found themselves asking at the turn of the last century as this dapper yet enigmatic figure flitted in and out of an astonishing array of the era's most noteworthy events—scandalous trials, unexpected disappearances, diplomatic controversies—most linked in one way or another to Latin America. Uncertainties about his ethnicity did not confine themselves to his 1909 border crossing at Eagle Pass. During his years in the public eye, commentators proffered a kaleidoscope of possibilities. The *New York World* observed that Eliseo "has the looks and dash of a Spaniard and speaks several languages." Denver's *Evening Post* asserted that Eliseo was a "wealthy Mexican"—in fact, "without doubt the wealthiest resident of the City of Mexico." Others maintained that he was "of Hawaiian blood" or "a Cuban gentleman of high degree." Editors at the *Kansas City Star*, however, cautioned that "the stories of his Hawaiian ancestry are not to be credited," while an equally suspicious correspondent to the *Baltimore Sun* discounted the rumors that Eliseo was of "Cuban, Brazilian, Mexican and no one knows what other Latin-American extraction." Concluded the *New York Sun*: "Just where [Eliseo] came from no one hereabouts seems to know."

My introduction to the riddle of Guillermo Eliseo and what contemporaries termed "his life of romance and adventure" came through the records of the US State Department. Reading through old consuls' reports from Mexico, I stumbled across a long-forgotten diplomatic exchange from the 1890s concerning Eliseo's attempt to resettle thousands of African Americans on Mexican haciendas. Many in the United States and Mexico alike believed that this effort presaged a mass migration of Southern blacks to Mexico, setting in motion a reconfiguration of labor conditions and race relations that would have dramatic consequences for both nations. As officials struggled to make sense of a movement that seemed to emerge out of nowhere, they wondered most of all about the elusive individual behind this audacious scheme. With little more to go on than mere conjecture, however, the State Department's investigations soon trailed off, leaving most of the puzzles connected to Eliseo unanswered.

Faced with a century-old mystery, one that conjured up a borderlands rife with mistaken identities, outrageous rumors, and unexpected migrations from North to South, I resolved to unravel Eliseo's story myself. I soon found, however, that over time this once-famous figure had slipped through the cracks of history into oblivion. Eliseo's efforts to obscure his background had, it seems, succeeded all too well. "Mystery," observed the *Los Angeles Times* in 1904, "hides the greater part of [his] life history." The truths, half-truths, and outright fabrications swirling around him frustrated most attempts to write a study of him, and in at least one case, family members, anxious to avoid being linked to such a disruptive character, apparently destroyed papers relating to him. But Eliseo also slipped through the fault lines that run through our ways of imagining the past. Because the historical discipline and nationalism have often worked hand in hand, the US-Mexico border divides not only two nations but also two historiographical traditions. Even today, most everything that happens north of the border is considered American history, while everything occurring south of the border remains Latin American history. The creation of two such separate containers means that those who move between the United States and Mexico like Eliseo tend to elude historians, their experiences falling through the artificial partitions we impose on the past.

Nor is the US-Mexico border the only peculiar divide that Eliseo's story straddles: he likewise slipped through the fissures between the fast-evolving fields of African American and Mexican American history. Over the last few decades, both of these subjects have been fundamental to enriching our portrait of the past, especially Americans' complicated, contradictory relationship to the concept of race. Yet to date the two fields have experienced little cross-fertilization. Those few books that do look at the interactions between African Americans and Mexican Americans tend to focus on twentieth-century tensions between the two groups around such issues as whiteness and US citizenship rather than excavate the longer history of shared interactions and ethnic intermingling that Eliseo's experience brings to light, let alone explore Mexican ideas of blackness or the space that Mexico occupied in the African American imagination.

Not so long ago, such conditions would have ensured that the history of a figure like Eliseo remained all but irrecoverable. New methods of digital scholarship, however, made it possible to comb archives around the world for stray scraps of evidence connected to Eliseo and his various alter egos in a way that would have been inconceivable only a few years before. Likewise, powerful new Web-based genealogical tools facilitated the tracking of Eliseo's extended family, leading me to relatives in the United States and later Mexico, who possessed a wealth of family stories, papers, and photos relating to their astonishing ancestor. By an odd twist of fate, indicative of the invisible web of circumstance surrounding any historical project, the first members of Eliseo's family that I located lived just blocks from my former address in Los Angeles. Amid our day-to-day routines, we had passed one another without ever realizing our mutual interest in the mysterious Guillermo Eliseo.

The story that these various documents allowed me to piece together was almost too strange to be true. Gilded Age claims that Eliseo's climb to prominence read "like a fairy tale" were in fact far more accurate than their proponents ever imagined. The man known as Guillermo Enrique Eliseo, rumored to be the fabulously wealthy owner of countless Latin American mines and haciendas had, it turns out, begun life in one of the most marginal positions imaginable: as an enslaved African American named William Henry Ellis, born amid the sweltering cotton plantations of South Texas. With the coming of emancipation, he engaged in a virtuoso act of self-invention that, through the adoption of a variety of alternative personas, propelled him far from his birthplace to New York, Mexico City, London, Ethiopia, and beyond.

To travel so far, Ellis needed to cross many boundaries, for his world, like ours, was one of borders. Among the most fundamental barriers he confronted was the color line. Slavery's end in 1865 had liberated Ellis and four million other enslaved African Americans. But out of slavery's ashes there arose an increasingly rigid system of segregation, designed to demarcate whites from blacks and confine the latter to a second-class status. Ellis also had to cross—at times simultaneously, as his experience at Eagle Pass reveals—the evolving borderline between the United States and Mexico. Ellis's journey to adulthood took place as the US-Mexico borderland transitioned, as the historian Friedrich Katz once observed, from a frontier to a border: from a lightly populated, loosely controlled periphery to an increasingly important site for trade and resource extraction for both nations. This process, however, unleashed a storm of countervailing pressures. Economic integration was set against the heightened desire by each nation to police the flow of peoples, goods, and ideas from the other side. The United States' fears of an unstable southern neighbor vied with Mexico's concerns about American desires to annex Mexican territory. Under such conditions, Ellis's movement between the two nations required not only the ability to be fluent in two languages; it necessitated uncommon proficiency at translating between the economics, politics, and cultures of each country as well.

As skilled as he was in such transactions, Ellis's greatest gift lay in identifying—and, more often than not, exploiting—the unexpected porousness of the color line and the borderline. Both boundaries masqueraded as natural and inevitable, but their rigid exteriors masked unstable, uncertain cores. Race had only solidified as a concept in the nineteenth century, and it remained unclear how it should be determined. Appearance? Behavior? Social standing? Ancestry? What happened when, say, appearance was ambiguous? Social standing ambivalent? When ancestry combined several supposed races? Much as there were no clear-cut races, there were also no self-contained nations. Ecologies, family ties, trade relations: all flowed across the carefully mapped geographic boundaries that nation-states—like race, an invention of the nineteenth century—drew around themselves.

In theory, the color line and the borderline complemented one another, ensuring that all people were in their place and all places had a people. Even as a young man, however, Ellis had come to discern how each boundary could undermine rather than buttress the other. Race was supposed to be a biological fact, but it ultimately fell to government officials to sort human beings into distinct races and patrol the boundaries between these invented categories. The results only made the subjective character of race all the more apparent, for one nation might impose a strikingly divergent racial system from another. The African American writer Langston Hughes witnessed firsthand the transformative effect the border could have on race relations when he ventured into Mexico in the early 1900s: "It was strange to find that just by stepping across an invisible line into Mexico, a Negro could buy a beer in any bar, sit anywhere in the movies, or eat in any restaurant, so suddenly did Jim Crow disappear."

Designed to delineate and control, the color line and the borderline laid bare their era's deepest anxieties. The more whites in the United States tried to separate the races, the more they fretted that African Americans might elude segregation altogether by "passing" into white society. The ensuing preoccupation with blackness as something at once invisible yet all-powerful rendered passing one of the dominant themes of American arts and letters at the turn of the century, with writers as diverse as Mark Twain, Charles Chesnutt, and Nella Larsen parsing the color line's brutal realities. Similarly, the creation of national borders created incentives for those willing to smuggle goods or peoples across them, much to the outrage of Mexican and US authorities alike. The Gilded Age's tidy world of clearly defined boundaries, in other words, simultaneously conjured up a secretive realm of blurred lines and border crossers, one inextricably bound to the other.

An uncommonly gifted border crosser, William Ellis offers rare access to this shadowy realm, one that unites the micro and the macro: an individual story of racial passing with a larger account of the evolution of the US-Mexico borderlands. While often thought of as a single phenomenon, passing in fact encompassed a wide range of behaviors. Some passers did so unintentionally, when their ambiguous appearance caused others to mistake their "real" racial identity. Some passed only to gain short-term access to whites-only restaurants, hotels, theaters, and other facilities. Some passed during the day to work at whites-only jobs but returned back across the color line to their black families and friends at night. And some vanished completely into their new identities. (Many in the African American community dubbed this latter behavior going "on the other side" to differentiate it from other, more temporary forms of passing.)

Given the practice's secrecy, precise counts of the number of passers remain elusive. Noting apparent absences in the census, early twentieth-century sociologists calculated that several thousand peoples of African descent moved across the color line each year. Anxious whites worried that "no one, of course, can estimate the number of men and women with Negro blood who have thus 'gone over to white,'" although they brooded that "the number must be large." No less an authority than Walter White, the aptly named African American executive secretary of the NAACP, whose light skin color enabled him to pass to investigate lynchings for the organization, estimated that twelve thousand blacks per year passed into the white world: "Nearly every one of the fourteen million discernible Negroes in the United States knows at least one member of his race who is 'passing'—the magic word which means that some Negroes can get by as whites."

Most passers were thought to masquerade as Anglo-Americans. But posing as a Latin American, as Ellis did in fashioning his persona of Guillermo Enrique Eliseo, was more common than most people realized. Because of passing's clandestine nature, some of the fullest discussions of its subterfuges took place in the realm of fiction, where one could replace the ambiguities surrounding actual passers with concrete, if invented, storylines. The 1899 melodrama *Don Cosme* features a light-skinned African American who reinvents himself as the Mexican Cosme Olmedo. "The practice has always existed," explains the novel's narrator. "Any colored American above the mulatto grade and shade can go to Mexico, learn the language, adopt a Mexican name, and then return and locate in some state where they are not known; and, if his features will bear out the tale, he can, as a Mexican, be a respected member of society." Real-world knowledge of such practices circulated clandestinely throughout the African American community. As Louis Fremont Baldwin noted in his turn-of-the-century exposé, *From Negro to Caucasian*, scores of American blacks managed to "'get by'—not as a caucasian, but as a Mexican, [or] Italian. . . . It is interesting to note how many of this class of deserters are learning to speak a foreign language to assist them in making the journey 'across.'"

Such journeys "across" had as much to do with forgetting as with language or skin color. The success of Ellis's most frequent alternative persona—the Mexican businessman Guillermo Enrique Eliseo—can be attributed to the fact that few during the Gilded Age associated African Americans with the US-Mexico borderlands. Yet for much of the nineteenth century, the spread of chattel slavery into the former Mexican province of Texas and the ensuing conflicts over fugitive slaves, territory, and emancipation dominated the politics of both nations. Expansionist pressure from the American cotton kingdom led the United States and Mexico to wage a full-fledged war with one another in the 1840s, to undergo contemporaneous and bloody civil wars in midcentury, and to engage in mutual—and increasingly intertwined—processes of national reconstruction in the decades following.

Telling the story of a border crosser like Ellis requires us to expand our frame of analysis and bring such events, usually separated into distinct US and Mexican histories, into focus alongside one another. In so doing, we can glimpse the past anew. The deeply entangled histories of the United States and Mexico contain both striking similarities (most obviously, the conquest of indigenous societies and centuries of racialized slavery) and profound disjunctures (ecologies, economics, and demographics among them). The goal of *The Strange Career of William Ellis* is to probe these continuities and ruptures to craft a truly American history—that is, a history not of the United States or Mexico, or even of their shared border region, but rather a history that encompasses the North American continent in its entirety.

———

ELLIS LIVED A life shrouded in mysteries—most of his own devising, some that he took to the grave with him. He left no diary, and only a few of his most candid documents—his photos and his correspondence with immediate family members—survive. Compensating for this paucity of sources, especially as to Ellis's early years as a slave, however, is the richness of the milieu in which he operated, with its startling blend of peoples and places. To reveal this context in its full complexity, the pages that follow are organized into three parts. As the parts progress, each expands in scale, from the local to the regional to the international, charting the increasing interpenetration of the United States and Mexico across time and space.

The first part analyzes Ellis's birthplace of Victoria, Texas, during its transition from a small Mexican village to an integral part of the antebellum South's booming plantation economy. This flourishing outpost of the Cotton Kingdom would be beset by deep tensions because of its proximity to the Mexican border, which rendered slavery vulnerable in ways that the slave owners rushing into the area from the Upper South had not foreseen. The second part brings together the US state of Texas and the northern Mexican states of Durango and Coahuila in the years after 1880 as the extension of the railroad brought the American South and the Mexican North into far more intimate contact than ever before. It was at this moment, as US-style cotton plantations began to take root on Mexican haciendas, that Ellis launched his experiment of relocating African American farmhands from the United States to Mexico—an event that would be greeted with alarm by the US State Department and the Mexican Senate alike.

The final part focuses on the early twentieth century, when

Ellis maintained dual residences in the two great North American metropolises of New York and Mexico City. This was an era of profound mutual engagement between the United States and Mexico. Americans seeking raw materials and cheap labor avidly sought out investment opportunities in their southern neighbor. Mexicans looked north to the United States for capital and possible models of modernization. From his offices on New York's Wall Street and Mexico City's *zócalo*, Ellis helped orchestrate this exchange, until the outbreak of the Mexican Revolution in 1910 brought the once-flourishing economic ties between the two nations to an abrupt halt. Ellis would suddenly find himself caught between the US government, which, preoccupied about radicalism seeping across its southern border, would investigate Ellis as a potential saboteur, and a volatile Mexican politics that, newly concerned with foreign intrusion, threatened to undo his life's work.

To some, Ellis was, as one State Department official put it, little more than "a smart, unscrupulous scamp"—a smooth-talking, multilingual rogue with a "hypnotic power" of persuasion. Such assessments, however, diminish Ellis's achievements in a world that all too often treated African Americans with disdain. Rather than representing some marginal character, Ellis in fact embodied the signature figure of his era: the Gilded Age's self-made man. Like most self-made men, he would ascend from poverty to wealth, becoming one of the first blacks on Wall Street (even if most people at the time were unaware of his African American ancestry). But he was self-made in another sense, too: his reinvention as a member of any number of ethnicities from Mexican to Cuban to Hawaiian.

Despite such refashionings, Ellis, unlike many passers, never completely vanished into his new personae. (This proved fortunate for a historian like myself, as the perfect passer would be unrecoverable—a fact that explains why there are many more novels than histories about passing.) Throughout his life, Ellis remained in contact with family members who continued to identify with the African American community. He also exhibited an almost extravagant disregard for his carefully crafted new identities by periodically engaging in projects relating to African American politics that raised awkward questions about his ethnicity. Rather than adopting a form of passing, then, that involved a complete, often traumatic, erasure of the self—the trading of one's "birthright for a mess of pottage," as James Weldon Johnson so tellingly put it in his classic 1912 novel of passing, *The Autobiography of an Ex-Colored Man*—Ellis engaged in codeshifting, the hallmark of the trickster from African American folklore. This figure deployed the quintessential weapons of the weak—charisma, deflection, improvisation—to advance his interests in a hostile world. In Ellis's case, he succeeded against great odds in subverting the dominant society's notions of racial authenticity, crafting a counterfeit persona that simultaneously represented a deeper, truer self.

To say that Ellis resembled a trickster does not mean he intentionally modeled himself on this figure. (Although, given the time and place in which he lived, it would have been impossible for him not to possess some familiarity with the era's rich corpus of African American trickster folklore.) The trickster, as Lewis Hyde reminds us, is an "abstraction. . . . Actual individuals are always more complicated than the archetype." Viewing Ellis through the lens of the trickster, however, enables us to understand the contradictory whirl of emotions—affection and suspicion, pride and dismay—he inspired among those who knew him, not to mention Ellis's uncanny ability to sense others' stereotypes and preconceptions. "[Those] who 'pass,'" observed the Harlem Renaissance writer Heba Jannath, "are usually past masters at detecting the slightest change in the thoughts and emotions of people around [them]."

In African American folklore, tricksters served simultaneously as hero and antihero—characters who through charm and guile managed to bring low the powerful, yet also figures whose self-interest rendered them disruptive and unpredictable. By passing, Ellis, much like the trickster, raised a host of challenging questions. Was passing, as Langston Hughes once put it, a joke on white supremacy: "Most colored folks think as long as white folks remain foolish, prejudiced and racially selfish, they deserve to be fooled"? Or was passing an egotistical act that harmed one's fellow African Americans by eroding family and cultural ties? Much as the trickster at once erased and erected boundaries, Ellis and passers like him operated in contradictory ways, undermining the color line while at the same time demonstrating its continued power.

Ellis's passing cast in sharp relief not only the peculiar tensions running through race relations in the United States but elsewhere as well. South of the border, Ellis's activities brought to the surface the persistence of racial thinking in Mexico, even as that country insisted that it remained free of the racism of its northern neighbor. In his curious foray into Ethiopia in the early 1900s, Ellis's encounter with Emperor Menelik II called into question the viability of a pan-African identity linking US blacks and the inhabitants of Africa. And everywhere, the fact that Ellis worked along the fringes of US empire placed him in the paradoxical position of aiding the expansion of American interests overseas even as he searched outside the United States for a refuge from his homeland's rising tide of segregation and white supremacy.

Like other tricksters, Ellis had few resources to call upon in negotiating these challenges beyond his powers of imagination and self-presentation. The stories that he spun in response may have been rife with facts masquerading as fictions and fictions pretending to be facts. But they nonetheless illuminate stark truths about North America's fraught transition from slavery to wage labor and its deeply intertwined peoples and places. Many across the continent may have sought to simplify this messy, hybrid reality through the imposition of clearly defined boundaries between nations and races. Ellis, in contrast, sought to test these emerging limits. As he confided to his sister not long after his forced relocation to the Jim Crow car at Eagle Pass, "My fight in life is hard, but I will win out, and the world will know your brother."

❈ PART I ❈

VICTORIA

1

GONE TO TEXAS

IKE MOST FABLES, the story that Ellis told about his origins said as much about its time and place as it did about its main character. Gilded Age Americans, living amid increasingly concentrated wealth and economic power, teeming cities, and labor unrest, sought refuge in reassuring tales of rugged frontier manhood and hard work rewarded. On the popular level, these impulses found expression in the burgeoning dime-novel market, cheap newsprint filled with Wild West adventures and the rags-to-riches tales of Horatio Alger and his imitators. For those with a more serious bent, there were the directories of prominent individuals churned out by numerous publishers. Bearing titles such as *The Successful American, One Thousand American Men of Mark of To-Day*, and *Builders of our Nation*, these works brought together in a single volume illustrative biographies of "America's foremost leaders": well-known, respected individuals whose life stories offered valuable lessons as to what could be achieved through "industry, energy or cleverness." As the editors of *One Thousand American Men of Mark of To-Day* promised their readers, "The careers herein described will be found stimulating to patriotism; and a potent factor in cheering and inspiring the efforts of rising generations."

Those who consulted such volumes seeking more information about the man known alternatively as William Henry Ellis, Guillermo Ellis, and Guillermo Enrique Eliseo would have found numerous entries, all painting a remarkably consistent portrait of their subject. The present-day "Banker, Broker and Miner," readers learned, had been born June 15, 1864, "on the Mexican frontier" to a rancher named Carlos Eliseo and his wife, Marguerita Nelsonia Eliseo. Eliseo's lineage could be traced back to Cuba, his maternal grandfather having lived on the island before relocating to Mexico. After being educated at "schools in Mexico," Eliseo, as befitted the son of a humble Mexican *ranchero*, "spent his early days as [a] cowboy on cattle ranches." Beginning modestly, "trading horses, cattle, etc., between Texas and Mexico," he went on to "pioneer . . . [the] cotton industry in Mexico" and achieve a string of remarkable successes developing mines and haciendas south of the border. Before long, Eliseo, having Anglicized his name to Ellis for the ease of his new English-speaking acquaintances, could be found mingling in the upper reaches of Manhattan's financial and social circles. "Mr. Ellis upon his arrival in New York was an utter stranger," explained the *Successful American*. "But with letters of introduction from and to some of the very best people in the city, and, through the kindness of [railroad tycoon] Collis P. Huntington and through his recommendations has been able to build up quite a business."

The directories listing Ellis's biography aspired "to present facts only," all the better to illustrate for their readers the "subtle influences which . . . go far in the determination of characters that are successful." Through such veracity, the guides transformed "utter strangers" like Ellis into individuals with known pedigrees. Yet in Ellis's case, the entries borrowed from the era's pulp fiction far more than the editors cared to acknowledge. His public biography blurred together the Wild West story and the Horatio Alger novel into a peculiar concoction, one part frontier heroics and two parts moral exemplar, in which Ellis, the proverbial young man from the provinces, managed through perseverance and strength of character to impress a powerful benefactor and climb up the social ladder.

To be convincing, however, Ellis's story could not be a complete invention: it needed to contain enough veracity to lend his performance the aura of truth. His parents' given names thus bore a close resemblance to the ones he listed in his biography. And he was not lying when he asserted that he had grown up amid peoples of Mexican ethnicity, spoke fluent Spanish, possessed a familiarity with ranching and cotton cultivation, and had gotten his start as a transborder merchant. But in each of these instances, Ellis rearranged key features of his upbringing to make the narrative of his life align more closely with what his audiences wanted to hear about his role in advancing what the editors of *Twentieth-Century Successful Americans* termed the Gilded Age's "moral, spiritual and material prosperity."

There was one detail that Ellis erased altogether in this chameleon-like process of shapeshifting. This fact was not some minor facet of his life story but one essential to understanding who he was and where he came from—and even how he acquired his light skin and ethnically ambiguous appearance. What had brought his mother and father to South Texas was not the story of burgeoning independence along the frontier so celebrated in American culture—the very narrative that Ellis invoked by wrapping himself in the image of the cowboy. To the extent that Ellis's parents were pioneers, they were unwilling ones, brought to Texas in chains by one of the preeminent relocations of the antebellum era: the "Second Middle Passage" that uprooted over a million enslaved African Americans from slavery's original home along the Atlantic seaboard and transported them deep into the continent's interior. Unlike the era's other great relocations—the removal of the Cherokee and the other "civilized tribes" into Indian Territory or the migration of Mormons to the Great Salt Lake—the westward movement of slaves and slave owners unfolded according to no grand plan. Yet the lure of new lands on which to cultivate cotton for a seemingly inexhaustible world market was so enticing that throughout the 1850s, long files of enslaved African Americans— "mud-incrusted, wrapped in old blankets or gunny bags," in the words of one onlooker—could be found shuffling in chains down the rutted dirt roads leading to Texas.

Among those caught up in this river of enslaved humanity were a woman in her early thirties named Mary and her two sons: Charles, about ten, and William, some two years younger. As slaves—property rather than people—they left but the slightest of traces in the historical record, writing no letters, keeping no diaries, their names unlisted in antebellum censuses. Instead, most of what we can reconstruct of their lives comes by tracking the family who in the 1850s claimed Mary, Charles, and William as their human chattel: the Weisigers of Kentucky, headed at the time by a prosperous physician named Joseph. The Weisigers had possessed slaves for generations (although, in an effort to put a benevolent face on the "peculiar institution," Southern whites rarely uttered the word "slave": "They speak of their servants, their boy, their negroes, but never their slaves," reported one visitor). At the time of his death in 1823, Joseph Weisiger's father, Daniel, was the third-largest slave owner in Frankfort. By 1850, Joseph, who in addition to practicing medicine owned a plantation in the heart of Kentucky's Bluegrass region, presided over a household containing twenty-three slaves, the oldest a sixty-year-old man, the youngest a girl only one year old. Joseph's brother-in-law, who dwelled nearby, owned twenty-two people similarly spanning the range from toddlers to middle-aged. Even Joseph's aged mother, Lucy, near eighty years old, held seven enslaved African Americans.

In 1852, at the unlikely age of fifty-eight, Joseph Weisiger elected to abandon his Kentucky homestead for the new territory, more than a thousand miles away, opened up by the United States' annexation of Texas. The doctor's enthusiasm for fresh horizons may have been prompted by the death of his wife, Isabella, only a few months earlier—the second time Joseph had outlived his spouse, and no doubt a potent reason for seeking a locale with fewer painful memories. Even more, it reflected the era's mania for cotton, a crop that grew poorly in Upper South states like Kentucky but flourished in Texas. "There was a fever going round, leastways it was like a fever," recalled one slave. "Everyone was dying to get down south and grow cotton to sell."

Weisiger's status as a slave owner meant that his bout with "cotton fever" would have consequences far beyond his immediate household. Not only did it affect his youngest children, his new wife, whom he wooed when she came to Kentucky to sell slaves from her Alabama plantation, and even his widowed mother, who joined her son's journey to the Lone Star State; it radiated out to the more than fifty African Americans bound to the Weisigers through the institution of slavery.

For Weisiger, the move to Texas represented new opportunities. But for his slaves, it inspired terror. Enslaved spouses and children, their relations not recognized by law, risked separation across impossibly vast distances whenever plantation owners headed for new lands. As a result, observed one planter, there was "a very great aversion amongst our Negroes to be carried to distant parts, & particularly to our new countries." Mary, Charles, and William had the good fortune to remain together during the move to Texas, but they could have just as easily been torn from one another forever. And the move may have involved a sundering of ties with grandparents, cousins, or siblings on nearby plantations—rendering these family connections all but irretrievable given the incompleteness of the historic record.

Relocating to Texas produced at least one identifiable separation for Mary and her children. As slaves, Mary, Charles, and William were not afforded the privilege of surnames, a situation that did not change until slavery's collapse amid the bloody chaos of the Civil War. Yet when Mary, Charles, and William chose legal last names for the first time in 1865, they did not, unlike many other ex-slaves, select the surname of the family owning them. In place of Weisiger, Mary and her sons opted for Ellis—which happened to be the surname of Hezekiah Ellis, the white overseer who had once worked for Lucy Weisiger in Frankfort. A hired hand, Hezekiah remained in Kentucky rather than joining the Weisigers and their slaves for the journey to Texas. But even two decades later, Mary retained memories—the full nature of which we can only imagine—of the white man who apparently impregnated her with at least two children when she was in her early twenties.

The Ellis surname that Charles's son, William Henry Ellis, would later transform into the Spanish-sounding Eliseo thus linked him not to Mexico or Cuba but instead to one of antebellum slavery's most brutal realities: the sexual exploitation of black women by white men. Such behavior had left its traces across multiple generations of the Ellis family; not only did Charles and his brother, William, appear in documents after the Civil War as mulattoes, but so, too, did Mary herself, meaning that her mother most likely was also a victim of sexual predation. This dark truth bequeathed to William Henry Ellis the light skin and ethnically ambiguous appearance that facilitated his passing as Guillermo Enrique Eliseo. But this opportunity was only available to him because of the abuse across the race line that his grandmother and great-grandmother—and no doubt other females in his family as well—had endured during generations of enslavement.

———————

IN RELOCATING HIS plantation from the Upper South, Joseph Weisiger became a small player in a big process: the transformation of Texas into a landscape dominated by cotton and slaves. In 1845, when the United States annexed Texas, the number of slaves within the rogue nation that Mexico still claimed as a rebellious province totaled a mere 27,000. Following admission to the United States, however, Texas's slave population soared, reaching 180,000 by 1860. Even so, Texas legislators continued to insist on the necessity of more "slave labor to meet the wants of the State in reducing its almost unlimited acres of sugar and cotton land to cultivation," and Texas newspapers proclaimed, "We want more slaves. We need them."

For many Americans, this explosive growth underscored an unmistakable fact: slavery's destiny lay along the border. Most immediately, that future meant the newly cultivated cotton fields of Texas. But just as Texas had slipped out of Mexican control in 1836, so, too, did it seem that other sections of the continent would soon fall into the American grasp, as California, New Mexico, and Arizona had in 1848. Many saw no reason why Mexico should not relinquish more territory in the near future, or why the tropical isle of Cuba, so suited to slave agriculture and so close to US shores, should not become another state. Expansionists thrilled to the prospect of transforming the entire Gulf of Mexico into a basin ringed with US territories: a

"great American lake." "I want Cuba," enthused Senator Albert Gall-
atin Brown of Mississippi. "I want Tamaulipas, Potosi, and one or two
more Mexican States; and I want them all for the same reason—for
the planting or spreading of slavery."

Joseph Weisiger's move brought his family and slaves to the very
outer limit of this expanding Cotton Kingdom: the onetime Mexican village of Villa de Nuestra Señora de Guadalupe de Victoria
Nombre de Jesús, known to most in the 1850s simply as Victoria,
Texas. Here Dr. Weisiger, patriarch from Kentucky, encountered
Doña Luz Escalera De León, matriarch of Victoria's leading Tejano
family, from whom he purchased one of the town's signature properties, Rancho Escondido, for $13,284. ("Tejano" was the term most
Texans of ethnic Mexican descent used to describe themselves at
the time; their Anglo-American counterparts in turn adopted the
term "Texian" for themselves.) In return, the doctor received not
only some 4,400 acres of land but also a ranch house, barns, and
outbuildings, all located along the bank of the Guadalupe River,
amid the tall-grass prairies and live-oak forests that spread inland
from the coast.

Joseph Weisiger was far from the only newcomer to Victoria with
dreams of transforming a Tejano cattle ranch into a Texian cotton
plantation. Scores of other transplants from the Upper South likewise
moved to this farthest periphery of slave society during the 1840s and
1850s, chasing the fertile soils and humid conditions favored by the
cotton plant. A town with only 3 slaves within its boundaries in 1838,
Victoria could by 1860 boast of 1,533 slaves laboring in fields that,
not so long before, had been open grasslands, grazed by long-horned
Mexican cattle.

Ecological boundaries as much as political ones situated Victoria on the frontier of the Cotton Kingdom. The cotton plant grows
best when it receives twenty to twenty-five inches of rainfall annually,
with few dry spells or sharp swings in temperature—conditions that
trail off amid the arid chaparral to the south and west of the Guadalupe River. In contrast, the broad plain leading from the coast inland
to Victoria—"almost Belgic in its level and rich repose," in the words

of one newcomer—was well watered and abounded in the loamy soils in which the cotton plant thrived.

But it was not only access to the rich, untapped soil beneath Victoria's prairies that attracted the Weisigers and other slave owners to Texas. The journey to Texas also promised greater security for slave owners' human property. To Americans at the time, Kentucky was a border state: for some six hundred miles, all that separated the slave plantations of Kentucky from the free communities of the North was the wide, slow-moving waters of the Ohio River. In cold winters, the river froze, and enslaved African Americans could escape simply by walking across the ice—a scenario Harriet Beecher Stowe dramatized in *Uncle Tom's Cabin*, published the very year the Weisigers departed for Victoria.

Those slave owners who relocated to Texas, however, soon came to an unwelcome realization: slavery was if anything more vulnerable in the Lone Star State than in the Upper South. Newcomers like the Weisigers had anticipated Texas would be just the next step in an ever-expanding Cotton Kingdom. But when further annexations of Mexican territory stalled, slave owners found themselves once more along a border. This time, though, they faced not the Mason-Dixon line between regions but rather the boundary line between nations. Moreover, while in the United States the Fugitive Slave Act of 1850 enabled slave owners to reach into the North and recapture escaped slaves, Mexico's status as an independent country meant that enslaved peoples who reached Mexico were beyond official recovery. As a result, explained the *Galveston Weekly News*, slave labor was "not safe" throughout much of Texas "because the Mexicans steel [*sic*] them. Mexico is a storehouse for the thieves, and Mexican laws shield the offenders."

Most slaves, of course, did not need to be "stolen" to recognize the opportunities that flight across the border presented. Runaway ads in antebellum Texan newspapers document the steady flow of slaves across the border, each notice a miniature portrait of sorts. Many fugitives, judging by their descriptions, bore traces of the omnipresent physical violence of slavery ("His right ear has been cropped . . .

and an upper nick out of the left"; "has lost some of his front teeth"; "his first finger on the right hand is off at the first joint"; "bears the marks of the whip on his back. . . . His right arm has been broken"). Almost all were young men, as in the ad that appeared under the title "Stop the Runaways" in the *Victoria Advocate* just before the Weisigers' and Ellises' joint arrival in town. P. D. McNeel promised a "liberal reward" for anyone who apprehended the three slaves who had fled from his plantation armed with a rifle and two double-barreled shotguns: Sam ("yellow complexion, about twenty two or three years old, kinky head, thick lips"), Frank ("coal black, white eyes, thick lips, trim made . . . about twenty years old"), and John ("about twenty seven or eight years old . . . hair tolerably straight, a scar in the corner of his eye"). "I have no doubt they are aiming for Mexico," opined McNeel.

If Sam, Frank, and John evaded the omnipresent "nigger dogs" that plantation owners in Victoria and elsewhere used to hunt runaways, they would have joined an estimated four thousand slaves who fled from the United States into Mexico prior to the Civil War. The sheer number of escapees across the international border reoriented the vector of freedom for enslaved persons throughout the Deep South, for whom Mexico became the newest and closest refuge. "'Round our part of the country," explained one former Texas slave, "iffen a nigger want to run away, he'd light out for old Mexico. That was nigger heaven them days." "Sometimes someone would come 'long and try to get us to run up North and be free," remembered another former Texas slave, Felix Haywood. "We used to laugh at that. There wasn't no reason to *run* up North. All we had to do was to *walk*, but walk *South*, and we'd be free as soon as we crossed the Rio Grande. . . . Hundreds of slaves did go to Mexico and got on all right," added Haywood. "We would hear about 'em and how they was goin' to be Mexicans." As one Texas plantation owner summarized in 1851: "The negroe he has got Mexico in his head."

The destinations for such runaways were the isolated villages dotting the border states of Coahuila and Tamaulipas. In 1849, in a rare act of three generations fleeing together, a slave named David

Thomas made his way from Texas to the Mexican town of Allende with his daughter and three grandchildren, freeing his entire family from bondage. In 1854, Frederick Law Olmsted, as well known at the time for his antislavery writings as for his landscape architecture, visited Piedras Negras, the next village over from Allende. Located just across the Rio Grande from Eagle Pass, Texas, Piedras Negras was a favorite gateway for fugitive slaves fleeing into Mexico. Olmsted encountered several runaways in the settlement and noted that escaped slaves "were *constantly* arriving" in Mexican border towns, with forty or more having made their way to Piedras Negras alone in the past three months.

One fugitive in Piedras Negras reported to Olmsted that "the Mexican government was very just to them, they could always have their rights as fully protected as if they were Mexicans born." But runaways in Mexico in fact occupied a legal gray zone. Under Mexican law, all male foreigners had to carry a visa from their home country, a statute that applied even to escaped slaves. (Female foreigners, assumed to have a husband, father, or other male guardian accompanying them, did not face the same requirement.) US consuls in Mexico, however, refused to grant fugitive slaves the necessary *carta de seguridad*. This denial left runaways in legal limbo, neither Mexican nor American, and vulnerable to arrest and fine or imprisonment. Unlike maroons elsewhere in the Americas, who tended to establish self-sufficient communities, fugitive slaves in Mexico tried instead to insert themselves into as many institutions of their host nation as possible. Marriage into a Mexican family, conversion to Catholicism, militia service: all were eagerly sought by runaways to demonstrate their usefulness to Mexico and to earn the tolerance of local authorities, who could enforce the law as they saw fit. When the fugitive slave Peter Towns reached Piedras Negras, for instance, he transformed his name into Pedro Tauns, started a family with a Mexican woman, found employment as a mason, and entertained with his fiddle at local *fandangos*. The calculus behind such actions, however, eluded outraged US slave owners, among whom Mexico became known as simply a "paradise of runaway slaves."

IN ESCAPING FROM Texas into Mexico, slaves also engaged in a flight from history that obscured Mexico's deep connections to chattel slavery. For much of its existence, Mexico had, like the United States—indeed, most of the Americas—been a slaveholding society. African slavery existed in Mexico as early as 1519, a full century before the arrival of the first documented slave ship at Jamestown, and during the colonial era, over two hundred thousand enslaved Africans landed in New Spain, exceeding the number of immigrants from Europe to reach Mexican shores during these same years. Eighteenth-century Mexican newspapers sported runaway notices with more than a passing resemblance to those that later appeared in Texas: "Joseph Polomo Urrutia, slave, native of the town of Aguas Calientes, fled from the Capital on the 12th of this month: regular build, brown [*cocho*] color, one eye cloudy, normal hair: his clothing leather pants, linen shirt, shoes, black hat, and he may be in possession of the two gray blankets [*fresadas cenicientas*] with which he ran away."

Most slaves labored in plantations along Mexico's Atlantic and Pacific coasts, but the institution even permeated the colony's far north. The 1783 census of the province of Texas revealed the presence of some 36 enslaved peoples of African descent, as well as 404 peoples *"de Color Quebrado"* (a category meaning "broken color" into which mulattoes were typically slotted), constituting 1.3 percent and 14.5 percent of the population of the province, respectively. A census at the same time of Saltillo, capital of the neighboring province of Coahuila, tallied 82 slaves of African descent, most working as domestic servants in elite households.

If Anglo-Americans were not the first to introduce African slavery to Texas soil, they embraced it on a scale that dwarfed their Spanish predecessors. Even so, Mexico's response when slave-owning Anglo colonists began to settle the newly merged state of Coahuila y Tejas in the 1820s manifested considerable ambiguity. Mexico's decade-long war of independence from Spain had assumed an abolitionist tinge, with insurrectionist leaders such as Miguel Hidalgo and José María Morelos issuing edicts calling for an end to slavery. After independence in 1821, Mexico took steps to prohibit the slave trade and to emancipate all slave children under fourteen. But contradictorily it also issued a law in 1823 granting extra land to colonists who brought large numbers of slaves with them to Mexico, designed to encourage Americans from the southern United States to settle in Coahuila y Tejas as a barrier to the powerful Comanche and Apache raiding parties devastating the new republic's northern frontier. Even after Morelos's onetime lieutenant-turned-president, Vicente Guerrero, issued a proclamation in 1829 abolishing slavery, he followed it up two months later with a measure excepting Coahuila y Tejas from the new law. The state government in Coahuila y Tejas was similarly erratic, enacting several statutes in the 1820s designed to bring about slavery's decline but also establishing a new contract law in 1827 that permitted masters to sign their slaves to ninety-nine-year contracts of indenture, a legal fiction that preserved slavery in everything but name.

Far less equivocal were the new republic's efforts to undo the complicated *casta* system. During the Spanish colonial period, peoples had been divided into a complex hierarchy of racial categories, arranged with European *criollos* at the top and *mulatos, pardos, morenos*, and *negros*—all terms for individuals with some degree of African ancestry—clustered at the bottom. After independence, however, Mexico attempted to erase the vestiges of Spanish colonialism. Mexican government documents no longer tracked people by race and, unlike in the United States, Indians were made full citizens of the new nation.

The disappearance of official racial categories did not necessarily mean the disappearance of the idea of race. But even before Independence, one outgrowth of the *casta* system's efforts to delineate the precise proportions of an individual's white, black, and Indian ancestry had been the erection of a bewildering thicket of racial identities. Because of their arbitrariness, these definitions had ironically facilitated movement from one category to another, with individuals ascending or descending the racial hierarchy as they moved up or down the socioeconomic ladder. During the struggle for independence, this dynamic allowed some individuals of Afro-Mexican descent, such as Presidents Morelos and Guerrero, to attain positions of prominence with little public comment, even as the idea of blackness and black peoples themselves (almost a tenth of Mexico's population in the early 1800s) began to evaporate from the Mexican national consciousness.

———

THE INTERTWINED WEISIGER and Ellis families arrived in Victoria at the moment when the paradoxes of Texas slavery were at their most pronounced. By all objective measures, the annexation of Mexican territory had infused the Cotton Kingdom with renewed vigor. A prime field hand in Texas (the term a telling reminder of the extent to which slavery reduced the enslaved to mere collections of useful body parts) might be worth as much as $1,800 in the 1850s (over $50,000 in current dollars)—a sum that explains the steady sale of surplus slaves from the Upper South to Texas as well as the outrage of Texian slave owners at their loss of capital when slaves escaped across the border into Mexico. In Victoria, Texas's cotton boom spurred the construction of a railroad to Port Lavaca, some thirty miles away. Local merchants did a thriving business supplying nearby plantations with everything from hoes, shovels, and padlocks to cheap goods for slaves ("negro blankets," "negro clothing of all kinds"). As a result of the prosperity brought by cotton, land in Victoria doubled in value by 1853, the year of the Wesigers' and Ellises' arrival.

Yet even amid this boom, many Texians had grown apprehensive about slavery's future. The same persons who envisioned themselves plantation masters also imagined themselves the victims of the dangerous currents swirling around slavery along the border. Since Texians believed slavery to be a benign institution—slaves, according to the Texas legislature, offered "the white man . . . willing obedience and affection"—it followed that any threat to slavery had to be external. By far the leading source of outside provocation was the neighboring nation of Mexico. Not only did the Mexican republic refuse to cede more of its northern territory to American slave owners; it had repeatedly declined to negotiate a treaty allowing for the return of fugitive slaves to their US owners.

Having already lost half its national territory to the United States, Mexico had good reason to be wary of the expansive republic to its north. Throughout the 1850s, the United States would press repeatedly for further sales of Mexican land. In the Gadsden Purchase of 1854, Mexico conceded a narrow strip of what became southern Arizona for a transcontinental railroad line. But American negotiators had been authorized to purchase much, much more—the northern states of Tamaulipas, Coahuila, Nuevo León, Baja California, Sonora, and Chihuahua—and in the years following, Americans would periodically clamber for further land acquisitions from Mexico. For those unwilling to await a negotiated purchase, the 1850s proved the heyday of filibustering, with US-based adventurers launching periodic invasions of Mexico, Cuba, and Central America in the hopes of creating new slave states along the Cotton Kingdom's outer fringes.

Faced with such pressures, Mexico saw little incentive to return escaped slaves. Such a policy would only strengthen the American threat along the republic's northern border while depriving the sparsely populated Mexican North of potentially useful inhabitants. In 1850, in a further effort to people its outer periphery at the United States' expense, Mexico entered into an agreement with some bands of Seminole Indians led by Wild Cat ("Gato del Monte" to his new Mexican allies), who relocated from Indian Territory to the border state of Coahuila. These peoples, whom the Mexicans termed Mascogos, settled around Nacimiento, El Moral, and San Fernando de Rosas and served as Mexican Army auxiliaries along the republic's northern *frontera*. To Texians, however, the "black Seminoles," who had incorporated large numbers of fugitive slaves when they inhabited their original homeland in the Everglades, represented one more unnerving facet of the borderlands—an armed maroon band that would only encourage more slaves to flee into Mexico. It did little to help matters that one of the most visible members of Wild Cat's band, his English-language translator, was a "full-blooded negro" and escaped slave nicknamed "Gopher John."

The perception that Mexico not only tolerated but encouraged the flight of fugitive slaves precipitated numerous Texian attempts to cross the international boundary and take the law into their own hands. In 1851, outside the border village of Guerrero, Coahuila, locals stumbled across a Texian who had seized a fugitive slave living in town and tied him to his saddle, apparently as a prelude to forcing the man back across the border to Texas. The mayor of Guerrero ordered the Texian to release his captive, triggering a shootout that ended in the would-be slave catcher's death. Four years later, a force of some two hundred Texians, demanding the return of fugitive slaves, crossed the border into Mexico. Pushed back by Mexican troops and their Mascogo allies, the invaders burned Piedras Negras to the ground before returning to the United States.

Not everyone in northern Mexico welcomed the slaves fleeing across the border. Not only did their presence invite Texian intrusion; desperate runaways occasionally stole supplies from Mexican homesteads. As the Mexican Army officer Emilio Langberg observed in 1855, "In all the settlements along this frontier, I have found among their inhabitants the best disposition not to accept any negroes, who, far from being useful, are very burdensome." Cross-border attacks like the ones in Guerrero or Piedras Negras, however, diminished what little sympathy existed for American slave owners, leading the US consul in Matamoros to observe that Mexicans along the border were "deadly hostile to every American, unless he is a Negro or mulatto."

As tensions along the border increased, Mexico embraced the notion of itself as the United States' opposite: a society where slavery not only did not exist but was unthinkable. When it came time for Mexico to rewrite its constitution in 1857, delegates opened the document with the statement that the "rights of man are the foundation and the objective of all social institutions." The constitution's next article reaffirmed Mexico's prohibition on slavery and added that all "slaves that set foot on national territory recover their liberty by this fact alone." Since the only contiguous territory from which slaves might enter into Mexico was the United States, this measure represented a clear rebuke to the republic's northern neighbor.

To Mexicans, such resistance to slavery became a source of national pride, confirming the emancipationist legacy of Hidalgo and Morelos. Mexicans celebrated incidents such as the one that took place in 1858, when a US ship carrying slaves ran aground at Cabo Rojo near Veracruz, requiring the captain to land all his passengers to repair the ship. Shortly afterward, Mexican officials showed up to proclaim that the slaves on the ship were now free because of their presence on Mexican soil. Manuel Rejon, military commander along the US-Mexico border, employed similar logic in 1862 to deny yet another Texan attempt to reclaim slaves in northern Mexico, stating to his American counterpart that "according to the laws of the Republic they [slaves] are considered free as soon as they step on Mexican territory."

To Texians, in contrast, Mexico's new constitution was "too outrageous . . . to bear." "So you see that our neighbors, if we may dare to call them such, are doing all they can to injure the Texians' cause: striving to break down our slave institutions by holding the false banner of liberty to our slaves," contended plantation owner H. M'Bride Pridgen, one of the Weisigers' new neighbors in Victoria. Hundreds of furious Texians signed petitions to Congress, calling for the United States to negotiate an extradition treaty with Mexico—or, failing this, to "wage war to the cannon's mouth" with Mexico until it returned fugitive slaves.

It did not take much for this ire at the Mexican government to bleed over into suspicion of Texas's ethnic Mexicans. Many Tejanos, having supported the Texan revolt in the 1830s or having fled peonage or military service in northern Mexico in the years hence, had their own disagreements with the Mexican government. Nonetheless, Texians erased such distinctions, rendering all persons of Mexican descent, whatever their citizenship or past behavior, plotters conspiring to undermine slavery. Opined one Texian, "For five dollars you can hire the Mexican to murder his next-door neighbor; but all the gold in the Southwest would not hire him to return a fugitive slave."

Even had Mexico not pursued policies detrimental to US slavery, Tejanos by their very presence posed a problem for slaveholding Texians. Proslavery ideology in the United States pivoted on maintaining a sharp dichotomy between white and black, free and slave, each category separate and immutable. In the words of an 1857 report from the Texas House of Representatives: "All experience hath shown that while an inferior being, the negro is indisputably adapted by nature, to the condition of servitude to the white man." In most other slave states, the absence of any significant population outside the black/white racial divide allowed such logic to go unquestioned. But this was impossible in Texas, which had more than twenty-five thousand Tejanos within its boundaries in 1850.

As peoples who were free but not necessarily white, Tejanos confounded the binaries at the heart of the proslavery defense. Ethnic Mexicans, in the words of one Texian, could be "as black as niggers"; nonetheless, they annoyingly considered "themselves just as good as white men." Editorialized the *San Antonio Standard*: "A peon Mexican can claim the political and civil privileges of a white man and may thus become instrumental to much mischief." Anglo anxieties about Tejanos' uncertain racial status manifested itself in the widespread use of the epithet "greaser," with its connotations of indeterminate color. "A 'greaser,'" explained one Texian, "was a Mexican—originating in the filthy, greasy appearance of the natives." Embedded within these allusions to hygiene were deeper Anglo obsessions with racial mixing. Spanish colonialism had created in Mexico a population that combined European, African, and native backgrounds; by the end of the eighteenth century, in fact, some 80 percent of Mexicans possessed some degree of African or indigenous ancestry.

Racial mixing had also taken place in the United States, of course. Of the eleven slaves in Joseph Weisiger's household at the time of the 1860 census, more than half, like Mary, Charles, and William, were described as mulattoes. And, although the fact was deeply obscured for obvious reasons, there were those whites whose fore-

bears included Native Americans or blacks. But as proslavery think-
ers increasingly turned to the idea of racial difference to justify the
enslavement of African Americans, mixing across racial lines became
an anathema, abhorred because it demonstrated that the races were
not, in fact, so separate after all. Slavery's defenders might assert that
black-white offspring were like mules, the product of the sexual congress of two different species and destined not to reproduce themselves—the mulatto *"cannot extend his race for he has no race,"* insisted
one proslavery writer; "there is no place for him in nature." But a
quick stroll through any slave quarter or plantation kitchen told a
quite different story.

As if their racial indeterminacy were not problem enough, "greasers" also blurred slavery's social boundaries. Texians responded with
alarm to scenes of "Peons and slaves [together] . . . playing at monte,
smoking cigars, and drinking liquor." Not only did such familiarity
instill an unhealthy sense of freedom in the Texians' property; it
also was thought to encourage Mexicans to guide their newfound
acquaintances across the border. "It is notorious everywhere," editorialized the *Colorado Citizen*, "that the peons or greasers—forming about nine-tenths of the Mexicans—consort with negroes and
continually incite them to murder their masters and escape into
Mexico." Tejanos, concluded another Texas slave owner, encouraged
slaves "in all their bad habits, married them . . . and ran them off
every day to Mexico."

Above all, Tejanos posed the most basic challenge any racial order
confronted: how to differentiate so-called races from one another.
Newspaper accounts from the 1850s hint at the uncertainties of
distinguishing blacks from Mexicans (a good number of whom, of
course, possessed some African ancestry, however forgotten by
Americans and Mexicans alike): horse thieves described as a "Mexican or a Mulatto"; runaway slaves who, it was warned, might "attempt
to pass . . . as a Mexican" or who in "form and color . . . [could] well
[be] taken for a Mexican Greaser."

Not only could physical appearance be ambivalent; so, too, could
cultural markers. Runaway ads often noted slaves who were familiar

with Spanish, as in an 1851 ad for "Jim," who reportedly "speaks a few words of Spanish." For a few of these slaves, Spanish may even have been their native tongue: during Texas's near decade-long interlude as an independent nation, planters regularly smuggled in slaves from nearby Cuba. But in other cases, the acquisition of Spanish speaks to the intimacy of interactions between slaves and Tejanos. "One of my grandfadders [was] a old Mexican man call[ed] Old Man Caesar [César]," explained former slave Virginia Newman. Another Texas ex-slave attributed his wife's light appearance to the fact that "her papa's name was Juan and he was a Mexican."

In antebellum Texas, of course, the stakes in differentiating African Americans from Mexicans remained profound, as a peculiar court case from the 1850s illustrates. In October 1857, the San Antonio sheriff arrested a woman named Dolores Brown on the suspicion that she was a runaway slave. At first glance, the evidence against Brown appeared overwhelming. Not only did she have an Anglo surname and "associate . . . with negroes"; local Tejanos "said she was not a Mexican." Brown, however, contended that none of these findings constituted proof that she was a fugitive slave and filed for habeas corpus. In court, she offered up the story that she had been born near Victoria "upon the Guadalupe River, of Mexican parents." As a young girl, she had traveled through Georgia and Alabama with a man named Brown, whose last name she adopted. When no one stepped forward in court to identify her as having escaped from their plantation, and with some witnesses deciding upon closer examination that Brown had "none of the features of a negro," the court ruled "in favor of freedom." Brown was, it concluded, "a free person of Mexican descent" and to be "discharged by the sheriff from further imprisonment." As this ruling highlighted, as ambivalent as the racial identity of Mexicans might be, only blacks could be slaves in Texas—a judgment that opened up a space for at least a few African Americans to escape slavery by fleeing not to Mexico but to an ethnic Mexican identity instead.

Unable to resolve the challenges of racial classification that Tejanos represented, Texians opted instead to eliminate them. Beginning in the 1840s and with gathering fury in the 1850s, Anglo Texans expelled Tejanos from scores of communities. One of the earliest expulsions took place in Gonzales County in 1845, after an ill-fated Mexican, accused of assisting a slave to escape, was given one hundred and fifty lashes and then branded on the forehead with the letter *T* for thief. Nine years later, the movement spread to Austin. An influx of Mexican laborers into the state capital triggered a mass meeting chaired by the city's mayor. Claiming that "we have among us a Mexican population who continually associate with our slaves, and instill into their minds false notions of freedom, and make them discontented and insubordinate," those gathered vowed to expel all of Travis County's Mexicans, save those "vouched for by some *responsible* American citizen." That same year, Seguin County, too, expelled its Mexican "peons." Matagorda and Colorado Counties followed in 1856, and Uvalde in 1857, the latter adding for good measure that "no Mexican should pass through that county without a pass from some reliable white man." The result was a piecemeal policy of ethnic cleansing that inhibited African American contact with Tejanos across a substantial portion of the state.

The same fears behind the expulsion of ethnic Mexicans also breathed life into one of the greatest terrors of any slave-owning society: an uprising of the enslaved. In the 1850s, repeated rumors of rebellion and flight to Mexico roiled Texas. In September 1856, in Colorado County, several slaves were accused of hiding guns and ammunition in a creek bottom with the intention to launch an uprising and "fight their way to Mexico." The county's Vigilance Committee whipped two supposed ringleaders to death before turning on the local Mexican population. The committee charged "every Mexican in the county" with being connected to the plot, even contending that one Tejano had served as the revolt's "prime mover." Committee members demanded that all the Mexican residents of Colorado County leave, never to return, upon pain of death.

The following month, the panic reached the Weisiger plantation. In October 1856, Anglos in Lavaca, DeWitt, and Victoria Counties unearthed a seemingly vast conspiracy: hundreds of slaves who planned to seize weapons and fight their way to Mexico. It was even said that the slaves had taken the precaution of "kill[ing] off all the dogs" so the canines could not warn whites when the slaves launched their attack. Unlike in nearby Colorado County, however, in Victoria these fears of a supposed slave insurrection did not transform into a vendetta against the ethnic Mexican community. Texians remained convinced that any uprising among their otherwise contented slaves required an outside agitator. But in Victoria, this role fell not to Tejanos but instead to a local white: the supposed ringleader of the slave revolt, he was "severely horsewhipped" before being ordered to leave the county.

This deviation from the usual script underscores the unique conditions prevailing in the Weisigers' and Ellises' new home. Scholars have observed that Texas represented a crossroads where the Mexican North and the American South bled into one another. But within the state itself, the spaces where the two regions overlapped were, in fact, quite small. Eastern Texas had been settled primarily by Southern whites and enslaved blacks, beginning with Stephen Austin's first colonization grant in 1821. The vast swath of western Texas between the Nueces and the Rio Grande Rivers, a perilous no-man's-land during the 1840s when it had been claimed by both Mexico and the United States and plagued by Comanche raids, remained predominantly Tejano, with ethnic Mexicans outnumbering Anglos almost nine to one in the 1850s. Only in a small portion of central Texas did Anglo Americans, African Americans, and Tejanos overlap with one another to any appreciable extent—and this section shrank considerably in the 1850s, as many counties expelled their Tejano communities.

At the heart of these intersecting regions lay Victoria. The town had begun its life as the only predominantly Mexican colony in Texas. On April 13, 1824, the former military officer Martín De León obtained a grant from the Mexican government to settle with forty-one followers on the lower Guadalupe River. As the grant's *empresario*, De León was empowered not only to plot the new town's central plaza and streets, for which he selected a wooded bluff overlooking the Guadalupe, but also to distribute land to the colonists. Since many of those accompanying De León were his family members, including his wife and ten children, the result of Martín's contract was, as he no doubt intended, to convert his clan into the town's largest property holders.

Not all of the required forty-one colonists accompanied De León from Tamaulipas, however, so Martín ended up filling his quota with outsiders from Ireland, France, Germany, Canada, the United States, and elsewhere who had drifted into the region. This move drew the ire of Mexican officials, who preferred to settle De León's grant exclusively with Mexicans as a buffer against the growing Anglo colonies of Austin and others, but Martín's open-handed policy ended up serving his family well. After the Texan Revolution of 1835, many Tejanos lost their holdings as newly ascendant Anglos used everything from cash purchases to physical violence to wrest land from ethnic Mexicans. In contrast, Fernando De León, Martín's oldest son, successfully waged a series of lawsuits that removed scores of Anglo squatters from the family's property. Key courtroom testimony supporting Fernando was provided courtesy of Victoria's early non-Mexican colonists, such as the Irish-born John "Juan" Linn, a former business partner of Martín's turned state senator, and Linn's brother, Edward, a local surveyor.

Fernando's legal triumph ensured that the De León family would remain one of Victoria's largest landowners for much of the nineteenth century. With property came other rewards. In a region where interactions between Texians and Tejanos could be rigidly circumscribed—only a handful of possible intermarriages between Anglos and ethnic Mexicans show up in Victoria's 1860 census, for instance—the De Leóns enjoyed a rare social acceptance. They were treated less as Tejanos and more as one of the town's "old Spanish families." Younger male members of the family adopted Anglo nicknames, with Francisco De León, Fernando's adopted son, becoming "Frank" and his cousin Silvestre De León being known as "Sil," and both socialized and did business with Anglo partners. Tejanos and Texians alike addressed older members of the family as "Don" and "Doña."

The De León family's tenacity in retaining its lands played a pivotal role in making Victoria the point at which the Anglo-dominated plantation belt in Texas transitioned to the Mexican-dominated ranching zone. The 1860 census captured this divide with great clarity. Census tallies showed slaves representing 34 percent of the population in Victoria. To the east, in the heart of the Anglo-dominated plantation zone, Wharton and Brazoria Counties recorded slave populations as high as 80 percent—rates that were among the highest in the nation. But to the west, between Victoria and the border, percentages plummeted. Only nearby San Patricio had any appreciable population of slaves (15 percent of the population). Many counties along the Rio Grande had few slaves or none at all.

The overlap in Victoria between Anglo plantation slavery and Mexican ranching produced a number of curious juxtapositions. Although census data record no Tejanos serving as overseers—a position instead dominated by white men from the Deep South, possessing little property but skilled with a whip or club—there existed a handful of ethnic Mexican slave owners. For years, the patriarch of the De León family, Fernando, had a black manservant, purchased during a trip to New Orleans. According to the 1860 census, Fernando's widow, Luz, owned a twenty-three-year-old mulatto woman, while Carlos De La Garza, Frank De León's neighbor, owned three slaves.

For their part, some Anglos incorporated the ranching lifestyle of their Tejano neighbors. As one early county history noted, although cotton was Victoria's "chief agricultural export," many of the "principal planters," including the Weisigers, were also involved in ranching. Joseph and Daniel registered a brand for their cattle in June 1854, not long after their arrival in Victoria, and Joseph Weisiger appears in the 1860 census as the proud possessor of one of the town's largest herds: 1,600 cattle and 60 sheep. Many plantations in the area became hybrid operations, mixing cotton cultivation and ranching together, and relying upon a labor force that combined both slaves and Mexican ranch hands. During his 1854 trip to Texas, which included several stops in Victoria, Frederick Law Olmsted noted slaves "working indiscriminately with hired Mexicans" in the region's cotton fields.

When Ellis later depicted his birthplace in works such as *Herringshaw's American Blue-Book of Biography* as "the Mexican frontier," he was engaged in an obvious attempt at obfuscation, designed to conjure up a background more acceptable than the slave quarters of a Texas cotton plantation. But it nonetheless contained a grain of truth. Victoria did, in fact, demarcate a significant boundary point. In theory, the post-1848 Mexico-US border was located some two hundred miles to Victoria's southwest. In practice, however, it was Victoria rather than the international boundary where many of the era's most prominent fault lines evinced themselves: the demographic transition from a predominantly English-speaking Anglo-American and African American population to one that was Spanish speaking and ethnically Mexican; and the economic shift from cotton cultivation and plantation slavery to cattle ranching and haciendas.

———

JOSEPH WEISIGER AND his slaves experienced Victoria's cotton boom in profoundly different ways. For the doctor, moving to Texas allowed him to capitalize on a seemingly insatiable global demand for cotton fiber. It fell to the Ellis family, however, to perform the backbreaking labor of transforming acre upon acre of tall-grass prairie into a monoculture of densely packed cotton plants. Cotton flourished in river bottoms that ran through the Weisiger plantation, where frequent floods left behind rich layers of silt. But there was only so much bottomland available, and such terrain could be irregular and difficult to till. To plant cotton on a large scale, it was necessary to cultivate the plains as well—and to do so, one had first to rip up the thick mat of roots binding together the head-high grasses that grew there, so that one could reach the topsoil beneath. Although this was occasionally done through the simple human labor of digging with a shovel, more often sod busters used a powerful wrought-iron plow drawn by several yokes of oxen, one of the few animals with the strength to tear through the dense roots underlying the prairies.

Once the soil hidden under the prairie grass had been uncovered, it was transformed into the base for a new ecosystem, one devoted exclusively to the cotton plant. Most plantations began the yearly cotton cycle in February and March, when seeds were selected and planted. The young cotton plants that sprouted soon afterward needed to be "chopped" periodically. Gangs of slaves would move along the rows, using heavy hoes to uproot ("chop") any weeds growing among the cotton seedlings. Chopping dominated most of the hot summer months: as the cotton plants grew in the Texas sun, so, too, did the cotton's competitors for soil and light. The cotton plants bloomed in August, a creamy white blossom that soon darkened to a deep red. As the petals dropped off, they left behind pods nestled in a dense cluster of cellulose fibers. Over time, these seedpods opened into bolls, exposing the fibers within. At this point, labor on the plantation transitioned to the all-important task of picking. Toting baskets or dragging long sacks, slaves walked between the rows of cotton plants for as long as there was light to see, selecting by hand the ripe bolls for transportation to the ginning house, where the cotton fibers would be mechanically separated from the seeds via a cotton gin. The resulting "lint" would then be packed into bales using an enormous screw press, which generated bales of some 400 to 500 pounds. Since bolls matured unevenly, picking lasted well into winter, as slaves took multiple passes over the same rows of cotton plants.

When conditions were right—when there was enough rain but not too much, when frost did not come too early and the sun did not shine too hot, when the insects and other pests that flourished in monocultures did not damage too much of the crop—a cotton plantation could generate extraordinary returns. In 1860 alone, the Weisiger plantation produced ninety bales of cotton, worth approximately $4,000 (over $115,000 today). Just one fragment of the Lone Star State's total output of 431,000 bales, the Weisigers' harvest, like those on neighboring plantations, was destined for the booming textile mills of New England and Great Britain. Every almost weightless boll of cellulose consumed by the cotton industry, however, reflected the vast input of human labor essential to sustaining an unnaturally simplified ecosystem devoted to the cultivation of a single plant—labor provided overwhelmingly by enslaved peoples like Mary and her sons, Charles and William.

Any hope of escaping the Cotton Kingdom by running to Mexico faced daunting obstacles. After Victoria's supposed slave revolt in 1856, Texians tightened their surveillance of local slaves. Every night at 9 p.m., watchmen rang the town bell, after which, according to Victoria's curfew law, "all slaves, or persons of color, Mexicans excepted, [were] required to be at their respective houses." Any slave violating the curfew was subject to five to twenty lashes. To enforce these measures, Victoria created a patrol to "discipline . . . our colored community" and exercise "special vigilance" over interactions between slaves and Tejanos.

Family circumstances further constrained the Ellises. The most likely slaves to hazard a dash for the border were young men like Charles and William. But fleeing would have meant leaving behind their mother, Mary, perhaps the sole family member from Kentucky with whom they retained a connection. Moreover, after 1858, Charles had a new commitment to consider: he had fathered a daughter, Elizabeth, with one of the other slaves on the Weisiger plantation, a young woman named Margaret Nelson (later, her son William would rework her name into the more Mexican-sounding Marguerita Nelsonia). Recognizing that eluding patrollers and bloodhounds across the miles of forbidding chaparral between Victoria and the border with an infant child in tow was next to impossible, Charles and Margaret settled for a more discreet form of resistance: giving their new-born daughter the middle name Reina, Spanish for "queen," subversively suggesting both forbidden contact with ethnic Mexicans and the elevation of a slave to nobility.

As the Ellises looked to Mexico as a potential escape, the Weisigers glanced longingly to the south as well. *Gossypium hirsutum*, the cotton cultivated in the Southern states, was a hybrid created in the 1820s through the introduction of seed from Mexico. Resistant to rot and quick growing, so-called Mexican cotton was prized above all for the size of its pods. "The superiority of the Mexican," explained the *Year-*

book of Agriculture in 1856, "consists in . . . the size of the boll . . . affording a facility for gathering by which three times the quantity above any other cotton can be picked in a given time." As a result, all other varieties in the US South had by the 1840s "given way to the Mexican," and newspapers in Texas regularly advertised the availability of "White Mexican Cotton Seed."

For Texians, planting "Mexican cotton" on land that not so long ago had been part of Mexico underscored the Cotton Kingdom's expansive possibilities. As observers in the 1850s pointed out, "about one-half of Mexico lies within the tropics," the same zone that was the natural home of the cotton plant and African peoples. If cotton was a "native of the tropics," so, too, was the Negro, "and the instinct of his nature prompts . . . him onward to his original and final home." The cotton plant, the slaves who cultivated it, and the masters who oversaw them: all seemed destined by nature itself to spread across the continent together.

Yet if Texian planters envisioned expansion as a natural process, ethnic Mexicans saw it as an all-too-human grasp for land. These pressures operated not only across the border, with many Anglo-Americans openly desiring more of northern Mexico, but also within Texas itself, where Texians continued to displace Tejanos from their property. In 1859, these tensions erupted into open conflict when a Tejano rancher named Juan Cortina organized an armed group that briefly occupied the border town of Brownsville in protest against Anglo attacks on Tejano landowning. "Many of you have been robbed of your property, incarcerated, chased, murdered, and hunted like wild beasts, because your labor was fruitful, and because your industry excited . . . vile avarice," Cortina told his fellow ethnic Mexicans. *"Our personal enemies shall not possess our lands."*

To Texians, Cortina, who soon sought refuge across the border in Mexico, was little more than a simple "robber." Nevertheless, his actions seemed to risk spiraling beyond mere banditry into a plot, in the words of one Texian, to "reconquer our country as far as the Colorado River" and ignite a new war between the United States and Mexico. "Events have carried us forward," editorialized San Antonio's *Ledger and Texan,* "until what commenced in a foray of banditti, is now become a war of races, and is becoming a war of nations." Within a matter of months, US Army troops—including a then-obscure lieutenant colonel named Robert E. Lee—would be venturing across the border into Tamaulipas in search of Cortina, where they hazarded colliding with elements of Mexico's National Guard.

When war came, however, it was not between the United States and Mexico. Rather, internal instead of external conflicts tore each nation apart. North of the border, the United States' westward expansion into areas once belonging to Mexico exposed deep tensions over slavery that erupted into the Civil War. South of the border, the national contraction that followed defeat at the hands of the United States resulted in the War of Reform, pitting Mexican liberals and conservatives against one another as both sought to rebuild Mexico along competing models. Usually thought of as distinct defining traumas, these events might better be approached as simultaneous civil wars (or, if one prefers, simultaneous wars of reform). For all the issues distinguishing the two conflicts—the role of the Catholic Church in Mexico, the existence of slavery in the United States—they were linked by shared tensions over the meaning of citizenship and the question of how to create a national government that struck the appropriate balance between federal and local power.

Mexico's war came first. The Revolution of Ayutla deposed the dictator Antonio López de Santa Anna in 1854; armed conflict between liberals and conservatives soon followed. North of the border, hostilities came in 1861 after Texas and ten other Southern states left the Union and created the Confederate States of America. In its formal declaration of secession, Texas not only decried the prospect that the Northern states might tamper with the "beneficent and patriarchal system of African slavery" but also pointed to its vulnerable condition as a border state. Mexico had long harbored an alarming mix of escaped slaves, Mascogos, followers of Juan Cortina, and Comanche Indians. Yet the federal government, charged Texas's Secession Convention, had "almost entirely failed to protect the lives and property of the people of Texas against the Indian savages on our border, and more recently against the murderous forays of banditti from the neighboring territory of Mexico."

Victoria voted overwhelmingly in favor of secession (313 in favor versus 88 opposed), and many of the town's young Texians enlisted in the Confederate Army. Dr. Joseph Weisiger's son Robert served as aide de camp for General Arthur P. Bagby of the 7th Regiment of Texas Mounted Volunteers. Another son, William, raised a company of mounted men for "Special Service on the Western frontier." In contrast, most of Victoria's Tejanos, viewing the great contest between North and South as an alien affair, enrolled not in the regular Confederate Army but instead in units like the Victoria Cavalry Company, a militia dedicated to defending the nearby coast. There were exceptions, however. As befitted his closer contacts with the Texian community, "Sil" De León volunteered for the same cavalry unit as Robert Weisiger and saw service in the bloody Louisiana campaign before being captured by Union forces and spending the rest of the conflict in a prisoner of war camp.

The departure and, in some cases, death of Victoria's young men was not the only change war brought. The Union naval blockade of the Texas coast made the previous practice of shipping cotton via Port Lavaca impossible. Many planters turned to the only remaining option—the overland route to Mexico—dispatching long convoys of oxcarts south toward the border. The lone sea outlet not just for neighboring Texas but for the entire Confederacy, the border port of Matamoros, just across the Rio Grande from Brownsville, soon became one of the most commercially vibrant locales in all of Mexico—a bustling hub of intrigue, awash in all manner of refugees and hustlers: Southern deserters, Texan unionists, Union and Confederate agents, runaway slaves, and European dealers in cotton, armaments, and other supplies.

Matamoros served as an important entrepôt, too, for Mexico. In 1862, the War of Reform gave way to foreign intervention. Under the pretext of forcing Mexico to repay the debts incurred during its recent conflict, the French invaded and installed an Austro-Hungarian noble named Maximilian as the "emperor" of Mexico.

President Benito Juárez and his supporters retreated to the Mexican North, where Juan Cortina, now the governor of Tamaulipas and a general in the Mexican Army, oversaw the flow of customs fees and foreign arms into Matamoros.

———

IN JUNE 1864, the conflicts in the United States and Mexico were grinding through another year of bloodshed. The massed armies of Grant and Lee were engaged in brutal siege warfare to the north of the Confederate capital of Richmond, Virginia. In Mexico, Emperor Maximilian and his wife, Carlota, had just arrived in that nation's capital to assume their short-lived throne, while Juárez collected his forces along the US-Mexico border in Chihuahua. Not far across the boundary line, in Victoria, Margaret, then about nineteen, had begun to feel the swelling abdomen and faint, first kicks that revealed that she was pregnant with her and Charles's second child. This time, the infant would be a boy, named William Henry Ellis after his uncle.

A slave born to slaves, Margaret's newborn possessed no birth certificate recording his exact birthday. Later accounts would give varying dates, from June 10 to June 15 to June 24. But whatever the precise day, because of luck or fate or some other reason, his birth took place at a moment when the old order was beginning to collapse around him and the new had yet to take shape. As his parents cradled their newborn son in their arms amid the crude slave cabins on the Weisiger plantation and imagined what his future might hold, they had no way of knowing that in a little more than a year, the centuries-old institution of slavery would collapse in the United States, bringing to an end the largest and most profitable slave society in the Western Hemisphere. Nor could they have known that after decades of political tumult, Mexico would establish a new regime that would invite renewed US involvement in its affairs. A child born along the fault line where the United States and Mexico merged into one another, where black blended with white, where slavery was in its death throes but where its replacement remained uncertain, the infant William would find himself inhabiting a world filled with pressing questions as he grew to adulthood. If he was not to remain a slave, what was he to become? What race should he identify with given his mixed background and ambiguous appearance? Did his future lie in the United States—or across the border in Mexico?

2

JUNETEENTH

N OT UNTIL THE summer of 1865 did William Henry Ellis, then a toddler, witness the final moments of slavery for himself and his family. Change came in the form of a troop of US Army soldiers, sweating in the Texas heat beneath their wool uniforms and heavy rucksacks, trudging up the long, dirt road to the main yard of the Weisigers'. Typically, upon arriving at a new plantation, the troops assembled all the resident slaves and explained to them that they were now free—the meaning of this crucial term often left tantalizingly undefined amid the moment's joyous celebrations—before moving on to the next plantation. But the unit's officers took an apparent liking to the shady grove of live-oak trees that lined the Guadalupe River as it ran through the Weisigers' property. Rather than departing, they decided to bivouack their forces there for the next few months, the men swatting mosquitoes and listening to the hum of cicadas as they camped not far from the cabins of the Ellises and others of the Weisigers' former slaves.

The end of the Civil War had come late to Texas. The Lone Star State's remoteness from the war's main theaters not only spared it the physical devastation that afflicted the rest of the South; visions of victory and slavery lingered far longer in Texas than the rest of the Confederacy. Even in October 1864, the *Victoria Advocate* predicted a Confederate military triumph—"We feel that the South has achieved substantial advantages in the recent operations . . . and that the prospect of military success was never more bright"—and as late as the spring of 1865, Texian plantation owners were purchasing new slaves and driving them into the fields to cultivate yet another crop of cotton. At the very moment, however, that Charles, Margaret, and other slaves in the Lone Star State began to chop around the new cotton sprouts, General Robert E. Lee surrendered his Army of Northern Virginia at Appomattox. Even with this loss, the secessionist government held out hopes of reconstituting itself in Texas. Jefferson Davis planned to relocate to Houston and continue the fight from there—a scenario that sparked fears of a wider war, with Confederate Texas allying itself with its borderlands neighbor, imperial Mexico.

The Confederate president, however, never made it to Texas: US forces captured him in southern Georgia during his flight west. Soon afterward, enlisted men in the Lone Star State, unpaid because of the Confederacy's collapse, began to melt away. A remaining handful fought the Civil War's final battle on May 13 at Palmito Ranch along the Mexican border. In this curious coda to the secessionist conflict, Confederate soldiers, most of whom had spent the war guarding against "bands of banditti in Mexico," defended the border town of Brownsville from a motley US force composed of the all-white 34th Indiana Volunteer Infantry, the 62nd United States Colored Infantry, and a party of Texan Unionists, many of them Tejanos. The fighting took place so close to the international boundary that it attracted the attention of French soldiers stationed outside Brownsville's Mexican sister city, Matamoros, who were rumored to have alerted the Confederates to the US advance.

Even as the last official casualty of the Civil War fell at Palmito Ranch—a dubious honor that goes to one private John Jefferson Williams of the 34th Indiana—the few Confederate civilian leaders west of the Mississippi called upon their military to cease hostilities. Days after Williams's death, General Kirby Smith surrendered the remaining Confederate troops in Texas, then promptly fled to Mexico to offer his services to Maximilian. US forces did not arrive in appreciable numbers for several more weeks, and not until June 19, 1865, when Major General Gordon Granger landed at Galveston, did the federal government take its first steps to end slavery in Texas.

In a terse message bearing the nondescript title of General Order Number Three, Granger pronounced: "The people of Texas are informed that, in accordance with a proclamation from the Executive of the United States, all slaves are free."

Once word of Granger's order reached San Antonio, the sheriff released the eight runaway slaves locked in the town's jail. These one-time fugitives were left to ponder whether to continue their flight to Mexico or to return to the plantations that they had escaped not much earlier—a dilemma that encapsulated the uncertain conditions confronting African Americans throughout Texas. All over the Confederacy, Reconstruction raised momentous questions as to the political and legal status of the South's former slaves. These issues, however, took on special urgency in Texas, where the state's isolation had left slavery unusually entrenched—in fact, the number of enslaved people in the state had increased during the war, as planters relocated their human property to the Lone Star State to escape the fighting elsewhere in the Confederacy—and where the recent confrontation between US and Confederate forces at Palmito Ranch was considered a Southern victory. Four months after Granger's announcement of the supposed end of slavery in Texas, Brigadier General Edgar M. Gregory, the newly appointed assistant commissioner of the Freedmen's Bureau for Texas, found it necessary to issue a circular restating that African Americans were no longer to be kept in bondage. Even so, in Victoria and many other parts of Texas, actual emancipation did not take place until sufficient US troops arrived to enforce the policy.

For William and his family, the arrival of the US Army at the Weisiger plantation assumed a special poignancy: many of the first soldiers stationed to Texas were African Americans, enlistees in the United States Colored Troops. The sight of armed black men, dressed in uniforms that invoked the authority of the federal government, occupying Victoria's leading homes thrilled the newly freed slaves, but the town's whites found this same image deeply unsettling. "The idea of a gallant and highminded people being ordered and pushed around by an inferior, ignorant race," complained one local newspaper, "is shocking to the senses." For their part, the newly arrived soldiers loathed their Texas service. As Colonel James Shaw Jr., commanding officer of the 7th Infantry Regiment, United States Colored Troops, explained, when his men were slaves, Texas had "been held up to them as a sort of hell to which they would be sold if they misbehaved."

————

FOR THE ELLISES and other ex-slaves in Texas, freedom remained a new and fragile possession. Their vulnerability evinced itself almost immediately: in September 1865, the Victoria County Court passed a series of laws imposing harsh new burdens on local African Americans. According to the measures, all "indigent colored persons"—a status left solely to the court to determine—could be hired out as laborers to "such persons as may be willing to take said indigent colored persons at such price and on such conditions as he may see fit . . . and for such length of time as to him may seem just and proper." In addition, Victoria levied a tax upon all freedpeople, ostensibly to cover the costs of the flood of vagrant blacks Emancipation had unleashed upon the town.

   This effort to narrow the scope of freedom for Victoria's ex-slaves was paralleled across Texas just a few months later. As a condition for its readmittance to the United States, Texas was required by President Andrew Johnson's Reconstruction plan to rewrite its constitution in February 1866. The all-white delegates to the convention granted African Americans the most basic of rights—to acquire property, to negotiate contracts, to testify against other blacks in a court of law—but produced a constitution that limited the franchise and public office to "*white* citizen[s]." The disempowered freedmen could only watch in dismay as statewide elections produced an all-white legislature that, in one of its first acts, passed a restrictive set of Black Codes designed "to reenslave the negroes" in all but name. "I concede them [African Americans] nothing but the station of 'hewers of wood and drawers of water,'" explained State Senator W. C. Dalrymple. "God Almighty has placed a sufficiently broad line of demarcation between the races, and it does not seem the part of wisdom to attempt to obliterate it."

Where the Black Codes did not suffice, Texians maintained their dominance through physical intimidation. Slavery in the Lone Star State had long been permeated by violence; as Frederick Law Olmsted observed in 1854, "In Texas, the state of war in which slavery arises, seems to continue in undertone to the present." But slaves had also represented valuable investments whose deaths entailed a significant loss of capital for their owners. The lives of freedpeople, in contrast, came cheap. Within weeks of Emancipation, Texas's new, federally appointed governor reported that hundreds of "dead bodies of freedmen" had been "found here and there throughout the State— some found in waters in creeks, others floating down streams, others by the roadside, and elsewhere."

In Victoria, the terror rippling through the African American community was palpable to representatives of the newly created Freedmen's Bureau, the federal agency charged with supervising the former slaves' transition from bondage. "The disposition of the lower classes of Whites towards the freed peoples is not friendly," wrote Agent Edward Miller to his superiors. "They seem to be jealous of the freed people." William Neely, Miller's replacement, found the situation had only worsened. "There is a silent bearing down upon them [African Americans in Victoria] to the extent that freedmen are fearful of personal injury."

Such fears flourished amid incidents such as the one that took place in January 1867, when plantation owner Alex Cromwell Jr. shot and killed Martin Cromwell, one of Victoria's new freedmen. The quarrel that precipitated this murder is unknown, but given that the two shared the same last name, Martin likely was a former slave of Alex's. Confrontations between plantation owners and ex-slaves often erupted when freedmen, hoping to exercise their new liberty, attempted to negotiate over wages or seek work elsewhere. After Martin's murder, a group of African Americans ringed Alex Cromwell's house in hopes of capturing the assailant, while two others rode into town to report the slaying to authorities. When Victoria's law officials arrived, however, they arrested the freedmen for riot rather than pursuing the killer.

One of the few checks keeping the violence in Victoria from spiraling even further out of control was the presence of US troops. Initially, these forces had stayed on the outskirts of town at the Weisiger plantation. But in the spring of 1867, the US Congress, outraged at the return of former Confederates to power and the imposition of Black Codes on ex-slaves, repudiated President Johnson's relatively lenient policy toward the secessionist states, voiding Texas's new constitution and placing the entire South under military rule. This shift in policy expanded the army's presence in Victoria's center, with a US Army officer replacing the town's mayor, and the enlisted men relocating from the Weisigers' to the fairgrounds downtown. These developments remade Victoria's racial geography. African Americans—including the Ellises—fled into town to be close to military protection and the new schools for blacks (one Methodist and one Baptist) created by the Freedmen's Bureau. For their part, remembered one ex-Confederate, "most of the citizens of rebel proclivities secreted themselves in the country[side]" to distance themselves from federal oversight.

This later stage of Reconstruction witnessed the high tide of US efforts to protect the rights of ex-slaves. On the national level, Congress passed the Fourteenth and Fifteenth Amendments, making it clear for the first time that freedmen were to become citizens with "equal protection of the laws" and the right to vote regardless "of race, color, or previous condition of servitude," rather than laborers confined to an indeterminate, quasi-free status. Locally, Texas was obligated to revoke the most egregious aspects of its Black Codes and to rewrite its constitution to permit black suffrage and office holding.

These measures enabled a flowering of black politics in the Lone Star State. In 1860s and 1870s, some thirty-nine African Americans were elected to the Texas legislature; even more were voted into county governments. But the extension of suffrage to the freedmen did little to address the economic inequalities that forced most ex-slaves to grow cotton on whites' land for a portion of the harvest. By 1870, the overwhelming majority of African Americans in Victoria supported themselves as sharecroppers, and three-quarters of the county's black households possessed no wealth at all, making them far poorer than Victoria's white and Tejano residents. Even the US Army's expanded presence in town could not prevent all manifestations of racial violence. White vigilantes assaulted a teacher and students at one of the town's new schools for freedpeople; other whites killed two ex-slaves accused of cooperating with federal authorities.

Much of this violence took place in the open, so that everyone, including a young William Ellis, could bear witness to the risks of opposing white dominance in Victoria. In May 1870, a freedman named Charles Barnes was publicly tortured following his arrest for burglary. Originally confined to Victoria's jail, Barnes was turned over by the deputy sheriff to a gang of whites, led by the "most influential men of this town." The mob suspended Barnes several times by the neck, inducing near-strangulation, in an effort to get him to reveal where he had hidden his supposed loot. Barnes at last named a nearby ditch. But when it turned out to be empty, the group returned the following night and again removed Barnes from jail. After once more choking him with repeated hangings, the assembled men gave Barnes two hundred lashes with a rope. They then took the rope and tightened it with a stick around the luckless freedman's head until it "compressed his skull," leaving him "prostrate ever since."

———

THE CHAOS AND uncertainty of Reconstruction doubtless left a deep impression on Charles and Margaret, as well as their children, Elizabeth and William. Yet the most intimate glimpse of the effect the conflicts roiling Victoria had on their family comes through the Weisigers, who in freedom, as in slavery, remain better documented in the historical record. On May 1, 1866, not long after leaving the Confederate Army, Robert Weisiger, the youngest son of Dr. Joseph Weisiger, was shot while riding to his family's plantation. The assailant's bullet entered through Robert's mouth, shattering his jaw and tongue. Amazingly, despite this gruesome wound, the twenty-four-year-old managed to stagger home before succumbing two days later. His heartbroken father requested in his will to be buried next to Robert. Two of the dead man's older brothers, however, took harsher measures. After Robert described his assailant as a "colored person," Reed and Samuel Weisiger summarily murdered a local African American, leaving the man's bones to "bleach on the bleak prairie at the head of Spring Creek." Their vigilantism earned them the attention of federal officials, and the two fled to family back in Kentucky to avoid arrest.

History does not record the name of the freedman the Weisiger brothers lynched. But given that Robert's death happened close to the family's plantation and that the supposed killer seemed to have had some sort of preexisting quarrel with Robert, it is not at all unlikely that the freedman was a former slave of the Weisigers, as in the contemporaneous killing of Martin Cromwell. So even though the immediate Ellis family survived the violence of the Reconstruction period, it doubtless touched them close to home. Those enslaved on the Weisiger plantation had come to view each other as part of an extended family, a habit reflected in their custom of addressing one another as "cousin." The death of another ex-slave of the Weisigers would thus have been akin to the loss of a close relative—and a reminder of how, even in the aftermath of Emancipation, the actions of the Weisigers and other powerful whites like them still had a disproportionate impact on African Americans.

ACROSS THE BORDER, Mexico's civil war moved toward resolution. US leaders had long been disturbed by the French presence in Mexico, which they termed a violation of the Monroe Doctrine and, in the words of Ulysses S. Grant, "a direct act of war against the United States." During the Civil War, the United States had been hesitant to take aggressive action against the French for fear of causing them to support the Confederacy. Once the Confederacy collapsed in 1865, however, the United States lost little time in funneling muskets, ammunition, and other surplus military supplies from Texas to the forces under President Benito Juárez, who in the face of French military pressure had withdrawn to Paso del Norte, across from El Paso on the US-Mexico border. In addition, a surprisingly large number of discharged Union soldiers, anxious to support what they saw as a fellow republican cause in Mexico, made their way across the international boundary and enlisted in the *juarista* forces.

Ex-Confederates cast their eyes across the border, too, seeing in Mexico a possible new South. Perhaps as many as five thousand secessionists, building on earlier fantasies of adding northern Mexico to an expanded Confederacy, relocated across the border in hopes of reconstructing slavery on Mexican soil. At one time or another, the Confederates seeking refuge in Mexico included five ex-governors, seven ex-generals, and two ex-senators. These figures persuaded Maximilian, who aspired to create a whitened and Europeanized Mexico, to adopt a plan to colonize Mexico with Southern whites and their former slaves. The latter would be converted back into unfree laborers via oppressive "apprenticeship" contracts not all that different from the measures ex-Confederates had originally sought to impose in the US South via the Black Codes. The largest colony of the eight or so that took shape in Mexico was initially labeled "New Virginia." Although little more than a collection of bamboo huts outside Veracruz, the colony would soon, its supporters hoped, become "as large as Richmond." For their part, Mexican liberals fumed at the burgeoning alliance between Maximilian and ex-Confederates. "Not content with having conspired against the liberty of their own country," the American exiles, complained one *juarista* newspaper, were engaged in a "new conspiracy to destroy the liberty" of Mexico as well.

Other ex-rebels stayed closer to home but contented themselves with the thought that the United States' support for Juárez might trigger a war with the French. Southerners testifying before the US Congress's Joint Committee on Reconstruction admitted that they had "heard general exultation at the prospect of a war with Mexico and France, because it would cripple the United States." If "war [were] to occur between the United States and Mexico," added one, "thousands of young men would rush to Mexico" to fight "against the United States." As one former Confederate exclaimed at the end of the Civil War: "We are not conquered! We are on our way to Maximilian in Mexico!" Little surprise that Philip Sheridan and other US military leaders believed that "we never can have a fully restored Union, and give a total and final blow to all malcontents, until the French leave Mexico."

The most prevalent invocation of Mexico, however, was as an exemplar of the horrors of race mixing. With the end of slavery having cast their dominance into question, many white Texans feared that any step toward granting African Americans equal rights to education, employment, or the like would lead to marriage across the color line. As proof of the unnatural character of interracial liaisons, Texians singled out their southern neighbor, whose political turmoil was, they claimed, a result of its hybrid population. "A mongrel Mexico affords no fit example for imitation," exclaimed State Senator Dalrymple. "I desire the perpetuation of a white man's government." The "stubborn and sincere opposition" to extending voting rights to freedmen, added John Henninger Reagan, a Texian who served in Jefferson Davis's cabinet, could "be sustained by pointing to the examples of Mexico, and the Central and South American States, where by the enfranchisement of the Indians, and negroes . . . without reference to race or mental or moral fitness . . . they have been deprived of the blessings of peace, order, and good government."

This discourse on the perils of "Mexicanization" resonated far beyond Texas. Despite being a nation "blessed by nature"—"Her soil is rich; her climate is varied; the bowels of the earth are filled with the most precious metals"—Mexico was, asserted Democratic senator Thomas F. Bayard of Delaware, "a doomed and blasted country." "Mongrelism, the mixing of the bloods of different races, has destroyed it; and you no longer have a race there fit or worthy or capable of sustaining themselves under a government of law, and of protecting themselves in their persons and property as a civilized nation." If "negroes [are] included in our system," added New York's *Old Guard* magazine, "of course, like Mexico, etc., we become a mongrel people and incapable of upholding Republican institutions."

Ironically, at the very moment that Americans were depicting Mexico as racked by unending political chaos, Juárez was restoring the Mexican republic. France withdrew its troops from Mexico in early 1867. Within a few months, the luckless Emperor Maximilian, only thirty-four years old, was captured by Juárez's forces and executed by firing squad outside Querétaro, Mexico. Juárez's victory, commemorated by many in Mexico as the nation's second independence from European domination, in turn cemented the reforms that Mexican liberals hoped would convert their country into a modern nation-state, unfettered by the antiquated institutions and unequal privileges of the colonial era.

Much of the impetus for these reforms came from the trauma of the republic's repeated territorial losses in the 1840s and 1850s to the United States, which had demonstrated to *juaristas* that Mexico had yet to become a functional nation-state. Even so, Mexico prided itself on the fact that its own efforts at reconstruction exhibited none of the racial violence taking place with "alarming frequency" across the border in the United States. As the Mexico City newspaper *El Siglo Diez y Nueve* observed, the United States was just beginning to grapple with what it meant to create a unified nation out of a multiracial population, a step that Mexico had taken decades earlier: "We Spanish Americans have had the virtue of resolving, long before the Anglo Americans, the difficult problem of slavery and the political equality of our races and *castas*."

ONLY A FEW scraps of evidence capture the daily experiences of the Ellis family in Victoria as the momentous events in Mexico and the United States whirled around them. The first such fragment is the 1870 census, the earliest document in which appear the names of family members, now citizens rather than slaves, and the record that illuminates their ongoing memory of the Kentucky overseer Hezekiah Ellis. By 1870, the family had adopted the Ellis surname as its own, with the peculiar mix of pain and pride that doing so must have invoked. According to the census, the Ellis children Elizabeth and William—"Willie" according to the census—had been joined by a newborn girl, Fannie. Over time, two more girls, Avalonia and Isabella, followed Fannie as well as another boy, whom his parents, in another link to their time in Kentucky, named Hezekiah after his putative grandfather.

The 1870 census shows Charles and Margaret among the many freedpeople who relocated to Victoria's center, likely accompanying the US Army when the soldiers moved into town from the Weisiger plantation. The Ellis's immediate neighbors, who ranged from a French restaurant owner and a white lawyer to African American domestic servants, convey the jumble of races and classes living alongside one another amid the initial disruptions of Reconstruction. Somehow, Charles had managed to avoid the fate of the majority of freedmen in Victoria: rather than sharecropping, he was instead a low-level craftsperson, being listed in the census as a shoemaker. And while neighboring African American women found employment as seamstresses and washerwomen, Margaret had gained one of the hardest-won victories for freedwomen: instead of working outside the house in the cotton fields or in service to a white household, she was listed in the census as being "at home" with her growing family.

The next scrap of evidence relating to the Ellis family comes a year later, in August 1871, when property records document Charles Ellis and his younger brother, William, purchasing an acre of land together in Victoria. Sales of land to African Americans incited sharp controversy during Reconstruction, with many whites attempting to prohibit freedpeople from gaining economic independence via landownership. Tellingly, Charles and William bought their property not from a native-born Texian but rather from one of Victoria's German immigrants, a wheelwright named Dillman Mantz. Mantz sold the brothers only an acre of land and charged them seventy-five dollars, far above the prevailing rate at the time. One acre may not have been enough land to farm on, but it was enough for a house or two and a small garden, offering Charles and William and their families a potential haven in an uncertain world.

By the time of the 1880 census, however, the brothers were no longer living on their mutual plot. Charles had moved on from his work as a shoemaker and was listed as a "warehouseman," while William, living some distance away, remained a laborer. The family's neighborhood in Victoria had become more economically homogenous, composed overwhelmingly of working-class African Americans and German immigrants. Charles and William's mother, Mary, now lived with Charles's family, finding employment as a washerwoman. Taking in laundry was a common enterprise among African Americans at the time. Requiring few start-up costs, the work could be done at home, using the unpaid labor of family members, including, one suspects, Willie Ellis, now sixteen, and his sisters.

Even as a young man, however, Ellis did far more than wash other people's dirty linen. Unlike his parents or grandmother, who, according to the 1880 census, could neither read nor write, Willie could do both, having attended school in the past year along with his younger sister Fannie. Attending school up into one's teens was unusual in Victoria, where by necessity many adolescents from modest backgrounds, black and white alike, held full-time jobs. Willie and Fannie's first cousins—their uncle's children—were already working as farm laborers and domestic servants. But Willie and Fannie had an intimate connection to one of Victoria's "colored schools": in 1880, their oldest sister, Elizabeth, married a local African American schoolteacher named Greene Starnes. Presumably, the two youngsters attended their brother-in-law's institution, and one imagines that Starnes may have been forgiving when necessary about collecting school fees from his new family members.

If these documents capture the general contours of Ellis's early life, they remain silent on several key points. The first concerns how young Willie picked up the Spanish that he spoke, in the words of one observer, with "great fluency and considerable correctness." According to the 1870 and 1880 censuses, none of the Ellises' immediate neighbors were of Mexican descent. (Indeed, by the end of the Civil War, ethnic Mexicans had declined to 10 percent of Victoria's population.) A few Tejanos lived in downtown Victoria, but, with the lone exception of Joseph Lopez's Tienda Mexicana, Germans and Anglo-Americans owned all the businesses in the community's commercial heart, from its bakeries to its saloons to its blacksmiths' and wheelwrights' shops. In 1873, in a shift indicative of the literal and figurative displacement of Tejanos in Victoria, the town renamed its central roadways, setting aside such Mexican-era terms as Calle de los Diez Amigos in favor of English-language names like Main Street and turning De León Plaza into Constitution Square.

Those ethnic Mexicans who remained in Victoria clustered in the rural outskirts. Significant numbers of the extended De León family, for instance, still ranched in Mission Valley, close to the Weisiger plantation. It may have been from these onetime neighbors that older members of the Ellis family received an introduction to Spanish and learned to cook the tamales and other Mexican dishes that the family enjoyed preparing for itself in later years. But given that Willie was living in Victoria township by age six, these early interactions in Mission Valley could have had only a limited impact on him.

After Emancipation, Texians, still anxious about a possible "war of races," discouraged contacts between blacks and Mexicans, their fears spilling over into periodic panics or lynchings when relations between blacks and Tejanos seemed too cozy. Yet despite these apprehensions, Texas's mixed cotton-plantation/ranching economy may have played an unintended role in bringing such contacts about. By far the most labor-intensive part of the cotton cycle came in the early fall, when it was time to pick the fresh cotton bolls. Although the Ellis family now lived in town, in autumn the children still picked cotton on nearby plantations to raise money for school. During this seasonal labor, they would have found it hard to avoid coming into contact with ethnic Mexicans, who constituted a significant portion of Victoria's agricultural laborers. Such interactions increased with the arrival of barbed wire in 1875, as a number of local plantation owners, including the Weisigers, expanded their stockraising, an industry that often relied on experienced Tejano ranch hands. It was no doubt during his annual trips to plantations like the Weisigers' to pick cotton that Ellis acquired the familiarity with livestock that allowed him to later boast in such rarefied venues as *Herringshaw's American Blue-Book of Biography* that he "spent his early days as [a] cowboy on cattle ranches."

Over time, Willie's first, fumbling conversations in Spanish blossomed into something far more momentous, for with a new language came the potential to reinvent one's self. Ex-slaves in Texas reported that it was not unknown for them to be mistaken for an ethnic Mexican. "I am taken for a Mexkin [Mexican] very often," explained one, who, knowing Spanish, usually opted to "jes' talk Mexkin back to 'em." What new horizons must have beckoned to the young William Henry Ellis if, one day, a stranger, seeing a youth speaking Spanish, assumed him to be Mexican and addressed him as such? This moment would have represented Willie's first, unprompted opportunity to pass—to cross the color line by finding opportunity in another's mistake. For a young African American of ambition and intelligence, chafing at the limited roles of field hand or laundry worker—and all too aware of omnipresent threat of white violence—mastering Spanish represented the first step in creating a new identity and a new life.

The other point the documents remain silent on is how Willie and his family approached the issue of racial identity. All the Ellises appeared in the 1870 and 1880 federal censuses as mulattoes, as did a considerable portion of the other African Americans in Victoria—a subtle reminder that even as white Americans debated the perils of Mexican "mongrelization" during Reconstruction, race mixing had in fact existed in the United States for generations. (Although Texas had long prohibited marriage between whites and blacks—defined in the state's 1858 antimiscegenation statute as any person "descended from Negro ancestry to the third generation"—it never outlawed interracial sex, as this would, of course, have required policing the sexual exploitation of black women by white men.) From the point of view of the Texan legal system, unlike the Spanish *casta* system from which the term had been borrowed, "mulatto" did not signify a distinct group between black and white, with intermediate rights and privileges. Instead, it was the proverbial distinction without a difference, for the law collapsed all of those who possessed more than one-eighth "African blood" into the category black, whatever their social standing and however ambivalent their physical appearance. Whether the Ellis family felt any distinctions between themselves and other freedmen is uncertain. Perhaps not, given that there were many others living in Victoria whom the census recorded as mulattoes and the shared confinement of blacks and mulattoes alike in the bottom tier of the labor market. Elsewhere, however, African American communities did draw distinctions based on skin color. In neighboring Louisiana, for instance, fairer-skinned peoples with mixed African and Native American or European ancestry often described themselves as "colored" or "creoles," and for much of the nineteenth century enjoyed rights unavailable to those defined as "Negro." And, in the future, members of the Ellis family would end up selecting labels as varied as African American, white, and Mexican, as the family negotiated the racial fault lines running through American life.

———

THE WITHDRAWAL OF the Freedmen's Bureau in 1870, followed by a string of electoral setbacks that caused both houses of the Texas legislature to shift from Republican to Democrat, spelled the end of federal oversight in the Lone Star State. In its wake, Reconstruction left an ambivalent legacy. Emancipation had elevated African Americans from slaves to citizens. Under slavery, teaching slaves to read and write had been illicit; now freedmen could attend schools. The end of slavery had deprived the town's cotton planters of one of their largest capital investments, their human chattel, and with it, much of their wealth. In 1860, there had been thirty-three families with property worth more than $20,000 in Victoria; by 1870, just three families could boast of similar holdings. Land prices, too, collapsed from the belief that free African Americans could not farm as efficiently as slaves.

Beneath these profound shifts, however, many patterns of life exhibited but modest changes. Property in Victoria remained concentrated in Texian and a few Tejano hands, while the majority of African Americans owned no land, the foundation of wealth in a predominantly agricultural economy. Most of Victoria's whites continued to be partisans of the Democratic Party, which dominated local politics (among the party's avid supporters was Reed Weisiger, who by the 1870s had returned to town and become chair of Victoria's Democrats). The only schools open to African Americans were separate, poorly funded "colored" institutions. In 1876, the town's whites even established a "protection company" to watch over Victoria that echoed the slave patrol of the antebellum period.

One other continuity running through the antebellum and postbellum periods was Victoria's proximity to the international boundary. If slaves fleeing to Mexico were a thing of the past, enough other controversies remained for the *Victoria Advocate* to publish a regular column about "our outraged frontier." As in the antebellum period, Victorians retained a fascination with the tropical resources of their "neighboring republic." Hoping to diversify beyond the old crops of "'corn and cotton' and 'cotton and corn,'" some farmers in Victoria in the 1870s argued that, given the ecological continuities in the borderlands, the town could repeat its earlier success with Mexican cotton by cultivating Mexican coffee. Others in Victoria looked across the border as a possible site for agricultural expansion—not for cotton or coffee but for their burgeoning ranching operations. In the early 1880s, two cattlemen from Victoria purchased twelve leagues of land in Coahuila, not far from Piedras Negras, and transferred much of their herd south of the international boundary.

Mexico greeted such American overtures with unease. When Maximilian had attempted to become Mexico's emperor in the 1860s, Americans and Mexicans had united in common cause to remove the French from the continent. Once this goal was achieved, however, the long-standing tensions between the two republics reemerged. Americans complained of Indians, smugglers, and other criminals venturing across the Rio Grande into Texas—none more than the Texians' old rival Juan Cortina, who had survived the twists and turns of Mexican politics to be appointed commander of Mexican federal troops along the Rio Grande in 1870. When Cortina had troubled Confederate Texas, US officials had encouraged his activities. But now that Texas was again part of the United States, Cortina once more found himself a "bad Mexican" in American eyes. "Bands of Mexican robbers continue their depredations on the Texas side of the line," opined the *New York Times* in 1871. "War seems imminent." The Mexican press retorted that American newspapers overlooked similar incursions into Mexico by cattle thieves and Indians from the US side of the border in favor of articles designed to "flatter the passions of filibusters." Mexicans fretted that Texan expansionists intended to provoke the US Army into "grave conflict" along the border. "The result will inevitably be war; that is, intervention, a protectorate, and annexation," concluded a glum *El Siglo Diez y Nueve* in 1872.

The fear that the United States and Mexico would once again go to war with one another shaped the career of the man who would lead Mexico for the next quarter century, Porfirio Díaz. An acclaimed general in the war against the French, Díaz launched a coup against Juárez's successor, Sebastián Lerdo de Tejada, in 1876. Although Díaz continued many of Juárez's reforms, he initially met with disdain from his northern neighbors. Perceiving Mexico's new president as sowing chaos along their mutual border—in part because Díaz struck an early alliance with the Texians' nemesis, Cortina—the United States refused to recognize his government. Instead, the War Department dispatched troops to Texas, with orders to cross the international boundary, "punish" any marauders found in Mexico, and confiscate any property believed to have been stolen from US citizens.

For Mexicans, the US War Department's instructions signaled that nothing less than their "national honor [was] in question." Díaz's minister of war branded the policy allowing US soldiers to cross the border a violation of the "rules of international law, and even with the practice of civilized nations." Mexican units were rushed to the nation's northern boundary with orders to prevent any effort by "the troops of the United States [to] enter our territory. . . . [R]epel with force the insult that it is being sought to inflict on Mexico by the invasion of her territory."

Despite such saber rattling, Mexican and US forces carefully avoided one another as they patrolled their respective sides of the border, preventing a full-fledged war. The ultimate dissipation of such tensions, however, required years of skillful diplomacy by the Díaz administration. The new president developed a policy of defensive modernization, designed to open Mexico's economy to US investors while preserving the republic's political independence. The project had to strike a difficult balance. By allowing Americans greater access to natural resources, Mexico hoped to encourage the United States to forgo its ambitions to acquire more Mexican territory. As Matías Romero, the secretary of *hacienda* (treasury) who would go on to be Díaz's diplomatic representative in Washington, DC, explained, "The best means of impeding annexation is to open the country to the United States . . . with the objective of making annexation unnecessary and even undesirable." At the same time, increased American investment would strengthen Mexico so that it would be better able to oppose any future aggression from its northern neighbor if necessary.

The ensuing paradox—resisting the United States by opening Mexico up to American development—would bedevil the republic throughout the Porfiriato, as the decades-long era of Díaz's rule came to be known. Wary of being swallowed up by the United States, Mexican elites cast their eyes abroad for alternative models of modernization. It was in Europe, and, surprisingly, in Mexico's former imperial occupier, France, that Mexicans found the most compelling response. Even as they rejected the imperial implications of France's nineteenth-century neologism "Latin America," Mexicans found the notion of *latinidad*—a common civilization based on Romance languages and Catholic culture that united Mexico with such European countries as France, Spain, Portugal, and Italy—seductive. Mexico might be economically less advanced than the United States. But reimagined as part of the Latin world, it was the heir to a cultural tradition that, from the Mexican perspective, remained far richer than the brash commercialism of Protestant Anglo-America.

In the meantime, the opening to the United States continued apace. The Díaz administration inaugurated an ambitious program of railroad construction, allowing American railroads for the first time to penetrate the Mexican interior and to link the republic to the burgeoning US rail network. By the early 1880s, American-backed interests were constructing a number of railroads across the rugged deserts separating the two countries, three of them breaching the border in Texas (Eagle Pass, Laredo, and El Paso), another in Arizona (Nogales). In addition to subsidizing rail construction, Mexico also offered generous concessions to foreign companies to develop mines, plantations, and other export-oriented enterprises. The US and Mexican militaries cooperated on campaigns against the Apaches and other Indian peoples, who had long hindered investment along both sides of the border. Bowing to American pressure, the Díaz administration even arrested Juan Cortina, confining him to house arrest in Mexico City. (The United States reciprocated by detaining Mariano Escobedo, a Díaz rival who had been organizing in Texas against the Porfiriato.) Mexico even sought to emulate the United States' success in immigration. In one of his first presidential addresses, Díaz identified attracting immigrants to Mexico to settle in the nation's *terrenos baldíos* (vacant lands) as "one of our most imperious necessities."

This last policy, however, brought to the surface the fraught dilemmas Mexico faced in its rush to blend its modernization with the United States'. Leery of the Texas debacle of the 1830s, in which American colonists had seized the province and precipitated war, Mexican colonization law prohibited US citizens from acquiring public land in its "frontier states," cutting off Mexico's most obvious sources of immigration. Instead, Mexico desired to "increase the population with hardworking and useful people" from Europe, especially those from countries like France or Italy that shared Mexico's newfound "Latin" background. "Theirs is the same Latin race as ours and will come to counteract the [Anglo] Saxon migration that over-flowing us from the north could absorb us," opined Mexico City's *La Libertad* in 1882. Ideally, such colonists would settle along Mexico's frontier, simultaneously developing an underpopulated region and providing the buffer between the republic and the United States that Mexico had sought ever since the colonial period.

Mexico's low wages, however, caused the immigrants stream-ing across the Atlantic from Europe to favor the United States or Argentina over Mexico. Those immigrants who did arrive in Mexico tended to come from more unexpected shores. In the early 1880s, the American corporations constructing Mexico's new railroads imported thousands of contract laborers from the Caribbean, espe-cially Jamaica. The arrival in Mexico of large numbers of blacks for the first time since the colonial period sparked a heated controversy. Some commentators pointed to the Mexican Constitution's embrace of human rights, which gave the Jamaicans and other blacks the right to "enter, leave, and reside in the country," and to the repub-lic's pressing need to use whatever workforce was necessary to attain that "emblem of civilization," the railroad. But many others wor-ried that the presence of peoples of African descent would undo the nation's nascent modernization efforts. "Now is not the time, when the current of European immigration has started to establish itself," contended *El Monitor*, "when it is appropriate to attract blacks. We judge this conduct to be unpatriotic and we hope that the Secretary of Public Works will put an end to the evil that threatens us." The editors at *El Nacional* concurred: "We unswervingly put ourselves on the side of those battling black immigration. No one can obscure the vices of the African race, especially when it is so opposed to the needs of our homeland to mix this race with that of the Indian."

Others comforted themselves with the thought that Caribbean immigration grew out of private initiatives rather than government policy and that blacks might be better suited to lay tracks in Mexico's fever-ridden tropical lowlands than Mexican workers. But opposition to black migration did not confine itself to the Mexico City press. As the first Caribbean newcomers landed in Tampico, the town's

Department of Health "saw itself obliged to take serious measures" and bar the laborers from the local hospital "because of the fear of an epidemic in our port." Other Caribbean workers found themselves charged with public drunkenness. Two were even accused of raping a woman in Tampico, and the town's residents, as one Mexican observer put it, "showed themselves imitators of our North American neighbors and applied the Lynch law to them."

Such *"inquietudes,"* as the Mexican press put it, toward Caribbean immigration underscored the reconceptualization that race had undergone in Mexico. If the colonial *casta* system had slotted peoples of African descent to the bottom of the racial hierarchy, at least it had acknowledged their existence. Since independence, however, Mexico had abandoned the idea of *castas* for a new vision of itself as a *mestizo* nation. To many Mexicans, racial mixing promised to assimilate the republic's restive indigenous majority. (Mexican Indians launched some forty-four rebellions between 1840 and 1860 as they struggled to retain their communal lands, which had become imperiled by Mexico's post-Independence policy of treating Indians as individual citizens rather than members of self-governing native communities.) One unintended consequence of this focus on Mexico's indigenous population was that *mestizaje* came to be defined as occurring solely between Europeans and Indians, erasing the republic's centuries-old African presence. "Mexico is inhabited by descendants of the conquerors of Mexico and other European races, by native Indians found there during the Spanish conquest, and by a mixture of the two," contended Matías Romero. "There are so few inhabitants of African descent that it is hardly worthwhile to speak of them." Such formulations imagined Mexico on a trajectory from a diverse *casta* past to a homogenous *mestizo* future—and confined the black immigrants arriving in the 1880s to the status of disruptive newcomers, rather than representatives of an ethnic group with a centuries-long presence in the country.

THE SAME WEB of steel tracks creeping its way across the Mexican landscape soon enmeshed Victoria, too. On July 4, 1882, the New York, Texas, & Mexican Railway officially reached the town. The teenaged William Ellis would have been among those crowding Constitution Square to witness the arrival of Victoria's first train, the centerpiece of that year's Independence Day celebrations: "Bells were rung, cannons fired and welcomes and huzzas were shouted." Within a matter of years, another line, the Gulf, Western Texas & Pacific Railway, also connected Victoria to the outside world. Victoria was now but a short railroad ride away from Texas's largest cities—Galveston, Houston, and San Antonio—as well as the Mexican border. Not only did the railroad integrate Victoria more fully into national and, in the case of Mexico, international markets; it offered, as one Mexican railway promoter put it, "the suspension of time, distance, cost, and danger." Journeys that were once measured in days if not weeks now took hours. To coordinate train schedules over their new continental rail system, the railroads even created four North American time zones in 1883, unilaterally supplanting local timekeeping in Victoria and elsewhere with centralized clocks set by the railroads.

As the era's preeminent emblem of modernity, the railroad also emerged as a leading venue for shaping race relations. If south of the border discussions of race and railroads focused on their workforce, north of the border the debate concerned ridership. By throwing the residents of previously separate settlements into close proximity with one another, the railroad generated intense anxiety among whites, for how were they to know the race of those seated beside them? In response to such concerns, railways endeavored to draw the color line from their very creation, despite vigorous African American resistance. In Victoria, these tensions played themselves out in a notable early court case. In September 1886, a pregnant young woman from Victoria named Lola Houck, off to visit family members in Rosenberg, Texas, some ninety miles away, purchased a ticket in the Victoria station, as she had done several times before. Observers, describing her as "ladylike," noted that by "casually looking at her or her husband it would be difficult to distinguish either of them from white persons." But, it emerged later in court, Houck had "some degree of negro blood in her veins": in fact, she and her husband, Leon, a merchant, were pillars of Victoria's African American community.

The carrier had sold Houck a first-class ticket. Once she boarded the train, however, the brakeman locked the door to the first-class car and directed her to the Jim Crow car in the front, intended "for the use of colored people." (The brakeman later admitted that Houck's "real" race was invisible to him: "When she [Houck] had traveled before with him he did not know she was a negro. . . . He only knew she was a colored woman [this time] after the bootblack on the train told him.") Houck refused to accept the change in accommodations. Conditions in the Jim Crow car were clearly inferior, with unpadded seats and male passengers, black and white (who could sit wherever they wanted), "boisterous[ly]" drinking and smoking—an improper setting for a respectable woman of any race. Moreover, she had paid the extra money for a first-class ticket. The brakeman, aided by the train's conductor, nonetheless repeatedly denied Houck's efforts to gain entry to the first-class car, even ripping her dress in one tussle. Houck ended up making the entire journey from Victoria to Rosenberg standing outside on the platform between the two cars in a cold rain. Three days later, she miscarried her child, a misfortune Houck attributed to her rough treatment by the Southern Pacific Railway.

Outraged, Houck sued the railroad and won $2,500 in damages. Her victory, however, did not come because the court ruled racial segregation illegal but rather because she was denied access to first-class accommodations despite purchasing a first-class ticket. In the eyes of the court, had Houck been identified as black in the Victoria train station and prevented from buying a first-class ticket, or had the conditions in the Jim Crow coach equaled those in the whites-only coach, the discrimination against her would have been perfectly acceptable. The ruling thus did nothing to alter the railroad's policies. The railway continued to set aside the first-class car exclusively for white passengers and even promoted the brakeman who had so vigorously barred Houck's entry.

Houck's constrained victory revealed with stark clarity the rising tide of segregation seeping across Texas in the years after Reconstruction. By 1891, rather than relying on corporate policies to separate blacks and whites, the Texas legislature mandated segregation on all railroads. Yet Houck's trial offered a less obvious lesson as well. The railroad might want to keep African Americans out of its first-class cars, but to what extent was it possible to determine whether someone was black or not? Lola Houck, after all, had ridden in the first-class railway car on previous occasions; she would have continued to do so had the local bootblack not identified her. For those who did not look or behave in ways believed to be "black"—and who could escape the gaze of nosy neighbors intent on enforcing the color line—there were, it seemed, fissures in the emerging post-Emancipation racial order.

———

WILLIAM H. ELLIS was eighteen when the train first reached Victoria, and twenty-two when Lola Houck's conflict with the Southern Pacific dominated local news. Although we do not know precisely when he began experimenting with presenting himself as a member of a different ethnic group—passing—the first evidence of his doing so comes from this period. The connection between these two events, passing and the coming of the railroad, was more than coincidental. For young blacks like William Ellis, the railroad encapsulated the paradoxes of life after Reconstruction. The steam engine opened up vast new horizons, allowing African Americans, a group only just emerging from the stifling confinements of slavery, to transcend space at a speed and scale previously unimaginable. Little wonder that with its connotations of motion and transformation—not to mention its propulsive rhythm—the train became a favored motif of the blues, the new African American musical genre taking shape in the South in the aftermath of Emancipation. Yet for all its promise, the railway, with its inferior, Jim Crow cars, simultaneously symbolized the novel humiliations that whites sought to impose on African Americans. Segregationists even converted that novel feature of local geography, the railroad track, into a divider between black and white: in Victoria, as in so many other Southern towns, "the Bottom," the town's African American neighborhood, was located on the proverbial wrong side of the tracks. If the railroad represented the dawning of a new era, it was one in which the color line threatened to become the defining feature.

One obvious solution to such discrimination was to exploit the instability of racial categories and portray oneself as a member of a different race altogether. Revealingly, the only time that Ellis publicly acknowledged passing (an 1891 interview with a Chicago newspaper), he pointed to railroad travel as his impetus for doing so. "In passing through Texas from Mexico," he contended, "I am forced to pass as a Mexican in order to obtain the ordinary comforts of a white traveler." Doing so involved deploying stereotypes that whites might conveniently misinterpret. On a train trip in Florida, the African American writer James Weldon Johnson managed to remain in the first-class compartment by speaking Spanish and wearing a distinctive Panama hat. Likewise, when the teenaged Langston Hughes changed trains in Texas in the early 1900s, he pomaded his hair "in the Mexican fashion" before entering the segregated waiting room and ordering a ticket in Spanish for the whites-only sleeper car. As with Johnson—and no doubt Ellis—the clerk never inquired as to his customer's background. Rather, as Hughes put it, he "mistook" the traveler's race based on language and appearance. " '*Dame un boletto Pullman to Chicago*,' will get you a berth in Texas," observed Hughes, "when often plain English . . . will not."

Passing required anonymity—the presence of strangers who, knowing little about the passer beyond appearance and behavior, were vulnerable to misdirection. In a small town like Victoria, however, anonymity was a scarce commodity. Only 6,200 people lived in the entire county in 1880, and William's family had inhabited the community for several decades. As Lola Houck's experience underscored, in any purely local effort to reinvent yourself, you ran the risk that a random passerby like a bootblack might recognize you and reveal your "real" racial identity. The unprecedented mobility opened up by the railroad, however, made it easy to distance oneself from one's hometown and, if one so desired, one's ethnicity as well. At some point in the 1880s, this is precisely what Ellis did.

For several years prior to his transformation, Ellis had been employed in the shop of William McNamara, one of Victoria's leading cotton and hide dealers. A recent immigrant from Ireland, McNamara managed in just a few years to build a well-appointed home for himself and his four daughters in downtown Victoria and become prominent in local politics, serving three terms on the city council. Like many other dealers in agricultural staples in the rural South, McNamara served as a middleman. His ads, promising "Highest cash prices paid for cotton, hides and wool," were a regular feature of the *Victoria Advocate* in the 1870s and 1880s. Buying directly from ranchers and plantation owners, he resold his wares to the Northern factories that were turning Texan cotton and hides into calico, shoes, and other goods for a growing consumer economy.

McNamara was also the person who unwittingly introduced Ellis to the cross-border Mexican trade. Years later, Ellis informed interviewers that he first became intrigued with the idea of selling cotton south of the border when "employment with a leather and hide merchant . . . took him on business trips into Mexico." Noting that even though cotton commanded a higher price across the border, many Americans, unfamiliar with the language and laws in Mexico, were "timid" about doing business there, Ellis seized on this opportunity to sell to Mexican buyers and "in that way laid aside a tidy little sum of several thousand dollars."

Ellis's duties in McNamara's shop are unclear, but given his precocious language skills and McNamara's status as a newcomer, the most likely scenario is that Ellis served as a Spanish interpreter for his boss. Once he became accustomed to conducting business in Spanish for his employer, it was but a small, if momentous, step for Ellis to repurpose these skills to his own ends. Rather than living out his expected role as a black man—a lifelong assistant in someone else's enterprise—William, then in his early twenties, undertook a stunning reversal. Boarding the

train to San Antonio and taking what he had learned watching McNamara (and, for all we know, many of McNamara's contacts and clients
as well), he switched his era's racial codes. Now it was Ellis who was
the entrepreneur, bargaining for cattle hides and cotton across the US-
Mexico border and employing others to work for him.

William was not the only member of his family to journey over
the new railroad tracks linking Victoria and San Antonio. His sisters preceded him: Fannie appears in the 1885 San Antonio directory, listed as teaching at the city's school for African Americans and
boarding with her brother-in-law, Greene Starnes, by this time a successful doctor in the Alamo City; Avalonia shows up the following
year. William may well have visited San Antonio regularly at this
time, both to check in on relatives and to test the possibilities of this
new setting. But only in 1888 does the city directory feature him as a
full-time resident.

William's listing, however, differed dramatically from those of his
relatives. He did not share the same address as his sisters and brother-
in-law nor—unlike the entries for Fannie, Avalonia, and Starnes—
was his listing followed by the telltale *c* that identified its bearer as
"colored." William instead told his new acquaintances that he was an
ethnic Mexican named Guillermo Enrique Eliseo and that "William
Henry Ellis" was just a translation of his name for the convenience of
English speakers. (As one commentator explained helpfully—albeit
in mangled Spanish that only aided William's efforts—there were
two names by which the new arrival was known, "Ellis in the North
and Guillaume Enriques Ellisio in Mexico.") Moreover, upon moving
to the Alamo City, Ellis announced his presence in as public a way as
possible. The directory in which his name first appears also includes
a full-page ad—far grander than any of McNamara's announcements
in the *Victoria Advocate*—for "W.H. Ellis & Co.," a dealer in "hides,
wool, and cotton . . . green salted hides a specialty." The business's
offices were located in the heart of San Antonio: the west side of Military Plaza, only a few steps away from the seat of local power, San
Antonio's new city hall. In his spare time, William frequented the
nearby Menger Hotel, San Antonio's most exclusive establishment,

which featured a mahogany-lined bar that was a favorite spot for local entrepreneurs to negotiate deals.

Ellis's choice to pass in plain sight demonstrates not only his remarkable self-confidence but also the odd quirks in how race was lived in the post-Reconstruction South. Texas law suggested that race could be easily measured: anyone with at least one black great-grandparent was "colored." But since it was almost impossible for anyone, black or white, to prove the race of ancestors across multiple generations (especially when these ancestors, more often than not, were dead), in practice Texians tended to rely on "commonsense" ways of assessing race. Skin tone alone rarely settled the issue; as one commentator put it in the late nineteenth century, although "our Southern high-bred people will never tolerate on equal terms any person who is even remotely tainted with negro blood . . . they do not make the same objection to other brown or dark-skinned people, like the Spanish [or] the Cubans." Instead, Americans invoked a plethora of factors: physical traits such as hair, feet, voice, and smell, but also dress, social standing, and community reputation.

Ironically, once this evaluation assigned an individual to a certain racial group, it became almost impossible to revisit the decision. Given that race was imagined to be so powerful, how could one have made a mistake earlier? Revising racial categories was all the more challenging if one were to accuse a person of being African American. So damaging was such a charge in the nineteenth century that whoever made it could be sued for slander. One unintended consequence of the stigma attached to blackness, then, was that unless one felt certain that the ancestry of another's great-grandparent was provable in a court of law, legal practice discouraged reassessing a racial classification once it had become widely accepted. "A white man fears to insult another in the South," contended one African American who, like Ellis, experimented with passing. "When in doubt, he lets you alone." Louis Baldwin, the author of *From Negro to Caucasian*, concurred: "There is an extreme delicacy about accusing a person of being a Negro. It is so degrading to be thus identified that people hesitate to make the accusation . . . . Unless therefore there are distinct evidences that the individual in question is a Negro, he may go his way without interference."

For William, these peculiarities meant that once he passed successfully for the first time in San Antonio—something facilitated by the city's thousands of ethnic Mexicans, who made up over 20 percent of the population—later attempts became that much easier. Otherwise, his new associates would have to admit to the embarrassing reality that they had been in close contact with an African American yet been unable to recognize their new companion's blackness. This also explains the counterintuitive logic to the young hide merchant's taking offices in the city center and issuing large advertisements for his firm in the city directory, rather than skulking in the shadows. The more widespread his acceptance, and the more he eschewed the low-level positions held by African Americans like his father and uncle in favor of activities that were seen as unimaginable for blacks, the more compelling his new persona became.

In reinventing himself as Guillermo Enrique Eliseo, Ellis crossed not only racial lines but class lines as well. As he had observed firsthand in Victoria, the status of peoples of Mexican descent in Texas hinged on their economic condition. Texians treated those ethnic Mexicans with property, such as the members of the De León family, as "Spanish," with all the privileges of whiteness that this term invoked, while they dismissed landless Tejanos as mere "greasers." In crafting a Mexican persona, Ellis thus took care to convey an image of himself not as an impoverished peon but rather as a member of the Tejano commercial elite, linked to well-placed family members across Mexico and Cuba.

At this point, one might expect Ellis to settle into a comfortable existence in San Antonio, selling cotton and cattle hides back and forth across the US-Mexico border, perhaps surreptitiously dropping in on his nearby family members from time to time. By the 1880s and 1890s, after all, William's siblings and brother-in-law lived on Blum, Bonham, and then Crockett Streets, all mere blocks away from William's Market Street residence, while Starnes's medical dispensary on Commerce Street was literally around the corner from William's office on the old Spanish colonial Plaza de las Armas ("Military Plaza" to the town's English speakers). But Ellis selected a far different path. Within a remarkably short period of time, he would throw himself into a number of activities that would imperil his new identity and propel him far beyond the plazas of San Antonio.

PART II

SAN ANTONIO

———

TLAHUALILO

3

MILITARY PLAZA

GEOGRAPHICALLY, ELLIS'S NEW hometown, situated almost exactly the same distance from the border as Victoria, marked the spot where the Texas hill country met the state's vast coastal plain. Economically, however, it lay at the heart of the commercial nexus between Mexico and the United States. As early as the 1830s, San Antonio, the onetime capital of Spanish and Mexican Texas, had served as a flourishing hub for transborder exchange—so much so, in fact, that most antebellum San Antonio merchants opened branch offices across the border in Chihuahua. With the passage of time, this relationship only deepened, helped along by a steady influx of Mexican refugees fleeing the War of Reform, which ensured that "almost everyone" in San Antonio, in the words of one observer, "spoke Spanish and most of the business was conducted in this common language."

By the time Ellis set up shop there near the close of the nineteenth century, Anglo and Mexican entrepreneurs had repurposed the elegant stone houses lining Military Plaza, once the homes of leading Tejano families, into offices and warehouses for a thriving transborder trade with Mexico. In the daytime, the hard-packed dirt of La Plaza de las Armas was crowded with mule- and oxcarts carrying goods into Mexico. At night, the inhabitants of the neighboring "Mexican quarter"—"Laredito" or "little Laredo"—replaced wagon trains bound for the border with an impromptu marketplace. Such conditions rendered La Plaza de las Armas "the heart of Mexican life.

The small vendors, the freighters, the pastores, peones, and vaqueros, all congregated here." Commentators opined that even though "the political border was at the Rio Grande . . . Military Plaza was the commercial and social border between the countries."

In relocating to San Antonio's plazas, where the dust of wagons bound for Mexico and the scent of Mexican cooking hung heavy in the air, Ellis once again inhabited his era's most liminal space between the United States and Mexico. If Victoria had represented the antebellum border between the American slave plantation and the Mexican cattle ranch, San Antonio—and especially Military Plaza—signified the deepening economic bonds between the two countries set in motion by the Porfiriato. As American trade and investment flowed south, increasing numbers of wealthy Mexicans traveled north along the new railroads linking the two countries to shop in San Antonio's stores, bank at its financial institutions, and visit its doctors. (Ellis's brother-in-law, Starnes, was the only African American doctor in the Alamo City in the 1880s, but the community included several Tejano physicians.)

Juxtaposed against this expanding relationship between the United States and Mexico were the narrowing possibilities for African Americans in Texas during these same years—a development that William observed firsthand from his office in La Plaza de Armas. San Antonio had a reputation for being less hostile to freedpeople than other communities in Texas, perhaps because of its physical remove from Texas's plantation belt, perhaps because of its relatively small black population (15 percent, compared to close to 40 percent in Houston and Austin). Even so, African Americans in San Antonio found themselves relegated to "negro work": demeaning, dirty, and sometimes dangerous employment as janitors, servants, cart drivers, ditch diggers, and other positions of the sort typically filled by slaves in the antebellum period. As a result, African Americans in San Antonio experienced little of the upward mobility of the city's European immigrants or Mexican Americans in the decades after 1870. For evidence of this harsh reality, William had to look no further than to his own family: his recently widowed father, Charles, and younger brother, Hezekiah. Both relocated to San Antonio soon after Fannie and William, only to be confined to menial positions, Charles as a porter and Hezekiah first as an elevator "boy" and then as a janitor like his father.

William's response to this situation would draw him out of his carefully created new persona into the dizzying maelstrom of Mexican and US politics in the 1880s and 1890s. Over time, Ellis would craft a unique approach to the dilemmas confronting African Americans. He began, however, by apprenticing himself to a pair of powerful mentors, Norris Wright Cuney and Henry McNeal Turner, influential politicians with compelling, if opposed, visions of how African Americans should advance in a hostile white world. Both had emerged out of the era's preeminent crucible for black politics, the Union League. Founded in the North in the early 1860s to rally support for the war effort, the league spread throughout the South during Reconstruction, where it attracted freedmen into local lodges aligned with the Republican Party through a blend of the secular (national symbols such as the flag, the Constitution, and the Declaration of Independence) and the sacred (outreach from the African Methodist Episcopal Church and other religious groups).

Ellis was drawn into Cuney's orbit first. Born on the Sunnyside plantation near Hempstead, Texas, in 1846, Cuney was the son of a slave mother and a slaveholding father. Cuney's father, Philip Minor Cuney, also had a white family (in fact, he would outlive three white wives). Unlike many other slave owners, however, he acknowledged his mulatto offspring, manumitting the thirteen-year-old Cuney in 1859 and sending young Norris along with several of his brothers to George B. Vashon's School for Colored Youth in Pittsburgh, Pennsylvania. As they grew to adulthood, some of Cuney's siblings, such as his sister Jennie, took advantage of their light complexions to pass into the white community. But Cuney opted instead to return to his home state to participate in Reconstruction. He settled in Galveston, Texas's leading seaport and the headquarters for the state's Freedmen's Bureau.

One of the few African Americans in Texas with higher education, Cuney quickly emerged as a community leader, first with the Union League and then among black workers on Galveston's docks. In 1883, he helped African American stevedores break the exclusive hold that whites had long exercised over dock work by founding the Galveston Colored Screwmen's Benevolent Association (so named because stevedores at the time used a tool called a screwjack to pack cotton into ship holds). Building on the support of this new African American union and his skills as an orator and organizer, Cuney rose through the ranks of the Texas Republican Party, acquiring the post of Galveston's customs collector—an important position from which to distribute federal patronage—and becoming in 1886 the chairman of the Texas Republican Party, the most prominent party post held by any African American in the South in the nineteenth century.

Politics in post-Emancipation Texas was a harsh business. Not only did partisan divisions persist between Democrats, dominated by ex-Confederates, and Republicans, the party of Lincoln and the Union; the Republican Party itself was fractured along racial lines. Although African Americans made up only a quarter of Texas's population, they constituted a majority of the state's Republican voters. Even so, many white Republicans proved unwilling to accept the blacks flocking to their party as anything other than mere voters. Other, even more extreme Republicans, whom Cuney dubbed the "Lily Whites," feared that the party would be confined to secondary status if freedmen "Africanize[d]" it. The solution, argued San Antonio's appropriately titled new newspaper, the *White Republican*, was simple: purge the party of all African Americans. Doing so "would effectively remove from the republican party. . . the stigma that is now attached to it, of being . . . called the 'negro party.'" (The *White Republican*'s effort to purify Texas politics also extended to ethnic Mexicans: the paper accused "Mexican cotton pickers," many of them recent immigrants, of being pliant tools of the Democratic Party.)

Although the Lily Whites did not succeed in their efforts to exile African Americans from the Republican Party, their presence made for bitter party meetings throughout the 1880s and 1890s. It was in this milieu of fierce intraparty struggles that William Ellis emerged as an important Cuney backer. As he did so, however, Ellis could not avoid becoming entangled in the color line that the Lily Whites were drawing through Texas politics. The first record of Ellis's venture into politics comes from the presidential election year of 1888, when newspapers reported that Ellis, then only twenty-four years old, gave a spirited speech in support of Cuney at one of the pillars of Victoria's African American community, its "colored Baptist schoolhouse." Ellis's charisma and flair for language—the same skills that facilitated his passing—also assisted his budding political career, for he succeeded not only "in carrying his point" with the assembled throng but also in getting selected as a delegate to the Republican Party state convention in Fort Worth. Five months later at the convention, Cuney repaid Ellis's support by appointing him to the Texas Republican Party's Committee on Resolutions.

In the presidential election year of 1892, Ellis was even more active in rallying support for Cuney. According to press reports, when Cuney came to Victoria for the Republican district convention, he was met at the train station by "W.H. Ellis and the Victoria colored brass band." Rumors floated around Victoria that a group of disgruntled Lily Whites planned to crash the district convention and take it over. But, observers noted, Ellis had gotten wind of the plot and "has been actively manipulating things here in the interests of Cuney for several days past. . . . It is the general belief that at the powwow to-morrow the Cuneyites will have things their way."

Events did indeed go Ellis and Cuney's way at the district convention. Not only did Ellis stave off the Lily Whites; in recognition of his leadership, local Republicans selected him "by acclamation elector for this district," a role that propelled Ellis further up the ranks of the Texas Republican Party. At the Republican convention several months later, Ellis reached what in retrospect represented the apogee of his involvement in electoral politics: the assembled delegates nominated him to represent the 83rd District in the Texas legislature. Soon the energetic young candidate could be found circulating through Victoria and the neighboring counties of Calhoun, Jackson, Refugio, and Bee, speaking to "considerable applause" at Republican assemblies.

When Ellis began his foray into politics, local newspapers had accepted his self-portrayal as "'Mexican' Ellis." "W.H. Ellis, from Mexico, was up from Galveston," observed the *San Antonio Daily Light*, and "made a red-hot speech." But over time, Ellis found himself branded a "colored aspirant for legislative honors." As such references made clear, Ellis's involvement in electoral politics had come at a cost: the undermining of his efforts to pass. It was almost impossible in the charged politics of post-Reconstruction Texas to avoid racial issues. Ellis may have clung to the hope that since his home district did not include San Antonio, he could compartmentalize his identities, serving as a black politician in Victoria yet remaining a Mexican entrepreneur in San Antonio. But Ellis's double life was not easy to maintain once press coverage spread word of his political involvement across the state. Moreover, it received little support from Cuney. With his straight hair and olive complexion, the Republican Party chair easily could have passed had he wanted. Observers at the time described him as "look[ing] like a Mexican" or a native of "Italy's sunny clime."

Cuney refused, however, to conceal his racial background, as his daughter, Maud, related in a revealing episode. Around 1890, Maud was traveling with her father to a political meeting in New York City. As she waited at a restaurant for her father to join her for breakfast one morning, the waitress mistook Maud, whose mother, like Cuney, was the product of a relationship between a white slave owner and a black slave, for "Spanish." Maud corrected the waitress, then explained the situation to her father when he arrived. "He said: 'You did right in declaring your race,'" remembered Maud. "He abhorred above all things the supposedly easier way of 'passing for white,' and instilled in my young brother and me a hatred and contempt for the cowardly method which is upheld by many who can successfully disown their negro blood." (Ironically, in 1898, Maud Cuney would marry J. Frank McKinley, an African American doctor, who insisted that the couple take advantage of their light complexions to pass as "Spanish Americans." Ellis may have even served as the catalyst for their decision: newspapers at the time reported that "W.H. Ellis of Mexico" was a guest at the nuptials.)

Ellis's venture into politics, however, exposed his double life. Even worse, it was a gamble that had not paid off. The rise of the People's Party, which under the leadership of the light-skinned mulatto John B. Rayner forged an unlikely black-white alliance in Texas through appeals to shared economic concerns, had unexpectedly complicated the 1892 election. Although never an overwhelming presence in Victoria, Rayner's "Colored Populist Clubs" siphoned off enough of the black vote to cause Ellis to lose his bid for the legislature to A. G. Kennedy, a white Democrat from Beeville.

Although Ellis continued to support Cuney, he never again ran for public office. Instead, over time he disengaged from the Republican Party and turned to another, quite different political figure: Henry McNeal Turner. Born free in South Carolina in 1834, Turner was also of mixed background, his father being the offspring of a liaison between a white woman, Julia Turner, and one of the black overseers on her plantation. When he was only nineteen, Turner became an evangelical minister, first for the Methodist Episcopal Church and then for the African Methodist Episcopal Church. In these roles, he traveled through much of the antebellum South until new legislation designed to enslave free blacks caused him to move north of the Mason-Dixon line. During the Civil War, Turner served as the first African American chaplain in the US Army. Afterward, he helped to organize the Republican Party in Georgia, working through the Union League and black mutual aid societies, much as Cuney had done in Texas.

Yet while Cuney retained a belief in the political process despite his tangles with the Lily Whites, Turner grew more skeptical. His encounters with the era's virulent racism, which included his being expelled from the Georgia House of Representatives by white legislators who refused to accept the presence of Turner and other elected black officials, caused him to sour on the possibility of African Americans ever achieving true equality in the United States. By 1876, he had become an honorary vice president of the American Colonization Society, the preeminent organization dedicated, in the language of the day, to "colonizing" African Americans overseas, and had begun to preach the need for blacks to leave the United States for Africa. "I would make Africa the place of refuge, because I see no other shelter from the stormy blast, from the red tide of persecution, from the horrors of American prejudice," declared Turner. "I do not believe any race will ever be respected, or ought to be respected, who do not show themselves capable of founding and manning a government of their own creation."

Ellis's introduction to Turner may have come from reading Turner's pamphlets, which enjoyed a wide circulation by the early 1880s. Or it could have come in 1887 when Turner, touring Texas, spoke in San Antonio. What is certain is that by 1889, Ellis had begun to entertain ideas of emigration himself, although not in quite the same vein as Turner. Whereas Turner looked to the African past in his search for a sanctuary for African Americans, Ellis instead envisioned a future for American blacks that was located across the border in Mexico. To further this goal, in August 1889, Ellis and Henry Ferguson, another African American supporter of Cuney's, traveled south on the new rail line to Mexico City, bearing letters of introduction from the Mexican consul in San Antonio to Mexico's secretary of foreign affairs, Ignacio Mariscal, and secretary of *fomento* (public works), Carlos Pacheco Villalobos. Ferguson and Ellis persuaded Pacheco, a grizzled former general who had lost both an arm and a leg in the war against the French, to grant them a ten-year contract to colonize up to twenty thousand settlers in Mexico. Although the race and nationality of the colonists were not specified in the contract—only that each colonist would have a certificate attesting to his or her "morality, honesty, and diligence"—Ellis and Ferguson's comments to the press left little doubt that they intended to fill the colonists' ranks with African Americans.

Of all the unexpected features of this agreement, perhaps the most surprising was that it was negotiated by two of Cuney's close allies in the Texas Republican Party. The colonization movement represented one of the most divisive fault lines running through African American politics in the late nineteenth century. Even as they defended the right of blacks to live wherever they pleased, most black leaders, from Frederick Douglass to Cuney, decried efforts to relocate African Americans. These figures charged that emigration not only diminished the pool of African American voters; it also encouraged long-standing white fantasies of solving the United States' "race problem" by ethnically cleansing all blacks from the nation. Even the great liberator Abraham Lincoln had briefly entertained thoughts of colonizing freed slaves on Mexico's Tehuantepec isthmus or Yucatán peninsula. Above all, by presenting blacks' real home as elsewhere, emigration diverted attention from what many African Americans perceived as the more pressing task: achieving their full civil rights in the United States. "I cannot see wherein [African Americans] would gain anything [by emigration]," contended Cuney. "They are so thoroughly identified with the perpetuity of our American institutions, that it seems to me to be rather late for them now to seek homes in a new country with the customs, government and people of which they are thoroughly unacquainted. There is much more glory, honor and gain for the colored man here in the land of his birth, and here he should stay and fight his way to the front."

Still, Ellis's colonization scheme possessed more resonances with Cuney's thought than may first appear. Cuney's entry into politics had come through organizing African American stevedores on the docks of Galveston. Ellis's plans likewise hinged on establishing the economic independence of working-class African Americans. Under the terms of the contract, the Mexican government was to sell land at a prearranged rate to Ellis and Ferguson, who would then redistribute it to the colonists, along with tools and seeds, in lots of 100 to 150 acres. "The idea of Mr. Ellis," explained one observer, "is that the colonists will become self-sustaining farmers."

Under such circumstances, relocating to Mexico did not necessarily represent the retreat from politics cited by so many of colonization's critics. Rather, it engaged in the inherently political act of highlighting the failures of Reconstruction—in particular, the federal government's failure to support blacks economically. Whites blamed the poverty in which African Americans found themselves

mired after Emancipation on a lack of work discipline. Ellis, however, underscored that blacks were in fact uncommonly gifted cotton
farmers—"the best in the world," as he boasted to Díaz. The cause of
black privation lay not with African American talents but rather with
the barriers that white society placed in their way. Blending in elements of Turner's thought, Ellis maintained that African Americans
could serve as agents of uplift for Mexico, much as Turner believed
Negro colonists would do in Africa. "The results of this movement,"
opined Ellis, "will not only benefit the African race, but the people
of this country [Mexico] will learn from our success lessons in agriculture which will increase the production and open up new fields of
labor for the poorer classes of native Mexicans."

Emigration tended to draw its support from the most marginalized
members of the black community—those, unsurprisingly, who suffered the worst oppressions and therefore had the least to lose in relocating to an unfamiliar land. Even before Ellis and Ferguson finalized
their contract with the Mexican government, they had compiled a list
of several hundred families from four adjoining Texas counties—Fort
Bend, Matagorda, Brazoria, and Wharton, all "places where the colored people have been having trouble," in Ellis's apt phrase—who had
expressed interest in moving to Mexico. These counties, located just
to the northeast of Victoria, were home to the largest African American majorities in all of Texas. These conditions led unsympathetic
whites to dub the region "Senegambia"; they also spawned significant racial strife as local whites endeavored, despite the demographic
imbalance, to "free . . . themselves from Negro rule."

The experiences of Ellis's partner, Henry Ferguson, in Fort Bend
illuminate the bitter conflicts giving rise to the emigration movement. In the 1880s, Ferguson had been elected Fort Bend's tax asses-
sor and his brother, Charles, the county clerk. In 1888, however, a
mob of local whites, styling themselves the "Jaybirds," vowed to wrest
Fort Bend from Republican control. As the next round of elections
approached, the Jaybirds issued a list of seven African Americans,
Ferguson's brother among them, whom they deemed "odious." All
were to leave Fort Bend within forty-eight hours or suffer the con-

sequences. Even with such brazen intimidation, the Jaybirds lost the subsequent vote. They responded with violence, giving the Democratic governor an excuse to send in the state militia. By the time the troops withdrew, the Democrats had gained control of the county, primaries in Fort Bend were restricted to whites only, and the commanding officer of the militia warned that next time he came to town, "it would not be as an official, but . . . [to] help kill every Negro in the county." Although Henry had not been on the Jaybirds' initial list, he soon joined his brother in fleeing Fort Bend. Little wonder that he and many other African Americans in "Senegambia" found Ellis's idea of a new start in Mexico so appealing.

———————

As BLACKS AND whites in the United States debated the merits of colonization, so, too, did their counterparts across the border in Mexico. For Mexicans, however, the question of colonization possessed profoundly different connotations. In a country that had long perceived itself at risk of being swallowed up by its more populous northern neighbor, colonization meant not the expulsion of entire categories of citizens but rather the attracting of new immigrants. As *El Siglo Diez y Nueve* asserted in 1881, colonization was one of Mexico's "great projects," essential to producing "a happy future for our homeland." New immigrants would "not only increase the scant population that we possess" but also aid in "the exploitation of our agricultural elements, whose richness will pour out . . . in the principal markets of the world."

Even though the Porfiriato could boast of arrivals from around the world, the total number of immigrants to Mexico remained modest. Commentators reported that even though "representatives of most every other nation are also found in Mexico, such as Turks, Arabs, Greeks, and Swedes . . . they are in small numbers and scattered all over the country." Forced to compete with the United States in immigration as in so much else, Mexico decided in the late 1870s to adopt more aggressive measures. Porfirio Díaz's government negoti-

ated nineteen colonization contracts between 1878 and 1882, offering a generous package of subsidies—free passage, land, tools, and
freedom from taxes, custom duties, and military service—to organizers who agreed to plant colonies of immigrants on Mexican soil,
especially in the republic's less inhabited, more vulnerable northern
states. Once this initial investment primed the pump, it was hoped
that an increased flow of immigrants would come to Mexico of their
own accord.

The Mexican government identified a range of ethnic groups, from
Egyptians to Canary Islanders, as possible colonists. But it placed
particular emphasis on attracting immigrants from Italy, who supposedly shared Mexico's "Latin" identity. "The Europeans who most
identify with our habits and our way of life are, without doubt . . . , the
Italians," opined one observer. The goal in drawing large-scale Italian immigration was to whiten Mexico's population—in part through
intermarriage with its indigenous population and in part by infusing
European culture into the republic's Indian countryside. "The Aztec
and Latin races will give rise, if we manage the situation properly,"
noted José Yves Limantour, Porfirio Díaz's influential finance minister, "to a strong, enlightened, and prosperous race."

In October of 1881, the first steamships bearing Italian colonists
arrived at Veracruz to shouts of "¡Viva México!" The government settled the Italians on sites around Mexico, taking care to mix in Mexican settlers among the colonists so as to Europeanize the natives
while Mexicanizing the newcomers. Despite the Mexican government's investment of millions of pesos in the project, however, the
Italian newcomers did not precipitate the mass influx of immigrants
that Mexico had anticipated. Some colonists did climb into the ranks
of independent artisans or become successful agriculturalists. But
before long the Mexican press told of colonists who had not been
issued the farming equipment, livestock, or homes promised in their
contracts. "We have been lodged in barracks like beasts of burden,
instead of houses," contended the members of one Italian colony, who
described the labor brokers who had arranged their passage to Mexico
as "merchants of human flesh." Italian colonists also found themselves

unwittingly drawn into conflicts in their new homeland. In Puebla, for example, the Mexican government expropriated land from Otomí Indian communities to give it to the newly arriving colonists, creating friction between the two groups. Dissatisfied Italians soon drifted away from the colonies, taking advantage of their newfound proximity to the US border to leave for Mexico's northern neighbor. "Some of the assisted colonists, especially Italians," reported the US consul at Matamoros, "have walked and begged their way across and out of the country."

These disappointing results created an opening for Ellis and Ferguson. For reasons of race and nationality alike, Porfirians had never viewed African Americans a desirable group for colonization. In 1879, the intellectual Francisco Pimentel, responding to an inquiry from Mariscal's predecessor as secretary of foreign affairs, contended, in a position that once again overlooked the republic's historic Afro-Mexican population, that the presence of blacks would "increase one of the ills our country suffers from, the heterogeneity of population." The Mexican press echoed this stance, with commentators contending that, given the "natural differences" dividing the races and Mexico's need to "improve its social, economic, and political status . . . which is still not at the enviable level of the principal European nations . . . , the immigration that we need is that of the enterprising, robust, [and] civilized white race."

Yet despite this hostility toward peoples of African descent, it was not long after Ellis's arrival in Mexico City that reports began to circulate that "Gen. Pacheco, Minister of Public Works, is greatly interested in Ellis's plan, and heartily in favor of granting the concession." If this startling departure from the Porfiriato's goal of whitening Mexico's population offers compelling evidence of Ellis's charm and powers of persuasion, it also underscores the challenges he faced in making his plans a reality. Pacheco's proposed contract restricted Ellis and Ferguson's colonies to low-lying regions of Veracruz, Oaxaca, Guerrero, Michoacán, and San Luis Potosí, where tropical diseases had long hindered development. "The object of this colonization is to populate and cultivate the hot and unhealthy places along our coasts that cannot be cultivated by our nation's inhabitants," asserted Mexican officials. "It will be convenient to see, as way of a test, if by bringing some blacks to these coasts it will be possible to transform them from uncultivated to productive." In addition, the Departamento de Fomento (Public Works) structured its contract so that rather than making a large initial investment, as had been done with Italian immigrants, most of Mexico's contributions came later, only after Ellis and Ferguson had established one thousand colonists in the republic and the president determined that the newcomers had farmed or mined successfully for at least a year. Such measures imposed on Ellis's colony the greatest constraints of any such project in Mexico. "No colonization company," stated Mexican politician Alfonso Lancáster Jones, "has been more restricted, more limited in its privileges and its rights."

Given the powerful role of the executive in Porfirian politics—Díaz had adopted a policy of preselecting all legislative candidates for office—the contract's acceptance was all but certain once Ellis secured the president's and Pacheco's approval. Even so, when the agreement came before the usually pliant Mexican legislature, it sparked a heated discussion that lasted several days. In the face of charges that black colonization would be a "scandal" for the country ("We are going to bring blacks to our coasts," warned Senator José María Couttolenc Cruz; "we are going to populate them with a contemptible, abject, and degraded race. ... The Mexicans in these places will be forced to flee"), other legislators rejected such assessments as tainted with the "despotism and tyranny" of Mexico's northern neighbor. In the words of Senator Pedro Díez Gutiérrez: "In the United States there still exist racial fears that violate human dignity, the foundation of true liberty; over there one encounters the fears of the American union's southern states, in whose sources it seems that my honorable colleague has imbibed his inspiration against the black race."

On November 7, 1889, Ellis's contract surmounted its final legislative hurdle, passing the Mexican Senate, where opponents had manipulated quorum rules to delay a vote. As if to signal the dawn of a new era in the borderlands, the approval of Ellis's colonization plan occurred within days of two other events that highlighted the expanding role of the Mexican and US federal governments along the international boundary: the death of Juan Cortina, the onetime "terror of the frontier" who had spent the last decade under house arrest by the Díaz administration; and the passage of a convention between the United States and Mexico to create a more accurate survey of the almost two-thousand-mile-long borderline between the two nations.

Despite the limitations that the Díaz administration had placed on Ellis and Ferguson, Mexican critics opposed this latest colonization project even more than they had the importation of black workers from the Caribbean a few years earlier. The laborers on the new railway lines had at least been brought in on a temporary basis by private corporations. Ellis's colonists, in contrast, were to be subsidized by the Mexican government and to become permanent citizens of the republic. "[We cannot] believe that the Secretary of the Interior would adopt a project that would bring about . . . grave difficulties for the Government and would be the breeding ground of riots and perhaps the engenderer of a race war," warned *El Monitor Republicano*. "Certainly we need arms [*brazos*] to exploit the resources of our rich territory, but as good and productive and desirable as the cultivation of cotton is, peace is better."

For more than a few Mexicans, Ellis's contract revealed Mexico's need to distance itself altogether from the US model of modernization. The editors of *El Tiempo* opined that Mexico should take "satisfaction" in having avoided "a population of tramps [*vagos*] like those that swarmed in the great centers of the United States." The recent mass migrations to its shores had left the United States with "a great diversity of races" that inhibited the creation of a coherent nation-state. In contrast, Mexico with its *mestizaje* was "among those American nations who have progressed with considerable speed in the unification of the races that inhabit our territory."

FERGUSON AND ELLIS were not the first African Americans to con-
template the emigration of their people to Mexico. As early as 1852,
Frederick Douglass's colleague at the *North Star*, Martin Delany,
argued passionately (if inaccurately) that since there has "never
existed in the policy of any of the nations of Central or South America, an inequality on account of race or color," Mexico and its fellow
Latin American nations should serve as "the ultimate destination and
future home of the colored race on this continent." During these same
years, a handful of free blacks from Florida and New Orleans, fleeing
rising restrictions in the antebellum South, settled in Tampico and
Veracruz. In 1882, according to reports in the Mexican press, a group
of African Americans from Mississippi visited Chihuahua to investigate resettling there. Four years later, African Americans in Washington, DC, organized the Afro-American Colonization Association
and entered into a correspondence with Mexican ambassador Matías
Romero about moving to Baja California. At much the same time
as Ellis and Ferguson were in Mexico City meeting with Pacheco
and other Mexican officials, African Americans in California incorporated the "Colored Mexican Colonization Company" for the purpose of "owning, selling, colonizing, and farming lands, [and] raising,
buying, and selling stock . . . in the Republic of Mexico."

Yet if Ferguson and Ellis were far from the only African Americans to portray Mexico as a refuge from US racism, they were the
first to negotiate a formal colonization contract with the Díaz government. This unprecedented turn of events reflected in part Ellis's
borderlands upbringing: his fluency in Spanish, his familiarity with
Mexican culture, his longtime contacts with Mexican merchants and
consuls in San Antonio. Even so, there remains something almost
preternatural about Ellis's precociousness—his ability as a young
man in his midtwenties to transcend his modest beginnings as a slave
born along the Guadalupe River in South Texas and operate at the
highest level of Mexican society. His uncanny self-confidence and

ability to present himself as others wished to see him—the same skills that enabled Ellis to pass so successfully in Texas—were now being employed for a very different purpose: to forge new linkages between Mexican and African American aspirations for the future.

If most other African Americans lacked Ellis's easy familiarity with Mexico, they nonetheless followed events south of the border with great interest. Ferguson and Ellis's negotiations in Mexico City garnered extensive coverage in the black press. "The Texas exodus scheme to Mexico, led by Messrs. Henry Ferguson and W.H. Ellis, of San Antonio, Texas, is progressing very satisfactorily," observed the *Southwestern Christian Advocate*. "The leaders are intelligent and well to do." The *Cleveland Gazette* featured repeated discussion of the plan in its "Race Doings" column. "As Mexico is an importer of cotton and comparatively free from the prejudice which is such a barrier to our progress . . . in the South, it would not be a bad idea to make successful this colonization scheme because both would benefit by it," noted the editors. "We are aware that arguments can and will be used against such a movement but, upon the whole, we believe it to be commendable."

The signing of the colonization contract, however, brought burdens as well as opportunities. Their agreement with the Mexican government committed Ellis and Ferguson to acquire croplands in Mexico and, within three years, to settle at least one thousand people on them. Every year afterward, the total number of colonists needed to go up by at least two hundred. Only after the colonists had reached Mexico and planted their second crop would the government pay Ellis and Ferguson fifty dollars for each adult immigrant. And only at the end of the contract's ten-year term would Ellis and Ferguson receive the handsome additional bonuses that the Mexican government had promised the two would-be immigration brokers.

The passage of the colonization act thus spurred Ellis to a frenzy of activity. He established an enterprise named the Mexican Coffee-Cotton Colonization Company, appointed himself director general, and tried to sell shares to finance his and Ferguson's colonization venture. He placed ads in San Antonio newspapers, offering free transportation to African American families who wanted to move to Mexico. In early 1890, Ellis expanded his activities to Houston and Waco, speaking to blacks in both cities. He was then off to Mexico City to speak with "members of a wealthy English syndicate" there about investing in his colonization project, before returning to Houston. A few months later, family members in San Antonio told of receiving letters from him bearing postmarks as disparate as Albuquerque, New Mexico; Flagstaff, Arizona; and San Francisco, California. Newspaper reports in 1891 located Ellis in New York City and Chicago. In the latter city, in an emboldened or perhaps desperate mood, he gave one of his rare extended statements to the white press about his colonization plans, contending that "the negro in Mexico with his American training could accomplish miracles. . . . The colored people are almost universally agriculturalists and they can not prosper in the southern states as much as they can in Mexico."

Ellis's urgency can be traced not only to his colonization contract but also to the exigencies of the cotton plant. Because of the cotton-cultivation cycle, which stretched from planting in the early spring to final picking in the late fall, there was only a limited window of time in the winter of each year when sharecroppers could leave their current arrangements for new homes in Mexico. Since the Mexican Congress had not approved the contract until November 1889, Ellis and Ferguson had had to scramble to assemble possible colonists almost immediately. When their plans did not cohere in time, they then had to wait until the following autumn before they could again have any realistic expectations of relocating African American field hands to Mexico. When they did not succeed over the winter of 1891, for the same reason that plagued so many black colonization efforts at the time—lack of start-up capital—their hard-won opportunity became all the more imperiled.

Almost as worrying was the fact that Ellis's colonization effort, like his contemporaneous involvement with Texas Republican politics, brought unwanted publicity—and the potential to let slip his carefully crafted mask of transborder Mexican entrepreneur. To most Americans, black and white, the mere fact of Ellis's interest in African

American colonization in Mexico did not necessarily signal that he was African American. There were also whites who supported colonization efforts, for reasons as diverse as wanting to purge the United States of all blacks to hoping to find an experienced labor force for the Gilded Age's growing trade in tropical goods. At the very moment that Ellis was in Mexico City negotiating with officials in the Departamente de Fomento, the white South Carolina senator Wade Hampton was issuing calls "to colonize the negro" to Latin America or Africa, out of supposed humanitarian concerns that blacks would be exterminated if forced to compete with the "superior" white race, and a coalition of white coffee dealers in New York City were floating a plan "to put . . . [American] negroes raising coffee and sugar" in Mexico. Even the black press contained a few references to Ellis and his project that betrayed an unawareness of the organizer's background. "A citizen of Texas, W.H. Ellis brings forward still another scheme of Negro colonization," complained one correspondent. "Of course the originator of the project had consulted everybody concerned except the Negroes."

Despite such confusion, astute observers could not fail to pick up on a number of revealing clues. The first was both partners' public association with Norris Cuney. In an interview in Mexico City designed to counter the negative images of African Americans circulating in the Mexican press, but subsequently reprinted by several Texas papers, Ellis emphasized the progress that American blacks had made since emancipation. Not so long ago, African Americans had been "slaves and deprived of all scientific instruction"; now, "many have become wealthy and have in every community schools of the highest order." In fact, continued Ellis, "the highest federal position in the state of Texas is held by Hon. N.W. Cuney, a personal friend of mine, and a member of the race." At a time when most Southern whites were Democrats—and those who were members of the Republican Party tended to support Cuney's archrivals, the Lily Whites—this connection alone hinted that Ellis and Ferguson were probably African American. Another clue could be found in Ellis's close ties to Ferguson, whose place at the heart of the racially charged confrontation in Fort Bend in 1888 had made him a figure of some notoriety in Texas. Even so, as the "negro exodus scheme . . . bec[a]me an all-absorbing topic throughout the union," some of the press coverage of Ellis, especially from newspapers outside of Texas, described him simply as a "promoter" without referring to his race. Within the Lone Star State, however, it became increasingly clear to many that Ellis was not the Tejano he claimed to be. As the *Galveston Daily News* revealed to its readers, "Mr. Ellis is an attractive mulatto, about 30 years of age, and is prominent in political circles in San Antonio." Confirmed the *Dallas Morning News*: "He is not a Mexican capitalist. . . . He is a rather shrewd republican politician."

This exposure of Ellis's racial subterfuges might have been worthwhile had his plan borne fruit. In the end, however, Ellis's aspirations exceeded his grasp. Although the plan to emigrate to Mexico excited considerable interest among blacks in Texas—by 1891, Ellis and Ferguson's list of potential colonists had reportedly grown from several hundred to several thousand—the two were never able to raise the funds necessary to get the project off the ground. Internal changes in Mexico hastened the scheme's collapse. In March 1891, General Pacheco, the head of the Departamento de Fomento and the leading champion of colonizing African Americans in Mexico, resigned his position because of ill health, only to pass away a few months later. Within days of his death, the Mexican government canceled Ellis and Ferguson's contract.

———

FOR A TIME, both Ellis and Ferguson drifted back into Texan electoral politics. Ellis would run for state representative in 1892. Ferguson would rise in the party ranks, ultimately contesting Cuney for the chairmanship of the state Republican Party in 1896. But while Ferguson never again returned to Mexican affairs, Ellis, after his electoral defeat, deepened his involvement with colonization. In 1893, he again surfaced in public debates about the movement, albeit in a strikingly different locale: as a delegate at a national convention that

Bishop Turner had called for the "colored people of the United States in anguish" to discuss the issue of "African repatriation."

Turner's meeting came at a high-water mark for African American emigration. The early 1890s witnessed Turner's first visit to Liberia, about which he wrote a series of glowing letters in the African American press, extolling the virtues of relocating to Africa. The bishop's enthusiasm for emigration was matched at the grass roots. Trapped between a rising tide of segregation and the sinking economics of sharecropping, especially as the Panic of 1893 plunged the country into a four-year depression, African Americans all over the nation took to forming colonization clubs and dispatching letters to the American Colonization Society, inquiring about the possibility of leaving the United States. "We are in suffering conditions and kneed [*sic*] help," pleaded one would-be emigrant. "I don't want to stay here and make no more 7 cts. & 4 cts cotton in the U.S. of America."

Like this letter writer, many of the other potential colonists were desperately poor—the same obstacle that had derailed Ferguson and Ellis's proposed Mexican colonization project. Keenly aware of the financial hurdles emigration posed, Turner fashioned a unique solution to the problem. By his reckoning, the United States government owed freedpeople $40 billion dollars in uncompensated wages for their forced labor as slaves (a figure arrived at by factoring the labor of two million people for two centuries at $100 per year). Under such circumstances, was it too little to ask that the US Congress allocate $100 million to fund a line of steamships that would carry all those African Americans who wanted to emigrate to Africa? Recoiling at the violence roiling the post-Emancipation South, the bishop declared, "I am tired of negro problems, lynch law, mob rule, and continual fuss, and millions of other negroes are tired of it. . . . We want peace at some period in our existence, and if we cannot have it here . . . let that portion of us who choose to try another section of the world have a little help."

Turner's 1893 convention, his first devoted exclusively to colonization, was designed to build upon the movement's apparent momentum. Among the several hundred African American delegates from around the country gathering at the meeting's host city of Cincinnati was Ellis. He either had had some prior contact with Turner or made a powerful initial impression on the bishop, for he ended up playing a surprisingly large number of leadership roles in Cincinnati. When the conference opened, Turner appointed Ellis to his "permanent organization" as a vice president. (Even in this setting, Ellis insisted on being described as being from south of the border—"fourth vice president, W.H. Ellis, Mexico"—rather than representing a US community as the other delegates did.) Not long afterward, Turner selected Ellis, along with his son John T. Turner, to serve on the meeting's most important body, the Committee on Emigration.

Turner opened the conference in dramatic style. In a heartfelt address, he called for African Americans to escape "the reign of mobs, lynchers, and fire-fiends" in the United States by establishing their own country—a statement reportedly greeted with cries of "Africa!" "Canada!" and "Mexico!" from some in the assembled audience. Attention then turned to the conference's centerpiece, a lengthy report from the Committee on Emigration. Observing that the "oppressed of all ages have had recourse to revolution or emigration"—but quickly adding that for American blacks to "adopt the former is to court utter extermination"—Ellis and his other committee members recommended that "the colored people of the United States . . . turn their attention to the civilization of Africa as the only hope of the Negro race."

Even in this receptive setting, the report generated fierce debate. A string of delegates rose to argue that blacks should instead devote their energies to securing equality before the law in the United States. Rather than a monetary obligation that could be used to finance emigration, noted one, the "Nation's debt to the negroes is justice." Others added that "the negroes of the United States are citizens of the United States, and it is entirely foreign to American ideas that any citizen of the country shall leave it because he cannot have justice here. The negro citizens hold to this American idea as do the white citizens. They do not propose to be driven from their homes." Although Turner's handpicked committee unanimously favored emigration, the delegates as a whole proved far less receptive. The bishop found himself in the unexpected position of having to delay a vote on the report for fear that the very convention he had called would conclude with a measure opposing emigration.

As controversy flared around him, Ellis tried in vain to nudge the discussion toward the subject of colonization in Mexico. "A Mr. Ellis, of Mexico," commented one observer, "said Mexico and not Africa was the place." Ellis pointed to Mexico's proximity and relatively developed economy, while apparently keeping quiet about his own recent failed effort at colonization south of the border. His statements generated cautious enthusiasm from at least a few audience members, who, recalling Mexico's earlier history of sheltering fugitive slaves, voiced the belief that African Americans "would be welcomed in Mexico." Turner, however, postponed any vote on recommendations, leaving Ellis's suggestions to linger unanswered. The following day, the convention drew to a close with a whimper. Still seeking to prevent a possible negative outcome, Turner withheld the Committee on Emigration's suggestions from a floor vote and opted instead to send them to a new committee for further study.

Rather than the ringing endorsement of colonization that Turner had hoped for, the convention instead underscored the ambivalence about the movement that existed in the black community. More than a few African American commentators concluded that the convention's unsettled ending proved emigration's unworkability—an argument they made, ironically, by employing the same environmentalist logic that whites often used to depict blacks as a "tropical" people who should be expelled from the United States. "The climate of the south is best suited to the people of my race," posited J. A. Baily of Bonham, Texas. "They do better here physically than in any other zone of the earth. Canada is too cold for them and the land is less productive. Mexico is more inviting than Canada, but there our people will have to battle against a language they do not understand and modes of soil culture and business transactions they do not understand. . . . Africa is less inviting than either Canada and Mexico."

As he boarded the train back to Texas in the aftermath of Turner's failed convention, Ellis had ample reason to feel discouraged. His political career had stalled. His experiment with colonization had yielded few concrete results. His position in San Antonio as a transborder entrepreneur and his claims of Mexican ethnicity were increasingly under scrutiny. Indeed, only the month before, in a preview of his 1909 experience at Eagle Pass, he suffered the ignominy of being refused entry to the whites-only sleeper car once his train from Mexico City crossed the border at Laredo. The train's conductor had become suspicious of Ellis's racial background, even though, in the words of one bystander, "it is claimed that he [Ellis] is a prominent Mexican politician, quite wealthy."

In the face of such challenges, Ellis demonstrated uncommon resilience. Within a year, he would be back in the Mexican capital, poised to breathe new life into his projects in the most spectacular manner yet. That he could do so speaks volumes not only about Ellis's unparalleled abilities as a border crosser but also about the rapidly changing world of the US-Mexico borderlands. Those like Ellis with the perspicacity to survey the new terrain shaped by the flow of railroads and capital alike across the international boundary could see that it remained a contingent space, ripe with multiple possibilities. Mexican and American officials might hope to strengthen their respective nations' hold over a distant periphery and to further capitalist development along the border. But as Ellis's next project would reveal, there were alternative possibilities to be found in the borderlands as well.

4

THE LAND OF GOD AND LIBERTY

I N JANUARY 1895, the small Southern town of Tuscaloosa, Alabama, hummed with a peculiar, almost invisible energy. Usually,
the beginning of a new year brought a lull to this community of
four thousand located in the rolling hills on the fringes of Alabama's
black belt. Cotton picking was finished, the holidays had come and
gone, and the spring cotton planting remained several months in the
future. This year, however, wherever the county's African Americans
gathered—be it in church, in town, or in the run-down sharecroppers' shacks that dotted the countryside—one subject dominated
their whispered conversations, carefully carried out beyond the reach
of white ears: Should they go?

For the past month, a number of newcomers, most prominent
among them the one-legged African American labor agent "Peg-
Leg" Williams, had been holding meetings with the area's blacks,
distributing flyers that told of a place quite unlike their native Alabama. It was, promised the circular, a land abounding in "all kinds
of fine game, such as deer, bear, duck, wild geese, and all manner
of small game, as well as opossum." This profusion of wildlife was
matched by the fecundity of the terrain. "The soil being rich and fertile, cotton has only to be replanted every four or seven years, and can
easily raise a bale to the acre, and corn 50 to 75 bushels to the acres."
Best of all, it was a land that "extends to all of its citizens the same

treatment—equal rights to all, special privileges to none. . . . They need labor badly, and prefer the colored people."

Where was this wondrous place? "Mexico," answered the circular, "which is better known as the country of 'God and Liberty,' and which offers unequaled inducements for agricultural laborers in the growth of cotton and corn." All those who wanted to leave, urged Williams, should "send in your lists of families and names at once." Otherwise, they would miss out on "the greatest opportunity ever offered to the colored people of the United States."

The success of William's surreptitious organizing efforts became clear on the day selected for departure from Tuscaloosa, January 25. To the shock of local whites, this otherwise normal Friday morning witnessed hundreds of blacks crowding into the railroad depot to board the "paradise train" to Mexico—a six-car special, routed direct for the border, complete with large signs on its sides spelling out MEXICO, TLAHUALILO, MEXICO—THE LAND OF LIBERTY FOR THE BLACK MAN and fluttering flags bearing similar messages. As befitted such an extraordinary event, the mood among the emigrants was jubilant. Informed by Williams that their Mexican sponsors would supply them with clothing, furniture, and farming implements, many had sold or given away whatever they could not carry with them. They now stood in the depot amid the meager possessions they hoped to use to rebuild their lives south of the border: piles of quilts and blankets, baskets of live chickens, old flintlock rifles, saddle bags, yapping dogs of all shapes and sizes. A few broke into song—an "old-time plantation jubilee"—to celebrate their near-biblical exodus from bondage, while others took advantage of their upcoming departure to express long-pent-up critiques of their oppressors. Local whites, drawn to the train station by the tumult, pronounced themselves unamused by "the most open and insulting abuse of the white men of the community." "Had it not been that they [the emigrants] were on the eve of what was sincerely hoped to be their permanent departure," noted one in a statement that made manifest the tensions the colonists hoped to leave behind, "they would have been roughly handled, for their utterances called for such treatment."

Stunned by the sudden appearance in their midst of a plan to "Mexicanize . . . the black labor of the south," Tuscaloosa's whites could only ponder whether the day's events represented the first wave in a much larger movement. Might "the Mexico emigration fever" spread far beyond Tuscaloosa, drawing much of the South's black labor into Mexico? This dawning realization electrified the region. Black migration, in the words of the *San Antonio Express*, "promise[d] . . . a solution of the labor question in the new cotton fields of Northern Mexico." But it threatened to do so by depriving the American South of the workforce it had depended upon for several centuries.

Even more mysterious was the riddle of who was behind the unexpected departure of so many of Tuscaloosa's African Americans. Peg-Leg Williams was well known throughout the ex-Confederacy—so much so, in fact, that in 1891, North Carolina passed the "Peg-Leg Williams Law" specifically to prevent the contractor from "taking negro laborers from the State." But Williams never worked alone, only for others. "It is not known exactly who is at the bottom of the movement," related one observer. "Several local colored men are working in the affair, but it is thought some enterprising railroad agent is the father of the whole scheme."

———

THE PERSON BEHIND this extraordinary exodus from Tuscaloosa, of course, was not some white railroad agent, intent on increasing the number of goods and peoples traveling along his rail line. Rather, it was William Ellis, who by design remained in the shadows, meeting quietly with interested emigrants in Tuscaloosa out of view of local whites, while Williams served as the movement's public face. More than four years after the Mexican government canceled his colonization contract, and little more than a year after the ambiguous close of Bishop Turner's conference in Cincinnati, Ellis had managed to orchestrate one of the most audacious African American emigration efforts in US history. Ellis's mentor Turner, famed as the nation's leading colonization advocate, had needed several decades to relocate a thousand or so African Americans to Liberia. (Noted Ellis: "Bishop Turner, it will be remembered, shipped 1096 negroes to Africa.") In contrast, in just a few short months in early 1895, Ellis colonized over eight hundred blacks in Mexico, with the promise of many more to come. In a little more than ten years, as many as "two-thirds of the Southern negroes will be in Mexico," predicted Ellis, who presented his "plan of shipping negroes . . . [as] the only solution of the race problem."

The development that made this unprecedented turn of events possible came about in late 1894. During one of his journeys through Mexico, Ellis learned about a vast hacienda in the Mexican North with an equally vast labor problem. Moreover, he realized that there might be a way in which the hacienda's needs and those of African Americans could be brought into alignment to the benefit of both. The hacienda that attracted Ellis's attention—La Compañía Agrícola Limitada del Tlahualilo—epitomized the transformations sweeping across northern Mexico during the Porfiriato. Located in the so-called Comarca Lagunera (lagoon region) along the Coahuila-Durango border, it had not so long before lain at the very heart of the vast "Comanche Empire" that dominated the American Southwest/Mexican North for much of the nineteenth century. Beginning in the 1830s, bands of Comanche Indians would depart the Great Plains and rendezvous in *la Laguna* before raiding deep into Mexico's interior in search of livestock and captives.

The hard-fought conflict with the powerful Comanche came to an end in the 1870s through the combined efforts of the Texas rangers and the US and Mexican militaries. The Comanches' decline and Porfirio Díaz's rise facilitated in turn the entrance of investors, many of them from Spain and England, into the region. These entrepreneurs sought to reengineer the Comarca Lagunera's desert landscape—long derided as little more than untamed "mesquite wilderness"—into sprawling estates, dedicated to cotton production. Although the region was among the most arid in all of Mexico, the Comarca Lagunera nonetheless experienced a short rainy season, which had generated the latticework of temporary lagoons that

Comanche raiders once relied upon to water their animals. The region's newly arrived investors planned to use the nearby Nazas River to irrigate the fertile beds of silt produced by these lagoons—but to do so, they needed to locate enough hands to work the hundred thousand acres of new farmland that they expected to bring into production.

The first of these problems was solved with help from Porfirio Díaz. Anxious to boost Mexico's cotton industry, which had prospered during the 1860s when the Civil War had expanded Mexico's access to US-grown fiber, and make the republic an exporter of cotton, the president raised tariffs on imported cotton goods. He also extended to a group of entrepreneurs led by the Spaniard Juan Llamedo access to water from the Nazas River and a right-of-way to construct a canal to their property some thirty miles distant. To prevent the sometimes-violent feuds that had arisen between different hacienda owners over access to the Nazas, in 1888 the Mexican federal government even assumed a new role as regulator of the region's scarce water.

In certain respects, Llamedo's enterprise looked across the border for inspiration, seeking to transplant technology and techniques from the most successful cotton-growing region in the world, the American South, to the Mexican North. But in others, it foreshadowed the spread of state-supported dam building and irrigation in the American West: not until the establishment of the Reclamation Service in 1902 would the US government inaugurate its first irrigation project for cotton cultivators along the Rio Grande. With irrigation in the borderlands in its infancy, Llamedo brought in José Farjas, a Spanish engineer, to oversee construction at Tlahualilo. Farjas employed some three thousand laborers to dig a massive six-foot-deep canal from the Nazas to the hacienda and to chop down acres of mesquite and cactus. In the meantime, the hacienda imported to the Comarca Lagunera the latest agricultural implements from the United States and Great Britain: a steam gin to clean and bale cotton; an oil mill to process the cottonseed from the ginning process; a factory to transform the cottonseed into oil and soap; an electric generator; seven

thousand American plows; and "modern sowing, weeding, and cultivating machines."

To many observers, the vista of cotton fields stretching toward the
horizon—"thousands of acres 'white to the harvest' . . . dotted with
Mexican laborers"—on what had been not so long before a barren
desert epitomized Porfirio Díaz's success in transforming Mexico.
Yale Scientific Monthly featured a glowing dispatch about the hacienda
that commended Mexico "for converting dry and waste lands into
fertile reproducing lands." *Engineering Magazine* carried a similarly
complimentary piece that labeled Tlahualilo an "impulse of progress" and "a typical modern enterprise . . . the largest as yet undertaken in the republic." Mexican commentators, as much in thrall to
the ideas of modernity and progress as their counterparts north of
the border, echoed this enthusiasm, hailing the region as "privileged
[and] prodigiously rich," a showcase for the works of "civilized man."

All across northern Mexico, one could find similar projects,
spurred by Mexican desires to link what had long been a remote hin-
terland, beset by indigenous raiders, to the rest of the nation, and by
American hopes of tapping the rich natural resources just across the
international boundary. With development came population growth:
some three hundred thousand Mexicans would immigrate to Mexico's North during the Porfiriato, as would more than fifteen thousand Americans and a scattering of other nationalities as well. Many
of these newcomers clustered in the region's surging cities, places like
Torreón, the closest urban center to the Comarca Lagunera. Torreón derived its name from the tower (*torre*) that its inhabitants had
constructed in the mid-nineteenth century to protect themselves
from Comanche raids. Although it contained just a handful of residents in 1883, in a mere decade and a half Torreón morphed into
Mexico's fastest-growing city—a booming industrial center and rail
hub, with a population of almost twelve thousand. Tlahualilo's proximity encouraged the construction of such factories as La Alianza,
a cottonseed-oil and soap producer founded in 1890, and La Con-
stancia, a textile mill that opened in Torreón the same year. Proud
residents took to calling their city "El Chicago de Coahuila" in honor

of its industrial prowess and the array of immigrants from Europe, China, and the United States strolling its dusty streets. "There [in Torreón] is forming a new society, the members of diverse nationalities, advanced together on the path of mutual respect and honoring the land of Mexico," enthused one of the city's first chroniclers, C. Amado Prado, in 1899. Torreón, observed another booster, was "a city of the *new* Mexico, not of the old."

Tlahualilo's population grew, too, during these years, albeit more slowly. In 1890, with the main canal from the Nazas complete, Llamedo decided to divide the corporation's sprawling property into ten separate *sitios*. Each was akin to a self-contained hacienda, complete with storehouses, barns, and housing for laborers. Telephone lines and wagon roads running alongside the freshly dug irrigation canals connected each *sitio* to the central hacienda of Zaragoza, where Tlahualilo's hospital, electric plant, and main offices clustered. By 1894, Tlahualilo had some four thousand workers scattered across its various *sitios*. Yet this number was not nearly enough to bring all the corporation's fields into production, especially as the expanding canal system brought water to more and more land. One obstacle to attracting *campesinos* may have been the "military discipline" that Tlahualilo's managers sought to impose on all workers in their settlements. But the more basic problem was that because of the area's virtual depopulation in the face of Comanche raids in the mid-nineteenth century and the preference of most newcomers for the region's fast-growing cities, there remained but a small pool of rural laborers from which to draw. Tlahualilo thus embodied in miniature what many during the Porfiriato considered Mexico's most pressing problem: the lack of sufficient labor to unlock the country's rich natural resources.

———

"THE YEAR 94–95 began auspiciously," Llamedo soon related to the Tlahualilo Corporation's shareholders. There was abundant water in the haciendas' canals, enough to irrigate even the recent "enormous extension of more than 125 square kilometers" of the company's holdings. Moreover, the labor problem finally seemed to be on its way to being solved. Although "the population [of Mexican workers] was not enough to cultivate so many fields," a promising new development augured the end of the Tlahualilo's woes. "In view of the scarcity of hands," explained Llamedo, "we considered a foreign immigration." And not just any migrants, but experienced sharecroppers from the American South. "The agitation of the negro colonization question, especially in the southern press," along with Ellis's descriptions of the virtues of African Americans as cotton cultivators, "gave [the corporation] the impression that the best type of negro labor was ready to emigrate from the States." On December 11, 1894, the Tlahualilo Corporation signed a contract with "*el señor Guillermo H. Ellis*," in which he agreed to bring at least "one hundred colored families, experienced in the cultivation of cotton," to the hacienda.

The passage of time has obscured the path that first brought Ellis into contact with Llamedo. Although the hacienda's cotton fields were in northern Mexico, the contract itself was signed at the Tlahualilo Corporation's headquarters in Mexico City. Ellis's apparent familiarity with both locales hints at the regularity of his visits south of the border, even in the wake of his first failed colonization attempt. For a black man, especially an aspiring and talented one like Ellis, the appeals of Mexico were multiple. South of the international border, Ellis escaped the constant artifice that passing required: the eschewing of contact with family members; the avoidance of other African Americans for fear they might reveal his deception; the constant, nagging worry about the consequences should his pose be unmasked. Ironically, it was in Mexico where Ellis most securely inhabited his American identity, for he never passed as a Mexican while south of the border. Rather, he took pains to emphasize his US citizenship, which, together with his position as a well-connected businessman, gave him a certain cachet at a time when Mexico avidly courted foreign investors. To elevate his status in Mexico all the more, Ellis sometimes asserted that he was not just any entrepreneur but in fact the illegitimate son of the railroad mag-

An abandoned sharecropper shack on the former Weisiger plantation in Victoria, Texas, where William H. Ellis was born and witnessed slavery's demise amid the chaos of Reconstruction.

W. H. ELLIS & CO.

DEALERS IN

HIDES, WOOL AND COTTON.

13 WEST SIDE MILITARY PLAZA.

Manufacturers' Agents for		Tanners' Agents for
TEXAS WOOL AND COTTON.		TEXAS HIDES, TALLOW AND SKINS.

GREEN SALTED HIDES A SPECIALTY.

LIBERAL CASH ADVANCES ON CONSIGNMENTS.

Telephone 257. | SAN ANTONIO, TEXAS. | P. O. Box 478.

☞ Names taken too late for regular insertion. See Addenda and Business Directory for proper Address.

Ellis's dramatic full-page ad in the San Antonio city directory, announcing his transformation into a transborder entrepreneur, buying and selling hides, cotton, and other goods across southern Texas and northern Mexico.

San Antonio's military plaza in the 1890s, with its mix of food vendors and wagon trains bound for Mexico. Ellis maintained an office on the plaza, the heart of San Antonio's commercial and political life, for almost a decade.

Norris Wright Cuney and Henry McNeal Turner, who would introduce Ellis to the fierce debates swirling around Republican Party politics and black emigration.

Ellis's home in Mexico City for almost thirty years: the Hotel Gillow.
Staying at the British-owned Gillow allowed Ellis to maintain his distance
from most other Americans in Mexico during the Porfiriato.

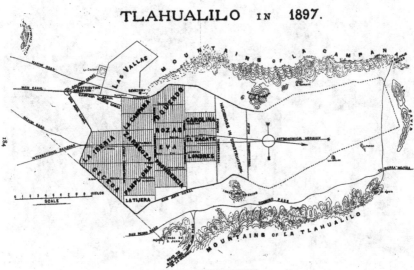

The Tlahualilo hacienda. The need for hands to work the hacienda's thousands of acres of
irrigated fields led its managers to sign a contract with Ellis in 1894 that would bring more
than eight hundred African American sharecroppers to Tlahualilo.

Mexican overseers in one of the Tlahualilo hacienda's cotton fields. Many of the sharecroppers who accompanied Ellis found the presence of such guards a disquieting reminder of the labor controls they had hoped to escape by emigrating to Mexico.

The former colonists from Tlahualilo during their internment at Camp Jenner outside Eagle Pass. Because of fears of smallpox, the US Marine Hospital Service quarantined all the returning colonists at the border.

William Henry Ellis as Guillermo Enrique Eliseo. Ellis's ability to persuade Americans of his Latin background depended not only on his fluent Spanish but also on his elegant dress.

A drawing of Ellis from the 1901 *New York World*. Such images convey Ellis's remarkable success in obscuring his African American ancestry and passing as an elite Latin American.

Maude Sherwood as she appeared at the time of her wedding to Ellis in 1903. There is no marriage photo of Ellis and Sherwood together, most likely because Ellis did not want to create a visual record of his transgressions against the color line.

The interior of Ellis's Wall Street office, located just down the street from the era's preeminent financial firm, J. P. Morgan & Company.

Emperor Menelik II and members of his court in a photograph taken just days after Ellis, the first African American to journey to Ethiopia, arrived in Addis Ababa.

Ellis's nephew Charles Starnes, who accompanied his uncle to Ethiopia. Following Ellis's example, Starnes would soon portray himself as Mexican and change his name to Carlos Eliséo Estarñez.

Ellis in Mexico City with his two oldest sons and his father, Charles. This image was taken in 1910, just before the Mexican Revolution disrupted Ellis's close ties with Porfirio Díaz's inner circle.

Maude in the backyard of the family's house in Mount Vernon, New York, with her and Ellis's four surviving children (from left): Victoria, Ermo, Fernando, and Sherwood.

Victoria Ellis dancing with José Manero in the 1936 Mexican melodrama *Irma la mala*, one of the numerous films from the golden age of Mexican cinema in which she appeared.

nate Collis P. Huntington. He and his alleged father, he intimated to acquaintances, were actively pursuing various railroad concessions throughout the republic.

Ellis's peculiar inversion of citizenship rights—claiming to be Mexican in the United States, and American in Mexico—highlighted the central, if contradictory, place of borders in his world. As much as the drawing of boundaries, be they political or racial, facilitated the creation of invidious distinctions, it also opened up opportunities for those who could move across them. Yet passing between black and white or moving between Mexican and US citizenship only acquired its utility by transgressing what were thought to be distinct, mutually exclusive categories. Thus, even as Ellis thrived by exploiting ambiguities, be they in his appearance or his personal history, he did not aspire to blur the boundaries in his world until they possessed no meaning. Rather, he sought to capitalize on their hidden vulnerabilities and inconsistencies.

Above all, it was Ellis's particular genius to grasp the advantages that could accrue to being a foreigner in whatever nation-state he happened to be inhabiting at the moment. If his alien status did not allow him access to local citizenship rights, it did permit him to step outside of the prevailing racial regimes in both the United States and Mexico. In addition, at a moment of growing economic engagement between the two countries, there were considerable advantages to being someone who could translate the desires of American investors and Mexican elites alike, facilitating their access to resources that otherwise hovered tantalizingly out of reach across the border.

Yet there was also a cost to Ellis's masquerades. Portraying himself as a well-to-do Mexican while in the United States and an American capitalist while in Mexico forced Ellis into the position of the perpetual outsider in both countries, never truly at home in either. This perennial sojourner status was one of the key distinctions between Ellis and his era's other signature border crosser: the "boodler," or embezzler. Much like the passer, the boodler embodied the late nineteenth century's unprecedented mobility, taking advantage of the new steamship lines and railways spanning North America to flee across the border and, if all went according to plan, escape prosecution by assuming a new identity. Ellis's time in Mexico City coincided with a number of noted boodlers. Charles Kratz, a former member of the St. Louis City Council, escaped to Guadalajara after being indicted for bribery, while Chester W. Rowe, a onetime county treasurer from Iowa, absconded with $30,000 in public funds and moved to the Mexican capital, where he opened a *cantina*.

Unlike such boodlers, Ellis did not seek a permanent refuge in Mexico. Yet even his temporary visits to the Mexican capital exposed him to a world far larger, older, and more sophisticated than his adopted hometown of San Antonio—a world, in fact, more cosmopolitan than most urban centers in the United States. In 1895, when San Antonio totaled sixty thousand inhabitants, Mexico City possessed well over three hundred thousand, making it the largest city in Mexico, and for that matter, one of the largest on the North American continent, exceeded at the time only by New York, Chicago, and Philadelphia. During his short-lived rule, Emperor Maximilian had initiated the process—continued by Díaz—of refashioning the Mexican capital into a more European-style metropolis, most notably by constructing the grand boulevard Paseo de la Reforma. Modeled on Paris's Champs-Élysées, Reforma cut diagonally across Mexico City, linking Chapultepec Park to the colonial *alameda* and expanding the capital west beyond its Spanish colonial core. Elegant new suburbs, required to maintain eight meters of garden space along their front facades, sprouted off Paseo de la Reforma for Mexico City's elite. Sewers, paved streets, and trolleys followed, giving the neighborhood the feel, in the words of one visitor, of "a little corner of Europe that was somehow transposed to Mexico." For its part, Reforma's eastern anchor, the *alameda*, was transformed into a site of upper-class leisure, complete with bandstand, fountains, and, after 1892, electric lights—the place for the well-to-do to see and be seen. In keeping with Mexico's vogue for "Latin" culture, the capital boasted several major theaters that hosted visits by French and Italian opera companies, while at the Jockey Club, the city's most exclusive resort, elite Mexicans showed off the latest Parisian styles: tight-waisted skirts and billowing blouses for the women, frock coats and top hats for the men—a sartorial style that Ellis soon adopted as his own.

For someone who had come of age in Victoria and San Antonio, towns with their own Spanish and Mexican legacies, there was much that proved familiar about Mexico City. Despite its antiquity and sophistication, the Mexican capital followed essentially the same layout as Ellis's dwelling places in Texas, albeit on a far grander scale: a grid radiating out from a handful of central plazas, upon which most of the city's commercial, religious, and administrative functions were concentrated. Yet as he wandered Mexico's metropolis, Ellis could not avoid noticing that he was in a very different place: two snow-capped volcanoes, Popocatepetl and Iztaccihuatl, jutted up to the capital's east; the city's enormous markets boasted a multitude of vendors selling a dazzling variety of products; along the streets, one could glimpse Mexico's indigenous peoples, clad in white cotton and speaking a number of different native tongues; beyond the central plazas beckoned the rougher pleasures of the capital's working-class districts, with their *pulquerías*, cheap eateries, and brothels. But most striking of all, the capital was notable for the absence of a color line. "Mexico has no race prejudice from a social standpoint," Ellis related. "The negro may occupy any position he is able to fill, and there is no discrimination against him either at hotels or places of amusements or in public conveyances."

Ellis took advantage of the color line's absence to become a regular at the Hotel Gillow, an elegant Italianate building situated only steps away from the *zócalo*. Opened in 1875 by the Englishman Thomas Gillow, the hotel catered to the capital's British colony, permitting Ellis to be in a setting known for English-speaking foreign visitors while simultaneously avoiding most other Americans, who might have raised troublesome questions about his life in the United States. Mexico City's American colony, which numbered some 1,400 in 1895, was not the capital's largest, being outnumbered at the time by the Spanish (9,000) and the French (4,000) alike. But it was arguably the most insular, with its own press, benevolent society, schools, and cemetery. One could shop for canned delicacies from the United

States at the American Market, enjoy ten-pin bowling at the American Club, and be treated by US-trained doctors at the American Hospital. As one observer put it: "[Members of the American colony] live as nearly as possible the life they would be living if they had never come to Mexico at all."

Dominated by US businessmen, the American colony mirrored class and racial concerns north of the border. Members of the American Club entertained one another with blackface minstrel productions, referred to the club's doorman—and sole African American employee—as "Big Joe," and even attempted to draw the color line against Mexico City's handful of African Americans. *The Massey-Gilbert Blue Book of Mexico*, an American-authored directory of the US citizens in Mexico City, following US custom, labeled all the capital's known African American residents (most of them Pullman car porters) with a "col." for colored. In 1895, the US-born owner of the café at the Hotel Iturbide—one of the city's principal hostelries, situated in a refurbished colonial palace—refused service to three American blacks, generating a firestorm of controversy. The Mexican press excoriated the "introduction into our soil of a concern [segregation] that has dominated our neighbor" and boasted that "on this point we are much more civilized than them." Even so, members of the American colony staged a protest against the arrest of the waiter who had denied the three men their drinks.

Such behavior caused Ellis to avoid the American colony whenever possible. He does not appear in *The Massey-Gilbert Blue Book*, and on those rare occasions when he mixed with other Americans, he finessed questions about his citizenship by asserting he was a "Cuban-American, born in Santiago de Cuba, but now of San Antonio, Texas." Ellis did manage, however, to forge relationships with European members of Mexico's foreign community, such as the Spaniard Llamedo and his British backers at the Bank of London. To Ellis, Llamedo's well-financed Tlahualilo Corporation at last seemed to offer a solution to the issue that had so bedeviled him and Ferguson (and, indeed, all of the era's colonizers, black or white): the shortage of funds. Upon signing the contract to furnish Tlahualilo with workers, Llamedo advanced Ellis $5,500 (some $150,000 today). Using this windfall, Ellis hired Peg-Leg Williams to recruit African Americans for Tlahualilo's cotton fields.

As news of Ellis's contract spread throughout Mexico, it reignited debates over the danger of US migration into Mexico—and of African Americans in particular—that had lain dormant since the signing of his first colonization contract in 1889. Mexican commentators trotted out the familiar argument that if even a small percentage of the United States' population of African Americans made its way across the border into Mexico, the results would be chaos: intermarriage between Indians and blacks, giving rise to a "degenerate race of *zambos*," increased crime, even armed uprisings. Layered on top of these concerns was worry that, as a foreign-owned corporation, La Compañía Agrícola Limitada del Tlahaulilo had prioritized its short-term economic gain over the long-term needs of the republic. "We grow tired of lamenting large enterprises like the one in Tlahualilo," complained *La Voz de México*, "that instead of cooperating for the well-being of the country, seek to attract a great threat to its interest." "It falls to the Compañía del Tlahualilo," added *El Tiempo*, "to install the first pipe to drain the African blood that exists in our neighboring country, leading it toward our weak and almost powerless nation!"

———

IF FOR MANY Mexicans Ellis's project evoked the specter of a "negro problem"—the contamination of the republic with unwanted African Americans—their counterparts across the border viewed the event through the prism of a national "negro problem" as well. Although the United States of the 1890s was home to some eight million African Americans, descended from peoples who had lived in the country for generations, white commentators persisted in casting blacks as alien to American life. Below the surface of such portrayals lurked the era's great unacknowledged paradox: the United States' dependence on black labor for much of its prosperity, even as the nation persisted in denying civil rights to this essential workforce.

The possibility that hundreds if not thousands of black sharecroppers might leave the South's plantation belt for Mexico thrust this
dilemma onto center stage, especially in the movement's epicenter of
Tuscaloosa. Peg-Leg Williams was reputed to have relocated eighty
thousand African Americans from the Carolinas to Texas just a few
years before, making the migration of even larger numbers of blacks
to Mexico an eminently plausible prospect. "A great deal has been
said about the wholesale exodus of southern darkies to other climes,"
warned the *Atlanta Constitution*, "but this scheme of Peg William's
is the biggest on record." "He [Williams] represents that section of
the state [Tlahualilo] to which they go as being the most productive
in the world, the natural home of the negro, and the final destination of the colored race," added New Orleans's *Times-Picayune*. "The
climate, he says, is entirely to the liking of the negro . . . and he finds
no reason why all the negroes of the south cannot be located there."

The specter of a mass African American emigration acquired additional power from perceptions of Mexico as a "tropical" country—the
ideal climate not only for tropical plants such as cotton but also for
African Americans (a "soft tropical man" in the language of the day).
These ideas reflected a prominent feature of Gilded Age thinking:
the use of climate to identify the proper homeland for each supposed
race. Even as this discourse naturalized divisions between peoples
and places, it remained capacious enough to encompass a wide range
of political positions. To white supremacists, the contrast between
the tropics of Africa and Latin America and the temperate climes of
Europe and the United States demonstrated "the superiority of the
white man to the negro in . . . the self-denial required . . . for carrying out great works" (the reasoning being that living in a temperate climate supposedly required more effort than living in the fertile
tropics). To Mexican commentators, climate explained the republic's
failures in attracting European colonization and offered the hope
that African American immigration might be confined to the republic's *"climas tropicales,"* where blacks could withstand conditions that
Mexico's *mestizos* could not. And to Bishop Turner and his followers,
the tropics represented a locale uniquely suited for peoples of African

descent, the region's fecundity a blessing rather than a curse. "We . . . know that the torrid regions give us a more prolific vegetation than the temperate or northern. Since nature is true to itself, it will do for man, surely, what it has done for both flora and fauna."

Contemporary events only furthered the perception that Latin America and Africa shared a common climate and common racial destiny. At the very moment that blacks in Tuscaloosa were boarding the "freedom train" for Mexico, the International Migration Company of neighboring Birmingham was loading a fruit steamer with two hundred "negro colonists" for Liberia—a place, like Mexico, perceived to be a tropical land in need of the uplift that African Americans could provide. Ellis's venture had become woven into a larger set of stories about climate and progress, about race and the destinies of the United States, Mexico, and Africa. Lost amid such formulations was the fact that while Liberia was a self-governing republic, in which American blacks and their descendants controlled the political and economic life, Tlahualilo was a European-owned commercial operation, located in one of the most forbidding deserts in all of North America.

THE FIRST TRAINLOADS of colonists for Tlahualilo departed from Alabama and Georgia in early February. Upon reaching New Orleans, the colonists were confined to the blacks-only part of the depot while they waited to change trains for San Antonio and the border. During this brief layover, a curious reporter from the *Times-Picayune* ventured into the station to interview several of the participants in this unprecedented migration. The newspaper later published some of the encounters, using the thick dialect that whites at the time imposed on black speech: "Dey tole us dat Mexico was er land of liberty—a land whar the nigger could git all he wanted to eat, and habe something to wear. Dat's what dey told us, and that's why I'ze gwine dar." The lone exception was the journalist's interview with Ellis. This exchange was in itself a rare occurrence, as most reporters at the time focused on

Peg-Leg Williams—which was doubtless how Ellis preferred matters, as it allowed him to escape closer scrutiny. On those few occasions when Williams did discuss Ellis in public, he was careful to describe him as a "Cuban and Mexican." As a result, during Ellis's rare mentions in the press, he remained a shadowy figure: the "general agent" of the "Mexican Colonization Company," his race unmentioned.

Within the New Orleans train station, however, the *Times-Picayune* reporter managed to corner Ellis and speak with him at length. Through a virtuoso performance of passing, Ellis convinced the intrusive journalist that he was an "intelligent . . . native of Cuba." Their interaction highlighted Ellis's adeptness at utilizing not only his appearance—mustachioed in the Latin American style and dressed in the European formal wear favored by members of the Mexico City elite—but also subtle linguistic codes to signal his racial identity. In speaking with the reporter, he made sure to describe African Americans in terms that indicated their distance from him while simultaneously employing black dialect and veiled references to his own appearance to suggest a white status. Often, he pulled off this feat in a few sentences, as when he told the *Times-Picayune* that "within the next sixty days, or six months at least, I hope to move 10,000 of the black people to Mexico. They want to go. As our train came along from Birmingham, great crowds gathered along the road, and many voices were heard to exclaim: 'White man, when's dat liberty car comin' through here ergin?'" Ellis emerged from the interview as an accomplished entrepreneur who expected to do well while doing good: "While I admit that there is with me a sort of philanthropic spirit in the matter, still, with land which produces a bale of cotton to the acre, and seventy-five bushels of corn, we hope to make something out of the business as well as the negro."

After leaving New Orleans and crossing the border at Eagle Pass, the colonists reached the Comarca Lagunera via the new Southern Pacific rail lines running through Torreón. They then traveled the last twenty-four miles in horse-drawn carts to Tlahualilo, where the hacienda managers placed the colonists at the section of the estate called Santa Rosa. The speed of events, with Ellis bringing hundreds of sharecroppers to Tlahualilo scarcely two months after signing his contract with the hacienda, seems to have caught Llamedo and his staff by surprise. The two-room adobes for each family of colonists, to be built along the same lines as those of the hacienda's Mexican peons, remained unconstructed, so the newcomers were forced to spend their first weeks in Tlahualilo camping on the ground during one of the region's rare rainy periods, fashioning makeshift tents out of whatever bedding they had brought with them. Even so, the initial conditions at the colony appeared promising. Santa Rosa included a space for a school, which the newcomers' children could attend alongside Mexican youngsters, and a church, in which ministers from the three different denominations ("Methodist Episcopal, African Episcopal and Baptist," according to Ellis) represented among the colonists took turns preaching. The hacienda also allowed the colonists to craft their own rules for themselves and select several of their members to serve as policemen. Among the migrants was even a journalist who hoped to start a newspaper in Tlahualilo. All the institutions central to African American life after Reconstruction— family, school, church, and press—were thus reconstituted in some modest way on the hacienda. The colonists' new farmsteads had even been planted for them and were beginning to show the first green shoots of a new cotton crop.

Williams, who had never been to Mexico before, let alone seen Tlahualilo, pronounced himself delighted with the colony's prospects when he returned to the United States a few days later, sporting a newly acquired Mexican sombrero, to pick up another trainload of colonists. "The negroes seem to like their new homes, and well they may for the country is kind to them—gives them warm weather, good lands, comfortable homes, protection of the laws, and half they can make, with plenty to eat. This is as much as the average negro wants, and more than many of them get." Attracted by such news, scores of potential migrants lingered along the railroad tracks in Georgia and Alabama, hoping to join the next "paradise train" to Mexico. By early March, Williams was back in Tlahualilo, with another load of several hundred colonists, bringing the total on the hacienda to 816.

During Williams's absence, Ellis took up residence in Santa Rosa's largest building, an adobe structure located in the center of the community that featured the colony's lone store and warehouse and, on its second floor, a private apartment. It seemed as if all Ellis's plans were at last coming to fruition—not only the immediate project of bringing a thousand colonists a month to Tlahualilo under his contract with the hacienda, but also his larger goal of demonstrating the opportunities that awaited African Americans in Mexico. "The preachers began to perform marriages," Ellis later recalled. "Seven children were born and the dream of my life was being realized. I had lived to see the Afro-American in the Country of God and Liberty."

The first reports from the colonists were similarly favorable. The preacher S. F. Todd recounted that "we landed in Mexico in this vicinity the 5th day of February, 1895 and so far our experience has been that if a Negro desires his manhood recognized, and desires to live in a country where the laws are equally administered to all alike, Mexico is that land. We feel we are free men under a free government." A. A. Adams from Tuscaloosa echoed Todd's comments: "[Mexico] is a grand country for the negro race; the lands are rich, climate good and healthful. . . . Our people here are much pleased with the country and are satisfied and happy. Mr. Ellis, the gentleman who brought us out here, has done in every particular all that he promised to do. Each and every man is his own man and is his own boss. I framed the laws by which we are governed in our local affairs."

Migration to Mexico allowed the colonists not only to savor, as Todd put it, "a new part of the world" but also to build lives in a place free from the "lynch law" and the other "impositions placed upon us in the land of our nativity." Yet Ellis's project rested upon a fragile foundation. To create his colony at Tlahualilo, Ellis had melded two discourses on colonization that had previously existed in isolation from one another across the US-Mexico border: Mexico's desire for skilled immigrants and African Americans' hopes for a homeland where they could live free from discrimination. Doing so, however, meant marrying an African American politics of liberation with the labor needs of a private corporation. Both the colonists and the hacienda had every reason to hope for the union to succeed, but it did not take long for the first fissures in the relationship to manifest themselves. Tlahualilo's managers found the colonists unaccustomed to irrigation and anxious to preserve one of their few gains of the Reconstruction era—their power as sharecroppers to manage their own time and labor—rather than working in gangs as the hacienda had hoped. For their part, Ellis's followers became increasingly unsettled by their new surroundings. In the words of John Washburn, a colonist from outside Birmingham: "[Mexico] is a different kind of country entirely from what any of us had ever been used to." Not only were Mexico's language and foods unfamiliar; in an era when both Mexico and the United States imposed high tariffs along the border, manufactured goods proved far more expensive than in Alabama and Georgia, eroding many of migration's economic advantages.

Most troubling of all, as construction on the lodgings at Santa Rosa progressed, the colonists' dwelling place took on an increasingly disconcerting appearance. The adobe structure gradually assumed the shape of a hollow square, with the housing for each family along the exterior, facing a common plaza. There were only a few exits to the fields beyond and no windows on the peripheral walls—common features in a region that had only recently been subject to Comanche attacks. This same history of Indian raiding also led many of the corporation's managers to carry firearms and to post guards around the hacienda at night.

For a people with fresh memories of bondage in the United States, however, Tlahualilo's fortified housing, armed overseers, and isolated position gave it an uneasy resemblance to a prison. Rumors soon surfaced among the colonists that the Mexicans planned to take advantage of Tlahualilo's remote location to reenslave them. (This was not an entirely unreasonable fear: farther south, on the republic's henequen and rubber plantations, Mexican *hacendados* fashioned a brutal debt-peonage system that approximated slavery in all but name.) The emigrants' discontent became intense enough that in March Peg-Leg Williams returned to San Antonio and publically denounced the colony. A trickle of colonists soon followed. Unable to afford railroad tickets, they walked over three hundred miles back to the border, following the same train tracks that had brought them to Tlahualilo only a few months before. Startled passersby in El Paso, Eagle Pass, San Antonio, and other border cities encountered small knots of "half starved and scantily clad" colonists begging for supplies as they retraced their route all the way back to Alabama and Georgia.

As this flight demonstrated, Mexico could excite fears as well as fantasies among African Americans. In theory, the colony should have been able to weather such challenges, with the departure of the loudest voices of discontent strengthening the bonds among those remaining. The colonists had the unexpected misfortune, however, of being colonized by an unknown microbe. As spring gave way to summer, the migrants, weakened by the lack of shelter, the unusual food, and the stress of recent controversies, began to exhibit symptoms of a mysterious malady: shootings pains, swollen joints, fever, diarrhea. After several died, the Tlahualilo Corporation turned to the borderland's medical center and brought Henry Trollinger, a white physician from San Antonio, to the hacienda. (One wonders at the complex family dynamics such an act invoked. Did Ellis ever consider hiring his brother-in-law, Greene Starnes, by now the leading African American doctor in the Alamo City, instead of Trollinger? Or did he avoid Greene because enlisting him might bring Ellis's connections to San Antonio's black community to light? To compound the irony, other African Americans in Texas, once they heard about the illnesses plaguing Tlahualilo, publically urged Starnes to go to Mexico and help the colonists, apparently without knowing that Ellis was Starnes's brother-in-law.)

Trollinger diagnosed most of the colonists as suffering from "a disease resembling malaria," but his prescribed treatment—mercury and quinine—offered little relief. The doctor reported that the mystery illness had left the colony "panic stricken. . . . The victims are afraid to go to bed, for they say that no one has ever arisen who has done so." By late July, as temperatures surged into the 100s and the deaths among the colonists mounted to over forty, most of the survivors elected to flee. A few, adopting the strategy of the prior wave of departing colonists, followed the railroad tracks north, feeding themselves on mesquite pods that they foraged along the way. Most, however, headed to the closest large town, Torreón.

"El Chicago de Coahuila" not only offered stores, supplies, and medical facilities; it also contained the closest representatives of the US government. In the wake of the United States' growing investment in Mexico, consuls' offices had sprung up across the republic until most major towns, especially in the North, possessed an American charged with reporting on local affairs to the State Department. Usually, the consuls' concerns centered on US-owned enterprises, such as the American mining operations near Torreón. Now, however, much to his surprise, the consular agent in Torreón, Lenious F. Poston, found himself meeting with a delegation of colonists, who insisted that despite their emigration to Mexico they remained US citizens—and that as such, the US government should cover the cost of their transportation back to their homes. Although the consul tried to get the colonists to accept positions at some of the US-owned firms in the area—"Mr. W.L. Eaton of El Oro [Mine] was wanting twelve or fourteen teamsters besides other laborers. He preferred negros"—most of the refugees, having soured on life in Mexico, preferred to stay together rather than scatter to different enterprises.

By heading for Torreón, the colonists also unintentionally engaged representatives of the Mexican state. The republic's health services had preceded their US counterparts in accepting the germ theory of infection, with the result that Mexico's Consejo Superior de Salubridad established quarantine and fumigation facilities in border towns such as Nogales, Ciudad Juárez, Nuevo Laredo, and Piedras Negras in the early 1890s, well before similar facilities existed on the US side of the line. Because of Torreón's import as a rail hub, it became the centerpiece of the republic's efforts to control the spread of infectious diseases from the frontier into the interior. Little more than a year before Ellis's colony arrived, Mexican health officials had responded to an outbreak of smallpox and typhus in Torreón with an aggressive campaign of pesticide application, street cleaning, and compulsory vaccination. The arrival of scores of potentially sick African Americans from Tlahualilo threatened to undo all these efforts. In response, Mexican authorities ordered the police to detain every colonist they could locate and test them for disease.

Fifteen came back positive for smallpox, compounding what was fast turning into a diplomatic crisis between the United States and Mexico. President Grover Cleveland issued orders for the War Department to ship rations to the colonists from the US Army depot at San Antonio. But Mexican authorities, in an apparent effort to force their US counterparts to remove their sick citizens from Mexico, refused to let the rations across the border without the payment of an onerous customs duty. After some initial hesitation because of the expense involved, the US government eventually saw no other option than to transport the colonists back to US soil, with the assistance of the Mexican International Railroad Company (despite its name, an American-owned enterprise).

The return of the colonists to Eagle Pass in late July revealed the extent to which questions of border security and of public health had increasingly become intertwined. When the colonists reached the boundary line, no longer traveling in passenger trains emblazoned with banners proclaiming TLAHUALILO, MEXICO—THE LAND OF LIBERTY FOR THE BLACK MAN but rather in crowded boxcars, they were shunted onto a separate rail spur. They were then escorted four miles out of Eagle Pass to an isolated patch of chaparral along the Rio Grande, where they were placed under quarantine. Since the US federal government, unlike its counterpart in Mexico, assumed almost no responsibility for enforcing health measures along the border, the burden of supervising the colonists fell instead to the state of Texas. As transborder trade and migration surged during the Porfiriato, Texan officials grumbled at their expanding role as the nation's sanitary guardians, especially since many of the goods and peoples crossing over from Mexico were no longer bound for the Lone Star State but for points deep in the US interior. It was as if, with Cortina and other Mexican bandits no longer troubling the Texas border, a new, microbial cast of raiders had arisen in their place. "Great as the importance of removing all needless obstacles to trade between the states and with foreign countries undoubtedly is," proclaimed the *Galveston Daily News*, "even greater is the importance of . . . protect[ing] the country against invasion and diffusion of pestilence. . . . As the matter is now arranged Texas stands guard, at her expense, for the benefit of the whole United States."

Reluctant Texas authorities expended as few resources as possible on the returning colonists, dispatching just four men to oversee the more than four hundred individuals quarantined outside Eagle Pass. These men served solely as guards, charged with preventing contact between the colonists and the residents of Eagle Pass/Piedras Negras, and did nothing to treat the infected migrants, who languished beneath mesquite bushes on tattered rags in the burning summer Texas sun. Nor did the guards do a particularly thorough job: passersby noted ethnic Mexicans coming to the camp to sell *sandia* (watermelon) as well as parties of colonists roaming the railroad tracks outside of town.

With many in the United States expressing concern about the "danger of the negroes stampeding and escaping to the interior," spreading disease in their wake, federal authorities decided to take a more active role in casting the border as a medical barrier. In early August, the Marine Hospital Service, long the quarantine agent for the nation's ports, assumed control of the camp outside Eagle Pass— its first venture into protecting the nation's terrestrial boundaries. The Marine Hospital Service quickly instituted "military rule" over the colonists. Using an expanded force of seventy guards, the quarantine supervisor, Dr. George M. Magruder, separated the sick and the healthy into separate campgrounds, then, through the use of a tightly patrolled picket line—a border within a border—isolated the former colonists from the outside world. Within this quarantined space, dubbed "Camp Jenner" in honor of the British physician who developed the smallpox vaccine, Magruder and his aides exercised near-total control. Medical officers burned the clothes, bedding, and other belongings of the colonists, forced them to bathe with highly toxic mercury bichloride, and inspected them twice a day for signs of smallpox. Those who exhibited any symptoms of illness were then segregated with the other infected individuals. This heightened control even extended to the colonists' immune systems: seizing upon the quarantine as "an opportunity not to be lost," the Marine Hospital Service and the National Hygienic Laboratory, extending a long and unsavory American tradition of using blacks as medical test subjects, experimented on the colonists with a new, unproven serum for smallpox derived from the blood of calves immunized with the variola virus.

Despite—or perhaps because of—this experimental treatment, Camp Jenner exhibited a disturbingly high mortality. Of the 411 colonists interned at Eagle Pass, 178 developed smallpox. Fifty-one died from the disease (a fatality rate of 29 percent), the oldest casualty being the sixty-five-year-old Henry Thompson and the youngest a baby born in quarantine and named Jenner after the camp. Little discussed amid this tragic loss of life was the question of whether the border represented the vulnerable entry point for disease that many Americans believed it to be. Other than the cases in Camp Jenner, there were only fifteen other cases of smallpox in Texas in 1895, despite the fact that the state possessed "hundreds of miles of boundary touching upon a foreign country in which smallpox and yellow fever to a greater or less extent are always present, owing to the habits of certain classes of the people and certain climatic conditions." Instead, the locales with the most pox cases that year were Chicago (432), Milwaukee (422), and Philadelphia (382)—all places distant from the Mexican border. Certainly from the perspective of Mexican health authorities, it was the United States, with its erratic quarantine process, that constituted the true disease threat in North America. Shortly after the departure of most of the colonists, Mexico dispatched military medical personnel to Tlahualilo, who, after burning or boiling whatever of the former colonists' possessions they could locate, vaccinated the small community of African Americans remaining on the hacienda. Convinced that African Americans were particularly susceptible to smallpox, the officers expressed a willingness to expand their measures across *la frontera* should the onetime colonists remain much longer in the border region.

IN EARLY AUGUST, Ellis, who had avoided falling prey to either smallpox or the mystery malady of the colonists, left Tlahualilo for the United States. His dream of African American colonization in Mexico had transformed itself into a nightmare, and he needed to manage the fallout, by either locating new colonists or persuading those who had left to return. His efforts at cajoling the ex-colonists collected at Camp Jenner to rejoin him, however, were rebuffed, and Ellis soon came to perceive the US government's actions in repatriating the colonists as hostile rather than humanitarian, designed to undercut not only the Tlahualilo colony but the entire project of black migration to Mexico. "The steps the American government had taken in one sense of the word was a good one," Ellis told the *San Antonio Express*, "and in another sense will prove disastrous to the entire negro race; for if their passage had not been paid hundreds of them would have remained until the harvest of this crop and would have averaged from $500 to $1000 to each family clear profit, and thus my enterprise would have been a success and proved a great benefactor to every American negro."

As Ellis circulated through the borderlands attempting to reconstitute his colony, the former colonists at Camp Jenner languished in quarantine. Not until late October, when the Marine Hospital Service finally issued them certificates documenting that they were free of smallpox, were they allowed to leave the camp. The sight of the pox-scarred colonists, dressed in ragged clothing and clutching their meager remaining possessions—some "old dirty blankets, [and] black pots and pans"—disembarking at the same railroad stations in Alabama and Georgia they had departed from with such high expectations less than a year earlier inspired considerable comment in the Southern press. A few whites had celebrated the colonists' departure. "They are the riff-raff of the county," contended the *Tuskaloosa Gazette*. "It was an occasion for universal rejoicing when they left." But most seized with relief upon the colonists' experience in Tlahualilo to counter the critique of US race relations contained within the colonization movement and to dismiss what had seemed not so long before like the very real possibility of a mass migration of African Americans into Mexico.

In justifying his colony, Ellis had juxtaposed an intolerant US South, where, in his words, African Americans were "suffering more . . . than at any time since the days of slavery" with the far more welcoming conditions in northern Mexico. Coverage of the colony's collapse in the white press inverted this contrast, suggesting that it was Mexico that represented a land of slavery for African Americans, while the United States was the land of freedom and opportunity. The *Victoria Advocate* (which somehow failed to recognize that the colony's organizer had spent his early years in the town) labeled Tlahualilo "prison-like . . . a thousand times more barbarous than slavery." Other papers were no less hyperbolic. The colonists thought "they would be treated as equals," chided the *Galveston Daily News*. Instead, they were subjected to "inhuman treatment and cruelty." The lesson to be drawn from the event was a simple one. "This is the home of the negro," editorialized the *Alabama Courier*. "He should better accept the southern sun and cotton fields and make of himself a more useful citizen."

The simultaneous return of several blacks who had left for Liberia at the same time as Ellis's colonists departed for Tlahualilo only reinforced such visions of the tropics as the graveyard not only of individual colonists but of the entire colonization movement. "The fate of another negro colony out about the same time appears to have been similar," asserted one commentator. "Three negroes have arrived . . . from Liberia . . ., reporting that ninety-seven colonists who sailed for the land of promise last spring were simply dumped on the shore by the colonizing society and left to shift for themselves." The supposedly salubrious tropical climate had, in fact, proven devastating to the colonists, "and this three, seeing no hope of obtaining a living in Africa, shipped for home on a passing steamer." Now, however, "the negroes are at home again and happy."

Across the border, Mexico drew its own lessons about the failure of Ellis's colony. Unsurprisingly, most observers concluded that the problem lay not with conditions in Tlahualilo but rather with African Americans themselves, who, as predicted, had made poor material for colonization. The immigrants, it was charged, lacked the promised agricultural skills—in fact, Llamedo went so far as to claim that many of the colonists Ellis brought to Tlahualilo were "bootblacks and other undesirable elements." The illnesses that had plagued the colonists provided further proof of their unsuitability for life in Mexico. "The climate [in Tlahualilo] for Europeans and Mexicans is unsurpassed, so that they are hardly sick at all," contended Llamedo. "[But] for blacks it was dreadful, causing them at first to become sick to their stomach because of the water and later to develop a special kind of small pox that only affects colored people." The Mexican press called once again for colonization to be limited solely to "the healthy, robust and hard-working people of the Latin countries of Europe, who only need to amalgamate with our race and to consider this land, with time, as their second homeland." Others spoke in favor of repatriating ethnic Mexicans from the United States—an act that would provide the republic with workers familiar with "all the modern mechanical systems in agriculture" while simultaneously rescuing them from the discrimination they faced north of the border.

Few thought to ask the returning colonists themselves about their experiences, so we know little about how the people most intimately involved with the Tlahualilo experiment assessed their time in Mexico. As the survivors settled back into their homes in Alabama and Georgia, they may have welcomed being once more among familiar peoples and places. But given the limited options available to them in the American South, there must have been days when they cast their minds back to Tlahualilo's endless cotton fields and cloudless skies and wondered at what might have been had disease and dissent not upended Ellis's experiment.

For all of the United States' and Mexico's fears of a mass transborder migration, the relocation of tens of thousands of American blacks to Tlahualilo seems unlikely. Ellis might contend that migration to Mexico opened up new avenues for land ownership and other forms of economic advancement. But such upward mobility was far more accessible to a bilingual, border-crossing entrepreneur than to share-croppers unfamiliar with Mexico or the Spanish language. Despite Ellis's promises—"my motive and sole object in the entire enterprise was for the good of everybody"—the colonists' immediate prospects were to remain as a landless workforce, much as they had been north of the border, relegated to a position not that different from a Mexican peon.

Even so, given the violence and discrimination roiling the post-Reconstruction era, Mexico retained an allure. "[As long] as the negro is suppressed as he is in the United States," explained Ellis, "the better class of them will seek new fields, and Mexico, standing at the very doors of the United States, offering inducements to all alike, will prove a welcome home." With the Tlahualilo Corporation having eliminated one of the preeminent obstacles to black migration—the costs of traveling to and settling in a new country—Ellis's colony had the potential to attract, if not tens of thousands of emigrants, at least a steady trickle. After all, in spite of the illness and turmoil that engulfed the colony, some sixty of the colonists elected to stay behind when their compatriots fled in 1895. As a result, even today, there are *tlahualilenses* who trace their ancestry to the African-American share-croppers in the Comarca Lagunera—to people who, after moving to the land of "God and Liberty," decided that Mexico did indeed represent the fresh start that Ellis had promised.

In the end, the colony's fragility can be attributed not only to bad luck but also to some of the unforeseen consequences of Ellis's decision to pass. Ellis had begun life in circumstances not dissimilar to those of the Tlahualilo colonists, laboring in his family's laundry and picking cotton in the fields. But his subsequent refashioning of himself into Guillermo Enrique Eliseo opened up a chasm between himself and the colonists that in retrospect proved almost impossible to bridge. Even had he attempted to identify himself as sharing the same background as the colonists, they could not have failed to note the ease with which Ellis circulated among elite European capital-ists south of the border—or the fact that, according to his contract with Llamedo, Ellis was slated to receive a portion of the hacienda's crop and stood to profit handsomely should the colony become a success. Nor could it have escaped the colonists' attention that when the reporter from the *Times-Picayune* chanced upon Ellis at the New Orleans depot, he took pains to portray himself as Cuban rather than as black. Ellis's behavior as an accomplished passer, in short, rendered his allegiance to other African Americans suspect. When bad times came, the already uneasy colonists proved unwilling to rally to Ellis's leadership and trust the genuineness of his concern for them—for it was no longer clear whether the colonists' fate and Ellis's fate were one and the same.

———————

ELLIS'S COLONY MAY have been short-lived, but the relationship between the US South and the Mexican North proved enduring. Together, the two regions came to constitute interlocking pieces of a massive North American cotton belt, organized around the parallel institutions of the plantation and hacienda. For additional evidence of the era's new cross-border interconnections, one needed only to note the unexpected migrant heading north at much the same time that Ellis and the colonists were heading south: the Mexican boll weevil. A quarter-inch-long beetle, the weevil was native to Mesoamerica, where it had been found on pre-Columbian cotton plants as early as 900 CE. The spread of cotton cultivation across northern Mexico and the southern United States, however, dramatically expanded the insect's range. By the 1890s, the weevil had hopscotched north across the Rio Grande; by the early twentieth century, "this enemy from Mexico" could be found throughout the US South.

The beetle's ravenous appetite for seedpods and leaf buds devastated the American cotton crop. Yet even as they watched their plantings wither away before the weevil's onslaught, many African Americans admitted a grudging admiration for the tiny, dark insect that had managed to bring low so many of the South's most powerful whites. "They were a proud and selfish people, those plantation

owners," recalled the gospel singer Mahalia Jackson. "I believe that
... God finally sent the boll weevil to jumble them. When the boll
weevil came, it ate right through thousands of fields of cotton and
most of those big plantation owners went bankrupt." Soon, throughout the South, one could hear blues songs that incorporated the
weevil—a seemingly defenseless insect who nonetheless managed to
triumph over his larger, more violent opponents—into the extensive
African American folklore on the trickster.

> The boll weevil is a little black bug
> Came from Mexico they say,
> All the way to Texas
> Just a-lookin' for a place to stay
> Just a-lookin' for a home, just a-lookin' for a home.
> . . .
> So they took the little boll-weevil and put him on the ice
> He sez to the farmers, "I say, but ain't this nice!
> But it ain't my home, though; no, it ain't my home."
>
> Then he took the little boll-weevil and put him in hot sand.
> He sez to the farmers, "Will, and I'll stand it like a man,
> Though it ain't my home, Baby; no, it ain't my home."

The linkages between Mexico and the US South inscribed themselves not only into the rough new music circulating through the
sharecroppers' shacks and juke joints of the plantation belt but also
into some of the era's most celebrated public events. In 1895, just
as most of Ellis's would-be colonists were returning to the United
States, Atlanta hosted the Cotton States and International Exposition. The event's backers intended it to showcase the rise of a "New
South"—one rooted in cotton cultivation but with industry and foreign trade playing increasingly prominent roles.

This New South, however, continued many old habits. The desire
to claim Latin American resources had not vanished, even if calls for
annexation were now supplanted by the vision of an informal empire

based on economic exchange. "The central idea of the 'Cotton States and International Exposition,'" maintained the event's promoters, "is to increase the trade and secure closer commercial relations between this country and Central and South America, Mexico, and the West Indies"—a concept exemplified by a widely circulated map that pictured Atlanta as the hub of a hemispheric trade network, with Mexico and Cuba its subsidiary spokes. The sense of Mexico as a tropical nation, with all that implied, remained as well. Although the Mexican government constructed an elegant pavilion on the fairgrounds, designed to showcase Mexico's modernization under Díaz, it proved far less popular than an unsanctioned three-acre "Mexican village" created by the American concessionaire James Porteous. (In a gesture toward authenticity, Porteous had collected his original curios and workers in Mexico, passing through Eagle Pass on his way to Atlanta at the very moment that the Marine Hospital Service was quarantining the Tlahualilo colonists.) With its burros, mock-up of Mayan ruins, and simulated coffee plantation, Porteous's village proved to be one of the fair's most popular exhibits, attracting crowds of whites and blacks alike. Most of the latter viewed the village through the prism of the recent news about Ellis's experiment, wondering aloud at the dangers for blacks in Mexico and whether the Mexican government had given the colonists on Tlahualilo smallpox on purpose.

As might be expected, an event labeled a "cotton exposition" was as much about race as it was about plant fiber. The fairgrounds included an exhibit from the Smithsonian Institution demonstrating the four "types of mankind"—black, red, yellow, and white—a schema that in its rigid divisions signaled the uncertain place of *mestizos* from Mexico or mulattoes like the Ellis family in the US racial order. The centerpiece of the campaign to demonstrate that the US South had surmounted its "negro problem" was the address delivered by Booker T. Washington at the fair's opening ceremony. Before a mixed audience, albeit one seated in separate black and white areas, Washington offered what came to be known as the Atlanta compromise: in exchange for white support for black education and employment, African Americans would accommodate themselves to Southern segregation. "In all things that are purely social," proposed Washington in the speech's best-known phrase, "we can be separate as fingers, yet one as the hand in all things essential to mutual progress." Although the "Wizard of Tuskegee" did not reference Tlahualilo by name, recent events in Mexico and Liberia were clearly on his mind. Instead of "bettering their condition in a foreign land" through colonization, Washington contended, African Americans should instead "cast down your bucket where you are." (While the exposition is best remembered for Washington's speech, both of Ellis's mentors featured in it as well: Bishop Turner delivered a lecture at the convention's "negro building" in favor of emigration and—in a possible rebuke to his one-time protégé—against those "miscegenated [African Americans who] pass for white," while Cuney served as one of the fair's "negro commissioners.")

Among those who refused to follow Washington's advice to cast down their bucket in their present location was Ellis. The winds of notoriety surrounding events in Tlahualilo had blown away whatever shreds of credibility still clung to his persona as a Mexican businessman. In April 1896, Ellis and Cuney entered a *cantina* on San Antonio's Alamo Plaza, located just down the street from Ellis's longtime office, only to be refused service because of their race. Shortly afterward, the new city directory for San Antonio was released. For the first time, Ellis's name appeared with a *c* after it for "colored."

Some individuals might have felt a certain relief at such revelations, which offered an end to the endless webs of deception inherent to passing. "There aren't any more secrets, nothing to be afraid of," related one passer upon finally acknowledging his African American ancestry. Ellis, however, followed a far different path. Rather than remaining in San Antonio and living in the African American community with the rest of his family, he vanished. He would not reappear until he was hundreds of miles from Texas, in a locale where he believed it would be safe for him to reinvent himself—and his connection to Mexico—once again.

PART III

MANHATTAN
—
MEXICO CITY

5

A PICTURESQUE FIGURE

IN EARLY APRIL 1897, passersby at Denver's Union Station glimpsed a stylishly attired figure alight from an incoming train and hail a cab to one of the city's premier addresses. The traveler's destination was the Brown Palace Hotel, a soaring edifice of Colorado granite and Mexican onyx located in the heart of downtown. Even though he was a regular at the Brown Palace, the guest's dramatic arrival—complete with multiple "boxes of cigars . . . and a large amount of luggage"— caused a minor sensation. Holding court in the hotel lobby before a large audience of curious spectators and reporters, he entertained various queries as to recent events in Latin America before retiring to one of the Brown Palace's deluxe suites.

The newcomer was known throughout town as the enormously wealthy Mexican investor Guillermo Enrique Eliseo. According to rumors, he owned many mines, including several in Colorado, and was involved in a project with Armour and Company to export Midwestern corn overseas. His purpose in coming to Denver, however, was to advance a new project involving several financiers in New York and $10 million of capital. With progress on the massive, decades-long Panama Canal project stalled, Eliseo and his partners were planning an alternative: a high-speed railroad line across the isthmus, which would in turn connect to a fleet of steamships plying the Pacific Coast. "It is claimed," enthused one commentator, "the scheme would be a great money-maker."

SUCH SCENES, WITH minor variations, played themselves out in numerous locales at the turn of the century. Sometimes the mysterious new arrival would be Mexican, as during his visit to Denver. Other times he would be Cuban—or even Hawaiian. On occasion, he might blur the categories, as when he claimed to own "sugar estates in Hawaii, coffee plantations in Cuba, [and] copper mines in Old Mexico," or to be "the son of a Cuban gentleman and of a Mexican mother." His name, too, might blend together Anglo- and Latin America, ranging as it did from William Ellis to Guillermo Enrique Eliseo to Guillermo Ellis. The character's one constant remained his role as a facilitator of investment in the American tropics. By the early 1900s, from his office on Wall Street (cable address: "Eliseo, New York") Ellis was listed as the president of a welter of such firms: the Mexico and Toluca Light and Power Company, La Compañia Mexicana Consolidada de Hule de Palo Amarillo, Eliseo Gold and Silver Mining Company, Mexican Securities and Construction Company, Cuban Central Unidad Sugar Company, Two Brothers Gold and Silver Mining Company, and the America, Mexico, West Indies, and Puerto Rican Company.

That it was on Wall Street, amid the new skyscrapers probing up into the skies above lower Manhattan, where Ellis resurfaced after his disappearance from San Antonio speaks volumes about the United States' deepening involvement with Mexico. By the close of the nineteenth century, the frenzy of American investment south of the border had caused the United States' Gilded Age and Mexico's Porfiriato increasingly to become one and the same. "Mexico is, in short, the coming country," enthused one American investor. "The resources of the country are almost illimitable."

Mexican officials took pains to advance the idea of the two nations as "sister republics," twin American democracies engaged in a mutual endeavor. But beneath this rhetoric, older divisions lingered, with the United States serving as the standard of development against which Mexico reluctantly, if inevitably, measured itself. Even Romero, the leading proponent of the "sister republics" concept, was not immune from presenting Mexico as the provider of raw materials to its more advanced northern neighbor. "Mexico has the shape of a cornucopia, with . . . its widest end towards the north, or the United States, and this has been considered allegorically as a sign that it will pour its wealth and products into this country. I look forward to the time, which I do not think far distant, when we shall be able to provide the United States with most of [its] tropical products."

Among US entrepreneurs, the imagined divide between a temperate, developed United States and a tropical, backward Mexico played itself out even more starkly, with the growing economic penetration of their southern neighbor invoking images not of "sister republics" but rather of conquest and domination. The monthly magazine *Modern Mexico*, headquartered just down the street from Ellis's Wall Street office, spoke for many in casting Latin America as the newest arena for the United States' fabled frontier:

> So far the triumphs of modern civilization the world over have been chiefly in the temperate zone. . . . The scene is changing, however. . . . The amount of money, for example, that is being put into plantations and ranches, not to mention mines, in Mexico and Central America runs into hundreds of millions. All through those wonderfully fertile lands are plantations owned and operated by Americans with American agricultural machinery, fast displacing the antiquated methods of the natives. . . . The same pioneer blood that developed the great farms of the West and Northwest is to-day helping to clear and plant the tropical fields of the extreme South.

Nearly every facet of the United States' booming consumer economy depended upon Mexico. The growing fleet of cars rolling along US roads did so on tires composed of Mexican rubber. The electricity and telephone calls flowing into US homes and businesses utilized wires of Mexican copper. Even the rising number of processed foods aimed at the American sweet tooth relied upon Mexican ingredients, from chocolate, vanilla, and sugar to the chicle used to make chewing gum. As the 1898 study *The Control of the Tropics* concluded: "If we turn at the present time to the import lists of the world and regard them carefully, it will soon become apparent to what a large extent our civilization . . . draws its supplies from the tropics."

One result of this reliance on the tropics was a staggering growth in US-Mexico commerce. In 1880, annual trade between the United States and Mexico totaled $15 million; by 1910, it had multiplied more than ten times to $166 million. Not only did total cross-border exchange soar; each nation dedicated an increasing proportion of its trade to the other. Mexico persisted with its hopes of cultivating European partners as a counterweight to a potentially acquisitive United States. By 1900, however, the republic's trade with the United States exceeded that with all of European countries combined; by 1912, the United States supplied 50 percent of Mexico's imports and purchased more than 75 percent of its exports.

This commercial expansion triggered a geographic reorganization. No longer was it solely border cities like San Antonio that were deeply entangled with affairs in Mexico. Now, involvement stretched all the way to the very epicenter of North American capitalism, New York City. Turn-of-the-century trade directories listed 122 New York City–based companies—among them Ellis's—dealing in exports to Mexico, far more than the next leading US cities: San Francisco with fifteen and New Orleans with ten. Direct investment in Mexico was harder to measure, but as the US State Department reported in 1895: "It is not extravagant to state that, in the last ten years, citizens of the United States have invested in Mexico, in mines, railroads, lands, and other undertakings, sums much larger in the aggregate than the whole amount of money in circulation in the [Mexican] Republic." US consuls estimated that the amount of American capital invested in Mexico by the early 1900s ranged between $500 million and $1 billion. Among these investments was the Tlahualilo Corporation: in 1896, British and American creditors assumed control of the company, and James Brown Potter, a New York–based financier, replaced Llamedo as Tlahualilo's director.

Given the vast sums and distances involved, some of this frenzy of US investment spilled over into fraud. The tendency toward questionable business practices emerged most dramatically in the era's rubber bubble. As America's mania for automobiles drove the price of a pound of rubber from fifty cents in the 1890s to over two dollars by 1910, US investors funneled millions of dollars into Mexican plantations, where the lowly rubber tree had long been used to shade coffee and cacao plantings. As promoters ripped out coffee and cacao bushes to increase their rubber plantings, overcapitalized new firms sprouted faster than new rubber seedlings, many promising staggering returns based on optimistic—or in some cases fabricated—yield assumptions. Even though few of these new companies met the accounting requirements necessary to list on the New York Stock Exchange, they could still market shares directly. Many firms targeted small-time investors who, lacking the means to inspect Mexico's plantations in person, relied instead on the assurances of the US Interior Department and the Departamento de Fomento as to the surety of the rubber industry. Such buyers responded enthusiastically to prospectuses promising that "of all the countries of the world, Mexico offers the greatest advantages for profitable investment." If the plantation did not yield as expected, however—or, as was sometimes the case, existed only on paper—the investors risked watching all their funds vanish like a shimmering tropical mirage.

With the relevant financial records having long since vanished, it is difficult to determine whether any of Ellis's corporations participated in the less savory aspects of the era's Mexican investment boom. The sheer quantity of firms in Ellis's name, as well as their involvement in mining and rubber, two frequent areas of corruption, raises the possibility. So, too, does the fact that the capitalization of his companies exceeded most reasonable assessments (the America, Mexico, West Indies, and Puerto Rican Company alone carried a value of half a million dollars). Ellis did not appear averse to spreading distorted information about his other business dealings: none of the rumors about Colorado mines or a trans-Panama train and steamship company that shadowed his visit to Denver have any documented foundation in reality. R. G. Dun & Company's credit report on Ellis from the turn of the century summed up the mysteries surrounding his new life on Wall Street: "He is either a Mexican or Cuban by nationality, and is otherwise known as Guillerine Enriques Elesio [*sic*]. . . . His operations in this city [New York] seem to be largely in the promoting line, principally in the organization of different Cuban and Porto Rican enterprises. . . . Authorities consulted apparently have no knowledge of his resources at this time and careful inquiry made could not indicate that he was a man of any definite standing and credit."

At least some of Ellis's misdirection, however, may not have been intentional. The line between deceiving others and deceiving oneself can be a blurry one—especially if a corporation's director had long harbored images of Mexico as an unparalleled land of opportunity and shared in the runaway optimism of his outside investors. Ellis had already sunk years of his time and much of his money into colonization attempts in Mexico; there was no reason why he should not likewise possess an outsized enthusiasm for speculating in Mexican enterprises, particularly when so many other Americans did as well.

What we do know is that whatever income Ellis generated in Mexico during these years came from far more prosaic sources than long-lost gold mines, tropical plantations, or Pacific steamships. In 1896, Ellis purchased the mortgage on the Edward Butts Manufacturing Company, a factory located on Mexico City's Avenida Balderas, only steps away from the capital's *alameda*. Butt's facility was the largest furniture factory in all Mexico, with a workforce of 120. Its chimney, reputed to be the tallest in the capital, served as a prominent Mexico City landmark. The firm specialized in making American-style beds, mattresses, desks, and other furniture for sale throughout the republic. Once more exhibiting his trickster-like tendency to hide in plain sight, the new owner boldly renamed the concern Ellis Manufacturing and promised to invest "a heavy amount of capital" in it over the next few years.

At much the same time as he purchased the factory, Ellis also became the Mexican representative for the Hotchkiss Arms Com-

pany, a French-based weapons manufacturer, apparently by charm-
ing the founder's elderly, American-born widow. Hotchkiss had
supplied arms to Mexico ever since the *juaristas* of the 1850s. By the
early 1900s, the Mexican Army featured several units armed with
Hotchkiss machine guns, presumably purchased with Ellis's assistance. What Ellis was learning to cultivate in Mexico, it turned out,
was not coffee or rubber plants but a different resource altogether:
well-placed capitalists and politicians, a skill for which he had already
shown great flair in his interactions with Mariscal, Pacheco, and Llamedo in the 1880s and 1890s.

———

ELLIS TOOK CARE to project a Hispanic persona from the moment
he arrived in New York. In the Manhattan directory, he listed
himself as "Ellis, Wm H broker" with offices at 29 Wall Street—
conveniently next door to the era's most powerful investment firm,
J. P. Morgan & Company, based at 23 Wall Street—and, in a separate entry on another page, as "Eliseo, Guillermo E," residing first
at the Hotel Imperial on Broadway and then at 153 West Eightieth
Street. These latter addresses placed him well outside the era's African American neighborhoods: the community of "San Juan Hill"
on the far west side of Manhattan and the newer cluster of black
households taking root in Harlem. Although New York State had
passed the Malby Law in 1895, prohibiting segregation in "places
of public accommodation or amusement," in Manhattan the law
tended to be observed in the breach. It was the rare restaurant
that denied African Americans entrance. But by offering desultory
service, such establishments managed to communicate their hostility
toward black customers all the same. By the early 1900s, W. E. B. Du
Bois could only identify one place "where a colored man downtown
can be decently accommodated"—revealingly, not Ellis's haunt, the
Hotel Imperial, but rather the Marshall Hotel, celebrated by James
Weldon Johnson as "the headquarters of Negro talent." Moreover,
the Malby Law left untouched New York's pernicious discrimination

in employment and housing. Thousands of blacks squeezed into San Juan Hill's few square blocks because of the limited number of rental properties available to them elsewhere. Outside such neighborhoods, African Americans often met hostile white mobs; in fact, it was to the frequent racial confrontations along its periphery that San Juan Hill allegedly owed its moniker.

In passing as Hispanic in New York, then, Ellis was once again eluding the racial barriers constraining African Americans. But unlike his earlier experience in Texas, in Manhattan Ellis was engaged in a process of reinventing not only himself but an entire ethnicity as well. San Antonio's large Tejano population had given him a preexisting community to blend into. By contrast, according to the census, there were fewer than three hundred Mexicans living in New York City in 1900. The city's Cuban population was slightly larger—just over two thousand—but it, too, remained a small shard in Manhattan's sprawling ethnic mosaic. These modest numbers meant most Manhattanites possessed little if any direct experience of Mexicans or Cubans prior to their encounter with Guillermo Enrique Eliseo. It was therefore up to Ellis to embody Mexico and/or Cuba for his new acquaintances, a process that involved refashioning preexisting American stereotypes to fit the role he sought to play.

Foremost among these stereotypes was the perception of Latin America as a tropical wonderland of tremendous riches—an image that Ellis embraced almost to the level of parody through his carefully waxed mustache, impeccable tailoring, ostentatious jewelry, and lavish distributions of Cuban cigars and Mexican leatherwork. "With fingers bedecked with massive gold rings of odd design, set with apparently valuable jewels, a slight mustache and very good English," noted the *Washington Times*, "Mr. Ellis . . . is a picturesque figure." Ellis "wears rings on both hands with a heavy gold chain with an immense diamond pendant, makes a big splurge among white men, and retains their friendship by giving handsome presents to them and their wives of jewelry and valuable curio's [*sic*]," added another observer. "In the mere matter of cigars he expends from $5 to $10 per diem." As both Cuba and Mexico were lands of social extremes—in the US imagination and in reality—Ellis did not claim to be just any Cuban or Mexican but rather a member of Latin America's upper class. Ellis modeled his exterior self on the elite Mexicans he had for years watched parade along the capital's Paseo de la Reforma and *alameda* (figures who, for their part, were attempting to emulate the latest fashions from Europe). But his pose was also designed to appeal to the acquisitiveness of his American audience—especially those who hoped to discover in Guillermo Enrique Eliseo a well-connected entrepreneur who could facilitate their access to the hemisphere's abundant natural resources.

The commercial undercurrent to Ellis's persona explains why he flitted between Mexican, Cuban, and, briefly, Hawaiian identities. Together, these three composed what might be considered the United States' late nineteenth-century imperial periphery: spaces on the country's very borders that, ever since the era of the filibusters, had beckoned to expansionists as incipient new American territories, destined by the forces of history and progress alike to be incorporated into the United States. As such, they differed from more distant Latin American nations like Argentina or Brazil—a fact that may explain why Ellis never attempted to pass as being from either of these two countries, despite such convenient models of self-invention as the hit Broadway play of the 1890s *Charley's Aunt*, which featured an American man masquerading as a Brazilian woman.

By the turn of the century, each member of this imperial periphery had assumed its own particular valence. Hawaii, dominated by American sugar planters from the mid-nineteenth century onward, would formally become part of the United States in 1898. Mexico limited US involvement to its economic sphere—although as late as 1903 *Harper's Weekly* would advocate the purchase of "Chihuahua and two or three others of the northern and thinly-peopled Mexican States" as a destination into which the United States could deport its "negro problem." The status of Cuba, however, remained an open question. One of the few remaining fragments of Spain's once vast New World empire, Cuba had been racked by political turmoil for decades as the island's population launched repeated campaigns for independence with the support of US-based clubs of Cuban émigrés. US audiences immersed themselves in events on the island, their motivations ranging from enthusiasm at the thought of displacing the final vestiges of European colonialism from the continent to a long-standing desire to annex Cuba to the United States.

These impulses came to a head in 1898, transforming what had been a localized rebellion in Cuba into a multifront war between Spain and the United States. American troops invaded not only Cuba but also the Philippines, Guam, and Puerto Rico. For the United States, the ten-week-long Spanish-American War—a "splendid little war" according to Ambassador John Hay—represented an overwhelming triumph for American arms, albeit one that raised unwelcome questions as to the United States' status as an imperial power. For Ellis, however, the era's sympathy toward all things Cuban provided an enticing new opening. Although neither Ellis's name nor that of any of his alter egos appears on the membership rolls of the Cuban émigré clubs in New York City, he nonetheless adopted the mantle of the Cuban *insurrecto*. In 1897, he planted an article in the press that depicted him as the leader of an expedition of Mexicans that slipped out of the Mexican port of Tampico and "joined the insurgents," bringing with them "a large quantity of arms and ammunition." "Ellis has the rank of Captain in the insurgent army," continued the account. "He will return to Mexico in a short time to plot another expedition to Cuba." In interviews, Ellis expressed a deep engagement in Cuban affairs. "Cuba, 'Cuba libre,'" he enthused, "is destined to be free. Her people are fighting with an idea that liberty is dawning on the horizon and we in Mexico extend our heartiest sympathy." He placed a large portrait of the *insurrecto* leader Antonio Maceo in his office, and before long had the pleasure of seeing himself depicted in the New York press as "an enterprising Cuban, who has been successful as a banker and business man in Cuba and Mexico. He was a member of the Cuban volunteers under Maceo during the last revolution."

Ellis's dalliance with Cuba reflected more than the mere desire to harness himself to the United States' most recent Latin American adventure. Racially, Cubans enjoyed a status as among the whitest of Latin Americans—a condition achieved by conveniently excluding peoples of African descent from the US definition of Cubanness. As the Bureau of Immigration and Naturalization put it: "The term 'Cuban' refers to the Cuban people (not Negroes)." Echoing this erasure of Cuba's African peoples—in reality, one-third of the island's population—the US Immigration Commission's *Dictionary of Races or Peoples* asserted that "in race . . . the population of Cuba is mainly composed of pure Spanish stock."

By identifying himself as a Cuban or of partial Cuban ancestry (as when he insisted he was "the son of a Cuban gentleman and of a Mexican mother"), Ellis sought to affirm his whiteness in a way potentially even more secure than masquerading as a Mexican. After all, in recognition of Mexico's *mestizaje*, the same US Immigration Commission's *Dictionary of Races or Peoples* concluded that "the Mexican population, unlike that of Cuba, is mainly of Indian or mixed origin." Further proof of the fragile racial status of Mexicans could be found in a controversial lawsuit that took place in Ellis's onetime hometown at the very moment he was essaying his first efforts at Cubanness.

In 1896, Ricardo Rodríguez, a Mexican immigrant to San Antonio, made a routine application to become a naturalized citizen. The leaders of the local Republican and Populist Parties, however, opposed his bid on the grounds that Rodríguez—and by implication all Mexicans—did not meet the racial qualifications for US citizenship, which had been restricted to "free white persons" until 1870, when Congress broadened the law to include African Americans as well. Compelled to testify to his origins, Rodríguez parried all efforts to designate him a member of "the original Aztec race" by claiming he was a "pure-blooded Mexican." Although the presiding judge, Thomas S. Maxey, ruled in Rodríguez's favor, he did so using a logic that made manifest the tenuous place of Mexicans in the US racial order. Maxey concluded that since the Treaty of Guadalupe Hidalgo of 1848 stipulated that Mexicans could become US citizens, Mexicans like Rodríguez were legally white, even though "if the strict scientific classification of the anthropologist should be adopted, he would probably not be classified as white." Rodríguez's victory was thus at best partial, for it slotted Mexicans into a new, nebulous category: people who did not meet a commonsense or scientific definition of whiteness but who nonetheless possessed its legal privileges.

Beyond his desire to craft the whitest persona possible in the shadow of the Rodríguez case, there was another, more subversive reason for Ellis to seek out a Cuban identity. Americans may have excluded Afro-Cubans from their definition of Cubanness, but many of the leaders of the Cuban independence movement, such as Antonio Maceo, were in fact of African descent (Maceo's nickname was *el Titan de Bronce*, the "Bronze Titan"). Claiming to be an *insurrecto* gave Ellis license to celebrate an individual of African descent—indeed, put a large portrait of him on the wall of his Wall Street office, right beside a similarly impressive portrait of Porfirio Díaz—while simultaneously opening up the plausible deniability that since Maceo was Cuban rather than black, Ellis's actions bore no connection to US race relations. Once again, Ellis had figured out how to exploit the ambiguities in the American racial order. Cuban or Mexican might be a nationality, and each country, like others in the Americas, might be composed of peoples of diverse backgrounds. But in claiming to be Cuban or Mexican, Ellis had discovered how to manipulate Americans' limited knowledge of each country to make subtle assertions as to his racial status.

———

ELLIS'S LIFE OF reinvention in New York City was not an isolated case, as he learned in a jarring episode soon after his arrival. Among his earliest acquaintances in the city was an actress named Fayne Strahan. Like Ellis, Strahan was a newcomer to Manhattan, having grown up in Atlanta with her widowed mother. Ellis became enamored of the young white woman, whom contemporaries labeled "a ruinous beauty," and wooed her with a sealskin coat and other expensive gifts. Little did he know, however, that all the time he was courting her,

Strahan was sizing him up for the "badger game," a grift designed for shallow men with deep pockets. After gaining the mark's trust, the female member of the con team would lure her target into a compromising situation. At this point, a male accomplice would burst in and, claiming to be the woman's husband (or in some variations, her brother or father), demand money to hush up the apparent outrage. In an age in which adultery carried considerable stigma, this "badgering" was often an effective ploy, securing money from the mark while discouraging him from going to the police, where he would have to confess to an awkward intimacy with the female member of the team.

After months of toying with Ellis, however, Strahan and her partner (and secret husband), William A. E. Moore, elected to spring their trap on Martin Mahon, the well-to-do proprietor of the New Amsterdam Hotel, instead. Apparently, Strahan and Moore had caught wind of Ellis's masquerades long before he picked up on theirs. (Such skills of detection were important in their line of business: one of the other marks they cultivated and then abandoned, the supposed Hungarian count Aurel Batonyi, turned out to be nothing more than an impoverished riding instructor named Kohen.) Mahon, however, was that rare mark who pursued prosecution, perhaps because Moore gratuitously clubbed him on the head with a revolver upon surprising him with Strahan. The subsequent trial dragged a reluctant Ellis into the public spotlight, threatening to undo his Hispanic persona. Called into court as a witness, Ellis identified himself as "a Cuban and a broker in Wall street" and dazzled audiences with his refined appearance: a "long brown overcoat of costly texture, . . . [a] thick white silk handkerchief around his neck . . . fingers sparkl[ing] with many valuable diamonds." Although trial testimony raised doubts as to Ellis's background, it soon became clear that he was not the only figure in the courtroom with an interest in seeing his Hispanic identity maintained. Mahon recalled Moore declaring that at least it was the Irish-born hotelkeeper, rather than "that nigger," Ellis, who had stolen his wife's affections. But Strahan, no doubt anxious to preserve an image of herself as a proper white woman, remained adamant throughout the trial that Ellis was not her "negro friend" but in fact a "high toned Cuban gentleman." So, too, did Strahan's mother in her interviews with a New York press corps consumed with the scandal.

With Strahan and her mother serving as unexpected defenders of his Cubanness, Ellis managed to weather the trial. He returned to Wall Street, where he soon launched one of his greatest business successes—albeit one that, ironically, bore only the slenderest connection to either Mexico or Cuba. A few years previously, Ellis had crossed paths with a businessman named Moses R. Crow, most likely when the latter was in Mexico City to assist the Díaz administration with one of its signature programs, a massive public works project to drain the wetlands ringing the capital. Crow had previously dabbled in municipal water works in the United States. Upon his return from Mexico, however, he went on a spree, buying up a slew of water companies near Manhattan using funds advanced by the widow Hotchkiss—an arrangement set in motion by his new acquaintance, Ellis, who became the president of the resulting conglomeration, the New York and Westchester Water Company, in 1899. Crow and Ellis would fall out following Hotchkiss's death as they struggled to unsnarl the convoluted stock deals behind their new enterprise. But in the meantime their actions created a corporation valued in the millions, complete with a sprawling network of reservoirs, pumping stations, and real estate holdings. Ellis was at last the wealthy, influential entrepreneur that he had long held himself up as being, rendering his stories of Latin American riches all the more believable to audiences in Manhattan and beyond.

———

FOR ANYONE INVOLVED in passing, one of the most fraught decisions involved marriage and children. Passing almost always involved distancing oneself from one's birth family: those nearest and dearest were also a vulnerability, the people most likely to betray the origins that passers were attempting to keep secret. For this reason, many African Americans referred to passing as a death of sorts. "By inquiring . . . what become of the 'Blank' family or of Old Mr. X's daughter," noted Louis Baldwin, "information was obtained which when followed up, showed that the family or daughter ... had 'gone on the other side' which did not mean that they had departed this life, but that they had 'become white.'" Creating a new family, however, posed its own dilemmas. Should one tell a potential spouse about one's hidden identity? Did one have children, knowing that offspring sometimes exhibited features phenotypically at odds from the race claimed by the passer?

After leaving Texas, Ellis, unlike most passers, maintained contact with his family, sending them money from time to time as well as requests to "place flowers on mother's grave from her boy." But he did so clandestinely: through the relative anonymity of the mail (as Langston Hughes once observed, "There's nothing to stop letters from crossing the color-line") and by meeting relatives in Mexico, far from his new acquaintances in Manhattan. From such ongoing family connections, Ellis learned of the controversy that had greeted his youngest sister, Isabella, when she attended Northwestern University in 1901. Perhaps because she was the darkest of her siblings, perhaps for other reasons, Isabella did not attempt to pass during her time in Evanston. She had initially been assigned a white roommate at Northwestern, but "when a shapely, handsome, and intelligent octoroon arrived and announced her identity," all the other students refused to room with her. The following fall, "the faction in favor drawing the color line won by a decisive majority." On the pretext that there was not enough space for her to stay by herself, as she was forced to do during her first year at Northwestern, Isabella was denied access to the university's dormitories. Soon afterward, she withdrew and returned home to San Antonio.

Ellis doubtless compared Isabella's humiliations with the contemporaneous experience of Anita Florence Hemmings at Vassar. A light-skinned African American, Hemmings, unlike Isabella, hid her black ancestry when she enrolled at the women's college outside New York in 1893. Dubbed the "beautiful brunette" by her classmates, most of whom "supposed ... that she was a Spaniard," Hemmings flourished at the college, becoming a campus leader, prominent "at the

Founders' Day, Philalethian Day and commencement day exercises."
She was unmasked only days before graduation when the father of
a jealous classmate dispatched a private detective to investigate her
background. Seeking to avoid a scandal, Vassar awarded Hemmings
her diploma, but news of her subterfuge still seeped out. "Society and
educational circles in this city," observed the *New York World* in the
summer of 1897, "are profoundly shocked by the announcement in
the local papers to-day that one of the graduating class of Vassar College this year was a Negro girl, who concealing her race, entered the
college." Despite all the unpleasantness Hemmings had to endure,
however, Ellis would have noted that by passing, Hemmings, unlike
Isabella, had managed to receive a college degree. And, as Ellis may
have witnessed firsthand, Hemmings soon resumed her career as a
passer. A few years after her graduation from Vassar, she married
Andrew Jackson Love, a light-skinned African-American doctor.
The two moved to New York City, where they lived out their days
as upper-class whites, sending their children to the exclusive Horace
Mann School and all-white summer camps.

It is tempting to picture Ellis and the Loves strolling past one
another on Manhattan's streets, a subtle flicker of recognition passing
between them. But Ellis did not always exhibit the same caution as
other turn-of-the-century passers, as his erratic route to matrimony
underscores. In his thirties by the time of his move to Manhattan,
Ellis appeared intent on selecting a fair-complexioned white woman
for a marriage partner. Three years after his disastrous courtship of
Fayne Moore, he made unwanted advances toward a young white stenographer with blue eyes and "light and wavy" hair named Frances
Sauer. On the pretext of interviewing her for a job at his firm, Ellis
invited her to his Wall Street address late one afternoon. After she
joined him in his private office, however, he uttered a few "expressions
of undying affection" and lunged for her. Sauer went to the police
the following morning, accusing Ellis of attempting to assault her.
In a stunning demonstration of both his financial resources and his
ability to pass, Ellis hired one of Manhattan's most prominent attor-
neys, George Gordon Battle, a white Southerner who had attended

Columbia Law School, to represent him. Battle wasted little time in accusing Sauer of blackmail, while Ellis pled for "the newspapers . . . [to] treat me kindly." "It is a shame," he declared, "that a man's reputation should be broken down in such a manner after he has struggled so hard to establish it."

Although the police eventually dropped the charges against Ellis for lack of evidence, this disquieting episode casts in sharp relief the distortions passing imposed on the passer's personal life. On his own in a new city, isolated from the family networks that under different circumstances would have facilitated introductions to young women, Ellis resorted to utilizing a routine job interview as a cover for his advances. Selecting a woman a decade younger than himself from a modest background, he no doubt hoped to overawe her with the trappings of his Wall Street milieu. If this attraction to the light-complexioned Sauer speaks to the erotics of the color line—especially the long-forbidden coupling of white women and black men—it fulfilled a practical purpose as well, ensuring that any possible children would be as light as possible.

As fortunate as Ellis may have been in avoiding attempted rape charges after his encounter with Sauer, his subsequent tactics seemed to have changed little, at least to judge by the woman he ended up marrying in May 1903: Maude Sherwood. In the press release that Ellis issued announcing the nuptials, he claimed that he and his bride had met in Great Britain on the estate of the Hotchkiss family and that Sherwood was descended from English nobility: "Bride—Only daughter of Thomas Clark Sherwood of Mayport, England . . . grandniece of Lord George Armstrong (deceased) . . . grandniece of Sir William Hy. Watson (deceased) at one time Baron of Exchequer. Related to Sherwoods of Nottingham, Clarks, Lightfoots and Watsons." But the truth was considerably more prosaic. Census data reveal that Sherwood was not born across the ocean in Great Britain but across the Hudson River in the working-class seaport of Jersey City. It was true that her father was from England, having emigrated in 1870. But he was no aristocrat, working instead on the docks as a clerk and shipping agent for a steamship line. By 1900, around the time when Maude first met Ellis, she and her widowed father were living in a boardinghouse in lower Manhattan, and Maude's profession was listed as "stenographer." Given her profession, age (thirteen years younger than Ellis), and working-class, New York background, Sherwood and Ellis, rather than meeting at a soiree on the Hotchkiss estate, must have first encountered each other in his office or some other work setting.

New York did not have any laws barring marriage between blacks and whites in 1903, making it one of the few states not to draw the matrimonial color line. But intimate relations across the color line nonetheless remained fraught. As the *North American Review* explained, "Even in commonwealths where mixed marriages are lawful they are extremely rare, and are visited with the severest social reprobation." Campaigns against Manhattan's vice districts invariably focused their horror on the city's "Black and Tan" clubs where black men and white women mingled with one another—a phenomenon, in the words of Police Commissioner William McAdoo, that ran "counter to violent racial prejudices and traditions. . . an unmitigated and disgusting evil." In 1900, a ferocious race riot, sparked in part by questions of interracial intimacies, gripped Manhattan, with white vigilantes pursuing African Americans throughout the city. Ten years later, the New York State Legislature debated a measure that would have voided all marriages "contracted between a person of white or Caucasian race and person of the negro or black race." Such incidents made Ellis's Hispanic identity valuable for romance as well as business. On his and Sherwood's marriage certificate, Ellis made sure to list the Spanish and English versions of his name and to give his parents' names as Carlos Eliseo and Marguerita Nelsonia. During the ceremony, held at Grace Episcopal Church (even though, as a proper Mexican, Ellis publicly identified as Catholic), he insisted on being referred to as Guillermo Enrique Eliseo. Recalled the minister: "I had great trouble pronouncing Mr. Eliseo's name, and we had a laugh over it."

While Ellis managed to convince the minister of his Hispanic background, it is less certain whether Sherwood—whose pet name for Ellis was "Gerry," an Anglicized diminutive of Guillermo—shared this belief. By most any measure, there was simply too much contact between Sherwood and the rest of Ellis's relatives for her to remain unaware of his African American ancestry. Immediately after the wedding, Ellis's sister Isabella made an extended visit to her brother and his new bride in New York City, and in later years, his niece Marguerite stayed with the couple for several summers while studying piano at Juilliard. Moreover, while it is not clear that Ellis and Sherwood ever visited San Antonio together, they nonetheless remained tethered to family affairs there. Shortly after his wedding, Ellis assumed the mortgage on his family's home in the Alamo City. Then, using a Manhattan notary, he transferred the title to Sherwood (listed on the deed as "Maude Ellis [Eliseo]"). Why he did so is uncertain. Perhaps he thought that the house would be more secure in the hands of a person whose white status was less open to question than his own; perhaps he wanted to hide the asset from potential creditors. But the transfer does underscore that Ellis placed a great deal of trust in Sherwood—enough to put in her hands not just any piece of property but the one that linked him to his greatest secret: the African American family whose existence he had striven to keep carefully hidden ever since his move to San Antonio in the late 1880s.

And what about Sherwood? Ellis may have found her whiteness appealing for multiple reasons, but what did she hope for from the relationship? Much about matters of the heart, of course, resides beyond the reach of historians. Nonetheless, for a young woman with few resources, marrying an older, well-to-do businessman may have seemed like a step up in the world. Often the leading impediment to marrying across the color line—beyond state laws prohibiting such unions—was the resistance of family. But by 1903, Sherwood had few such ties: she was an only child; her mother had died years before, and her father of tuberculosis just three weeks before her nuptials with Ellis. (Ellis promptly interred his would-be father-in-law in style in Woodlawn Cemetery, the most elegant graveyard in New York City, where the onetime shipping clerk from Jersey City lay alongside assorted titans of the Gilded Age, including Ellis's putative mentor and father, Collis P. Huntington.) One measure of Maude's isolation can be found in the fact that her wedding ceremony included only two guests. The first was Ellis's private secretary, the second—and Sherwood's only possible invitee to the event—according to the minister, a "Miss Gilbert, from out of town somewhere."

The story that arose around Sherwood as minor British nobility even raises the question of whether, as with Fayne Moore earlier, it was in fact Ellis the trickster who was tricked. If this appears unlikely, given their probable manner of meeting, it does suggest that Sherwood was far from passive in shaping how she and Ellis were perceived by the outside world. For most Gilded Age Americans, passing was limited solely to the move across the color line from black to white. Yet as Ellis discovered first with Strahan and now with Sherwood, New York bubbled with figures involved in various forms of self-shaping, all seeking to cross class or ethnic lines in pursuit of a more privileged position in Gilded Age society. "Because of America's particularly fierce taboo on the Negro, we have come to think that 'passing' pertains only to him," observed the Harlem Renaissance writer Heba Jannath. However, "it must be borne in mind that passing for something which one is not is a very common practice in America. Jews and Mexicans often pass for Spaniards (since to be Spanish is thought more desirable here). Jews, Russians, Germans, Italians, and Irish frequently change their names into 'acceptable' Anglo-Saxon."

Making such forms of shapeshifting especially common in Gilded Age Manhattan was not only the city's size—three and a half million souls, making it the largest city in North America and one of the largest in the world at the time—but also the fact that New York was composed overwhelmingly of newcomers from elsewhere. Forty-two percent of Manhattanites in 1900 were foreign born, with Germany, Ireland, and Russia the primary sources. A significant portion of the remaining inhabitants were either the children of immigrants or transplants from other parts of the United States. Among New York's African American community—only sixty thousand in 1900 (less than 2 percent of the city's population)—many had relocated from

Virginia, North Carolina, and other states in the Upper South. As these individuals left the closeness of rural communities in Europe, the United States, or elsewhere for the anonymity of urban life, they were presented with an opportunity to attempt new narratives about themselves—to perform daily life as someone else, in front of an audience that, more often than not, was involved in a parallel process of reinvention. "The task of passing, especially in our great cities," concluded Jannath, "is not so difficult as is supposed."

Manhattan's polyglot population offered particularly rich opportunities for African Americans to recast themselves as members of another ethnicity. "There are so many swarthy races represented in New York's population," reported Walter White, "that even colored people who could easily be distinguished by their own race as Negroes, pass as French or Spanish or Cuban with ease." Many blacks discovered that by speaking accented English, "jabbering off some French," or even resorting to gibberish and outlandish outfits, they could convince whites that they were not African American and thus gain access to venues that were otherwise closed to them. The ensuing dilemmas that black-white passing raised as to racial solidarity and individual freedom, exterior appearance and inner reality, animated the "New Negro Movement" taking shape in Manhattan in the early 1900s. Indeed, for many leaders of the emerging Harlem Renaissance, the predicaments surrounding passing were far from distant abstractions. As the literary scholar Ann Douglas has noted, Jessie Fauset, Jean Toomer, and other prominent artists in the movement were all light-skinned and "able to pass as white whenever they chose."

There could be deep pain in such passing, as individuals severed connections to family, culture, and community to further their masquerades. But passing also offered liberation from artificial constraints and even the chance to ridicule prevailing conventions, as an incident that occurred with Ellis and Sherwood shortly after their wedding reveals. A prominent merchant from Victoria, Texas, in Manhattan on business, found himself relaxing at a racetrack outside the city one summer weekend. Not long after he took his place

in the stands, a waiter showed up with a bottle of wine, explaining
that it was being offered to him "compliments of W.H. Ellis." Not
initially recognizing the name, the merchant asked for clarification.
The waiter pointed out Ellis, who was sitting nearby with Sherwood;
Ellis responded to the shocked stare of the visitor from Victoria with
a nod and a wave. (Although the name of the visitor is not recorded,
poetic justice would make him one of the Weisigers who had wielded
such vast power over Ellis and his family during slavery and Reconstruction—a not altogether impossible occurrence, given that many
of the Weisigers dedicated themselves to raising racehorses after the
war, entering their animals in events as far away as Saratoga Springs.)
The distance Ellis had traveled from Victoria to Manhattan could
be measured in many ways, but perhaps none more profound than
this simple exchange: the ability of a onetime slave to sit next to his
white wife and greet one of the leading figures from his birthplace as
a social equal.

ONE MIGHT EXPECT relocation and marriage to transform Ellis. In
the aftermath of his sudden disappearance from San Antonio, he had
managed against great odds to fashion a viable new life for himself
in New York—one that, with marriage, involved another individual
in his deceptions more intimately than ever before. Yet rather than
limiting himself to his new roles as a Wall Street entrepreneur and
husband, Ellis once again dipped into African American politics. The
first inkling in this direction came in the summer of 1902 when Ellis
went to Great Britain during the coronation of Edward VII. While in
London, Ellis crossed paths with Ras Makonnen, the Ethiopian general who was representing Emperor Menelik II at the British court.
Menelik's realm—also known at the time as Abyssinia—enjoyed great
prestige in the African American community as the sole country in
Africa to have defeated a European imperialist invasion (Italy in the
1896 Battle of Adwa) and retained its independence. Enthralled by
his encounter with Makonnen, one of the heroes of Adwa, Ellis fas-

tened on the idea of journeying to Ethiopia, at the time such a remote spot that reaching Menelik's capital of Addis Ababa required a three-week camel caravan over hundreds miles of forbidding desert terrain. Nevertheless, Ellis remained undaunted. After reading every book he could find about the country and collecting what he deemed suitable presents for its emperor (an elaborately tooled bit, spurs, and saddle, all inlaid with silver, that he commissioned in Mexico City; a gold-plated, pearl-handled revolver; a pair of Hotchkiss rapid-fire cannons; and a picture of black US soldiers in Santiago, Cuba during the recent war with Spain), he departed for Abyssinia only a few months after his marriage—the first but not the last time he would leave his bride behind in New York while he ventured off to some distant locale.

If Ellis's voyage reflected the same fascination with Africa that motivated his onetime mentor Bishop Turner, it was also shaped by his more recent experiences in Mexico. Like the Mexican republic, Ethiopia was in the midst of a conscious effort to modernize under a strong ruler so as to prevent possible dismemberment by outsiders—a process that in Abyssinia, as in Mexico, involved the construction of railroads, roads, and telegraph lines, the development of mines, and the export of such agricultural staples as cotton and coffee. Ethiopia's isolation and the fact that Menelik came to power some fifteen years later than Díaz, however, meant these processes were not as far along in Abyssinia as in Mexico. For Ellis, such conditions offered the opportunity to become a key architect of Ethiopia's economy in a way that he could only pretend to achieve in Latin America. He accordingly brought with him to Addis Ababa "specimen coins" for a new national currency and plans for a national bank—to be run, of course, by himself. He also sought to expand trade between the United States and Ethiopia, which at the time had no diplomatic relations with one another. Invoking the era's familiar tropes of tropical abundance, Ellis portrayed Abyssinia as a storehouse of natural resources awaiting American capital and technology: "The soil is the richest on earth. It has been found by experiments that American cotton grows as well there as it does in the delta of the Mississippi, and the climate is adapted to the raising of everything that grows in the torrid zone. I also consider it the richest mineral country in the world. There are gold and silver, rubies and some diamonds, as well as graphite and hard coal in large quantities."

Preoccupied with imperialist threats to his kingdom, Menelik ordered that the official chronicle of his rule include no records about foreign relations. We thus have scant documentation on how the Ethiopians viewed Ellis, the first African American to reach their homeland. But Ellis's sense of Ethiopia as a land of new possibilities was such that while in Addis Ababa he evinced no need to pass. His African ancestry, so often a liability in the United States or Mexico, represented, in Ellis's eyes, an asset in Abyssinia—proof of a common bond between himself and the Ethiopians that differentiated him from the other Europeans and Americans trickling into the region. Ellis enthused that "the Emperor and all the Rases received me like a brother" and that Menelik "was especially interested in the negro race." But whether the emperor and his subjects believed they shared an ethnic tie with the light-skinned American black who had suddenly appeared in their midst is less certain. Menelik, who regularly had foreign news releases translated into Amharic so that he could stay abreast of world events, was too savvy a leader not to grasp the role white supremacy played in justifying the colonial projects ringing his kingdom. Yet he was also acutely aware of the divisions that could exist between peoples sharing the same dark skin. When not fending off European intrusions, Menelik had expanded his realm by conquering several neighboring peoples. This fact explained in turn one of the less appealing features of his realm: slavery, which was sustained through raids on communities along Abyssinia's borders perceived as ethnically distinct.

Ellis was far from unique in casting Ethiopia as possessing a special tie to the African diaspora. Accompanying Ellis on his trip was the Haitian-born intellectual Bénito Sylvain. Sylvain had first ventured to Addis Ababa in 1897, envisioning Menelik as the potential leader not only of Ethiopia but also of a global movement to advance the rights of peoples of African descent. Menelik, accustomed to including educated outsiders in his court, soon found a place for Sylvain in his circle as an aide de camp. Sylvain's new duties included representing Menelik at the first Pan-African Conference. In July 1900, thirty-three delegates of African descent from the United States, Canada, Haiti, Liberia, Sierra Leone, the Gold Coast, and the British West Indies gathered at Westminster Town Hall in London "to deliberate solemnly upon the present situation and outlook of the darker races of mankind."

The movement marked a new stage in the diaspora's relation to Africa. The term "pan-African" was itself novel, having been coined just a few months prior by Henry Sylvester Williams of Trinidad, one of the conference organizers. Behind this neologism stood the realization that Bishop Turner's dream of an independent nation for New World blacks in Africa had ceased to be feasible, for the recent frenzy of European imperialism had subjected almost the entire continent to white control. It was therefore necessary to shift tactics from colonization to ensuring civil rights for African and African-descended peoples wherever they might be found. The conference's centerpiece was an "Address to the Nations of the World." Authored by W. E. B. Du Bois, the address opened with the phrase "The problem of the Twentieth Century is the problem of the color line"—the first appearance of the concept that Du Bois would elaborate in greater depth in his 1903 opus, *The Souls of Black Folk*.

In Sylvain, Ellis found a figure that connected him to an emerging global movement—intellectuals of African descent grappling with the rise of a worldwide color line. But Ellis was also joined by an individual who linked him back to his roots in Victoria. His caravan to Addis Ababa, Ellis explained to curious reporters, included not only bodyguards, servants, and Sylvain (whom Ellis depicted as his secretary) but also "Carlos Eliseo Starns." This was none other than Ellis's nephew Charles Starnes, the son of his older sister, Elizabeth, and the physician Greene Starnes. Until recently, Charles had resided in San Antonio with the rest of his family. He shows up in the 1900 census as a sixteen-year-old schoolboy. Census takers denoted his race—like that of the rest of his family and that of almost everyone else in his neighborhood—as black. Charles's mother, however, died in 1898. Not long afterward, Charles fell under the influence of his entrepreneurial uncle, moving up to New York to work in Ellis's Wall Street office. After traveling to Mexico with his uncle, he, too, set about crafting a Mexican persona, calling himself Carlos Eliséo Estañez and claiming that he had been born in Monterrey, Mexico.

Ethiopia received Ellis and his nephew as honored visitors. Officials made a large, thatched-roof guesthouse available to them. Their quarters were connected via the emperor's favorite new innovation—the telephone—to Menelik's palace, a multibuilding complex surrounded by sycamore trees that crowned one of Addis Ababa's most prominent hills. Although Menelik only spoke Amharic, Ellis, in a demonstration of his linguistic dexterity, seems to have picked up a working knowledge of the tongue by studying what he could find in English or Spanish about the language. But much of the communication between the two took place through one of the multilingual Greeks who served as translators for the Ethiopian royal family. Ellis found the emperor, who favored the loose-fitting white cotton garments of his countrymen (although in his case topped with a red velvet mantle and an imported felt hat), fascinated with the world beyond Ethiopia. He quizzed his visitor about Teddy Roosevelt's life and career, and listened with apparent interest as Ellis told him how Lincoln "set the black man free and united the country."

Ellis reached Addis Ababa only weeks before the first American diplomatic party, led by Robert P. Skinner of the US State Department. The proximity of these two expeditions was far from coincidental. Ellis had spent much of the prior year cultivating Francis Loomis, the assistant secretary of state and Teddy Roosevelt's confidant, with an eye toward acquiring some sort of diplomatic imprimatur for his trip to Addis Ababa. Yet even though Ellis introduced Loomis to Professor Enno Littmann of Princeton, the sole American at the time able to translate documents into the Amharic language of Ethiopia, the only tangible reward he received from Loomis was a letter of introduction to US consular and diplomatic officers abroad. During their interactions, however, Loomis also let slip the schedule for Skinner's trip. Ellis used this information to ensure that he preceded the American diplomat to Menelik's court, thereby giving him some exclusive time with the emperor while also creating the perception that he was laying the groundwork for the diplomatic encounter to come.

Ellis's efforts to blur the boundary between his undertaking and Skinner's official mission does not appear to have deceived the emperor. Many Americans, however, came to link the two visits. Skinner, who believed that "the true Abyssinian type contains no negro blood whatever, and none of the negro qualities, either physical or mental," took pains to excise Ellis completely from all accounts of the United States' diplomatic mission to Addis Ababa. Contemporary press reports, however, regularly spoke of "Ellis . . . [, who] has played an important role in all American relations with Abyssinia" and of "William H. Ellis, who paved the way for the commercial treaty recently executed between this country and King Menelik." Ellis had pulled off yet another masquerade, managing to pass this time as a diplomat on official US business.

The ensuing confusion as to private and public endeavors brings to the surface the central tension running through Ellis's mission to Ethiopia and, indeed, his entire career: his ambivalent relationship to American empire. Ironically, even though it was the injustices of the United States that propelled Ellis beyond its borders in search of an escape from the color line, it was along the frontiers of American commerce where he found his greatest opportunities. The title that he claimed for himself on Wall Street—broker—could not have been more accurate: in the final analysis, he functioned as a middle man, one who translated between the fears, hopes, and desires of Americans and foreign populations. Because of Ellis's background, the results of his efforts could be unique and unexpected, as in his attempt in 1895 to colonize African American sharecroppers in northern Mexico. But the contours of possibility within which Ellis operated were not of his own making. His gift lay instead in finding the unanticipated openings that the expanding American sphere of influence around the globe presented.

The opportunistic nature of Ellis's endeavors could make for unlikely pairings. Several of his Mexican schemes had involved an uneasy combination of the most impoverished and alienated of the South's African Americans and the most elite of Mexico's entrepreneurs and politicians. In Ethiopia, Ellis managed to forge a productive relationship with Sylvain, one of the leaders of the Pan-African Conference, even though Sylvain was preoccupied with diminishing white dominance over Africa and Ellis was endeavoring to open up Ethiopia to American investment. To be sure, there existed potential points of agreement between the two: one could argue that Ethiopia, by expanding its trade with the United States, increased its ability to resist the more proximate threat of European imperialism. Moreover, Ellis took pains to portray Menelik in a manner that upended white stereotypes about the dark continent, insisting that the emperor was "an extremely intelligent man" and "there is nothing suggesting barbarism in Menelik's court. The emperor wears European clothes and a felt hat of American shape. The empress and court ladies were dressed in Paris modes." Even so, there remained deep schisms between Sylvain's position as an anticolonialist and Ellis's efforts to further the reach of a United States that, at the turn of the century, was one of the globe's leading proponents of white supremacy. "King Menelik has got the impression that Ellis represents the intelligent Negroes of this country and that he is loyal to his race," grumbled the African American journalist John Edward Bruce privately to a friend. "The fact is he represents the white capitalists and they are using him to work King Menelik."

Thanks to his charm and charisma, Ellis managed to bridge the fissures between Sylvain and himself on an individual level. But he was unable to address such contradictions in a more systematic way. He never took the step, for example, of participating in the Pan-African Conference, of which Sylvain was such a prominent member and Menelik an honorary leader. Doing so would have not only removed the questions surrounding his racial background (all but one of the participants in the first meeting of the Pan-African Conference were of African descent); it would have also required him to clarify, for outsiders—and, potentially, for himself—the ambiguities surrounding his place in the United States' emerging global presence. In the final analysis, Ellis's business empire was too intertwined with American empire for the two to be completely disentangled.

————

HAVING BEEN APART from Maude for almost four months, Ellis returned to Manhattan in early 1904. Upon landing, he displayed to the reporters waiting at the dock several brightly colored flags from Menelik—said to be the first Ethiopian flags ever allowed to leave the kingdom—and a collection of agreements that paralleled the sorts of deals that he had been negotiating in Mexico for the past decade and a half. Ellis boasted that "I have obtained full concessions from the King for all the diamond mines in the country and 200,000 acres of land on the Nile to experiment in cotton growing. . . . I shall establish the Royal Bank of Abyssinia and control the financial affairs of the country." He claimed to have also secured an agreement to construct a series of trading posts across Ethiopia and, in an echo of his earlier efforts in Mexico, to colonize thousands of African Americans in the empire.

Skinner followed not far behind Ellis, bearing the treaty of commerce that he had negotiated with Menelik. Seizing upon this new opening, Ellis lobbied Loomis to be allowed to carry the treaty back to Ethiopia once it was ratified by the US Senate, even offering to undertake the journey at his own expense. Loomis again demurred, awarding the mission instead to his younger brother. Kent Loomis was neither a professional diplomat nor the possessor of any particular expertise on Africa. But he had been complaining of the strain of his job as a newspaper editor in West Virginia, and so the Loomis brothers concluded that "he might be benefited by a change of scenery, diet and rest"—even though the rugged trip to Menelik's capital would seem anything but relaxing.

Discerning yet another way to attach himself to the treaty, Ellis ingratiated himself with the younger Loomis, inviting him to combine his diplomatic mission with a "prospecting and hunting tour" in East Africa that Ellis proposed to organize. Soon, the two were constant companions, staying together at a whites-only hotel in Washington, DC, to which Ellis gained entrance by claiming to be a rich Hawaiian. In June 1904, the two shipped out on the first leg of what had become a joint journey to Ethiopia by boarding the *Kaiser Wilhelm II*, bound for France. On the steamer, the two roomed together, dined together, and by all outside appearances got along swimmingly. On the last night of their voyage, they shared a late supper, after which Ellis returned to his berth to pack for their upcoming landing and Kent retired to read in a favorite chair on one of the upper decks.

The next morning, as the *Kaiser Wilhelm II* steamed into port, Loomis was nowhere to be found. Despite a frantic search of the ship, he would not reappear until four weeks later, when his decomposing body washed up along the English coast. Upon examination, the corpse was found to possess a circular wound the size of a half dollar behind the right ear, likely produced before death.

To more than a few, these findings constituted proof of foul play; Loomis, so the argument went, must have been hit over the head and then thrown over the ship's railing. Others, however, noted that the would-be diplomat could have struck his head on the boat's fittings upon slipping or jumping overboard. Francis Loomis repeatedly dismissed any suggestion of suicide or murder in his younger brother's disappearance, claiming instead that Kent must have climbed onto the hurricane deck of the *Kaiser Wilhelm II* to catch a glimpse of the English coast and lost his footing. But for those who sought a conspiracy, the culprit could only be Ellis. He was the one who had spent the most time with Loomis right before his death; he also possessed the most obvious motive. Hadn't Ellis wanted to carry the ratified treaty himself back to Menelik? And hadn't Loomis's disappearance cleared the way for his doing precisely that? Indeed, following Loomis's mysterious disappearance, Francis Loomis instructed authorities in Great Britain to open the safe on the *Kaiser Wilhelm II*, extract the special tin box containing the treaty, and pass it along to Ellis to bring to Addis Ababa.

Suspicion of Ellis only heightened as Loomis's disappearance brought in its wake hints that Ellis was not what he seemed to be. "What greatly increases the mystery of the affair," opined the *Pacific Monthly*, "was the presence on the vessel of one W.H. Ellis, a Hawaiian or negro, of fabulous fortune." Added another commentator: "The whole affair is strange in the extreme. . . . Why should a messenger bearing a treaty paper from this Government to another choose for his companion and assistant a man of queer antecedents and 'off color' as to his skin?" Given the centrality of the color line in American life, many observers found it peculiar that Loomis, a white man, and Ellis, an individual with "a complexion so dark to make plausible the statement that he has been mistaken for a negro," not only "were constantly together, and were known as intimate friends" but had shared a confined stateroom during their trans-Atlantic voyage.

Yet, as had happened so often before, there was a resistance on the part of those with whom Ellis had managed to pass to admit that he had deceived them. Seeking to defend his brother's judgment, Francis Loomis found himself forced to defend Ellis, too. In public, Loomis insisted that "Ellis was Kent's friend. Their relationship was sincere," and dismissed all speculation that Ellis had killed Kent. In private, though, he admitted that not until Kent's death did he have "occasion to go very thoroughly into his [Ellis's] antecedents and to receive a very large amount of information about him."

> Ellis is a broker and promoter on Wall Street, and has been charged unofficially with some sharp practices in business matters, and I suppose he has the average morality or lack of morality in financial transactions on the street. He is said to be a man of considerable means and appears to have the confidence of some very well known businessmen in New York. It has been developed since this tragedy that he was implicated in certain woman scrapes prior to his marriage, and people who knew him in Mexico and Texas years ago speak of him as an adventurer, but how valuable their testimony is I have no means of knowing. I cannot see at this time, although I am searching for information on this point, that Ellis would have anything to gain by the death of his associate.

Those with a deeper knowledge of Ellis's career found themselves amused at the consternation sweeping the halls of American power. "It seems that Loomis' companion, W.H. Ellis, was formerly a negro politician and promoter in this section of Texas and was born and reared in Victoria," noted the *Fort Worth Telegram*. "In these write-ups he is generally credited with being a Cuban, as in the reports of the past few days, but here he is known as a negro. . . . He is, in fact, quite dark, and it is a puzzle to Victorians why there should be any doubt as to his race."

The black press's coverage of the case likewise revealed that for many African Americans, Ellis's race remained an open secret. The community had for years guarded the truth, in keeping with the observation in Nella Larsen's novel *Passing*: "It's funny about 'passing.' . . . We shy away from it with an odd kind of repulsion, but we protect it." "Mr. Ellis resided with his parents, sisters and brothers at San Antonio, Tex. and for many years was known as a colored man," noted Indianapolis's *Freeman*. "Having learned the Spanish language, he went to New York, where he became known as a Cuban 'gentleman of leisure.'" "The case of William H. Ellis has created consternation and chagrin in the nation's capital, because of the discovery that he is an Afro-American instead of a Cuban, Spaniard or Hawaiian," commented the *Appeal*, a "national Afro-American newspaper." "Mr. Ellis is a man with energy and a peculiar ambition, who found his interests best subserved by an intimate association with Caucasian men of affairs. His wealth, his general appearance and business sagacity brought him within the 'Enchanted circle,' and he used his opportunities well, and, in the language of the street, 'he got his.'"

For such observers, Ellis's ability to pass in such rarefied company demonstrated that white society, despite its commitment to the color line, was in fact riddled with peoples of African-American descent. "Although not generally known," continued the *Appeal*, "it is an interesting fact, highly incredible though it may seem to those whose intense race hatred precludes such possibilities, that there are men and women high up in the financial, social, political and education circles of this country, through whose veins course the blood of the despised race—not enough, perhaps, to show, but enough, if known, to cast a shadow of gloom over many a proud soul that believes itself 'untainted' or who has never included among their intimate friends or acquaintances a person of 'Negro' descent." Not only did the achievements of passers such as Ellis or Anita Hemmings and her husband give lie to the myth of black inferiority; the inability of whites to discern these peoples' racial background demonstrated how subjective and unstable the entire category of race truly was. For proof, one needed only ponder the absurdities that Ellis's story had brought to the surface: race was of vital importance to whites, yet these same people could not differentiate blacks from whites—and, because of passing's ubiquitous yet covert character, might even be of partial African descent themselves. As Du Bois put it: "The reason of all of this [white anxiety about passing] is of course that so many white people in America either know or fear that they have Negro blood."

FOLLOWING LOOMIS'S DEATH, Ellis continued on to Addis Ababa, delivering the ratified treaty to Menelik "carefully rol[l]ed in an American flag." In exchange, he assumed responsibility for a menagerie of animals—"the finest zebra in captivity, baboons, ostriches, [and] a Nubian lioness"—that the Ethiopian emperor sought to bestow upon President Roosevelt. Ellis returned to the United States in late October 1904. While the animals settled into their new home at the National Zoo in DC, Ellis engaged in lengthy debriefings at the State Department and at the White House with President Roosevelt himself. Hoping to avoid further scandal, all involved proclaimed afterward that Ellis had rendered exemplary service in the face of an inexplicable accident. "Mr. Ellis's explanations were of a satisfactory nature," proclaimed the State Department in its statement to the press. "No blame is attached to him in connection with the tragic episode which occurred on his trip from New York to France in June last." Yet a cloud of suspicion continued to hover over Ellis, and he wondered whether the same US officials that had undone his colony in Tlahualilo were seeking to thwart his efforts in Ethiopia. "I have a great fight on hand, some of the Governments are doing what they can to block me," he complained in a letter to his younger sister Fannie, who had gone on to marry Greene Starnes after the death of her sister Elizabeth. But, he added, "I am determined to finish my work and succeed in everyway so it makes no difference how hard the fight is or how difficult my task I *will* and *must* succeed."

The irony of the moment was not lost on Ellis. For a man who had devoted his career to cultivating powerful patrons, his return to the United States should have represented a moment of singular triumph. He had served in a highly visible diplomatic function, gained an audience with none other than the president of the United States, and even managed to parlay his connections with Menelik into introductions to such notables as Andrew Carnegie and Robert E. Peary. Instead, he faced not only the whispered rumors of his involvement with Loomis's death but also questions once again about his racial status. It was a situation that encapsulated one of the paradoxes at the heart of passing: only by obscuring his African American ancestry could Ellis realize his ambitions in a segregated society. Yet this same achievement brought increased scrutiny and a heightened possibility of being unmasked.

Even the African American community, the longtime guardian of Ellis's secret, could not restrain itself from commenting on his predicament, albeit in an indirect way. Gilded Age New York possessed a vibrant black theater, and shortly after Ellis's return from Ethiopia, black playwrights incorporated elements of Ellis's recent history into two musicals. One, *The Oyster Man*, was the first Broadway show to star and be produced by an African American. The plot followed Rufus Rastus—an oyster vender in Baltimore, played by the African American comedian and musician Ernest Hogan—who became enmeshed in a colonization scam. (Rastus was a stock name in the era's minstrel shows, usually designating a foolish, simple-minded character, although some representations hinted at the complexities beneath the stereotype.) Rastus sets sail for Africa at the invitation of a swindler who, it turns out, has sold him worthless shares in a colonization project. Once Rastus realizes he has been tricked, he throws the con man overboard and makes his way to the idyllic island of Blazasus, where after several misadventures he discovers gold and becomes the island's ruler.

If Rastus, like Ellis, found wealth and a new life beyond the bounds of the United States, *The Oyster Man* also hinted that Ellis might have a less savory side. Colonization swindles, in which organizers collected funds from would-be colonists yet never delivered the promised transportation or supplies, were an unfortunate fact of life in the African American community at the turn of the century. Ellis had not stooped to this sort of behavior in his Tlahualilo venture, but the colony's spectacular collapse had nevertheless fused itself in African American popular memory with other colonization scandals. Rastus's tossing of the con man overboard served as a form of symbolic revenge on these false colonizationists while simultaneously summoning up images of the Loomis disappearance—thereby hinting that Ellis might not have been as innocent as he professed to be. After all, if he could mislead others by passing, what else might he be capable of?

Ellis's experiences were satirized in a slightly different vein in the musical comedy *In Abyssinia*, staged by the black theater's first superstars, George Walker and Bert Williams. This play featured another Rastus character—Rastus Johnson—who wins the lottery. To celebrate, he takes his family and friends to Ethiopia, where Emperor Menelik mistakes him for an American prince. In contrast to many other contemporary presentations of Africa as a land of unredeemed primitivism, *In Abyssinia* portrayed Menelik as a dignified and powerful ruler and posited that rather than the Ethiopians needing to be uplifted, it was in fact African Americans—especially the status-conscious members of the black bourgeoisie—who stood to learn from the inhabitants of the land, as one of the play's songs put it, "Where My Forefathers Died." To make sure no one missed the point, the actor playing Menelik delivered his lines in perfect English, while the buffoonish Americans spoke in minstrel jive.

As much as the play's depiction of the encounter between African Americans and Ethiopia took its inspiration from Ellis's recent visits to Menelik's empire, *In Abyssinia*, like *The Oyster Man*, also conveyed a subtle critique. Ellis's efforts to profit from his connections with Menelik rather than foster a more equitable exchange between Africans and African Americans were, the play hinted, misguided if not counterproductive, cheapening what should have been a deeper connection between the two groups.

It was oddly appropriate that the most in-depth reckonings with Ellis's activities at the turn of the century came via the world of the theater. Not only was the theater a prominent arena of day-to-day efforts at passing, as African American audiences tried to bypass the segregation that confined them to the worst seats (the second balcony, or "buzzards' roost"), when it did not bar them from theatrical venues altogether; the central drama of Ellis's life—passing—was profoundly theatrical, requiring the passer to become akin to an actor playing a role. The theatrical quality of the African American experience was reinforced by the frequent (although by no means universal) tradition of blackface. African American actors such as Bert Williams regularly "blacked up" with burnt cork in an effort to transcend the minstrel tradition and evoke the humanity beneath the mask—to display that even when playing a black character they were inhabiting an invented and stereotyped role.

Best of all, because theater was a simulacrum of real life, it allowed for a discussion of passing at a safe fictional remove. For all their apparent humor, comedies such as *The Oyster Man* and *In Abyssinia* cast a doleful gaze on the painful reality that surrounded a trickster like Ellis—yet without unmasking him and leaving him vulnerable to the wrath of an unfriendly white world. (In a similar vein, the popular musical *Jes Lak White Fo'ks* featured a song entitled "The Vassar Girl" that alluded to Hemmings's recent experiences without naming her directly.) Theater functioned, in essence, as a veiled manner of discussing a veiled phenomenon. As such, it was perfectly suited to William Henry Ellis/Guillermo Enrique Eliseo, who every day performed his life not only along the border of the United States and Latin America but also along the border where fact and fiction formed a reality all their own.

6

THE CITY OF HAPPY HOMES

T HE SUMMER OF 1905 found New York immersed in one of the rites of a modern bureaucracy: the taking of a decennial census. Canvassers fanned out across the state, intent on tallying the name, age, race, and profession of each of its eight million residents. On the first day of June, census takers reached one of Manhattan's premier addresses, the El Dorado, an eight-story apartment complex located at 300 Central Park West. Here, canvassers noted, dwelled such prominent New Yorkers as William Strang, a railroad promoter, and Xavier Fontura, the consul general of Brazil. Each, as was customary among upper-class Manhattanites at the time, headed a household that included a cohort of European-born servants. Living between Strang and Fontura in apartment number 33 was a figure seemingly much like his neighbors: a prosperous banker and his young family. Census takers dutifully recorded the presence in the household of one William Ellis; his wife, Maude; their year-old son, Guillermo; and two maids, both German immigrants, Ida Werner and Clara Wite-kammen. Although one of the key categories the census was designed to measure was race, the canvassers discerned only one individual of color in the entire El Dorado: an African American maid employed by another neighbor, the cigar dealer Henry Cobb. Fontura, the Bra-zilian, was recorded as white, as were Ellis, Maude, and, of course, the infant Guillermo.

ONE OF THE factors that rendered the Gilded Age a golden era for passing was the limited nature of government record keeping. Even at the turn of the century, birth certificates, passports, and driver's licenses remained rare and little-used documents, meaning that there was almost no reliable way to verify a stranger's stated identity. The ensuing slipperiness between appearances and realities bewildered many Americans. Given the era's unprecedented mobility, which swept up individuals from near and far and tossed them into greater proximity with one another than ever before, how was one to know without official proof whether a new acquaintance was a respectable member of society—or a possible con artist, whose pleasant dress and demeanor masked a malicious intent?

Nascent efforts to fix identity by regularizing record keeping, however, possessed their own liabilities. If one could play the trickster and hack the process, these new bureaucratic procedures could be converted into potent tools of subterfuge. Such was the case for Ellis. Now the head of a growing family, he managed to persuade authorities to generate a stream of census reports, birth certificates, and other documents that established his and his children's status as white. Each record built on the other, each serving as one more brick in an ever-higher wall meant to keep his family safely on the white side of the color line. The boy who had been listed in the 1880 federal census as a mulatto had now ventured permanently across the border dividing the races. For the rest of his life, he would appear in the census and other official records as white. Ellis's passing now took place not only in the improvisational realm of day-to-day personal interactions but also on paper in the equally, if not more, important arena of state record keeping.

This new facet to Ellis's passing came at a moment of peculiar juxtapositions. Now in his early forties, Ellis found himself assuming the role of patriarch. Guillermo Jr. was soon joined by other children:

Carlos Sherwood, born September 10, 1905; Maude Victoria, born June 8, 1909; a pair of twins, Porfirio Diaz and Sherwood Ellis, who died shortly after their premature birth on May 25, 1912; and Fernando Demetrio, born on May 14, 1915. Ellis and Maude selected each child's name with care. Guillermo was, of course, named for his father (or, to put matters more accurately, for his father's Mexican alter ego). Carlos's given name was the Spanish version of his grandfather's name, Charles, his middle name an homage to his mother. Victoria's name included a sly reference to Ellis's hometown while simultaneously honoring her mother and making another veiled connection to Ellis's time in Texas: Norris Cuney's daughter, Maud. Porfirio was named for the Mexican dictator, while Fernando Demetrio's middle name summoned up a less obvious link to the Porfiriato: Ellis's longtime lawyer in Mexico City, Demetrio Salazar, the son-in-law of General Pacheco, the minister of *fomento* who had approved Ellis and Ferguson's colonization scheme in 1889. The children appeared as white on their birth certificates, their father's race recorded as "Mexican (Spanish)," "White Cuban," "Cuban White," or some variation thereof.

Like most parents, Ellis took great pleasure in his progeny. Previously, he had shied away from photographers, wary at creating a lasting image that might undermine his masquerades. (His 1900 entry in *The Successful American*, for instance, was one of the few in the entire volume not accompanied by a portrait, and although he splurged on an elegant studio photo of Maude on her wedding day, she appears in the image alone, without her new husband.) Once Ellis became a father, however, his vigilance relaxed. Of the handful of pictures of Ellis that do survive, almost all of them feature him proudly posing with his two oldest boys, Guillermo and Carlos. One shot from the early 1900s captures the children, outfitted in spats, belted tunics, and crushed velvet hats, while Ellis sits between them in his customary tailored three-piece suit, complete with watch fob and pocket square. In another, taken in Mexico City in 1910, the boys, again exquisitely costumed—this time, in matching sailor suits with embroidered collars—are joined by their grandfather Charles: rare photographic evidence of Ellis's continu-

ing contact with family members who identified as black (although
Charles appears light enough that he could have passed had he so
desired). Ellis signed a copy of this image "For Father, from his boys"
and sent it to Charles in San Antonio. As this inscription hints, Ellis
seems to have hoped the births of his children might mend relations
with the Texas branch of his family, who may well have suffered
bruised feelings from the distancing—geographic and emotional—
that Ellis's passing required. Confessed Ellis in a letter to his sister
Fannie: "Tell Dad I hope he [Guillermo Jr.] will not give me as much
trouble as I have given him."

With their brood growing, Ellis and Maude opted in the early
1900s to move out of Manhattan to nearby Mount Vernon. Nicknamed the "City of Happy Homes" for its comfortable single-family
houses and quiet tree-lined streets, Mount Vernon, just a thirty-
minute train ride north of New York, represented the first ripple
in an incipient wave of suburbanization washing over Westchester
County. The family settled into a three-story home at 540 East
Third Street. Theirs was an exclusively white neighborhood—a segregation achieved primarily by pricing homes beyond the reach of
African Americans, although racial covenants were not unknown in
the Westchester of the early twentieth century.

Once ensconced in their new home, the Ellis family settled into
the routines of suburban middle-class life. The pages of the local
newspaper, the *Mount Vernon Argus*, offer occasional glimpses of the
children's lives: birthday parties attended by all in the neighborhood;
piano recitals at the nearby Congregational church; YMCA athlet-
ics; amateur plays; graduations from school. The events are remarkable for their unremarkableness: there is not the faintest hint that the
family residing at 540 East Third Street was perceived as different
from any other family of upward strivers in Mount Vernon. (The fact
that Ellis, the least white-appearing member of the family, was often
away in Mexico on business may have facilitated the family's seamless
entry into Mount Vernon: "I was always alone . . . except for the children," recalled Maude.) Like their counterparts in San Antonio or
in the American colony in Mexico City, the compilers of the Mount

Vernon city directory in the early 1900s appended "(col)" after the names of all of the town's African Americans. Yet this designation never appeared next to Ellis's name or those of his family members. The songs that the children played at their recitals were not the spirituals or jazz tunes that might have been assigned to African Americans but rather ditties with names like "Dance Around the Snow Man," "Merry Boys," and "Honeybell Polka." When school board members visited their school, it was Carlos, a member of the honor club, whom the teachers selected to give a speech on "The Value of Good Literature." The boys even managed over time to shed their birth names for more Anglo-sounding alternatives, with Guillermo Jr. going by Ermo, and Carlos turning to his middle name, Sherwood.

Such suburban tranquility, however, masked the turmoil roiling Ellis's business dealings by the early twentieth century. His grand plans for Ethiopia had stalled. In 1906, Menelik suffered the first in a series of debilitating strokes that effectively ended his rule. Even before this unwelcome turn of events, however, Ellis found himself hamstrung by the same issue that had bedeviled his earlier colonization efforts in Mexico—lack of capital—and the harsh economic reality that it made little sense to develop mines or cotton farms in Africa when the same enterprises could be undertaken far more cheaply closer to home.

As if the collapse of his Ethiopian projects were not enough, Ellis had also begun to suffer money woes. He would continue to present an impressive front, maintaining an office on Wall Street and dressing himself and his family in the finest fashions. But legal records from the early 1900s reveal that his financial situation had begun to crumble—or, as Ellis admitted to his sister Fannie, "I have had some of the sweets out of life and am now reaping some of the bitters." In 1905, Ellis would be sued by two of his neighbors in Mexico City, Elena Blake and Florencia Blackmore, who demanded that Ellis brick up the windows in his Balderas Avenue workshop that opened onto their adjoining house. During the trial—which Ellis lost, requiring him to pay court costs and damages—it emerged that his furniture factory had been out of operation for some time. The following year witnessed Ellis back in Mexico City's *tribunal superior de justicia*, embroiled in a string of legal battles: a long-running case with the Mexican Alberto Niquet over a mortgage on this same Balderas Avenue property; a dispute with a US citizen named Elias Delafond over an option Delafond had taken on Ellis's La Olvidada mine in Michoacán; and a suit brought by two Mexicans against Ellis for nonpayment of the rent on an office he had opened on La Calle del Colegio de Niñas. By 1907, Ellis's woes had expanded still further to include a fine from the Mexican government for failing to pay the taxes due on his defunct factory. Even meeting personally with José Yves Limantour, the Porfiriato's powerful secretary of finance and an avid supporter of foreign investment, did little to help Ellis shore up his eroding position. By the end of the year, the Mexico City court declared "el Sr. Guillermo H. Ellis" to have defaulted on the mortgage on his Balderas Avenue holdings. The property and all its furnishings were sold at auction to help Ellis pay off a debt of $145,169.75.

Ellis's financial embarrassments did not confine themselves south of the border. In 1909, a bill collector named Leprelette Sweet appeared at Ellis's Wall Street office, demanding payment for a debt owed to a local coal company. When Ellis tried to hustle Sweet out the door, the two ended up in a physical altercation. Sweet's eyeglasses were broken in the scuffle, injuring his eye, and he sued Ellis for assault. The case bounced through various courts for close to a decade, running up legal fees and a $50,000 fine that further diminished Ellis's already fragile finances.

The growing instability in Ellis's life mirrored conditions in the country that had become his second home. Over time, the vaunted *orden y progreso* of the Díaz regime planted the seeds of disorder and chaos, for the Porfiriato proved unable to resolve Mexico's fundamental paradox: how to create a more modern nation, one that would be better able to resist US expansion, while also relying on its northern neighbor for the overwhelming majority of its trade and investment. By the 1900s, Mexico could point to multiple signs of progress under Díaz: an expanded federal budget; a rising export sector; an array of new factories churning out goods for a growing consumer market; a nationwide network of railroads and telegraphs. Yet in spite of these developments, Mexicans across the social spectrum believed that the fruits of their nation's economic expansion had been unevenly distributed. Observed *El Nuevo Mundo* in 1908: "There is prosperity in Mexico, but it is Yankee prosperity; there is poverty and misery in Mexico and that belongs totally to Mexicans."

In central and southern Mexico, the Porfiriato's policy of declaring vast expanses of the Mexican countryside *terreno baldío*—vacant land available for development by domestic or foreign investors— pushed hundreds of thousands of peasants off their lands. Cast into the republic's labor market, many of these newly landless *campesinos* drifted north to such booming new settlements as Torreón, finding employment in the region's US-owned firms. These companies, however, imposed a two-tiered wage system on their employees, paying Mexican workers far less than Americans for the same jobs. Unsurprisingly, Mexico's laborers loathed such pay scales for their economic unfairness and racism alike. By the early 1900s, outrage with the two-tiered wage system exploded into a spate of strikes, including a bloody uprising at the US-owned Cananea Consolidated Copper Company, the republic's second-largest enterprise. Strikers at Cananea distributed handbills targeting Mexico's outsiders: "Curse the thought that a Mexican is worth less than a Yankee; that a negro or Chinaman is to be compared with a Mexican. . . . MEXICANS, AWAKEN! The Country and our dignity demand it."

Over time, even segments of the Mexican elite came to side with working-class calls for *México para los mexicanos*. The Díaz administration's opening of the country to outside investors had had the effect of creating formidable rivals for the republic's homegrown capitalists. A leading illustration of the ensuing tensions could be found in the Comarca Lagunera, where the foreign-owned Tlahualilo hacienda proved a fierce competitor with Mexican *hacendados* for the region's limited supply of water and agricultural workers. A leader of the Mexican faction in these battles was Francisco Madero, the cotton-growing scion of a Coahuila family that traced its wealth back to cross-border dealings with the Confederates in the 1860s. By 1908, Madero's focus had expanded beyond the Comarca Lagunera to national politics as he spearheaded the movement to prevent Díaz's sixth reelection as president of Mexico. A lifelong vegetarian and tee-totaler, the moderate Madero sought only to institute a more demo-cratic politics in his homeland. But the removal of Mexico's longtime dictator unleashed a maelstrom that consumed Mexico for more than a decade, as the era's long-hidden pressures surged to the surface. Madero's revolution against Díaz became many revolutions, as rebel factions clashed with each other over their competing visions for Mexico. The ensuing conflict cost upwards of two million lives, sent hundreds of thousands of refugees fleeing north across the border, and once again raised the specter of US invasion and occupation of Mexico.

———

IF THE REVOLUTION possessed multiple meanings for Mexico, for Ellis it posed but a single puzzle. For more than twenty years, his strategy in Mexico had hinged on ingratiating himself with the Por-firiato's close-knit inner circle. In addition to his lawyer, Demetrio Salazar, Ellis's leading contacts included Luis Fernández Castello—a nephew of Díaz's whose father was Justino Fernández, Mexico's min-ister of justice—and Felix Díaz, Mexico City's chief of police and another of the president's nephews. The utility of such connections, however, depended upon the Porfirian regime remaining in power. Once political circumstances shifted, these onetime assets were transformed into potent liabilities, forcing Ellis to improvise his way in a strange new Mexico.

For Ellis, the 1910s were a particularly inopportune moment for his adopted homeland to be convulsed with popular unrest. Ellis's previous moneymaking endeavors—representing Hotchkiss Arms, directing the New York and Westchester Water Company, managing the Ellis furniture factory—had tapered off years earlier. As a result, he had recently thrown himself into a number of new projects, each of which promised to restore his tarnished luster as a Latin American entrepreneur.

The first of these targeted one of the nascent automobile age's most important resources and the favorite commodity of tropical speculators: rubber. At the time, this essential raw material could only be produced from a few plants, including the Brazilian rubber tree (*Hevea brasiliensis*), the predominant plant on southern Mexico's rubber plantations, and guayule (*Parthenium argentatum*), a low-lying shrub found in the deserts of northern Mexico—including on the Madero family's extensive landholdings in the Comarca Lagunera. Ellis, who bragged of "large rubber holdings in Africa," dedicated considerable time and money to searching for an alternative to these two sources, even going so far as to bring Professor Henry Hurd Rusby of Columbia University, the United States' leading tropical botanist, to Mexico to assist on his quest.

Finally, Ellis seemed to find what he was looking for in Mexico's palo amarillo (*Euphorbia fulva*). He licensed the patent on refining the tree's sap into rubber from its English inventor and established a number of companies dedicated to the process. The corporations' names varied from the Continental Palo Amarillo Rubber Company to the Compañía Mexicana Consolidada de Hule de Palo Amarillo; the associated board members ranged from Ellis's nephew Charles Starnes to Felix Díaz. The one constant, however, was Ellis's role as president and director. In January 1909, Ellis signed a ten-year contract with the Díaz government for the establishment of a factory "to extract, refine, and manufacture the rubber obtained from the *Palo Amarillo* and *Amate* trees." This agreement allowed Ellis to import all the necessary machinery for his factory duty free and exempted his company from all taxes for a decade—a boon for Ellis, but precisely the sort of sweetheart deal that caused so many Mexicans to grumble about the Porfiriato's preference for well-connected foreign capitalists.

A few months later, Ellis secured another concession, this time to construct hydropower dams on several rivers in the mountains west of Mexico City. "This is one of the most valuable water powers in the Republic," enthused Ellis, "on account of being situated so near this

Capital, also on account of the power not being dependent solely on rain fall, but on the snows melting from the Toluca mountains." Ellis named his new enterprise the Mexico and Toluca Light and Power Company. With the Díaz administration intent on electrifying cities across the nation as part of its modernization efforts, Ellis expected that within a number of years his hydropower plant would be worth "over Twenty million dollars, gold." Others in the republic, however, saw this concession as yet another valuable economic opportunity that had slipped into foreign hands.

In this same period, Ellis also managed to secure the rights to the fabled Manning and MacKintosh claim. This deed dated back to the 1850s when one of Mexico's short-lived, cash-strapped governments struck an agreement with two British entrepreneurs, Robert Manning and Ewen MacKintosh, for a loan of several million dollars. Later Mexican governments felt little inclination to cover an obligation run up by a fleeting predecessor, and the republic repudiated Manning and MacKintosh's claim in 1886. Nonetheless, Great Britain exerted periodic pressure on Mexico to honor its debt. To Ellis, this festering controversy offered a potentially vast opportunity. During a visit to Mexico in the early 1900s, Ellis tracked down the elderly heir to the claim, one Enrique G. MacKintosh, and—after consulting with his contacts in the Díaz administration as to the likelihood of Mexico's repayment—purchased MacKintosh's interest in the loan. Next, Ellis transferred the claim to one of the corporations he controlled, the Mexican Securities and Construction Company, and sold off shares in the company. With the funds raised, he hired the same high-powered law firm that represented J. P. Morgan & Company to recover Manning and MacKintosh's debt from Mexico. In the prospectus for possible investors, Ellis calculated that Mexico owed the holders of the Manning and MacKintosh claim more than $105 million in compensation to cover both the original loan and half a century of accrued interest. "A single claim of this size is conceded to be formidable," observed the *New York Times* in its extensive coverage of Ellis's latest Mexican sensation. "Wall Street regarded it as significant."

Each of these undertakings—the rubber factory, the hydroelectric plant, and the Manning and MacKintosh claim—positioned Ellis on the cusp of his greatest successes in Mexico ever. To be sure, measuring success in these cases required a different metric than in earlier projects. Ellis had never been averse to making money, but his 1889 colonization contract and his 1895 effort to resettle sharecroppers on the Tlahualilo hacienda had also embraced a liberatory politics that promised to transform the status of peoples of African descent on both sides of the US-Mexico border. In contrast, the objective of his current projects was limited to improving the financial status of Ellis himself. As if to celebrate his imminent return to prosperity, in the early months of 1910, Ellis took his only known trip south of the border with his entire family, even bringing along the family's Irish American maid. (To avoid potential embarrassments like the one at Eagle Pass in 1909, the family traveled together by steamship rather than by railroad.) During this same journey, Ellis met up with his father in Mexico City, and the three generations of Ellis men posed for their collective portrait.

Although Ellis had no way of knowing it as he and his family took in the sights in the Mexican capital, 1910 would prove to be a watershed year, one that altered forever the course of the republic's history. In July, an American named Edward Doheny drilled the first of several oil gushers in the jungles of Veracruz. Within a few years, Mexico would explode into prominence as the world's second-largest exporter of oil, attracting the interest of numerous American corporations intent on gaining access to Mexico's latest tropical riches. In September, the Díaz administration ushered in the hundredth anniversary of Mexico's independence with a gala celebration in Mexico City, complete with military bands, a forest of Mexican flags, and a massive display of red, green, and white electric lights that spelled out "1810 Libertad" and "1910 Progreso." And in October, after fleeing across the border to the relative safety of San Antonio—an escape made possible by the intervention of family friend José Yves Limantour—Madero issued the Plan of San Luis Potosí, calling for an armed rebellion against the Díaz regime to start on November

20. Even before Madero's deadline, uprisings erupted across northern Mexico. The revolution had begun.

———

IN THE FACE of Mexico's political upheaval, Ellis's agenda narrowed to a single goal: the restoration of a stable central government that would allow him to continue his development schemes. "The revolution in Mexico that has made my business awfully bad is no fault of mine," confided Ellis to his family, "but at the same time I am helping to . . . protect my own interest." Doing so required all of Ellis's considerable skill in navigating across borders, for he found himself forced to forge relationships with a shifting, mutually suspicious array of revolutionary cliques. Setting aside his ties to Díaz, Ellis began by entering into negotiations with the Madero administration over the Manning and MacKintosh claim. In 1913, however, the conservative general Victoriano Huerta deposed the president. Ellis quickly ingratiated himself with Mexico's new leader. Immediately after Huerta's coup, he telegraphed the general's co-conspirator, his longtime acquaintance Felix Díaz, to offer his support. "With your strong hand," Ellis wrote, "I hope that you and President Huerta will bring peace and prosperity to the republic. You will have no trouble in getting all financial assistance that you need." If accounts in the New York press are to be believed, Ellis was also part of a secretive circle of Mexican politicians and US businessmen that attempted to broker a rapprochement between Huerta and Woodrow Wilson, who had refused to recognize the new Mexican president and had discouraged Americans from traveling south of the border. In the press (which described Ellis as "a New York capitalist and personal friend of General Huerta"), Ellis depicted relations between the United States and Mexico in terms that spoke volumes as to his own situation. "The present administration did not take into consideration that by ordering these thousands of Americans out of the country it was ruining them financially," he contended. After years spent living south of the border, many Americans "have no connection to this country [the

United States], although it is their own." As for remedies, Ellis, like many American investors, longed for the days when a single strongman ruled Mexico. "Mexico is not wanting for intelligent men. But it is in want of a military leader. The people are accustomed to being ruled by an iron hand."

In late 1914, Venustiano Carranza, a former *maderista*, overthrew Huerta. Ellis promptly reached out to this newest Mexican president to offer his congratulations and to wish that "you will yet succeed in safely and soundly establishing your Government." "Having lived in Mexico, enjoying the hospitality of the country and people for over thirty years," Ellis continued, "being connected with no political party but simply at all times willing and ready to recognize and be loyal and royal to any government that the Mexican people chose . . . I offer you my heartfelt and earnest support to do anything to maintain your Government." When Pancho Villa's followers executed seventeen American mining engineers in the town of Santa Isabel in January 1916, Ellis contacted his "distinguished Friend" Carranza and promised to do all he could to dissuade the United States from intervening, provided the Mexican government issued an official statement "saying that these bandits would be immediately run down and put to death and good Americans in other parts of the Republic need not feel any alarm."

Events elsewhere, however, soon overwhelmed Ellis's attempts at backroom diplomacy. In March 1916, Villa attacked the border town of Columbus, New Mexico, killing sixteen more US citizens. President Wilson responded with a "punitive expedition," dispatching ten thousand soldiers led by General John J. Pershing, who had begun his military career chasing Apaches along the border, hundreds of miles into Mexico in a fruitless pursuit of Villa. This violation of Mexico's sovereignty brought the two nations to the brink of war. The US War College drew up plans "for the occupation and pacification of northern Mexico"; the Army Air Service enlisted the new technology of the airplane to patrol the skies along the border; and Senator Albert Fall, an influential member of the Committee on Foreign Relations, called for "the immediate organization of an army of 500,000 men, ostensibly for the policing of Mexico or for the invasion of that country to protect our citizens if necessary."

Carranza survived long enough to oversee the writing of the Constitution of 1917, which continues to govern Mexico today. This document built on the prior Constitution of 1857, even opening with the same injunction against slavery: "Slaves that set foot on national territory recover their liberty by this fact alone." In keeping with the revolutionary ferment of the time, however, the new constitution expanded the rights of all Mexicans to education, labor, and health care, rendering it one of the most progressive charters in the world at the time—a model eventually emulated by much of the rest of Latin America. The new constitution also proclaimed the right of the Mexican state to regulate property within the nation's boundaries. Article 27 stated that "all land and water within national territory is originally owned by the nation, which has the right to transfer this ownership to individuals"—a measure that empowered the state to nationalize resources or redistribute them through agrarian reform.

By itself, however, the new constitution could not end Mexico's instability. In 1920, Alvaro Obregón, a onetime chickpea farmer from the border state of Sonora turned revolutionary general, deposed his former ally Carranza. Joining Carranza as he fled Mexico City via train with a handful of supporters—and, according to observers, much of the gold from the national treasury—was none other than Ellis. Intent on having Carranza approve his latest Mexican development plan, a series of free trade ports, Ellis remained with the president's party until an attack by pro-Obregón troops forced them to abandon the train near the village of Aljibes. Carranza headed into the mountains on horseback, only to meet his death a few days later, while Ellis constructed a white flag from bedsheets purloined from the presidential train, requisitioned an automobile from the loot the *carrancistas* had loaded on the railroad cars, and made his way to safety. According to rumor, not only did he manage to secure Carranza's signature on his port agreement before he departed the train; he also pocketed a few coins from the Mexican treasury, which Carranza's forces had abandoned in their haste to escape.

Beyond these potentially apocryphal gold coins, however, Ellis's involvement in the Mexican Revolution yielded few tangible dividends. Indeed, the era's frequent changes in government made simply holding on to those assets he already possessed a profound challenge. "On account of the very disturbed conditions in Mexico I am at a loss to know what to do regarding certain mining properties that I own in that republic," complained Ellis in 1914. "I have one very valuable mine and several other claims that are very important. The taxes on these mines according to the last decree issued by President Huerta is over $1,676, Mexican money. . . . General Carranza has issued an order, so I am informed, that all taxes paid to the Huerta Government have to be repaid to him. The Huerta Government issued an order that if the taxes are not paid the mines will be confiscated, so I am at a loss to know what to do." Adding to the confusion was the fact that the various revolutionary factions all issued their own currency. "In what money . . . shall [I] pay the taxes [?]" inquired Ellis. "I am informed that Carranza refused to take the Huerta money and Villa now refuses to take the Carranza money."

Ellis's customary strategy to address such uncertainties—working his way into the good graces of whoever happened to be in power in Mexico City—posed its own risks. His contacts could all too readily transform into liabilities if the political landscape shifted, turning Ellis in the eyes of Mexico's new leaders into a meddlesome foreigner with dubiously acquired assets. In 1913, in fact, such a turn of events led to the cancellation of Ellis's Toluca hydropower contract. Ellis was outraged at watching his prized investment slip from his grasp—"One of the departments of the Federal Government of the Republic of Mexico . . . attacked [the] concession . . . [of] this Company [Toluca Light and Power]. . . .We have spent many thousands of dollars on these falls"— but he was powerless to change the government's decision.

Across the border, Ellis's involvement in Mexico subjected him to renewed scrutiny as well. American authorities had grown increasingly concerned that the chaos in Mexico might seep into the United States. For years, almost by its very existence, the international boundary had fostered dissent. US radicals fled across the border to escape the police or the draft; Mexican agitators crossed over to the United States, where they maintained a vibrant Spanish-language press devoted to criticizing the Porfiriato. Some of these activists, such as the Flores Magón brothers, the anarchist publishers of *Regeneración*, had endured raids and harassment by US law enforcement well before the outbreak of hostilities in Mexico. But as events across the border spiraled into greater violence, Congress, led by Senator Fall, launched investigations into the "radical socialism movement in Mexico," and the federal government empowered a raft of agencies to investigate possible violators of the era's newly expanded espionage and neutrality acts.

Among these new police forces was the Bureau of Investigation, the forerunner to the FBI. In 1916, agents charged with investigating "Mexican Revolutionary Matters" initiated surreptitious surveillance of Ellis. Agents dug through Ellis's finances and watched his offices in New York and Mexico City. They tracked his correspondence, noting that he "receive[d] many letters and telegrams from Mexico." Bureau employees even broke into Ellis's Wall Street headquarters to search for evidence of plotting with radicals. Although agents opined that Ellis was "a pretty slick institution" with "his lines out on practically every phase of Latin-American revolutions," they had little luck in making any definitive findings as to his finances or background. Agents reported inconclusively that Ellis was "apparently a negro married to a white woman." Or "may be a Mexican." Or perhaps "the illegitimate son of some white woman in Texas."

During his long career, Ellis had learned to be wary of strangers: each new person he encountered represented one more individual who needed to be convinced of his various identities. The caution he had acquired as a passer left him well prepared for his encounters with the Bureau. One agent, having arranged to run into Ellis on a Wall Street sidewalk, tried to lure him into a conversation about affairs in Mexico. Ellis, however, quickly detected something odd afoot. After telling the agent that "all he knew as regards happenings in Mexico he obtained from the daily papers," he excused himself, saying that he "was in a hurry" to deal with some pressing business.

Ellis had good reason for concern. By the 1910s, not only was the Bureau of Investigation rummaging through his affairs, so was at least one private detective agency. With the Mexican Revolution having made investment south of the border all but impossible, Ellis began to cast about for opportunities elsewhere. He seemed to find what he was looking for in Costa Rica, a nation that, like Mexico, was being torn apart by the twin disruptions of an oil boom and political unrest. In 1917, the president of Costa Rica, Alfredo González Flores, was overthrown in a coup headed by his minister of war, Federico Tinoco. González fled to New York City, where, together with his former consul general Francisco Montero, he began to organize a Costa Rican government in exile. Among the first members of González's inner circle was Ellis, who hoped to control Costa Rica's petroleum concessions should the former president be restored to power. A private detective hired by pro-Tinoco forces reported on Ellis's presence in Montero's quarters in Manhattan in April 1918:

> I noticed a gathering of 10 or 12 men, all speaking Spanish. None of them seemed to be of importance except one, whom by the description given me I at once recognized as Mr. Ellis, a Mexican, whose office is at 35 Nassau Street, and who, I had been told, was interested with Montero. I followed him to his office, where I left him.

A few days later, this same detective trailed Ellis to his home in Mount Vernon and then, presenting himself as a visiting Texas oilman, set up an appointment with Ellis in his Wall Street office. During the course of their conversation, Ellis told the detective that González was organizing a rebellion, and that several of Tinoco's generals were ready to join him as soon as Ellis hired a schooner in Mexico to smuggle arms and ammunition to the plotters.

Sharing this tale of Central American intrigue may have represented a momentary indiscretion on Ellis's part. Or it may have been an intentional fabrication in which Ellis, intuiting his visitor's identity, hoped to mislead Costa Rican authorities as to the plot against them. In either case, facing unrest at home and rumors of a coup abroad, Tinoco stepped down at the end of 1918. His departure, however, did not work out as Ellis had hoped. González failed to return to power, depriving Ellis of his anticipated access to Costa Rica's petroleum fields.

Offsetting such disappointments was the slow return of stability to Mexico. Bit by bit, Obregón consolidated control at the expense of the more radical wings of the revolution. In 1919, Emiliano Zapata, the charismatic peasant leader who had inspired Mexico's dispossessed with his calls for *tierra y libertad* (land and liberty), was lured into an ambush and assassinated. Four years later, the bandit-turned-revolutionary Pancho Villa suffered a similar fate while riding in his Dodge roadster through the dusty streets of Parral, Chihuahua. Obregón's rise to power, however, left unresolved the familiar question of the republic's relationship to the United States. The tensions that had defined affairs between the two countries before the revolution still loomed: Mexico desired American capital but worried about preserving its sovereignty; the United States sought Mexican natural resources—especially the precious new commodity, petroleum, which as the republic's minister of foreign affairs put it, now undergirded all "industrial development and, therefore, . . . military and naval power"—but questioned the stability of its southern neighbor. In particular, alarmed at what Article 27 of Mexico's new constitution might mean for American investments in the republic, the United States refused to recognize Obregón's government and instituted a ban on loans from American banks at a time when Mexico was desperate for funds to rebuild its war-shattered economy.

Such disagreements, of course, only impeded Ellis's plans, and he did what he could to mend relations between the two nations. In 1920, in an apparent effort to influence events, the usually reticent Ellis gave a lengthy interview to the *New York Times*, which labeled him a banker "who knows Mexicans." Ellis attributed the recent unrest south of the border to the fact that Mexico was "without a doubt . . . the richest spot on the face of the earth," and claimed that if Americans understood their neighbors better, they would see the wisdom of extending a "helping hand" to Mexico's new leaders. The following year, Ellis made a behind-the-scenes appeal to one of the leading opponents of Mexican recognition, Senator Fall, to see if he could ease tensions, possibly by setting up an in-person meeting between Fall and Obregón. Ellis managed to schedule a lengthy conversation about US-Mexico relations with Fall on the *Golden State Limited* as the train made its way from Kansas City to El Paso (an arrangement that, as so many times before, hinged on Ellis's ability to pass, as trains remained segregated in 1920s Texas). Afterward, the two maintained a correspondence, with Fall expressing interest in meeting Obregón "in a private way." Ellis accordingly introduced the senator to Ignacio P. Gaxiola, "a personal friend and Power of Attorney in private business of General Obregon." Gaxiola, explained Ellis, "has the absolute confidence of General Obregon although he is not officially connected with the Government."

By the time the United States finally recognized Mexico in August 1923, Ellis was already south of the border, working on his latest scheme: a free-port agreement. This was the same project he had risked his life to get Carranza to approve during his flight from Mexico City in 1920. After Carranza's death, the indefatigable Ellis had directed his appeals to Huerta before ultimately persuading Obregón of the wisdom of the plan. Under the agreement, Guaymas, Salina Cruz, and Puerto México, similar to free ports elsewhere such as Hong Kong and Singapore, were to reduce their taxes and customs duties in hopes of attracting trade and industry. Overseeing the ports was a board of five appointed managers, of which Ellis was the sole non-Mexican.

Mexico's renewed receptivity to Ellis's free-port idea brought to the surface the preoccupations that continued to dominate its relationship with the United States. The President of the Mexican Free Port Commission, Modesto C. Rolland, saw free ports as the way to solve the "serious problem of our northern border," which had if anything grown more acute in the aftermath of the revolution. "Very painful experiences in our history," opined Rolland, "should teach us that we need to proceed intelligently and efficiently to strengthen our people and to defend ourselves, no longer with weapons, but rather in the field of administration." By making Mexican labor and resources accessible to American firms—albeit under strictly controlled circumstances—the free ports held out the promise of assisting Mexico's reconstruction without sacrificing national sovereignty. "The free ports will be under the jurisdiction of a special commission, with police and other powers to protect American and Mexican interests," maintained Roberto Casas Alatriste, Mexico's financial agent in New York. "The whole system is principally devoted to the commercial relations of these two countries." Once again, Ellis had demonstrated his uncanny ability to sniff out the newest and most promising point of intersection between the United States and Mexico.

———

EVEN AS ELLIS returned once more to his familiar pose of transborder entrepreneur, he found himself forced to conceal a central aspect of his life from his new business acquaintances. This time, however, it was not his background nor his place of birth, but rather the troubling fact that his health had begun to falter. Ellis's life of disguise had extended not only to his tailored suits and glittering jewels but even to his very body, which had long exhibited the ample girth that those at the time expected of a well-fed capitalist who enjoyed all the best in life. Now, as he reached his late fifties, Ellis's weight, combined with the stresses of his double life, had begun to take a toll.

Ellis had gotten a hint that something was not right even before he reached Mexico. Complaining of "bladder trouble," he made a surreptitious stop in San Antonio on his way to the border so that his brother-in-law Greene Starnes could examine him. Once in Mexico, Ellis detrained at the northern city of Monterrey for a couple of days to seek further treatment before continuing on to Mexico City. But the capital's high altitude and thin air only exacerbated his woes, although he struggled to keep news of his condition secret. "Please do not let anybody know that I had a fainting spell the other night," confided Ellis to his lawyer in New York. "The doctor says that I am worked down and that if I do not get out of this climate within two or three days, my heart will stop. . . . The other night I sat on my bed trying to get my breath for several hours."

Even as he faded over the next eight months, Ellis remained intent on not letting his health problems derail his plans to rebuild his fortune. "I fell in the room and fell in the bank and [I had to] pick myself up," he explained to his sister Fannie. "Things here are not running smooth at all but I have got my fighting clothes on and am going to fight until the last." After suffering a nocturnal hemorrhage, however, which caused him to "wake up and f[i]nd the bed covered with blood," Ellis began to sense that his luck might running out. "I am beginning to fear the worst for myself," he warned his sister. "Don't be surprised at what may befall me, but there is one thing that you and everybody will say[:] he did the best he could, his fight in life was hard, he came into the world fighting for his rights and that of his wife and children and he went out of life doing the same."

Increasingly unable to hide his condition, Ellis made several trips to Veracruz to recuperate at sea level, followed by bed rest in his room at the Hotel Gillow. In September 1923, in a sign of his desperation, he forewent his lifelong avoidance of the American colony in Mexico and checked into Mexico City's American Hospital. A few days later, at 1:05 p.m. on the afternoon of September 24, under darkening skies as a hurricane gathered force in the Gulf of Mexico, he passed his final border, one that even the most consummate trickster could not evade: the divide between life and death. William Henry Ellis was fifty-nine.

EVEN IN DEATH, Ellis was not completely free of passing's masquerades. Ironically, given Ellis's aloofness from the American colony in Mexico City, it was the US embassy that supervised the initial response to his death, issuing a death certificate that listed Ellis as an American citizen—the pose, after all, that he had maintained in Mexico for over three decades—and telegraphing Maude to inform her of her husband's passing. The embassy staff made an inventory of the surprisingly modest collection of effects in Ellis's room in the Hotel Gillow. As might be expected, there was a large number of items of personal adornment: "1 gold watch, 1 gold chain with pendant, 1 gold pen, 1 gold pen-knife, 1 gold cigar cutter, 1 pair gold cuff buttons, 8 collar buttons, 2 gold rings, 1 gold pin, 1 gold pencil, 2 collar links, 1 silver case with nose-glasses." But Ellis had only fourteen pesos in his pockets when he died, and officials calculated that despite Ellis's reputed wealth, the value of all his belongings in the Hotel Gillow totaled less than a hundred dollars. Embassy staffers packed the deceased's possessions into the three well-worn trunks they found in Ellis's room for delivery to Ermo, who had arrived in Mexico City to take charge of his father's affairs.

The first public notice of Ellis's demise appeared five days after his death in the *Mount Vernon Argus*, the newspaper of his adopted hometown. The *Argus*'s obituary hewed closely to the script that Ellis and his family had followed for more than a decade in the City of Happy Homes. There was no direct discussion of Ellis's ethnicity, although the paper did note that Ellis was also known as "G.E. Eliseo" and was born "near the Mexican border" to "Carlos and Margarita (Nelsonia) Ellis." Instead, the *Argus* focused on Ellis's business undertakings in both Mexico and the United States (including the Manning and MacKintosh claim for "over a $100,000,000"), his adventures as a "great explorer and traveller," and his "personal friend[ship]" with Theodore Roosevelt. The obituary did little to disrupt the image of an elite Latin American entrepreneur that had long served Ellis as his public mask, at first in life and now in death.

But as word of Ellis's death spread beyond the tree-lined confines of Mount Vernon, this tightly controlled narrative began to unravel. The day after his obituary debuted in the *Argus*, the rest of the New York City press published its announcements. While they echoed the *Argus*, these later treatments expanded their coverage to highlight Ellis's connections to the Ethiopian treaty of 1904 and the still unresolved puzzle of Kent Loomis's disappearance. "William Henry Ellis, broker and promoter of this city and Mexico . . . , will best be remembered as the man who in 1904 took the commercial treaty between this country and Abyssinia to King Menelik," opined the *Times*. Ellis enjoyed a "spectacular career as a banker, promoter, and soldier of fortune," reported the *World*. "He and Kent J. Loomis, brother of the then Assistant Secretary of State, started with the treaty together, but Loomis was lost mysteriously at sea and his body was washed up on the English coast." On a more subtle level, these obituaries proved how successfully Ellis had obscured his early life in Texas. Most New York papers repeated Ellis's decades-old assertion that "in the early days he was a cowboy on Texas ranches," and none of the obituaries touched upon Ellis's ties to Cuney and Turner or conveyed the slightest whisper of controversy about his racial background. The sole reference to African Americans at all could be found in a few short sentences in the *New York Times*: "He promoted a scheme for negro colonization in Mexico. The colony failed."

The leading exception to this trend could be found in the African American press. Over the years, the *New York Age* had featured a number of articles on Ellis, always carefully excluding any discussion of his background (although astute readers surely realized why New York's leading black newspaper elected to cover such a figure). Following Ellis's death, however, the *Age* abandoned its discretion. The editors published an extended obituary on their front page of "Wm. Henry Ellis, a colored man" that explored the "career of adventure and financial success that brought him world-wide fame." "He was at various times a cowboy, ranchman, banker, broker, promoter, and finally diplomatic envoy to King Menelik of Abyssinia, as the bearer of a treaty of amity and commerce from the State Department at Washington. Ellis possessed financial genius of a high order and made several fortunes. . . . He was a well-known figure in Wall street [*sic*]. He posed as a Cuban, transforming his name into 'Guillermo Enrique Elliseo.'"

African American newspapers elsewhere followed suit. The enthusiasm of the nation's black press for revealing Ellis's secret laid bare the complicated emotions that passing evoked within the black community. On the one hand, there was a clear desire to show the world that an African American could beat the white man at his own game and attain the wealth and stature that defined success during the Gilded Age. "Though serviceable in small degree to the race of which he was a part," asserted the *Dallas Express*, "nevertheless, from the fact that his life was spectacular, filled with strivings in a big way among the greatest of the world, some degree of satisfaction must be ours in realizing that he was of us."

On the other hand, the alacrity with which the black press unveiled Ellis's deception sent a clear signal to other passers: as much as they might succeed in fooling gullible whites, they could not separate themselves so easily from African Americans, who had always known their true identities. Thus, when Chicago's *Broad Axe* published a wire-service obituary of Ellis, it appended an explanatory line to the otherwise boilerplate article: "Outside of transacting big business with some of the most prominent white business men in this country or the world, William Henry Ellis was a colored man." For its part, the *Chicago Defender* portrayed Ellis as a model passer: someone who achieved vast fame and fortune yet still maintained close connections with African American family members. "The announcement of the death of William E. Ellis in Mexico City recalls to mind an international figure who helped to make national Race history more than a decade ago," asserted the *Defender*.

[After his public role in bearing a] special message or important treaty to the court of Abyssinia . . .Ellis returned to this country and resumed his seat in the stock exchange, but dropped out of sight as far as our group was concerned. During his heyday he built his mother an elegant home in San Antonio and would occasionally return to his native home in his private car. . . .The death of Mr. Ellis brings to a close a life that was fought against many odds. But when it came to high finance he was always on the safe side of the ledger.

Even the *Crisis*, the preeminent black publication of the 1920s, planned a piece about Ellis, with whom the magazine's founding editor, W. E. B. Du Bois, had engaged in a sporadic correspondence about Abyssinia since the 1910s. Within days of Ellis's first obituary, Du Bois dropped a note to Judson Douglas Wetmore, inquiring, "Where can I get a picture of the late William H. Ellis and some account of his life? I trust you can help me." The historical record does not reveal how Ellis and his family knew Wetmore, a lawyer and very light-skinned African American, so white in appearance that he was rumored to have served as the inspiration for his childhood friend James Weldon Johnson's novel *The Autobiography of an Ex-Colored Man*. But in response to Du Bois's request, Wetmore dispatched a letter of sympathy to Maude and asked that she have "her son come in and see me." Wetmore evidentially hoped Ermo or Sherwood might provide the information Du Bois desired. The family, however, intent on preserving what it could of Ellis's fast-eroding pose as a Cuban or Mexican, seems to have proven unwilling to cooperate.

Even so, as word of Ellis's demise rippled out beyond New York, an increasingly suspicious tone began to filter into many obituaries. In an article that evoked Kipling with its title "Who Would Be King," *Time* magazine described Ellis as "prefer[ing] to style himself Guillermo Enrique Eliseo" and noted that even though Ellis "was born in Victoria, Tex., in 1864 . . . [he] claimed to be of Cuban parentage, on account of which he used the Spanish form of his name." "Tall, powerful, black mustached, and brown of complexion, [Ellis's] racial antecedents were doubtful in a region where racial antecedents count for so much," commented the *Milwaukee Sentinel*. "He professed himself to be a Cuban of Spanish parentage and said his name was rightly Guillermo Enriques [*sic*] Eliseo. . . . Texans were of the opinion that he was a native of San Antonio and was of mixed descent, largely Spanish with a dash of negro." The Associated Press obituary of Ellis, which was picked up by papers throughout the country, similarly called its subject's ethnicity into question. "Ellis was either a Cuban or of mixed parentage, but he preferred to be known as a Cuban, as he signed himself Guillermo Enrique Eliseo."

Even as Ellis's passing was posthumously called into question, his story, like all trickster tales, offered a few final surprises. Maude initially let it be known that Ellis would be interred in Woodlawn Cemetery, the same exclusive resting place the couple had selected for their short-lived twins, Porfirio Diaz and Sherwood Ellis, as well as Maude's father. In truth, however, Ellis never joined New York's elite in Woodlawn, but was instead buried in an unmarked grave in Mexico City's Spanish cemetery. (More unanswered questions: Could it be that even in death Ellis identified as Spanish more than American? Or did the American colony, catching wind of the controversy over Ellis's background, refuse to allow him into the American cemetery?) The family's inability to fulfill its promise to transport Ellis's body back to the United States can be explained by the shocking revelation that emerged after his death. Despite all the newspaper headlines as to how "The Story of the Life of W.H. Ellis Reads Like Fiction . . . Died Wealthy," it turned out that the man who had once controlled corporations valued in the millions left only $5,000 to Maude. "Much surprise is expressed that his estate should be so small," observed the *New York Age*. "It is all personal property, with no realty holdings."

Among those surprised by this turn of events was Maude. Her situation was in fact far more dire than most realized, for in addition to his almost nonexistent estate, Ellis left Maude a stack of unanticipated debts. He had stopped paying property taxes on the family's house in 1919, meaning that Maude was now several years in arrears to Mount Vernon. He had also taken out a second mortgage on the house without informing his wife. "I have found about $15,000 worth of debts that I shall have to pay off. . . . I feel I shall be paying off for the next hundred years," confided Maude to her sister-in-law Fannie. "I often wonder how we have managed. Gerry got a lot of money, but you know how it is in Mexico—he just had to have a lot there to keep himself going and he also had to give a lot away to get his business through."

While Maude contacted the State Department in a fruitless effort to determine the status of her husband's fabled concessions in Abyssinia, Ermo remained in Mexico City, pursuing the Manning and MacKintosh claim as well as attempting to regain the title to the family's hydropower concession in Toluca. Unlike his father, with his constant precautions against being unmasked as a passer, the far more white-appearing Ermo seems to have mixed freely with members of Mexico City's American colony, which in any event had shrunk almost by half because of the revolution. Within months of his arrival, he became the "chief instructor" of an American shooting club—"quite an honor for one so young," his mother enthused. "It is surprising how much the older men [in the American colony] like him," added Maude. "I received a lovely letter from a man down there who used to be the consul general from the United States. He speaks so highly of Ermo's conduct and character."

Ermo's efforts to restore the family's fortunes, however, ended almost before they began. In late April 1924, Ellis's oldest son began to experience a high fever, headache, and rash: the first signs of typhus. Like his father before him, Ermo checked into Mexico City's American Hospital. But there was little that the doctors could do to halt the disease. On May 2, 1924, at the age of only twenty years, Ermo passed away. In a measure of how different his experience of Mexico was from that of his father, Guillermo Enrique Ellis Jr. was interred in Mexico City's American cemetery rather than being buried beside his namesake in the Spanish cemetery. These separate burials represent the final, bittersweet fruit of Ellis's passing: his first-born son had gained the acceptance that Ellis had long sought for himself, but at the cost of remaining apart from his father for the rest of eternity.

THE YEARS AFTER Ellis and Ermo's deaths witnessed a slow splintering of the ties that had once bound together their extended family. Ellis's nephew Charles Starnes would never rejoin his relatives in Texas. The young man who in 1903 accompanied his famous uncle on his trek to Ethiopia lived out his days in far less glamorous circumstances, working as a clerk for a New Jersey railway company. He continued to maintain that he was born in Monterrey, Mexico, even taking the step of having his name legally changed to Carlos Eliséo Estarñez. Like his uncle before him, he appeared as white in the federal census, married a white woman, and lived alongside whites. Even more than Ellis, however, Starnes charted a journey to the other side of the color line. After his first child died in infancy, he never had any more offspring, perhaps because of the trauma of the baby's death, perhaps from the fear, common among passers, that any future child might possess physical features that would betray a parent's nonwhite ancestry. Estarñez also isolated himself from the rest of his family—so much so that he even lost touch with some of his siblings. His sister Marguerite recalled that "until 1925 she heard from him occasionally by letter," but since then she had "been unable to ascertain whether he is dead or alive. . . . her efforts to locate him have been unavailing." As for the few relatives who did know where he was, Estarñez only permitted those who were light enough to pass to visit him in whatever all-white neighborhood he happened to be inhabiting at the moment. Estarñez lived to the age of ninety, dying in Burlington, Vermont, in 1965. His death certificate, the final documentation of the earthly existence of the individual once called Charles Starnes, listed the deceased as a white man from Mexico, mother's and father's names unknown.

At the same time that Estarñez passed permanently across the color line, others in his family initiated a voyage of their own. Enticed by conditions on the West Coast, in the early 1920s the extended Starnes family moved from San Antonio to Los Angeles—a journey that made them pioneers in the newest migration to reshape African American life: the relocation of blacks from the rural South to the urban centers of the North and West. Greene Starnes opened a medical office at the intersection of Central Avenue and Twelfth Street, and his children, many of them by now married and beginning to start families of their own, settled nearby. Their new neighborhood was popularly referred to as LA's black belt, for its abundance of African American churches, restaurants, nightclubs, and shops, although the area contained significant numbers of Asians and Mexicans as well.

To newcomers like the Starneses, California held out the promise of being less encumbered by the color line than Texas. In the Golden State, blacks could vote, the Republican Party dominated state politics, and segregation in public places was prohibited. But shadows nonetheless lurked amid the Southern California sunshine. In 1781, the majority of the colonists who founded Los Angeles had been Afro-Mexican—a reflection both of how widespread the Afro-Mexican presence was in the colonial period and of the greater opportunities for blacks along Mexico's frontiers. By the dawn of the twentieth century, however, peoples of African descent represented only a small percentage of Los Angeles's population. As the Starneses and increasing numbers of blacks relocated to Southern California, local whites responded with racial covenants that constrained where African Americans—and, often, Asian and Mexican Americans as well—could rent or buy homes. African Americans also faced discrimination in employment. Even though Marguerite Starnes's husband, Richard Moore, had a college education, for instance, the best job he could find in Los Angeles was a position at the post office.

If Estañez transformed himself into a white man and the Starneses participated in African America's incipient urban migration and civil rights struggles, Ellis's immediate family charted a path that propelled them beyond the boundaries of the United States altogether. In 1926, Maude and her surviving children—Sherwood, Victoria, and Fernando—boarded a steamer in Manhattan bound for Veracruz. From here they made their way to the Mexican capital for what was intended as a temporary visit to resolve Ellis's Mexican estate. Like Ermo before them, Maude and the children easily inserted themselves into Mexico City's American colony. (Fernando even took the step of adopting the more American-sounding moniker Bill instead of using his Hispanic name.) They lived first at the Hotel Regis, which billed itself as "the only American hotel in Mexico"— complete with an "Amer[ican] barber shop" and "American food"— before settling into a shabby gentility in a series of rented quarters off Avenida de la Reforma. Encouraged by their mother, a talented pianist and dancer who had once harbored theatrical aspirations, all three children joined one of the new dance groups that had sprung up amid the cultural ferment sweeping postrevolutionary Mexico. Artists throughout the nation were grappling with how to articulate a more "authentic" *mestizo* identity—one less influenced by the European models favored by the Porfiriato and more accessible to the entire population. In fine art, this movement gave rise to the famed murals of Diego Rivera, David Alfaro Siqueiros, and José Clemente Orozco. In dance, it birthed *ballet folklórico*, which blended Mexican music and dress with trained choreography to produce a new "traditional" Mexican dance.

Sherwood and Bill only participated in the *ballet folklórico* for a few years, but Victoria, who had taken classes in tap and other dance forms in Mount Vernon, emerged as the premier dancer of her generation. In addition to touring throughout the republic, she extended the reach of her performances via the nascent Mexican film industry, many of whose popular melodramas showcased music and dance numbers. More often than not, it was Vicky (as she came to be called) who choreographed or performed the signature *bailes* in everything from *Una carta de amor* (A Love Letter), a period piece about a brave Mexican officer battling the French in the 1860s, to *El peñón de las ánimas* (The Rock of Souls), a drama about star-crossed lovers from two rival families, starring Jorge Negrete and María Félix, to *A la orilla de un palmar* (At the Edge of a Palm Grove), a romance set in a fishing village outside Veracruz.

For all their novelty, such films as *A la orilla de un palmar* also brought to the surface the odd continuities in Mexican racial thinking between the Porfiriato and the postrevolutionary era. *A la orilla de un palmar* was set in an area that had been a center of Afro-Mexican life since the 1500s. It showcased *son jarocho*, a musical style derived from African antecedents. Its publicity materials boasted that the movie was *"una película costumbrista"* (a folkloric film), with almost anthropological attention to local culture. Yet *A la orilla de un palmar* featured no identifiable Afro-Mexicans. As much as the Mexican Revolution had inspired a deeper appreciation of the nation's Indian roots, the ensuing recalibration of *mestizaje* to increase the focus on Mexico's indigenous peoples—a movement known throughout the republic as *indigenismo*—nonetheless continued the older pattern of obscuring the existence of Afro-Mexicans.

The ironies multiply all the more when one considers the prominent role of Vicky Ellis in diffusing this latest, more indigenous vision
of *mexicanidad*. As immigrants, Vicky and her family were required
to obtain visas from the Mexican government that recorded each
person's distinguishing characteristics, including color and race. In
both these categories, Vicky, her mother, and siblings were denoted
as *blanca* or *blanco* (white). Thus, not only was Vicky at the forefront in
defusing a new, more indigenous image of Mexican culture, despite
being an immigrant; she also helped embody the new ideal of *mestizaje*, even though by Mexican standards she was considered white
(an issue that was occasionally finessed by having her wear a dark wig,
as she does in the grand finale to *A la orilla de un palmar*). And despite
her own background as the daughter of a former slave, Vicky helped
solidify a notion of *mestizaje* that continued the marginalization of
Afro-Mexicans.

Ellis had spent a lifetime crisscrossing the borderline and slipping
back and forth across the color line. His children, however, made
but one transition. As one year passed into the next and the long-
anticipated settlement of Ellis's claims failed to materialize, the family's temporary visit to Mexico transformed itself into a permanent
stay. Sherwood became a newspaper reporter, only to die young, like
Guillermo before him, from typhus. Vicky remained single her entire
life, teaching in her mentor's studio, where she trained a generation of
Mexican dancers. Fernando worked in a medical laboratory, where he
met and married a young Mexican woman named Mercedes Irigoyen.
They raised four children, two boys (Guillermo and Peter) and two
girls (Andrea and Leticia). These children in turn had eight children of their own. Family members report that Vicky and Fernando
almost never spoke about their father. In her only known interview,
given to a dance magazine shortly before her death, Vicky mentioned
her father only once—and described him as a banker from England.
When Fernando's youngest son, Peter, chanced upon a photograph
of his grandfather seated in an elaborately carved wooden chair and
became curious about W. H. Ellis's appearance, Fernando emphati-
cally denied that the family had any African American ancestry. It

was, recalls Peter, as if his father "didn't like the idea of being related to a black person."

Ellis had passed as Cuban and Hawaiian, married a white woman, lived much of his life in Mexico, and maintained a lifelong interest in African American politics. Such fluidity, however, was rare in a world that sought to organize itself around clear racial divides—a reality cast in sharp relief by the gradual division of Ellis's family into separate ethnic affiliations. While his nephew crossed the veil to the white side of the color line and his sisters and their families maintained an identity as African Americans, Ellis's immediate descendants—his children, grandchildren, and great-grandchildren—came to think of themselves as Mexican. Eventually, the branches of this spreading family tree became so distant as to lose contact with one another. Toward the end of her life, the elderly Victoria Ellis relocated to Tijuana to live with her nephew Peter. Although she did not know it, through an odd twist of fate, she was now little more than a hundred miles away from her aunt and relatives in Los Angeles. By this time, however, a pronounced border had arisen between the two branches of the family. Its most obvious manifestation could be found in the tightly surveilled international boundary separating Tijuana from Southern California, with its banks of searchlights, coils of razor wire, and platoons of Border Patrol agents. But it could be found, too, in the accumulated layers of history that led the members of the same family to encounter one another across an ethnic divide.

Epilogue

TRICKSTER MAKES THIS WORLD

THE IMAGINED OFTEN has a way of proving all too real. Just as the stories that Ellis spun about himself took on a life all their own, shaping events on both sides of the border, so, too, did race, that momentous yet absurd human invention that had so defined Ellis's career, retain its power in the years after his death, becoming, if anything, more entrenched. Once it had been possible, as in the Texas legal code of 1866, to have some African American ancestry yet still be considered white. By the early twentieth century, however, the United States had come to embrace the "one drop" rule. Alarmed that "many thousands of white negroes . . . were quietly and persistently passing over the line," numerous states enacted laws classifying anyone with an African American forbear, no matter how remote, as black. By 1920, the Census Bureau, in accordance with this new logic, confined the category of whiteness solely "to persons understood to be pure-blooded whites," while classifying an individual of mixed black-white ancestry "as . . . a Negro . . . regardless of the amount of white blood." This relentless drive for racial purity undermined the viability of any intermediate category between black and white. As late as 1890, the Census Bureau utilized "mulatto," "quadroon," and "octoroon" to describe individuals of varying degrees of African ancestry. By 1930, however, these terms dropped from the census altogether. From now on, such persons were simply black.

Across the color line, some African Americans articulated their own versions of this doctrine. Marcus Garvey, the leader of the Universal Negro Improvement Association, the most popular organization among peoples of African descent in the early twentieth century, appealed for all persons with black ancestry, no matter how small, to join together as a "united Negro race." "We desire to have every shade of color, even those with one drop of African blood, in our fold; because we believe that none of us, as we are, is responsible for our birth," wrote Garvey in 1923. "We believe that every Negro racially is just alike."

Ironically, at the very moment that many in the United States sought to create purer, more discrete races, Mexico deepened its celebration of racial mixing. In 1925, Mexican intellectual José Vasconcelos published his influential *La raza cósmica* (The Cosmic Race), a work that argued that a "new universal era of Humanity" would only come about through the blending of races. "The ulterior goal of History," asserted Vasconcelos, "[is] to attain the fusion of peoples and cultures." Vasconcelos's work situated Mexico on a trajectory toward future glories while leaving its northern neighbor doomed to stagnation because of its "inflexible line that separates the Blacks from the Whites."

That two such different ways of thinking about race should arise along a shared borderline was more than mere coincidence. As neighboring New World republics, the United States and Mexico possessed a number of common historical features: participation in the Atlantic slave trade, wars of independence against European colonial powers, the expropriation of Indian lands. Paradoxically, however, these points of congruence rendered each nation an especially potent foil for the other—a mirror of sorts in which one could glimpse one's imagined other, and in so doing, oneself as well. As a result of this dynamic, the United States and Mexico's growing interaction during the nineteenth century led not to a blurring of distinctions but rather to a heightening of difference. This was particularly manifest in the realm of race relations. As the United States and Mexico engaged in parallel projects of national reconstruction, designed to forge a unified citizenry out of diverse collections of inhabitants, each conceptualized itself in opposition to the other. In portraying itself as a white nation, unlike "mongrel Mexico," the United States obscured the existence of its many nonwhite residents, not to mention the racial mixing and passing that rendered the very notion of a pure white race untenable. And in casting itself as a *mestizo* nation of Spanish and Indian origin, unmarred by the slavery that had fueled the violent land grabs of its northern neighbor, Mexico erased the presence of its considerable Afro-Mexican population as well as those other ethnic groups, such as Arabs and Asians, who likewise fell outside its definition of *mestizaje*.

This intimate interplay ensured that even though the border was situated on the physical perimeter of the two countries, it played a central role in each nation's process of racial formation. The periphery defined the core, and the borderline evinced the color line. Less than a year after Ellis's death, the United States passed the Johnson-Reed Immigration Act, establishing an intricate quota system for who could legally cross its borders that favored immigrants from Western Europe while outlawing the immigration of "colored races" from Asia. As befitted a measure that spawned vast categories of "illegal aliens," the act also established a Border Patrol to police the nation's boundaries and keep out unwanted migrants.

At much the same time, Mexican authorities similarly narrowed the scope of who could legitimately cross their nation's border. For all Vasconcelos's pronouncements on the "Cosmic Race," it turned out that the republic continued the old pattern of confining *mestizaje* to the mixture of Europeans and Indians. In 1925 (the same year, ironically, that *La raza cosmica* appeared), the Mexican congressman Gustavo Durón González opined in *Problemas migratorios de México* that "as we don't have a negro problem, it is a blunder to create one artificially" by allowing the entry of African Americans. Turning such pronouncements into policy, Mexico's Departamento de Agricultura y Fomento forbade the immigration of blacks as well as Chinese and South Asians. Zealous officials even barred African American tourists, leading Du Bois to complain that "Mexico discriminates between American citizens who wish to visit their country. . . . No person of Negro descent is allowed to make such a visit." (These rulings also meant that, by the standards of their homeland's one-drop rule, Ellis's children were engaged in their own form of passing when they entered Mexico on visas that declared their race as "white.")

In his long career journeying back and forth between Mexico and the United States—across the intertwined borderline and color line—Ellis the trickster had become a virtuoso in surmounting such boundaries and transforming them into opportunities. Moreover, as in the archetypical trickster tale, Ellis played a key role in creating the world that he inhabited. For more than three decades, he had served as the Gilded Age's leading proponent of African American immigration to Mexico, not to mention a prominent facilitator of cross-border trade and investment. By setting in motion many of the interactions that defined the US-Mexico relationship, Ellis generated the very terrain on which he operated.

Approaching Ellis's life through the figure of the trickster enables us not only to grasp the central roles that improvisation and dissembling played in his life as a border crosser; it also offers us a way out of the conceptual trap at the heart of the turn-of-the-century discourse on passing. Gilded Age Americans conceived of passing in dichotomous terms: the concealment of one's true racial identity to adopt a fake, invented one. According to such logic, the fact that an individual calling himself Guillermo Enrique Eliseo spoke fluent Spanish, lived much of his life in Mexico, dressed like a member of the Porfirian elite, circulated among Mexico City's leading politicians and entrepreneurs, and died and was buried in the Mexican capital counted for nothing. He remained what he had been at birth: an African American.

Once we realize, however, that race is a protean, ever-changing fiction, rather than an objective fact, it becomes impossible to parse identity so neatly into the authentic and the contrived. It is true that Ellis concealed elements of his background from outsiders. But the

features he showed insiders were equally revealing. In two of his surviving pieces of personal correspondence—a letter to his father and
another to his younger sister Fannie—Ellis signed himself "Guillermo." In identifying himself using his Spanish name, Ellis surely did
not expect to deceive his family into believing that he was Mexican.
Rather, his use of Guillermo even among his closest familiars hints
that his Latin American persona felt as real to him as his African
American one. And why not? For by the odd alchemy of American
racial thinking, in which Mexican blurred into Spanish, and Spanish
blurred into white, it was Guillermo Enrique Eliseo who opened up
the new worlds that would have been closed to William Henry Ellis
by the harsh realities of the color line. And after so many years spent
passing as Eliseo, might not the mask and the face, the person and the
persona, have begun to fuse into one another?

At the same time, Ellis evinced no contradiction in claiming to be
Mexican, Cuban, or Hawaiian yet being active in African American
politics. Even as he and his family settled into an all-white neighborhood in Mount Vernon, Ellis maintained a link to black political
life, replacing the electoral campaigns of Cuney and the colonization of Turner with the economic uplift and backroom negotiating
of Booker T. Washington. In 1917, Ellis offered "one of the principal
talks of the evening" at a dinner held at one of Manhattan's premier
restaurants to honor the Tuskegee Institute—an event attended by a
veritable who's who of New York's black community, including James
Weldon Johnson, author of *The Autobiography of an Ex-Colored Man*,
Fred R. Moore, editor of the *New York Age*, and clergyman Adam
Clayton Powell. That same year, Ellis took advantage of his ties to
Teddy Roosevelt, with whom he had maintained an intermittent correspondence since his foray into Ethiopia in the early 1900s, to urge
the ex-president to end the horrors of lynching: "We have asked the
Turks to spare the Armenians; we have asked the Russians to protect
the Jews and, yet, in our own house and under our own fig-tree, we
have allowed human beings to be burned at the stake. Such a thing
has never happened in Russia, Turkey or Mexico or in any of the
places that we are trying to reform." When a mob of whites murdered

at least eighteen blacks in Slocum, Texas, and forced many other African Americans to flee the town, Ellis dispatched a similar telegraph to President William Howard Taft, demanding that the federal government intervene: "Grover Cleveland Democratic President sent troops Illinois stop rioting. Cant you use Federal strength to stop massacre helpless blacks in Texas for humanity's sake if nothing else?"

By passing, then, Ellis was ultimately laying claim to an identity beyond a specific ethnic label, be it Mexican, Cuban, or Hawaiian. Rather, he was asserting his existence, in Earlene Stetson's apt phrase, "as a human person with all the rights and privileges thereof." After all, in a United States that sought to inscribe the color line through all facets of daily existence, to be caught on the black side of this boundary was to be deprived of the full measure of one's humanity, left with few if any civil rights that the larger society was obliged to respect. It was this tension between the particular and the universal that Du Bois explored so memorably in *The Souls of Black Folk* when he spoke of the "double consciousness" of being African American, "this sense of always looking at one's self through the eyes of others, of measuring one's soul by the tape of a world that looks on in amused contempt and pity." Ellis the trickster at once rendered this "twoness" singular—a transcendent humanity—and refracted it through a multiplicity of identities: white, black, Cuban, Hawaiian, and Mexican. Passing added a new layer of complexity to Du Bois's depiction of the African American predicament, one that required Ellis to preserve a coherent sense of self while also remaining exquisitely attuned to how his plethora of alternative guises was perceived by others.

This could be a difficult performance to sustain even in the best of circumstances. There were obvious reasons why Ellis—with his swarthy skin, black hair, and dark eyes, his childhood spent along the border, his fluent Spanish—favored a Mexican persona when passing. For "persons of *obviously* colored complexion," counseled Langston Hughes, passing as an individual of northern European origin could prove challenging. Far easier to "go to Mexico as colored and come back as Spanish." But Ellis's claims to *mexicanidad* may have resonated on a deeper plane as well. For all its problematic erasure of the Afro-

Mexican presence, the notion of *mestizaje* nonetheless allowed Ellis to express an identity that accessed whiteness's legal rights while also recognizing the existence of racial ambiguity and mixed ancestry. If the resulting formulation did not reflect every facet of Ellis's ethnic background, it nonetheless remained a far more attractive option than the constrained racial categories prevailing in the United States. Moreover, it hinted at the possibilities to be found in expanding *mestizaje* still further to embrace the totality of the North American experience and acknowledge the continent's centuries-long history of miscegenation, mixing, entanglement, and creolization. Recast from this perspective, Ellis's passing as Mexican represented not a form of social death but rather the birth of a truer, more complex self.

TODAY, MANY OF the landscapes that once would have been familiar to Ellis have changed almost beyond recognition. Former cotton fields outside Victoria now sprout the pumps and drilling equipment of the nation's newest resource boom: fracking for oil and natural gas. One no longer finds an informal ferry shuttling residents across the river from Piedras Negras to Eagle Pass. Travelers must pass instead through computerized checkpoints along the reinforced concrete bridge linking the two nations. Below, agents of the US Border Patrol guard the waters of the Rio Grande/Río Bravo del Norte in high-speed airboats, while a spiked, black steel barrier some twenty feet high dominates the riverbank along the US side of the border. Mexico City has metatastatized into the largest city in the Western Hemisphere, an agglomeration of some twenty million people that sprawls far beyond the nineteenth-century core where Ellis once strolled, absorbing the sights and sounds of the capital's busy streets. In the wake of the Mexican Revolution's land reforms, a patchwork of peasant *ejidos* has supplanted the vast, foreign-owned hacienda in Tlahualilo. The Manhattan that possessed only a handful of Mexican residents when Ellis first arrived in the 1890s is now home to hundreds of thousands of immigrants from Mexico, who constitute the city's fastest-growing ethnic group. Mount Vernon, an overwhelm-ingly white suburb when Ellis, Maude, and the children settled there, has become a majority minority community. One need only glance out the front door of Ellis's former address in the City of Happy Homes to chart the demographic transformation: located across the street is a Dominican bodega specializing in "comida Hispana."

Yet for all these transformations, the defining features of Ellis's world reside with us still. The borderline and the color line may have assumed new guises over the years, but their power has proven remarkably resilient. Transforming our divided world, it turns out, will require more than a lone trickster. It will require us to recognize that we all inhabit a *mestizo*, mulatto America—and that surmounting the boundaries that separate us is our mutual project.

AFTERWORD

IT GOES AGAINST the instincts of historians to insert ourselves into the stories we tell. Yet the past has a way of grabbing hold of the present in spite of our efforts to separate the two. Over the decades I spent researching William Ellis's life, I logged more time than I care to recall squinting at old documents, trying to make sense of faded words from a vanished era. With time, however, Ellis's twisting trail led not only to dusty papers in distant archives but also to living, flesh-and-blood members of his extended family—first his grand-nieces, descendants of Ellis's sister Elizabeth, and then his grandchildren, offspring of Ellis's youngest son, Fernando.

Almost as soon as I met them, it became clear to me that each side of the family was intensely curious about the other. The American branch had preserved a surprisingly large number of stories about William Ellis as well as a number of family names (Fanny, Marguerita) passed down from earlier generations. But they knew nothing about their cousins across the border in Mexico. For their part, the Mexican Ellises, although they were aware their grandfather was from the United States, did not realize that he was of African American descent until I shared this information with them during an early phone call.

So it was, through such unexpected interactions, that I, a historian, found myself setting in motion a transborder family reunion. One Saturday in the spring of 2015, twenty-five or so of William Ellis's long-scattered family members—the lone outsiders myself and my wife—gathered in the backyard of a suburban Los Angeles home. This meeting would be the first time in almost a century that the cousins, long divided by the international boundary, were once again in contact with one another. William Ellis's grandson and his wife had braved the Tijuana border crossing, the busiest in the world, to drive up and spend the weekend with the American side of the family, who had gathered from near (Pasadena) and far (Baltimore) to join the celebration. Under a brilliant blue Southern California sky, the family members mingled in the carefully tended garden of one of William Ellis's grandnieces, conversing in a jumble of Spanish and English, their words punctuated by laughter and hugs. After talks and toasts, those assembled produced treasured picture albums, filled with faded black-and-white photos, the images within revealing ancestors of varied hues in settings as disparate as Texas, Mexico, and New York. Other family members gathered around a television in the living room to watch a rare movie from 1940s Mexico, featuring a young Victoria Ellis tap-dancing across the classroom of a girls' boarding school in *Internado para señoritas*. The reunion began over brunch, but it ended up stretching into the twilight hours, as family members lingered over food and drink or sat quietly in the shade, contemplating a family circle restored. As the participants drifted off into the evening stillness, those present began to make plans to repeat the event again soon—only next time, in Mexico.

A crossing of borders, a search for connections, a conversation: these may seem like small acts. But even as the reunion laid bare the forces that had splintered William Ellis's family so many years ago—divides of citizenship, of language, of ethnicity—it also demonstrated the possibility of forging new connections. What will flow from such encounters? For now, the answer lies beyond the realm of history. It is a future waiting to unfold, a story still to be written.

ACKNOWLEDGMENTS

In my many years chasing William H. Ellis, I was fortunate enough to have had the assistance of a great number of accomplices along the way.

My first thanks go to the Moore family in Southern California and the Ellis family in Mexico. When I began to search for William H. Ellis's relatives, I was not at all certain I would ever find them, given the numerous obfuscations that Ellis had introduced into the historical record. I never dreamed that I would encounter such lovely people who have over time become like a second family to me. The Moore sisters—Susie Williams, Joan Williams, and Fanny Johnson-Griffin—have been incredibly gracious with their time; their support for this project has meant the world to me. Many thanks, too, to the rest of the family for their warm welcome: Robert Adan Williams, Angela Williams, Robin Wood, Jimmy Wood, Marguerita Drew, Dylan Drew, Cairo Collins, Adye Evans, Edison Griffin, Sheldon Johnson, Aaron Johnson, Portia Wood, and Savannah Wood, among others. I look forward to celebrating the publication of *The Strange Career of William Ellis* with all of you, seven long years after we first met.

When I encountered the Moore sisters in 2009, I told them that I would try to track down the long-lost Mexican branch of the family for them. Alas, for far too many years, this promise seemed a hollow one. Not until 2013, thanks to a remarkable string of coincidences set in motion by Sandra Pujals and Patricia Aulestia, did the final pieces of the puzzle fall into place. Having researched their elusive, border-crossing ancestor for so long, it was a profoundly moving experience to finally speak to members of the Mexican Ellises. This happy moment, however, soon became tinged with an unexpected sadness. Only days before I was to meet Peter, Liz, and their children, their only son, Christopher Guillermo, died in a freak accident in Mexico City. This book is dedicated to the memory of Christopher, William H. Ellis's great-grandson and Valeria and Paulina's beloved brother.

The Strange Career of William Ellis owes its genesis to an assignment that Emilia Viotti da Costa gave me in one of my first classes in graduate school. Knowing that I was interested in the US-Mexico borderlands, Professor da Costa suggested that I look at some of the US consuls' reports from northern Mexico and write a brief research paper on what I found there. Little did she or I know what this supposedly short assignment would ultimately become. One of the very first reports I encountered discussed William H. Ellis's 1895 effort to relocate African Americans to Tlahualilo. Fascinated by this unlikely tale, I returned to it again and again, even as I went on to write a dissertation about something else entirely. As I wrestled with my preliminary findings relating to William H. Ellis, Jim Scott and Gil Joseph at Yale were of great help, as was William Meyers of Wake Forest University.

Even so, this project might have languished in a desk drawer forever without repeated nudges from Sam Truett. First, Sam encouraged me to revise the essay I had written for Professor da Costa for inclusion in the anthology on new approaches to borderlands history that he and Elliott Young were editing, *Continental Crossroads*. Then, after I had finished my last book, *Shadows at Dawn: A Borderlands Massacre and the Violence of History*, Sam helped me think through how to make what still struck me as an impossible project into a coherent book. I am grateful for his boundless enthusiasm as well as his encyclopedic knowledge of borderlands history.

Marni Sandweiss, whose eye-opening book on Clarence King's black-to-white passing proved an inspiration to me, was equally generous in offering her support and expertise. Bill Deverell was a great help in facilitating my initial introduction to Joan Williams. Marsha Weisiger proved an invaluable sounding board and a wonderful traveling companion as our research interests unexpectedly intertwined with one another. In particular, she arranged a memorable trip to Victoria, where we met Craig Weisiger and Corky Goodman, who were kind enough to share their detailed knowledge of their hometown with two befuddled non-Texans. Native Texan Aaron Frith accompanied me on another indelible Texas trip, this time to Eagle Pass/Piedras Negras, and helped with several of the illustrations for *The Strange Career of William Ellis.*

In turning what had been a short article into a full-sized book, I relied upon numerous accomplished academics for advice and guidance. Special thanks to Erik Anderson, Adam Arenson, Blake Ball, Alwyn Barr, Mia Bay, Gerry Cadava, Gregg Cantrell, William Carrigan, Carlos Castañón Cuadros, Doug Cope, Sarah Cornell, Bill Cronon, Justin Castro, Grace Delgado, Anahi Douglas, Greg Downs, Ann Fabian, Eric Foner, Matt García, Adam Goodman, Greg Grandin, Matt Guterl, Ramón Gutiérrez, Steve Hahn, Douglas Hales, Françoise Hamlin, Martha Hodes, Jesse Hoffnung-Garskof, Evelyn Hu-DeHart, Andrew Huebner, Irvin Hunt, Nancy Jacobs, Valeria Jiménez, Ben Johnson, Jane Kamensky, Emilio Kourí, Chris Lamberti, Jessica Lee, Joel Lee, John Logan, Adrián Lopez Denis, Danny Loss, Monica Martinez, Jim McCann, Stephanie McCurry, Scot McFarlane, John Mckiernan-Gonzalez, Amanda McVety, Michele Mericle, Ed Morales, Dirk Moses, Rachel Newman, Mae Ngai, James Nichols, Andrew Offenburger, Jolie Olcott, Juan Antonio Padilla Compean, Dylan Penningroth, Pablo Piccato, Caterina Pizzigoni, Anthony Quiroz, Andrés Resendez, Annette Rodriguez, Bill Schell, Bill Scott, Larry Spruill, Charles Spurlin, Alexandra Stern, Andrew Torget, Ben Vinson, and Michael Vorenberg,

I also benefited from the assistance of a number of gifted research assistants. Susan Berlowitz and Billye Jackson showed me how much historians can learn from genealogists. Benjamín Alonso Rascón once again demonstrated his mastery of Mexican archives. Brown University students Khalila Douze, Elena Gonzales, Jonah Newman, and Danielle Slevens all provided invaluable help.

Over the years it took me to complete this book, I presented talks about William H. Ellis at a number of venues, including Arizona State

University, Brown University, the Massachusetts Institute of Technology, New York University, Oberlin College, Rutgers University, University of New Mexico, Indiana University, Southern Methodist University, Yale University's Agrarian Studies Program, and the Newberry Library's Borderlands and Latino/a Studies Symposium. I am grateful to all those who participated in these sessions for their thought-provoking feedback.

Without financial assistance from the John Simon Guggenheim Foundation and the Russell Sage Foundation, I would never have been able to take the pause from teaching necessary to write up my findings. At the Russell Sage, I was fortunate enough to be exposed to a unique community of gifted scholars, including Aliya Saperstein, Ann Morning, Elizabeth Cohen, Ellie Shermer, Mona Lynch, Susan Silbey, and Paul Osterman, as well as to receive the assistance of the foundation's accomplished research staff. My time as a scholar in residence at the Center for Borderlands Studies at Arizona State University, run by my good friend Matt Garcia, also proved an invaluable opportunity to think more deeply about the issues relating to this book.

For help in tracking down archival materials relating to William H. Ellis's life, I benefited from the efforts of Peter Blodgett at the Huntington Library; Lorna Owens at the Andrew Carnegie Birthplace; Evan Hocker at the Center for American History at the University of Texas at Austin; John Friend at the Wisconsin Historical Society; Janette Garcia at The University of Texas-Pan American Library; Mattie Taormina at the Stanford University Library; Susan Olsen at Woodlawn Cemetery; Fenta Tiruneh at the Library of Congress; Mandy Altimus Pond at the Massillon Museum; and Xóchitl Fernández of Agrasánchez Film Archive. Ulf Lindhal was my sage guide to the arcane yet fascinating world of Ethiopian stamp collecting.

Equally important support was offered by family friend Mary Kim, who with her husband, Jeff, generously let me stay at their home when I was doing research in Southern California. New York City friends Wendy Walters, Dan Charnas, Susan Ferber, Rachel St. John, Andrew Needham, Maria Montoya, Jared Farmer, Jerry Weinstein,

Suzy Kim, and others not only helped me think through some of the writing challenges associated with *The Strange Career of William Ellis*; they occasionally insisted I step away from my desk and enjoy my new Manhattan home. Magaly Polanco's loving care of Jason made coping with work/life pressures manageable most days.

My agent, Geri Thoma, skillfully guided this project to the desk of Tom Mayer at W. W. Norton, who has proven to be an uncommonly astute and insightful editor. I hope this will be the first of many, many books we work on together.

Having spent so much time thinking about William H. Ellis's family has made me treasure mine all the more. My love to you all— above all, to the tricksters who remain the heroes of the story of my life: Marie and Jason.

NOTES

PROLOGUE: THROUGH HISTORY'S CRACKS

xv   **Mexican North:** [A Gringo], *Through the Land of the Aztecs; or, Life and Travel in Mexico* (London: Sampson Low, Marston, 1892), 98–100; Michael Matthews, *The Civilizing Machine: A Cultural History of Mexican Railroads, 1876–1910* (Lincoln: University of Nebraska Press, 2013), 7–9; *Travelers' Official Guide of the Railway and Steam Navigation Lines in the United States, Canada and Mexico* (New York: National Railway Publication Company, 1897), 824–825.

xvi   **"sister republics":** S. G. Reed, *A History of the Texas Railroads and of Transportation Conditions Under Spain and Mexico and the Republic and the State* (Houston: St. Clair, 1941), 203.

xvi   **watches, and cigars:** [Ferrocarriles Nacionales de México], *Mexico from Border to Capital: A Brief Description of the Many Interesting Places to be Seen en Route to Mexico City via the Laredo, the Eagle Pass and the El Paso Gateways* (Chicago: Corbitt Railway Printing, n.d.); US Department of Commerce and Labor, *Immigration Laws and Regulations of July 1, 1907* (Washington, DC: GPO, 1908), 66–68; Peter Andreas, *Smuggler Nation: How Illicit Trade Made America* (New York: Oxford University Press, 2013), 183–190; George T. Díaz, *Border Contraband: A History of Smuggling Across the Rio Grande* (Austin: University of Texas Press, 2015), 51–57, 90.

xvii   **face value:** US Department of Commerce and Labor, *Immigration Laws and Regulations of July 1, 1907* (Washington, DC: GPO, 1908), 52; Craig Robertson, *The Passport in America: The History of a Document* (New York: Oxford University Press, 2010), 160–163, 197–198; US Bureau of Immigration and Naturalization, *Annual Report of the Commissioner-General of Immigration for the Fiscal Year Ended June 30, 1907* (Washington, DC: GPO, 1907), 7–10, 110; Erika Lee, *At America's Gates: Chinese Immigration During the Exclusion Era, 1882–1943* (Chapel Hill: University of North Carolina Press, 2003), 161–162; Anna Pegler-Gordon, *In Sight of America: Photography and the Development of U.S. Immigration Policy* (Berkeley: University of California Press, 2009), 196–197.

xviii   **"Jim Crow" car:** *Victoria Advocate*, March 16, 1909; *New York Tribune*, March 15, 1909; *New York Sun*, March 15, 1909. Although this is the first book-length study of Ellis, he makes brief appearances in a handful of other scholarly works. See Michele Mitchell, *Righteous Propagation: African Americans and the Politics of Racial Destiny After Reconstruction* (Chapel Hill: University of North Carolina Press, 2004), 37; Edwin Redkey, *Black Exodus: Black Nationalist and Back-to-Africa Movements, 1890–1910* (New Haven: Yale University Press, 1969); J. Fred Rippy, "A Negro Colonization Project in Mexico, 1895," *Journal of Negro History* 6, no. 1 (January 1921): 66–73; and Alfred W. Reynolds, "The Alabama Negro Colony in Mexico, 1894–1896, Parts 1 and 2," *Alabama Review* 5 (October 1952): 243–268, and 6 (January 1953): 31–58.

xviii   **"seems to know":** *New York World*, March 15, 1909; *Denver Evening Post*, April 6, 1897; "A Mysterious Disappearance," *Week's Progress* 24, no. 400 (July 9, 1904): 23; *Pittsburgh Press*, July 17, 1904; *Kansas City Star*, June 30, 1905; *Baltimore Sun*, July 25, 1904; *New York Sun*, September 21, 1903.

xix   **Eliseo unanswered:** *Saint Paul Globe*, July 10, 1904.

xix   **the past:** *Los Angeles Times*, July 27, 1904; Susie Williams, interview by author, March 12, 2012.

xx   **African American imagination:** Works on black-Mexican interactions include Neil Foley, *Quest for Equality: The Failed Promise of Black-Brown Solidarity* (Cambridge: Harvard University Press, 2010); Brian Behnken, *Fighting Their Own Battles: Mexican Americans, African Americans, and the Struggle for Civil Rights in Texas* (Chapel Hill: University of North Carolina Press, 2011); Brian Behnken, ed., *The Struggle in Black and Brown: African American and Mexican American Relations During the Civil Rights Era* (Lincoln: University of Nebraska Press, 2011); and Gerald Horne, *Black and Brown: African Americans and the Mexican Revolution, 1910–1920* (New York: New York University Press, 2005).

xxi   **and beyond:** *Baltimore American*, July 25, 1904; *Cleveland Gazette*, October 13, 1923.

xxi   **as well:** Friedrich Katz, *The Secret War in Mexico: Europe, the United States, and the Mexican Revolution* (Chicago: University of Chicago Press, 1981), 7–21; Juan Mora-Torres, *The Making of the Mexican Border: The State, Capitalism, and Society in Nuevo León, 1848–1910* (Austin: University of Texas Press, 2001), 3–5.

xxii   **"Jim Crow disappear":** Langston Hughes, *I Wonder as I Wander: An Autobiographical Journey* (Columbia: University of Missouri Press, 2003), 91.

xxii   **to the other:** Werner Sollors, *Neither Black nor White yet Both: Thematic Explorations of Interracial Literature* (Cambridge: Harvard University Press, 1997), 283–284.

xxiii   **forms of passing:** W. L. White, *Lost Boundaries* (New York: Harcourt, Brace, 1947), 60.

xxiii   **each year:** A useful overview of passing can be found in Randall Kennedy, "Racial Passing," 62 *Ohio State Law Journal* 1145 (2001). For estimates as to the number of black to white passers, see E. W. Eckard, "How Many Negroes 'Pass'?" *American Journal of Sociology* 52, no. 6 (May 1947): 498–500;

John H. Burma, "The Measurement of Negro 'Passing,'" *American Journal of Sociology* 52, no. 1 (July 1946): 18–22; and William M. Kephart, "The 'Passing' Question," *Phylon* 9, no. 4 (1948): 336–340. As compared with the plethora of literary studies of passing, there is surprisingly little historical scholarship on passing. Leading studies include Allyson Hobbs, *A Chosen Exile: A History of Racial Passing in American Life* (Cambridge: Harvard University Press, 2014); Daniel J. Sharfstein, *The Invisible Line: Three American Families and the Secret Journey from Black to White* (New York: Penguin Press, 2011); Martha Sandweiss, *Passing Strange: A Gilded Age Tale of Love and Deception Across the Color Line* (New York: Penguin Press, 2009); and Mary Frances Berry, *We Are Who We Say We Are: A Black Family's Search for Home Across the Atlantic World* (New York: Oxford University Press, 2015).

xxiii **"as whites":** Ray Stannard Baker, *Following the Color Line: An Account of Negro Citizenship in the American Democracy* (New York: Doubleday, Page, 1908), 164; Walter White, *A Man Called White: The Autobiography of Walter White* (New York: Viking Press, 1948), 3–4.

xxiv **"journey 'across'":** Troilus Hilgard Tyndale, *Don Cosme: A Romance of the South* (New York: G. W. Dillingham, 1899), 240; Louis Fremont Baldwin, *From Negro to Caucasian; or, How the Ethiopian Is Changing His Skin* (San Francisco: International Publishing, 1929), 10. For real-life examples of African Americans passing as Mexican, see Carolyn Ashbaugh, *Lucy Parsons: An American Revolutionary* (Chicago: Haymarket Books, 2012 [1976]), 14; and Rebecca J. Scott and Jean M. Hébard, *Freedom Papers: An Atlantic Odyssey in the Age of Emancipation* (Cambridge: Harvard University Press, 2012), 177.

xxvi **Hawaiian:** Jesse W. Sparks to Edwin F. Uhl, December 13, 1895 in Dispatches from United States Consuls in Piedras Negras (Ciudad Porfirio Díaz), Records of the Department of State, RG 59, M299, NARA–Microfilm Publications; *Akron Times* quoted in Richard Pankhurst, "William H. Ellis—Guillaume Enriques Ellesio: The First Black American Ethiopianist?" *Ethiopia Observer* 15 (1972): 103. Most accounts of Wall Street date the presence of African Americans financiers to the 1920s. Gregory S. Bell, *In the Black: A History of African Americans on Wall Street* (New York: John Wiley & Sons, 2002), 23–26.

xxvii **truer self:** James Weldon Johnson, *The Autobiography of an Ex-Colored Man* (New York: Hill and Wang, 1960 [1912]), 211. My thoughts on the trickster figure owe a great deal to Kevin Young, *The Grey Album: On the Blackness of Blackness* (Minneapolis: Grey Wolf Press, 2012), 26–27, as well as the classic statements of Lawrence W. Levine, *Black Culture and Black Consciousness: Afro-American Folk Thought from Slavery to Freedom* (New York: Oxford University Press, 1977); John W. Roberts, *From Trickster to Badman: The Black Folk Hero in Slavery and Freedom* (Philadelphia: University of Pennsylvania Press, 1989); Lewis Hyde, *Trickster Makes This World: Mischief, Myth, and Art* (New York: Farrar, Straus and Giroux, 1998); and Henry Louis Gates, *The Signifying Monkey: A Theory of Afro-American Literary*

Criticism (New York: Oxford University Press, 1988). The phrase "weapons of the weak" is from James C. Scott, *Weapons of the Weak: Everyday Forms of Peasant Resistance* (New Haven: Yale University Press, 1987).

xxvii **"around [them]"**: Hyde, *Trickster Makes This World*, 14; Heba Jannath, "America's Changing Color Line," in *Negro: An Anthology*, edited by Nancy Cunard (New York: Continuum Publishing, 1996 [1934]), 62. Jannath was the pen name of Josephine Cogdell Schuyler, a white woman married to Harlem's leading journalist in the 1920s and 1930s, George Schuyler. Carla Kaplan, *Miss Anne in Harlem: The White Women of the Black Renaissance* (New York: HarperCollins, 2013), 84.

xxviii **continued power:** Roberts, *From Trickster to Badman*, 23–28; Levine, *Black Culture and Black Consciousness*, 102–121; Langston Hughes, "Fooling Our White Folks," *Negro Digest* 8, no. 6 (April 1950): 41. See also Langston Hughes, "Jokes on Our White Folks," in *Langston Hughes and the* Chicago Defender: *Essays on Race, Politics, and Culture, 1942–62*, edited by Christopher C. DeSantis (Urbana: University of Illinois Press, 1995), 97–99. The classic statement of whiteness as property is Cheryl I. Harris, "Whiteness as Property," *Harvard Law Review* 106, no. 8 (June 1993): 1707–1791. Intriguingly, Harris opens her article with a discussion of passing.

xxviii **"your brother":** W. H. Ellis to Fannie Starnes, October 11, 1911, family letter shared with author.

1: GONE TO TEXAS

3   **"rising generations":** *One Thousand American Men of Mark of To-Day* (Chicago: American Men of Mark, 1916), i–ii; *Successful American* 1, no. 1 (January 1900): 3.

4   **"a business":** Thomas William Herringshaw, ed., *Herringshaw's American Blue-Book of Biography: Prominent Americans of 1919* (Chicago: American Blue Book Publishers, 1919), 171; Herman W. Knox, ed., *Who's Who in New York: A Biographical Dictionary of Prominent Citizens of New York City and State, 1917–1918* (New York: Who's Who Publications, 1918), 336; "William H. Ellis," *Successful American* 2, no. 2 (August 1900): 62; *New York Herald*, June 27, 1904.

4   **social ladder:** *Successful American* 1, no. 1 (January 1900): 3; Carol Nackenoff, *The Fictional Republic: Horatio Alger and American Political Discourse* (New York: Oxford University Press, 1994); Michael Denning, *Mechanic Accents: Dime Novels and Working-Class Culture in America* (New York: Verso, 1987); Marcus Klein, *Easterns, Westerns, and Private Eyes: American Matters, 1870–1900* (Madison: University of Wisconsin Press, 1994).

5   **"material prosperity":** *Twentieth-Century Successful Americans: Local and National* (N.p.: United Press Service Bureau, 1917?), foreword [unpaginated].

5   **to Texas:** Frederick Law Olmsted, *A Journey Through Texas; or, A Saddle-*

Trip on the Southwestern Frontier (New York: Dix, Edwards, 1857), 55–57;
Ira Berlin, *The Making of African America: The Four Great Migrations* (New
York: Viking, 2010), 99–116. First-person descriptions of the coffles can
be found in Andrew Waters, ed., *I was Born in Slavery: Personal Accounts of
Slavery in Texas* (Winston-Salem, NC: John F. Blair, 2003), 37, 50.

6   **African Americans:** Arthur James Lyon Fremantle, *Three Months in the
Southern States: April–June 1863* (New York: John Bradburn, 1864), 120;
Benjamin Boisseau Weisiger III, *The Weisiger Family: An Account of Daniel
Weisiger, the Immigrant, of Henrico and Chesterfield Counties, Virginia, and
His Descendants* (Richmond, VA: B. B. Weisiger, 1984), 12–15; 1850 US
Federal Census, Slave Schedules, Boyle and Woodward, Kentucky, M432,
NARA–Microfilm Publications; Estate of Lucy Weisiger, September 13,
1859, Victoria County Probate Book 5.

6   **"cotton to sell":** According to the 1850 agricultural census, Weisiger's plantation in Boyle County, Kentucky, cultivated corn, wheat, potatoes, and fruit,
but no cotton; 1850 US Federal Census, M1528, Agricultural Schedule, Boyle
County, Kentucky, 395, Microfilm Publication, Duke University Library.
Slave quoted in Edward E. Baptist, *The Half Has Never Been Told: Slavery and
the Making of American Capitalism* (New York: Basic Books, 2014), xx.

7   **institution of slavery:** J. W. Petty Jr., ed., *A Republishing of the Book Most
Often Known as Victor Rose's History of Victoria* (Victoria, TX: Book Mart,
1961), 25, 212.

7   **historic record:** Planter quoted in Adam Rothman, *Slave Country: American Expansion and the Origins of the Deep South* (Cambridge: Harvard University Press, 2005), 53. Using the WPA slave narratives, William D.
Carrigan has computed that 75 percent of the slaves in Texas reported
some sort of family separation, compared with just 20 percent elsewhere in
the South. William D. Carrigan, *The Making of a Lynching Culture: Violence
and Vigilantism in Central Texas, 1836–1916* (Urbana: University of Illinois
Press, 2004), 52.

7   **early twenties:** Herbert G. Gutman, *The Black Family in Slavery and Freedom,
1750–1925* (New York: Vintage Books, 1976), 230–256; Nettie Henry Glenn,
Early Frankfort, Kentucky, 1786–1861 (Frankfort, KY: N. H. Glenn, 1986),
90. Hezekiah Ellis shows up in the 1870 census of Frankfort as a fifty-eight-
year-old saloonkeeper, meaning he would have been in his early thirties when
Mary gave birth to Charles. 1870 US Federal Census, Frankfort, Kentucky,
99B, M593, NARA–Microfilm Publications. For a useful overview of the
role of the overseer, see Alan Taylor, *The Internal Enemy: Slavery and War in
Virginia, 1772–1832* (New York: W. W. Norton, 2013), 62–66.

8   **"We need them":** C. Allan Jones, *Texas Roots: Agriculture and Rural Life
Before the Civil War* (College Station: Texas A&M University Press, 2005),
138; *A Report and Treatise on Slavery and the Slavery Agitation: Printed by
Order of the House of Representatives of Texas* (Austin: John Marshall and
Co., 1857), 12; *Northern Standard* (Clarksville, TX) quoted in Randolph

B. Campbell, *An Empire for Slavery: The Peculiar Institution in Texas, 1821–1865* (Baton Rouge: Louisiana State University Press, 1989), 67; Randolph B. Campbell, *Gone to Texas: A History of the Lone Star State* (New York: Oxford University Press, 2003), 221.

9 **"spreading of slavery":** For Texan interest in annexing Cuba, see *Texas State Gazette* (Austin), May 19, 1855; Brown quoted in Robert E. May, *The Southern Dream of a Caribbean Empire, 1854–1861* (Gainesville: University Press of Florida, [1973] 2002), 8–9; Matthew Guterl, *American Mediterranean: Southern Slaveholders in the Age of Emancipation* (Cambridge: Harvard University Press, 2008).

9 **the coast:** Ana Carolina Castillo Crimm, *De León: A Tejano Family History* (Austin: University of Texas Press, 2003), 220; William T. Carter and C. S. Simmons, *Soil Survey of Victoria County, Texas* (Washington, DC: US Department of Agriculture, 1931). For further descriptions of the Weisiger ranch lands, see *Civilian and Gazette* (Galveston, TX), February 8, 1859.

9 **Mexican cattle:** Texas Slavery Project <http://www.texasslaveryproject .org/database/list.php?begin_year=1837&end_year=1845&county=Victoria &group=&include_estimated_data=1&submit=Submit> (accessed 9/28/11); Campbell, *Empire for Slavery*, 266.

10 **plant thrived:** Harry Bates Brown, *Cotton: History, Species, Varieties, Morphology, Breeding, Culture, Diseases, Marketing, and Uses*, 2nd ed. (New York: McGraw-Hill, 1938), 266–270; W. H. Johnson, *Cotton and Its Production* (London: Macmillan, 1926), 374–378; Mrs. William Cazneau [Cora Montgomery], *Eagle Pass; or, Life on the Border* (Austin: Pemberton Press, 1966 [1852]), 27.

10 **for Victoria:** Sharfstein, *The Invisible Line*, 78; Eric Foner discusses the prevalence of runaways from the upper South in *Gateway to Freedom: The Hidden History of the Underground Railroad* (New York: W. W. Norton, 2015), 16–25.

10 **"the offenders":** *Galveston Weekly News*, September 10, 1861.

11 **opined McNeel:** *Victoria Advocate*, August 14, 1851; *National Vindicator* (Washington, TX), February 3, 1844; *Ledger and Texan* (San Antonio), April 28, 1853, and May 25, 1854. Women may have fled less because their work was tied more closely to the plantation; childcare responsibilities posed an additional burden. Sylviane A. Diouf, *Slavery's Exiles: The Story of the American Maroons* (New York: New York University Press, 2014), 89–92.

11 **"in his head":** James Boyd in Waters, *I Was Born in Slavery*, 6; Felix Haywood in George P. Rawick, ed., *The American Slave: A Composite Autobiography* (Westport, CT: Greenwood Publishing, 1972 [1941]), 4:132; plantation owner quoted in Sean Kelley, "'Mexico in his Head': Slavery and the Texas-Mexico Border," *Journal of Social History* 37, no. 3 (Spring 2004): 709; Rachel Adams, *Continental Divides: Remapping the Cultures of North America* (Chicago: University of Chicago Press, 2009), 65–77; Diouf, *Slavery's Exiles*, 288–292. Based on estimates of runaway slaves, it seems that enslaved African

Americans were several times more likely to escape bondage from Texas
than from the South as a whole. Benjamin Johnson, *Bordertown: The Odyssey
of an American Place* (New Haven: Yale University Press, 2008), 69.

12   **three months:** Cuevas to Governor of Coahuila, April 23, 1849 <http://
ahc.sfpcoahuila.gob.mx/admin/uploads/Documentos/modulo11/c2f8e3
.pdf> (accessed 2/9/15); Olmsted, *A Journey Through Texas*, 323–325 (emphasis in the original). For more on fugitive slaves, see Ronnie C. Tyler, "Fugitive Slaves in Mexico," *Journal of Negro History* 57 (January 1972): 1–12;
Alwyn Barr, *Black Texans: A History of Negroes in Texas, 1528–1971* (Austin,
TX: Jenkins Publishing, 1973), 28–32; Kenneth Wiggins Porter, *The Negro
on the American Frontier* (New York: Arno Press, 1971), 424–435, 463–465;
and Quintard Taylor, *In Search of the Racial Frontier: African Americans in
the American West, 1528–1990* (New York: W. W. Norton, 1998), 60–61.

12   **as they saw fit:** Olmsted, *A Journey Through Texas*, 325; Sarah E. Cornell, "Citizens of Nowhere: Fugitive Slaves and Free African Americans
in Mexico, 1833–1857," *Journal of American History* 100, no. 2 (September
2013): 351–74; and James Nichols, "The Line of Liberty: Runaway Slaves
and Fugitive Peons in the Texas-Mexico Borderlands," *Western Historical
Quarterly* 44, no. 4 (Winter 2013): 413–433. For a rethinking of maroon
society in North America, see Steven Hahn, *The Political Worlds of Slavery
and Freedom* (Cambridge: Harvard University Press, 2009), 22–40.

12   **"runaway slaves":** Towns/Tauns appears in "Letter from the Secretary of
War, Communicating his Views in Relation to the Bill (S. 165) to Reimburse the State of Texas for Expenses Incurred in Repelling Invasions of
Indians and Mexicans," 45th Congress, 2nd Session, Senate Ex. Doc. 19,
156–157, 178, 189. It is possible that Towns escaped to Piedras Negras with
a female family member, as this document also shows a "Maria (Mary?)
Tauns," married to a Domingo San Miguel. "Modern Mexicans," *Chambers's Journal of Popular Literature, Science, and Arts* 389 (June 15, 1861): 380.

13   **"ran away":** Colin A. Palmer, *Slaves of the White God: Blacks in Mexico,
1570–1650* (Cambridge: Harvard University Press, 1976), 3–4; Patrick J.
Carroll, *Blacks in Colonial Veracruz: Race, Ethnicity, and Regional Development*, rev. ed. (Austin: University of Texas Press, 2001), 80–87; Dennis N.
Valdés, "The Decline of Slavery in Mexico," *Americas* 44, no. 2 (October
1987): 171; Herman L. Bennett, *Africans in Colonial Mexico: Absolutism,
Christianity, and Afro-Creole Consciousness, 1570–1640* (Bloomington: Indiana University Press, 2005), 1–2. Gonzalo Aguirre Beltrán, *La poblacíon
negra de México* (México: Fondo de Cultura Economica, 1972), 341, shows
how complicated racial categories became over time in New Spain. Runaway slave ad in *Gaceta de México* (Mexico City), April 22, 1788.

13   **elite households:** "A Census of Spanish Texas, December 31, 1783," in *Docu-
ments of Texas History*, edited by Ernest Wallace (Austin: Steck, 1963), 28;
Carlos Manuel Valdés and Ildefonso Dávila, *Esclavos negros en Saltillo, siglos
XVII–XIX* (Saltillo: Universidad Autónoma de Coahuila, 1989), 24, 82–84.

14   **everything but name:** Sean M. Kelley, *Los Brazos de Dios: A Plantation Society in the Texas Borderlands, 1821–1865* (Baton Rouge: Louisiana State University Press, 2010), 98–99.

15   **national consciousness:** Eric Van Young, *The Other Rebellion: Popular Violence, Ideology, and the Mexican Struggle for Independence, 1810–1821* (Stanford: Stanford University Press, 2001), 29–30; Ben Vinson III, "Fading from Memory: Historiographical Reflections on the Afro-Mexican Presence," *Review of Black Political Economy* 33, no. 1 (Summer 2005): 63–9; R. Douglas Cope, *The Limits of Racial Domination: Plebian Society in Colonial Mexico City, 1660–1720* (Madison: University of Wisconsin Press, 1994), 49–85.

15   **into Mexico:** David Brion Davis, *The Problem of Slavery in the Age of Emancipation* (New York: Alfred A. Knopf, 2014), 237; Walter Johnson, *River of Dark Dreams: Slavery and Empire in the Cotton Kingdom* (Cambridge: Harvard University Press, 2013), 151–54; Elizabeth Silverthorne, *Plantation Life in Texas* (College Station: Texas A&M University Press, 1986), 36. Computing relative values across time is a fraught process. The figure of over $50,000 comes by calculating the change in the Consumer Price Index from the 1850s. See <http://www.measuringworth.com> (accessed 8/15/15).

15   **Ellises' arrival:** Petty, *Victor Rose's History*, 33; *Texas Presbyterian* (Victoria), January 9, 1847; *Victoria Advocate*, November 14, 1850, and June 18, 1853.

16   **US owners:** *A Report and Treatise on Slavery and the Slavery Agitation*, 4.

16   **outer fringes:** Rachel St. John, *Line in the Sand: A History of the Western U.S.-Mexico Border* (Princeton: Princeton University Press, 2011), 40–43; Joseph A. Stout Jr., *Schemers and Dreamers: Filibustering in Mexico, 1848–1921* (Fort Worth: Texas Christian University Press, 2002), 7–8.

17   **"Gopher John":** Cazneau, *Eagle Pass*, 74–5, 145; Paulina del Moral, "Mascogos de Coahuila: Una cultura transfronteriza," in *Desierto y fronteras: El norte de México y otros contextos culturales*, edited by Hernán Salas Quintanal and Rafael Pérez-Taylor (Mexico: Playa y Valdés, 2004), 474–476.

17   **United States:** Guerrero was located some twenty-five miles to the south of Piedras Negras. Manuel Flores to el secretario de gobierno, March 20, 1851 <http://ahc.sfpcoahuila.gob.mx/ADMIN/uploads/Documentos/modulo11/C3F8E8.pdf> (accessed 2/9/15); *El Siglo Diez y Nueve* (Mexico City), November 12, 1855.

17   **"Negro or mulatto":** For African Americans stealing livestock, see Jesus Castillo to President of the Ayuntamiento of Guerrero, August 1, 1851 <http://ahc.sfpcoahuila.gob.mx/ADMIN/uploads/Documentos/modulo11/C8F1E1.pdf> (accessed 8/5/15). *Ledger and Texan* (San Antonio), October 10, 1857, features an ad describing a runaway slave caught riding a horse with a "Spanish brand." *El Siglo Diez y Nueve* (Mexico City), November 12, 1855; consul quoted in Jerry Thompson, *Cortina: Defending the Mexican Name in Texas* (College Station: Texas A&M University Press, 2007), 80.

18   **northern neighbor:** *Constitución Federal de los Estados Unidos Mexicanos, Febrero de 1857* <http://www.agn.gob.mx/constitucion1857/constitucion1857

.html> (accessed 7/30/11). The measure also represented a swipe at Mexico's onetime colonial ruler, Spain, which still controlled Cuba, where racialized slavery remained widespread.

18   **"Mexican territory"**: Raymond A. Hall, *An Ethnographic Study of Afro-Mexicans in Mexico's Gulf Coast: Fishing, Festivals, and Foodways* (Lewiston, NY: Edwin Mellen Press, 2008), 28; *El Siglo Diez y Nueve* (Mexico City), January 14, 1862.

18   **fugitive slaves**: H. M'Bride Pridgen, *Address to the People of Texas, on the Protection of Slave Property* (Austin: John Marshall, 1859), 10–13. For more on Pridgen's property holdings, see his ad in the *Victoria Advocate,* July 31, 1851.

19   **"fugitive slave"**: *Reports of the Committee of Investigation Sent in 1873 by the Mexican Government to the Frontier of Texas* (New York: Baker and Godwin, 1875), 19; *Liberator* (Boston, MA), May 29, 1863.

19   **in 1850**: *A Report and Treatise on Slavery and the Slavery Agitation,* 4; David Montejano, *Anglos and Mexicans in the Making of Texas, 1836–1986* (Austin: University of Texas Press, 1987), 31.

19   **indigenous ancestry**: Olmsted, *A Journey Through Texas,* 126, 164; *Standard* (San Antonio), October 21, 1854; Texian quoted in Arnoldo De León, *They Called Them Greasers: Anglo Attitudes Toward Mexicans in Texas, 1821–1900* (Austin: University of Texas Press, 1983), 16; Louise Pubols, *The Father of All: The de la Guerra Family, Power, and Patriarchy in Mexican California* (Berkeley: University of California Press, 2009), 15.

20   **different story**: 1860 US Federal Census, Slave Schedule, Victoria, Texas, 12, M653, NARA–Microfilm Publication; Sharfstein, *The Invisible Line*; Joshua D. Rothman, *Notorious in the Neighborhood: Sex and Families Across the Color Line in Virginia, 1787–1861* (Chapel Hill: University of North Carolina Press, 2003), 9–10, 204–234; Joe Mozingo, *The Fiddler on Pantico Run: An African Warrior, His White Descendants, a Search for Family* (New York: Free Press, 2012); Peter Arrell Browne, *Trichologia Mammalium; or, A Treatise on the Organization, Properties and Uses of Hair and Wool* (Philadelphia: J. H. Jones, 1853), 168.

20   **"to Mexico"**: *Texas State Gazette* (Austin), October 14, 1854, and May 26, 1855; *Colorado Citizen* (Columbus, TX), January 23, 1858; Olmsted, *A Journey Through Texas,* 65.

20   **"Mexican Greaser"**: *Texas Almanac* (Austin), May 23, 1863; *Texas State Gazette* (Austin), November 9, 1850; *Ledger and Texan* (San Antonio), August 4, 1853; *Nueces Valley* (Corpus Christi, TX), March 18, 1854. I am indebted to James Nichols for this last citation.

21   **"was a Mexican"**: *Texas State Gazette* (Austin), January 25, 1851; Kelley, *Los Brazos de Dios,* 48–51; Gerald Horne, *Race to Revolution: The United States and Cuba During Slavery and Jim Crow* (New York: Monthly Review Press, 2014), 14; Rawick, *The American Slave* 5:1, 149.

21   **Mexican identity instead**: *Ledger and Texan* (San Antonio), October 10, 1857. See also Walter Johnson, "The Slave Trader, the White Slave, and

the Politics of Racial Determination in the 1850s," *Journal of American History* 87, no. 1 (June 2000): 13–38.

22 **the state:** Wendell G. Addington, "Slave Insurrections in Texas," *Journal of Negro History* 35, no. 4 (October 1950): 432; *Texas State Gazette* (Austin), October 14, 1854, and May 26, 1855; Paul D. Lack, "Slavery and Vigilantism in Austin, Texas, 1840–1860," *Southwestern Historical Quarterly* 85, no. 1 (July 1981): 5–10; Montejano, *Anglos and Mexicans*, 28; *Colorado Citizen* (Columbus, TX), January 23, 1858.

22 **pain of death:** Addington, "Slave Insurrections," 414–416.

23 **the county:** Addington, "Slave Insurrections," 417; Herbert Aptheker, *Essays in the History of the American Negro* (New York: International Publishers, 1945), 56.

23 **Tejano communities:** Neil Foley, *White Scourge: Mexicans, Blacks, and Poor Whites in Texas Cotton Culture* (Berkeley: University of California Press, 1997), 1–4; Montejano, *Anglos and Mexicans*, 30–31.

24 **property holders:** Crimm, *De León*, 76–82; Ana Carolina Castillo Crimm, "Finding Their Way," in *Tejano Journey, 1770–1850*, edited by Gerald E. Poyo (Austin: University of Texas Press, 1996), 117.

24 **local surveyor:** Montejano, *Anglos and Mexicans*, 28; Crimm, *De León*, 190–192.

24 **"Doña":** 1860 US Federal Census, Victoria County, Texas, M653, NARA–Microfilm Publication, 15, 20, 25, 26, 32; Crimm, *De León*, 192, 210, 216, 221.

25 **none at all:** Edwin Hergesheimer, *Map Showing the Distribution of the Slave Population of the Southern States of the United States, Compiled from the Census of 1860*, engraved by Thomas Leonhardt (Washington, DC: GPO, 1861).

25 **three slaves:** Crimm, *De León*, 190; 1860 US Federal Census, Slave Schedule, Victoria, Texas, 4, 17, M653, NARA–Microfilm Publication. Slave censuses do not record family ties, but given the lack of an African American male in De La Garza's household, it is not impossible that the father of the young slaves was De La Garza himself.

25 **cotton fields:** 1860 US Federal Census, Agricultural Schedule, Victoria, Texas, "Selected U.S. Federal Census Non-Population Schedules, 1850–1880," online database (Provo, UT: Ancestry.com Operations, 2010); Petty, *Victor Rose's History*, 34–35; Brand Book, Victoria Town Records; Olmsted, *A Journey Through Texas*, 272.

26 **haciendas:** Herringshaw, *Herringshaw's American Blue-Book. . . 1919*, 171.

26 **the prairies:** Jones, *Texas Roots*, 140–141.

27 **cotton plants:** Jones, *Texas Roots*, 196–199; Olmsted, *A Journey Through Texas*, 42.

28 **Charles and William:** *New York Times*, July 27, 1866; 1860 U.S. Federal Census, Agricultural Census, Victoria, Texas, "Selected U.S. Federal Census Non-Population Schedules, 1850–1880 [Database On-Line]." The worth of the Weisigers' cotton harvest can be estimated as follows: 90 bales at 400 pounds apiece, with the wholesale price for cotton in 1860 11 cents

per pound wholesale equals $3,960. Adjusted for the changes in the Consumer Price Index, this sum comes to $116,000. Wholesale cotton prices from Susan B. Carter et al., eds., *Historical Statistics of the United States: Millennial Edition Online* (New York: Cambridge University Press, 2006), Table Cc205–266.

28 **slaves and Tejanos:** *Victoria Advocate*, July 20, 1848, and September 28, 1934.

28 **slave to nobility:** Susie Williams, interview by author, March 12, 2012.

29 **"Cotton Seed":** David Ames Wells, *The Year-book of Agriculture; or, The Annual of Agricultural Progress and Discovery for 1855 and 1856* (Philadelphia: Childs and Peterson, 1856), 232; *Texas Planter* (Brazoria), February 1, 1854; Mark Fiege, *The Republic of Nature: An Environmental History of the United States* (Seattle: University of Washington Press, 2012), 118–119; Sven Beckert, *Empire of Cotton: A Global History* (New York: Alfred A. Knopf, 2015), 115–116.

29 **continent together:** William Chambers and Robert Chambers, eds., *Information for the People* (London: W. R. Chambers, 1856), 2:320; Karl Jacoby, "Between North and South: The Alternative Borderlands of William H. Ellis and the African American Colony of 1895," in *Continental Crossroads: Remapping U.S.-Mexico Borderlands History* edited by Samuel Truett and Elliott Young (Durham: Duke University Press, 2004), 217; "Slavery Extension," *DeBow's Review* 15, no. 1 (July 1853): 6, 11.

29 **"our lands":** "Difficulties on Southwestern Frontier," 36th Congress, 1st Session, House of Representative Ex. Doc. No. 52, 72, 81.

30 **National Guard:** *Texas State Gazette* (Austin), June 8, 1861; *Ledger and Texan* (San Antonio), November 19, 1859, December 10, 1859, March 31, 1860; *Navarro Express* (Corsicana, TX), April 7, 1860; Benjamin Heber Johnson, *Revolution in Texas: How a Forgotten Rebellion and Its Bloody Suppression Turned Mexicans into Americans* (New Haven: Yale University Press, 2003), 23–25.

31 **"territory of Mexico":** "A Declaration of the Causes which Impel the State of Texas to Secede from the Federal Union" <http://avalon.law.yale.edu/19th_century/csa_texsec.asp> (accessed 9/13/11).

31 **war camp:** Crimm, *De León*, 230–231; Weisiger, *The Weisiger Family*, 15; Petty, *Victor Rose's History*, 44, 51; *Victoria Advocate*, October 1, 1864.

31 **other supplies:** Ronnie C. Tyler, "Cotton on the Border, 1861–1865," *Southwestern Historical Quarterly* 73, no. 4 (April 1970): 456; *Texas Almanac* (Austin), May 23, 1863; Mario Cerutti and Miguel González Quiroga, "Guerra y comercio en torno al Río Bravo (1855–1867). Línea fronteriza, espacio económico común," *Historia Mexicana* (October–December 1990): 217–97, 239; Miguel A. González Quiroga, "La puerta de México: Los comerciantes texanos y el noreste mexicano, 1850–1880," *Estudios Sociológicos* 11, no. 31 (January–April 1993): 218–219; *El Siglo Diez y Nueve* (Mexico City), December 7, 1862; David Montejano, "Mexican Merchants and Teamsters on the Texas Cotton Road, 1862–1865," in *Mexico and Mexicans in the Making of the United States*, edited by John Tutino (Austin: University of Texas Press, 2012), 141–170.

32   **into Matamoros:** Robert W. Delaney, "Matamoros, Port for Texas During
       the Civil War," *Southwestern Historical Quarterly* 58, no. 4 (April 1955):
       476–477; Thompson, *Cortina*, 106–112, 127–132.

33   **in Mexico?:** Steven Hahn, *A Nation Under Our Feet: Black Political Struggles
       in the Rural South from Slavery to the Great Migration* (Cambridge: Harvard
       University Press, 2003), 52.

2: JUNETEENTH

34   **former slaves:** Gregory P. Downs, *After Appomattox: Military Occupation
       and the Ends of War* (Cambridge: Harvard University Press, 2015), 50–51;
       Eric Foner, *Reconstruction: America's Unfinished Revolution, 1863–1877* (New
       York: Harper and Row, 1988), 77–78.

35   **imperial Mexico:** *Victoria Advocate*, October 17, 1864; Carl H. Moneyhon,
       Texas After the Civil War: The Struggle of Reconstruction (College Station:
       Texas A&M University Press, 2004), 12; Carrigan, *The Making of a Lynch-
       ing Culture*, 117; Brad R. Clampitt, "The Breakup: The Collapse of the
       Confederate Trans-Mississippi Army in Texas, 1865," *Southwestern His-
       torical Quarterly* 108, no. 4 (2005): 503–507, 522.

35   **US advance:** Jeffrey William Hunt, *The Last Battle of the Civil War: Palmetto
       Ranch* (Austin: University of Texas Press, 2002); Phillip Thomas Tucker,
       The Final Fury: Palmito Ranch, the Last Battle of the Civil War (Mechanics-
       burg, PA: Stackpole Books, 2001), 58, 70, 73, 83.

36   **"slaves are free":** Hunt, *Last Battle of the Civil War*, 126–127, 138–142;
       Randolph B. Campbell, "The End of Slavery in Texas: A Research Note,"
       Southwestern Historical Quarterly, 88, no. 1 (July 1984): 71.

36   **the policy:** *Houston Telegraph*, July 14, 1865; Diane Neal and Thomas W.
       Kremm, "What Shall We Do with the Negro? The Freedman's Bureau
       in Texas," *East Texas Historical Journal* 27, no. 2 (1989): 23–24; Rebecca
       A. Kosary, "'Wantonly Maltreated and Slain, Simply Because They Are
       Free': Racial Violence During Reconstruction in South Texas," in *African
       Americans in South Texas History*, edited by Bruce A. Glasrud (College Sta-
       tion: Texas A&M Press, 2011), 70; Downs, *After Appomattox*, 27.

37   **"they misbehaved":** Newspaper quoted in William L. Richter, *The Army
       in Texas During Reconstruction, 1865–1870* (College Station: Texas A&M
       University Press, 1987), 25; James N. Leiker, *Racial Borders: Black Soldiers
       Along the Rio Grande* (College Station: Texas A&M University Press, 2002),
       28; Shaw quoted in Charles D. Spurlin, "The World Turned Upside Down?
       The Military Occupation of Victoria and Calhoun Counties, 1865–1867,"
       in *Still the Arena of Civil War: Violence and Turmoil in Reconstruction Texas,
       1865–1874*, edited by Kenneth W. Howell (Denton: University of North
       Texas Press, 2012), 116; David Work, "United States Colored Troops in
       Texas During Reconstruction, 1865–1867," *Southwestern Historical Quar-*

terly 109, no. 3 (January 2006): 346; *Flake's Bulletin* (Galveston, TX), July 6, 1868.

37 **upon the town:** Codes quoted in Sharon H. Smith, "Victoria County, Texas, 1824–1870" (master's thesis, Southwest Texas State University, 1998), 91–92.

38 **"obliterate it":** *The Constitution, as Amended, and Ordinances of the Convention of 1866* (Austin: Joseph Walker, 1866), 6; for voting in Victoria in 1866, see Petty, *Victor Rose's History*, 63; Barry A. Crouch, "'All the Vile Passions': The Texas Black Code of 1866," *Southwestern Historical Quarterly* 97, no. 1 (July 1993): 34; *Report of the Joint Committee on Reconstruction, at the First Session of the Thirty-Ninth Congress* (Washington, DC: GPO, 1866), 95.

38 **"and elsewhere":** Olmsted, *A Journey Through Texas,*123; *Report of the Joint Committee on Reconstruction, at the First Session of the Thirty-Ninth Congress,* 88–89; Barry A. Crouch, "A Spirit of Lawlessness: White Violence, Texas Blacks, 1865–1868," in Crouch, *The Dance of Freedom: Texas African Americans During Reconstruction* (Austin: University of Texas Press, 2007), 95–117. By one count, 373 freedmen were killed in Texas between 1865 and 1868. Carrigan, *The Making of a Lynching Culture*, 116.

38 **"personal injury":** Report of Captain Edward Miller, January 11, 1867, and Report of William Neely, October 1868 in Crouch Collection, Box 8-B, Victoria Regional History Center, Victoria College/UH–Victoria Library.

39 **the killer:** Report of Captain Edward Miller, January 11, 1867, in Crouch Collection, Box 8-B, Victoria Regional History Center, Victoria College/UH–Victoria Library.

39 **federal oversight:** *Roll of Honor: Names of Soldiers Who Died in Defense of the American Union, Interred in the Eastern District of Texas; Central District of Texas; Rio Grande District, Department of Texas; Camp Ford, Tyler Texas; and Corpus Christi, Texas.* Quartermaster General's Office, General Order No. 32 (Washington, DC: GPO, 1866), 9–10; Robert W. Shook, *Caminos y Entradas: Spanish Legacy of Victoria County and the Coastal Bend, 1689–1890* (Victoria, TX: Victoria County Heritage Department, 2007), 452; Terry Hammonds, *Historic Victoria: An Illustrated History* (San Antonio: Historical Publishing Network, 1999), 27–28; Smith, "Victoria County, Texas, 1824–1870," 95; Petty, *Victor Rose's History*, 56–58.

40 **federal authorities:** The numbers of black legislators come from the appendix in Barry A. Crouch, "Hesitant Recognition: Texas Black Politicians, 1865–1900," in Crouch, *The Dance of Freedom*, 214–223; Smith, "Victoria County, Texas, 1824–1870," 86, 92. Only 11 percent of whites and 15 percent of ethnic Mexicans possessed no property of value in 1870. James M. Smallwood, *The Feud That Wasn't: The Taylor Ring, Bill Sutton, John Wesley Hardin, and Violence in Texas* (College Station: Texas A&M University Press, 2008), 30, 52; Kosary, "'Wantonly Maltreated and Slain,'" 72.

40 **"prostrate ever since":** J. M. Morse and Charles H. Porter to Governor of Texas, May 10, 1870, in Crouch Collection, Box 31-B, Victoria Regional

History Center, Victoria College/UH–Victoria Library. For other examples of violence against African Americans in Victoria at this time, see William L. Richter, *The Army in Texas During Reconstruction, 1865–1870* (College Station: Texas A&M University Press, 1987), 43.

41 **avoid arrest:** *Southern Intelligencer* (Austin), May 17, 1866; *Texas Countryman* (Belville), May 18, 1866; Petty, *Victor Rose's History,* 213; *Victoria Advocate,* September 28, 1934; Last Will and Testament of Joseph Weisiger, April 14, 1867; Item 7, File 400, Box 21, Sidney R. Weisiger Papers, Victoria Regional History Center, Victoria College/UH–Victoria Library.

41 **African Americans:** Susie Williams and Joan Williams, interview by author, October 2011. For a discussion of kinship and slavery, see Hahn, *A Nation Under Our Feet,* 17–18.

42 *juarista* **forces:** Grant quoted in Hunt, *The Last Battle of the Civil War,* 27; Jan Bazant, "From Independence to the Liberal Republic, 1821–1867," in *Mexico Since Independence,* edited by Leslie Bethell (Cambridge: Cambridge University Press, 1991), 46; Philip Sheridan, *Personal Memoirs,* vol. 2 (New York: D. Appleton, 1902), 227; Todd W. Wahlstrom, *The Southern Exodus to Mexico: Migration Across the Borderlands After the American Civil War* (Lincoln: University of Nebraska Press, 2015), 2–3; Robert Ryal Miller, "Arms Across the Border: United States Aid to Juárez During the French Intervention in Mexico," *Transactions of the American Philosophical Society* 63, no. 6 (December 1973): 7, 13, 37–41.

42 **Mexico as well:** Wahlstrom, *The Southern Exodus to Mexico,* 27–28; Andrew Rolle, *The Lost Cause: The Confederate Exodus to Mexico* (Norman: University of Oklahoma Press, 1965), 103–104; George D. Harmon, "Confederate Migration to Mexico," *Hispanic American Historical Review* 17, no. 4 (November 1937): 459, 462, 466, 469; *Monitor Republicano* (Mexico City), July 30, 1867. "New Virginia" came to be known as "Carlota" for Maximilian's wife.

43 **"leave Mexico":** *Report of the Joint Committee on Reconstruction, at the First Session of the Thirty-Ninth Congress,* 45; Carl Coke Rister, "Carlota, a Confederate Colony in Mexico," *Journal of Southern History* 11, no. 1 (February 1945): 35; Southerner quoted in Rolle, *The Lost Cause,* 9; Ex-Confederate quoted in Thomas David Schoonover, *Dollars over Dominion: The Triumph of Liberalism in Mexican–United States Relations, 1861–1867* (Baton Rouge: Louisiana State University Press, 1978), 195.

43 **"good government":** *Report of the Joint Committee on Reconstruction, at the First Session of the Thirty-Ninth Congress,* 95; John Henninger Reagan, *Memoirs, with Special Reference to Secession and the Civil War* (New York and Chicago: Neale Publishing, 1906), 290.

44 **"Republican institutions":** Thomas F. Bayard in *The Congressional Globe: Containing Speeches, Reports, and the Laws of the Second Session Forty-Second Congress* (Washington, DC: Congressional Globe, 1872), Part 6, Appendix, 356; "Restoration of Self-Government in the South," *Old Guard* 4 (July

1866): 424. For more on the "mongrel Mexico" discourse, see Benjamin H. Johnson, "The Cosmic Race in Texas: Racial Fusion, White Supremacy, and Civil Rights Politics," *Journal of American History* 98, no. 2 (September 2011): 408; and Gregory P. Downs, "The Mexicanization of American Politics: The United States' Transnational Path from Civil War to Stabilization," *American Historical Review* 117, no. 2 (April 2012): 387–409.

44   **colonial era:** Friedrich Katz, "The Liberal Republic and the Porfiriato, 1867–1910," in *Mexico Since Independence*, edited by Leslie Bethell (Cambridge: Cambridge University Press, 1991), 49–50.

44   **"races and *castas*":** *El Siglo Diez y Nueve* (Mexico City), January 13, 1868; May 20, 1863. See also *El Siglo Diez y Nueve*, November 10, 1867; *El Monitor Republicano* (Mexico City), July 2, July 27, 1867.

45   **putative grandfather:** 1870 Federal Census, Victoria, Texas, M593, 248A; 1880 Federal Census, Victoria, Texas, T9, 172C, NARA–Microfilm Publication.

45   **growing family:** 1870 U.S. Federal Census, Victoria, Texas, M593, 248A; 1880 U.S. Federal Census, Victoria, Texas, T9, 172C, NARA–Microfilm Publication.

46   **uncertain world:** Dillman Mantz deed to Charles Ellis and William Ellis, August 28, 1871, 169, Victoria Town Records; James M. Smallwood, *Time of Hope, Time of Despair: Black Texans During Reconstruction* (Port Washington, NY: Kennikat Press, 1981), 55; Keith J. Volanto, "James E. Youngblood: Race, Family, and Farm Ownership in Jim Crow Texas," in *Beyond Forty Acres and a Mule: African American Landowning Families Since Reconstruction*, edited by Debra A. Reid and Evan P. Bennett (Gainesville: University Press of Florida, 2012), 63–82. For more on lot prices in Victoria at this time, see Sara R. Massey, "After Emancipation: Cologne, Texas," in *African Americans in South Texas History*, edited by Bruce A. Glasrud (College Station: Texas A&M Press, 2011), 86.

46   **his sisters:** 1880 U.S. Federal Census, Victoria, Texas, T9, 172C, NARA–Microfilm Publication.

46   **family members:** 1880 U.S. Federal Census, Indianola, Texas, T9, 308A; Petty, *Victor Rose's History*, 74.

47   **Constitution Square:** *Baltimore Sun*, July 25, 1904; Smith, "Victoria County, Texas, 1824–1870," 121; Petty, *Victor Rose's History*, 59, 74, 76–79; Robert W. Shook and Charles D. Spurlin, *Victoria: A Pictorial History* (Norfolk, VA: Donning, 1985), 40–41.

47   **impact on him:** Susie Williams and Joan Williams, interview by author, October 2011.

48   **"cattle ranches":** Alwyn Barr, "The Texas 'Black Uprising' Scare of 1883," *Phylon* 41, no. 2 (1980): 181; Hammonds, *Historic Victoria*, 19–20; Petty, *Victor Rose's History*, 70; Herringshaw, *Herringshaw's American Blue-Book . . . 1919*, 171; Susie Williams, interview by author, March 12, 2012. The use of children as farm laborers dated from the very beginnings of Emancipa-

tion. As an agent in Victoria for the Freedman's Bureau reported in 1868, "Many scholars are kept from day school to pick cotton." Report of William J. Neely, August 1868, Crouch Collection, Box 8-B, Victoria Regional History Center, Victoria College/UH–Victoria Library.

48   **new life:** Rawick, *The American Slave* 4:100; Kathleen Pfeiffer, *Race Passing and American Individualism* (Amherst: University of Massachusetts Press, 2003), 7.

49   **American life:** Charles F. Robinson II, "Legislated Love in the Lone Star State: Texas and Miscegenation," *Southwestern Historical Quarterly* 108, no. 1 (July 2004): 68, 82; Steven W. Engerrand, "Black and Mulatto Mobility and Stability in Dallas, Texas, 1880–1910," *Phylon* 39, no. 3 (1978): 208–211; Arthé A. Anthony, "'Lost Boundaries': Racial Passing and Poverty in Segregated New Orleans," *Louisiana History* 36, no. 3 (Summer 1995): 291–312; Susan E. Dollar, "Ethnicity and Jim Crow: The Americanization of Louisiana's Creoles," in *Louisiana Beyond Black and White: New Interpretations of Twentieth-Century Race and Race Relations*, edited by Michael S. Martin (Lafayette: University of Louisiana at Lafayette Press, 2011), 1–16; Verna M. Keith and Cedric Herring, "Skin Tone and Stratification in the Black Community," *American Journal of Sociology* 97, no. 3 (November 1991): 760–778.

50   **as slaves:** Moneyhon, *Texas After the Civil War*, 188–9; Randolph B. Campbell, *Grass-roots Reconstruction in Texas, 1865–1880* (Baton Rouge: Louisiana State University Press, 1998), 22–23; Hammonds, *Historic Victoria*, 15; Petty, *Victor Rose's History*, 54.

50   **antebellum period:** Petty, *Victor Rose's History*, 74; *Indianola Weekly Bulletin*, April 25, 1871; *Victoria Advocate*, September 21, 1876.

50   **international boundary:** *Victoria Advocate*, October 5, 1876, October 12, 1876, August 9, 1884.

51   **in 1872:** Michael G. Webster, "Intrigue on the Rio Grande: The Rio Bravo Affair, 1875," *Southwestern Historical Quarterly* 74, no. 2 (October 1970): 150; *Victoria Advocate*, October 12, 1876; *New York Times*, August 10, 1871; *El Siglo Diez y Nueve* (Mexico City), April 25, 1872.

51   **US citizens:** Lars Schoultz, *Beneath the United States: A History of U.S. Policy Toward Latin America* (Cambridge: Harvard University Press, 1998), 236; "Papers Relating to the Foreign Relations of the United States, 1877," 45th Congress, 2nd Session, House Ex. Doc. 1, 413–415; Thompson, *Cortina*, 231; Charles W. Hackett, "The Recognition of the Díaz Government by the United States," *Southwestern Historical Quarterly* 28, no. 1 (July 1924): 46; Robert Wooster, "The Army and the Politics of Expansion: Texas and the Southwestern Borderlands, 1870–1886," *Southwestern Historical Quarterly* 93, no. 2 (October 1989): 151–167.

52   **"her territory":** Katz, "The Liberal Republic and the Porfiriato, 1867–1910," 68–70; "Papers Relating to the Foreign Relations of the United States, 1877," 417–418.

52   **if necessary:** Romero quoted in Richard J. Salvucci, "The Origins and

Progress of U.S.-Mexican Trade, 1825–1884: 'Hoc Opus, Hic Labor Est,' "
Hispanic American Historical Review 71, no. 4 (November 1991): 719.

53 **Anglo-America:** Walter D. Mignolo, *The Idea of Latin America* (Malden, MA: Blackwell Publishing, 2005), 57–61.

53 **"imperious necessities":** John H. Coatsworth, *Growth Against Development: The Economic Impact of Railroads in Porfirian Mexico* (Dekalb: Northern Illinois University Press, 1981), 33–46; Richard White, *Railroaded: The Transcontinentals and the Making of Modern America* (New York: W. W. Norton, 2011), 203–204, 215–216; David M. Pletcher, *Rails, Mines, and Progress: Seven American Promoters in Mexico, 1867–1911* (Ithaca: Cornell University Press, 1958), 24; Thompson, *Cortina*, 235–241; Mora-Torres, *The Making of the Mexican Border*, 58. Díaz's plans built on earlier Mexican calls to emulate US land and immigration policies. David K. Burden, "Reform Before *La Reforma*: Liberals, Conservatives and the Debate over Immigration, 1846–1855," *Mexican Studies/Estudios Mexicanos* 23, no. 2 (Summer 2007): 287.

54 **colonial period:** "Papers Relating to the Foreign Relations of the United States, 1879," 46th Congress, 2nd Session, House Ex. Doc. 1, pt 1, 798; *La Libertad* (Mexico City), March 4, 1882; Evelyne Sanchez-Guillermo, "Nacionalismo y racismo en el México decimonónico: Nuevos enfoques, nuevos resultados," *Nuevo Mundo/Mundos Nuevos* (2007).

54 **"the Indian":** Laura Muñoz Mata, "La migración afroantillana a México: Una historia olvidada," *Del Caribe* 24 (1994): 124–130; Laura Muñoz Mata, "Presencia afrocaribeña en Veracruz: La inmigración jamaicana en las postrimerías del siglo XIX," *Sotavento* 3 (1997–1998): 73–88; *La Libertad* (Mexico City), March 4, March 16, 1882; *El Monitor* (Mexico City), March 10, 1882; *El Nacional* quoted in *El Monitor*, March 8, 1882.

55 **"law to them":** *El Monitor* (Mexico City), February 17, 1882; *La Patria* (Mexico City), March 1, March 5, April 7, 1882; *La Voz de México* (Mexico City), April 5, 1882; Moisés González Navarro, *Los extranjeros en México y los mexicanos en el extranjero, 1821–1970* (México: Colegio de México, 1994), 185.

55 **in the country:** *La Libertad* (Mexico City), March 4, 1882; Agustín F. Basave Benítez, *México mestizo: Análisis del nacionalismo mexicano en torno a la mestizofilia de Andrés Molina Enríquez* (Mexico City: Fondo de Cultura Económica, 1992), 25–28; Edward Telles, *Pigmentocracies: Ethnicity, Race, and Color in Latin America* (Chapel Hill: University of North Carolina Press, 2014), 41; Matías Romero, "Mexico," *Journal of the American Geographical Society of New York* 28, no. 4 (1896): 348; Marisela Jiménez Ramos, "Black Mexico: Nineteenth-Century Discourses of Race and Nation" (Ph.D. dissertation, Brown University, May 2009), 81–82.

56 **the railroads:** *New York Herald*, July 20, 1882; A. W. Spaight, Texas Commissioner of Insurance, Statistics, and History, *The Resources, Soil, and Climate of Texas* (Galveston: A. H. Belo, 1882), 322; Jesús Cuevas quoted in Robert W. Randall, "Mexico's Pre-Revolutionary Reckoning with Railroads," *Americas* 42, no. 1 (July 1985): 9; José Margati, *A Trip to the City of Mexico* (Boston:

Putnam, Messervy, 1885), 7; William Cronon, *Nature's Metropolis: Chicago and the Great West* (New York: W. W. Norton, 1991), 79–81.

57 **African American community:** Grace Elizabeth Hale, *Making Whiteness: The Culture of Segregation in the South, 1890–1940* (New York: Pantheon Books, 1998), 128; Blair L. M. Kelley, *Right to Ride: Streetcar Boycotts and African American Citizenship in the Era of Plessy v. Ferguson* (Chapel Hill: University of North Carolina Press, 2010); *Houck v. Southern Pacific Railway*, in *Federal Reporter: Cases Argued and Determined in the Circuit and District Courts of the United States* (May–July, 1889) 38: 226–227; *Galveston Daily News*, March 2, 1887; Barbara Young Welke, *Recasting American Liberty: Gender, Race, Law, and the Railroad Revolution, 1865–1920* (New York: Cambridge University Press, 2001), 269–270, 283; Janice L. Sumler-Edmond, "Lola and Leon Houck Versus the Southern Pacific Railway Company," in *African Americans in South Texas History*, edited by Bruce A. Glasrud (College Station: Texas A&M Press, 2011), 133–150.

57 **Southern Pacific Railway:** *Houck v. Southern Pacific Railway*, 227–229; Kelley, *Right to Ride*, 46–47.

57 **Houck's entry:** *Houck v. Southern Pacific Railway*, 229–230; *Galveston Daily News*, December 13, 1888; *Fort Worth Daily Gazette*, December 12, 1888; *Waco Evening News*, December 15, 1888.

58 **racial order:** Alwyn Barr, *Black Texans: A History of African Americans in Texas, 1528–1995*, 2nd ed. (Norman: University of Oklahoma Press, 1996), 82.

59 **"will not":** *Chicago Herald*, August 17, 1891; Langston Hughes, *The Big Sea: An Autobiography* (New York: Hill and Wang, 1993 [1940]), 50–51; James Weldon Johnson, *Along This Way: The Autobiography of James Weldon Johnson* (New York: Viking Press, 1933), 87–88; Hughes, "Fooling Our White Folks," 40.

60 **Ellis did:** Spaight, *Resources, Soil, and Climate of Texas*, 321.

60 **consumer economy:** *Victoria Advocate*, September 25, 1923, August 10, 1876, December 9, 1882; Graham Davis, *Land! Irish Pioneers in Mexican and Revolutionary Texas* (College Station: Texas A&M University Press, 2002), 189–190; "History City of Victoria City Council and City Managers, 1839–2012," <https://www2.victoriatx.org/pdfs/historyofcouncil.pdf> (accessed 12/1/14). For more on McNamara, see 1880 US Federal Census, Victoria, Texas, T9, 141A.

60 **"thousand dollars":** "An American Promoter in Abyssinia," *World's Work* 7, no. 5 (March 1904): 99–100.

61 **full-time resident:** *Morrison and Fourmy's General Directory of the City of San Antonio, 1885–86*, 129. Page 299 lists a "George Starnes" who was a "colored" physician and surgeon; this was doubtless a misspelling of Greene Starnes's name. *Morrison and Fourmy's General Directory of the City of San Antonio, 1887–88*, 133; *Morrison and Fourmy's General Directory of the City of San Antonio, 1889–90*, 150–151.

62 **negotiate deals:** *New York Sun*, October 4, 1903; *Washington Times*, June

27, 1904; *Morrison and Fourmy's General Directory of the City of San Antonio, 1889–90*, 150–151. *H. H. Childers v. The State*, 30 Tex. Ct. App. 160; 16 S.W. 903; 1891 Tex. Crim. App. LEXIS 68. Docia Schultz Williams, *The History and Mystery of the Menger Hotel* (Plano, TX: Republic of Texas Press, 2000), 183–185.

62 **community reputation:** Commentator quoted in Ariela J. Gross, *What Blood Won't Tell: A History of Race on Trial in America* (Cambridge: Harvard University Press, 2008), 89.

63 **"without interference":** Gross, *What Blood Won't Tell*, 63–70; passer quoted in Earl Lewis and Heidi Ardizzone, *Love on Trial: An American Scandal in Black and White* (New York: W. W. Norton, 2001), 22–23; Baldwin, *From Negro to Caucasian*, 36.

63 **persona became:** Steven Ruggles, J. Trent Alexander, Katie Genadek, Ronald Goeken, Matthew B. Schroeder, and Matthew Sobek, *Integrated Public Use Microdata Series: Version 5.0*, machine-readable database (Minneapolis, MN: Minnesota Population Center, 2010).

63 **Mexico and Cuba:** Natalia Molina, "The Long Arc of Dispossession: Racial Capitalism and Contested Notions of Citizenship in the U.S.-Mexico Borderlands in the Early Twentieth Century," *Western Historical Quarterly* 45, no. 4 (Winter 2014): 431–447.

64 **San Antonio:** *Morrison and Fourmy's General Directory of the City of San Antonio, 1889–90*, 353; *Johnson and Chapman's General Directory of the City of San Antonio for the Year 1891* (San Antonio: Dodd, Johnson, 1890), 162, 368; *Jules A. Appler's General Directory of the City of San Antonio, 1895–96* (San Antonio: Jules A. Appler, 1895), 548.

3: MILITARY PLAZA

67 **border in Chihuahua:** González Quiroga, "La puerta de México," 216, 222; Raúl Ramos, *Beyond the Alamo: Forging Mexican Ethnicity in San Antonio, 1821–1861* (Chapel Hill: University of North Carolina Press, 2008), 17–18; Gerald E. Poyo, "Community and Autonomy," in Gerald E. Poyo, ed., *Tejano Journey, 1770–1850* (Austin: University of Texas Press, 1996), 2; Caroline Remy, "Hispanic-Mexican San Antonio: 1836–1861," *Southwestern Historical Quarterly* 71, no. 4 (April 1968): 564–565; Santiago Tafolla, *A Life Crossing Borders: Memoir of a Mexican-American Confederate*, trans. Fidel L. Tafolla (Houston: Arte Público, 2010), 38–39.

67 **"common language":** Quoted in Montejano, *Anglos and Mexicans*, 35–36. Immigrants from Mexico represented the largest immigrant group in Bexar County in the 1870s. Mason, *African Americans and Race Relations in San Antonio*, 25; Miguel A. González Quiroga, "Mexicanos in Texas During the Civil War," in *Mexican Americans in Texas History*, edited by

Emilio Zamora, Cynthia Orozco, and Rodolfo Rocha (Austin: Texas State Historical Association, 2000), 59–60.

68 **"the countries":** Edward King, *The Great South: A Record of Journeys in Louisiana, Texas, the Indian Territory, Missouri, Arkansas, Mississippi, Alabama, Georgia, Florida, South Carolina, North Carolina, Kentucky, Tennessee, Virginia, West Virginia, and Maryland* (Hartford, CT: American Publishing, 1875), 161; William Corner, *San Antonio de Bexar: A Guide and History* (San Antonio: Bainbridge and Corner, 1890), 24; Montejano, *Anglos and Mexicans*, 35–36.

68 **Tejano physicians:** Colin M. MacLachlan and William H. Beezley, *El Gran Pueblo: A History of Greater Mexico*, 3rd ed. (Upper Saddle River, NJ: Prentice Hall, 2004), 216–217; see the list of doctors in *Morrison and Fourmy's General Directory of the City of San Antonio, 1887–88*, 385.

69 **his father:** Larry P. Knight, "Defending the Unnecessary: Slavery in San Antonio in the 1850s," in Glasrud, ed., *African Americans in South Texas History*, 37; *Jules A. Appler's General Directory of the City of San Antonio, 1895–6*, 253–4; *Jules A. Appler's General Directory of the City of San Antonio, 1897–8*, 249; *Jules A. Appler's General Directory of the City of San Antonio, 1899–1900*, 241. The upward mobility rate was 22 percent for European immigrants, 20 percent for native-born whites, 11 percent for Mexican Americans, and only 6 percent for African Americans. Mason, *African Americans and Race Relations in San Antonio*, 24, 50–51.

69 **religious groups:** Hahn, *A Nation Under Our Feet*, 177–181.

69 **Freedmen's Bureau:** Douglas Hales, *A Southern Family in White and Black: The Cuneys of Texas* (College Station: Texas A&M University Press, 2003), 3–12, 15.

70 **nineteenth century:** Ernest Obadele-Starks, "Black Labor, the Black Middle Class, and Organized Protest Along the Upper Texas Gulf Coast, 1883–1945," *Southwestern Historical Quarterly* 103, no. 1 (July 1999): 54–55; Hales, *A Southern Family in White and Black*, 23–25; *Dallas Morning News*, August 7, 1889; *St. Louis Republic*, July 22, 1889.

70 **Democratic Party:** Hales, *A Southern Family in White and Black*, 52, 75; *White Republican* (San Antonio), September 2, September 10, September 17, November 12, 1890.

71 **Committee on Resolutions:** *Galveston Daily News*, April 15, September 21, 1888.

71 **"their way":** *Galveston Daily News*, April 7, 1892.

71 **Republican assemblies:** *Dallas Morning News*, April 10, 1892; *Galveston Daily News*, September 18, October 14, 1892; *Daily Herald* (Brownsville, TX), September 19, 1892.

72 **"sunny clime":** *San Antonio Daily Light*, April 2, 1896, February 29, 1892; *Galveston Daily News*, October 14, 1892.

72 **the nuptials:** Maud Cuney-Hare, *Norris Wright Cuney: A Tribune of the Black People* (New York: G. K. Hall, 1995 [1913]), 61, 154, 227; Willard B. Gatewood, *Aristocrats of Color: The Black Elite, 1880–1920* (Bloomington:

Indiana University Press, 1991), 181–182; *Washington Bee* (Washington, DC), October 1, 1898.

73 **from Beeville:** *Southern Mercury* (Dallas, TX), July 14, 1892, bemoans the lack of a strong Populist presence in Victoria. For more on Populism in Texas, see Hales, *A Southern Family in White and Black*, 84; Lawrence D. Rice, *The Negro in Texas, 1874–1900* (Baton Rouge: Louisiana State University Press, 1971), 68–85; and Omar H. Ali, *In the Lion's Mouth: Black Populism in the New South, 1886–1900* (Jackson: University Press of Mississippi, 2010), 98–102.

73 **in Texas:** Stephen Ward Angell, *Bishop Henry McNeal Turner and African-American Religion in the South* (Knoxville: University of Tennessee Press, 1992), 7; M. M. Ponton, *Life and Times of Henry M. Turner* (New York: Negro Universities Press, 1970 [1917]), 33–36.

74 **"own creation":** Charles Spencer Smith, *A History of the African Methodist Episcopal Church* (New York: Johnson Reprint, 1968 [1922]), 47; Hahn, *A Nation Under Our Feet*, 182; Kenneth C. Barnes, *Journey of Hope: The Back-to-Africa Movement in Arkansas in the Late 1800s* (Chapel Hill: University of North Carolina Press, 2004), 42–43; *Christian Recorder* (Philadelphia, PA), February 22, 1883.

74 **African Americans:** Henry McNeal Turner, *A Speech on the Present Duties and Future Destiny of the Negro Race* (N.p.: Published by the Lyceum, 1872); Henry McNeal Turner, *Civil Rights: The Outrage of the Supreme Court of the United States upon the Black Man* (Philadelphia: AME Church, 1889); *Galveston Daily News*, June 10, 1887; Hales, *A Southern Family in White and Black*, 88. For a copy of the contract that Ellis and Ferguson signed with Pacheco, see *El Monitor Republicano* (Mexico City), November 14, 1889. For a contemporary description of Pacheco, see Margati, *A Trip to the City of Mexico*, 67.

75 **"the front":** Eric Foner, *The Fiery Trial: Abraham Lincoln and American Slavery* (New York: W. W. Norton, 2010), 185; Thomas Schoonover, "Misconstrued Mission: Expansionism and Black Colonization in Mexico and Central America During the Civil War," *Pacific Historical Review* 49, no. 4 (November 1980): 607–620; N. Andrew N. Cleven, "Some Plans for Colonizing Liberated Negro Slaves in Hispanic America," *Journal of Negro History* 11, no. 1 (January 1926): 35–49; Michael Vorenberg, "Abraham Lincoln and the Politics of Black Colonization," *Journal of the Abraham Lincoln Association* 14, no. 2 (Summer 1993): 22–45; Cuney-Hare, *Norris Wright Cuney*, 31.

75 **"self-sustaining farmers":** *El Monitor Republicano* (Mexico City), November 14, 1889; *El Tiempo* (Mexico City), July 12, 1889; *Galveston Daily News*, November 13, 1889.

76 **"native Mexicans":** W. H. Ellis to Porfirio Díaz, October 16, 1889 in Colección Porfirio Díaz, Legajo 14, Docs. 010444–010450; *Galveston Daily News*, November 13, 1889. For more on African American ideas of cotton cultivation, see Andrew Zimmerman, *Alabama in Africa: Booker T. Washington, the German Empire, and the Globalization of the New South* (Princeton: Princeton University Press, 2010), 49–51.

76   **"Negro rule":** *Chicago Herald,* February 24, 1890; Cuney-Hare, *Norris Wright Cuney,* 84–91.

77   **so appealing:** Alwyn Barr, *Reconstruction to Reform: Texas Politics, 1876–1906* (Dallas: Southern Methodist University Press, 2000 [1971]), 197–198; Rice, *The Negro in Texas,* 121–122, 204; *Galveston Daily News,* October 14, 1889; Cuney-Hare, *Norris Wright Cuney,* 84–91; Hales, *A Southern Family in White and Black,* 70–72; Carlyle McKinley, *An Appeal to Pharoah: The Negro Problem, and Its Radical Solution* (New York: Fords, Howard and Hulbert, 1890), 169; *Christian Recorder* (Philadelphia, PA), October 1, 1891; *El Monitor Republicano* (Mexico City), July 16, 1889. Cuney would come to Ferguson's aid after the riots.

77   **"the world":** *El Siglo Diez y Nueve* (Mexico City), October 22, 1881.

78   **own accord:** *Emigration and Immigration: Reports of the Consular Officers of the United States* (Washington, DC: GPO, 1887), 618; Jan de Vos, "Una legislación de graves consecuencias: El acaparamiento de tierras baldías en México, con el pretexto de colonización, 1821–1910," *Historia Mexicana* 34, no. 1 (July–September 1984): 76, 83. Chihuahua would become the state with the most colonies.

78   **"prosperous race":** *Emigration and Immigration,* 629–631; *El Siglo Diez y Nueve* (Mexico City), October 22, 1881; Jürgen Buchenau, "Small Numbers, Great Impact: Mexico and Its Immigrants, 1821–1973," *Journal of American Ethnic History* 20, no. 3 (Spring 2001): 31–32; Limantour quoted in Michael Johns, *The City of Mexico in the Age of Díaz* (Austin: University of Texas Press, 1997), 59–60; Moisés González Navarro, "Las ideas raciales de los científicos, 1890–1910," *Historia Mexicana* 37, no. 4 (April–June 1988): 565–583.

79   **"the country":** *La Patria* (Mexico City), October 22, 1881; *El Siglo Diez y Nueve* (Mexico City), October 22, 1881; Moisés González Navarro, *La colonización en México, 1877–1910* (México: Talleres de Impresión de Estampillas y Valores, 1960), 24, 37–39, 43; *Emigration and Immigration,* 618–619, 621, 639, 643; "Colonization of Lower California," *Science* 13, no. 322 (April 5, 1889): 256; James J. Passarelli, "Italy in Mexico: Chipilo," *Italica* 23, no. 1 (March 1, 1946): 43.

79   **"white race":** Francisco Pimentel, "La colonización negra," in *Obras completas* (Mexico City: Tipografía Económica, 1904), 511; *El Monitor Republicano* (Mexico City), July 13, 1889; *El Tiempo* (Mexico City), July 12, 1889.

80   **"its rights":** *Toronto Daily Mail,* November 14, 1889; *Diario de los debates de la Cámara de Senadores decimocuatro Congreso Constitucional: Tercero y cuatro períodos* (México: Imprenta de gobierno federal, 1890), 90–91, 98. Lancáster Jones was descended from a British-Mexican family from Jalisco.

80   **"black race":** *Diario de los debates de la Cámara de Senadores decimocuatro Congreso Constitucional,* 97.

81   **two nations:** *Diario de los debates de la Cámara de Senadores decimocuatro Congreso Constitucional,* 94; *Daily Picayune* (New Orleans, LA), October 12,

1889; MacLachlan and Beezley, *El Gran Pueblo*, 157–159; *Galveston Daily News*, October 27, 1889, November 9, 1889.

81 **"peace is better":** *El Monitor Republicano* (Mexico City), July 16, 1889; *El Tiempo* (Mexico City), July 12, 1889.

81 **"our territory":** *El Tiempo* (Mexico City), July 11, September 25, 1889; *El Monitor Republicano* (Mexico City), July 13, 1889.

82 **resettling there:** Martin Delany in *African-American Social and Political Thought, 1850–1920*, edited by Howard Brotz, rev. ed. (New Brunswick, NJ: Transaction Publishers, 1992 [1966]), 82; *Weekly Herald*, (New York, NY), August 22, 1857; Stephen Kantrowitz, *More than Freedom: Fighting for Black Citizenship in a White Republic, 1829–1889* (New York: Penguin Press, 2012), 111–112, 255; Rosalie Schwartz, *Across the Rio to Freedom: U.S. Negroes in Mexico* (El Paso: Texas Western Press, 1975), 23–33, 40–41; *La Patria* (Mexico City), July 4, 1882.

82 **"Republic of Mexico":** H. G. Gussom et al. to Matías Romero, September 30, 1886. 15.6.65, Archivo de la Secretaría de Relaciones Exteriores; Articles of Incorporation of the Afro-American Colonization Company of Mexico, Colored Colonization Company, the Colored Mexican Colonization Company, and the Colored Colonization Association of Fresno County, California State Archives, Sacramento. See also Arnold Shankman, *Ambivalent Friends: Afro-Americans View the Immigrant* (Westport, CT: Greenwood Press, 1982), 61.

83 **the future:** For more on Ellis's letters of recommendation from San Antonio, see *Rocky Mountain News* (Denver), October 24, 1889.

83 **"be commendable":** *Southwestern Christian Advocate* (New Orleans, LA), July 25, 1889; *Cleveland Gazette*, June 29, July 6, July 13, 1889.

83 **immigration brokers:** *El Monitor Republicano* (Mexico City), November 14, 1889; *Cleveland Gazette*, November 30, 1889. See also W. H. Ellis to Anonymous, November 19, 1889, AF-Mexico, Missouri History Museum. I am indebted to Adam Arenson for bringing this letter to my attention.

84 **"in Mexico":** *Saint Paul Globe*, July 10, 1904; *El Regidor* (San Antonio, TX), February 22, 1890; *Weekly Times Herald* (Dallas, TX), February 1, 1890; *Galveston Daily News*, January 29, 1890; *Lethbridge News* (Lethbridge, Canada), March 5, 1890. *H. H. Childers v. The State*, 30 Tex. Ct. App. 160; 16 S.W. 903; 1891 Tex. Crim. App. LEXIS 68; *Chicago Herald*, August 17, 1891.

84 **more imperiled:** Mitchell, *Righteous Propagation*, 45.

85 **"the Negroes":** *Daily Picayune* (New Orleans, LA), August 31, 1889; *Daily Inter Ocean* (Chicago), August 6, 1890; *New York Times*, August 6, 1890; *St. Paul Daily News*, July 29, 1890; *Cleveland Gazette*, August 29, 1891.

85 **"of the race":** *Galveston Daily News*, November 16, 1889.

86 **"republican politician":** *Galveston Daily News*, October 1, October 25, 1889; *Brenham Weekly Banner* (Brenham, TX), August 20, 1891; *Fort Worth Gazette*, August 20, 1891; *Dallas Morning News*, October 11, 1893.

86 **Ferguson's contract:** *Fort Worth Gazette*, August 20, September 18, 1891.

87   **"African repatriation":** *Christian Recorder* (Philadelphia, PA), October
     19, 1893; *Freeman* (Indianapolis, IN), October 14, 1893; *Cleveland Gazette*,
     November 25, 1893.

87   **"U.S. of America":** Redkey, *Black Exodus*, 109.

87   **"little help":** Brainerd Dyer, "The Persistence of the Idea of Negro Col-
     onization," *Pacific Historical Review* 12, no. 1 (March 1943): 63; Turner
     quoted in William Laird Clowes, *Black America: A Study of the Ex-Slave
     and His Late Master* (London: Cassell, 1891), 189.

88   **Committee on Emigration:** *Galveston Daily News*, November 14, 1893;
     Daily Inter Ocean (Chicago), November 6, December 2, 1893; *Waco Evening
     News*, November 6, 1893; Redkey, *Black Exodus*, 186–188.

88   **"Negro race":** Herbert Shapiro, *White Violence and Black Response: From
     Reconstruction to Montgomery* (Amherst: University of Massachusetts Press,
     1988), 48; Redkey, *Black Exodus*, 187–188.

89   **opposing emigration:** *Daily Picayune* (New Orleans, LA), December 1,
     1893; *Daily Inter Ocean* (Chicago), December 2, 1893, and December 4,
     1894; Redkey, *Black Exodus*, 188–189; Mitchell, *Righteous Propagation*, 48.

89   **further study:** *Daily Inter Ocean* (Chicago), December 1, 1893; *Cleveland
     Gazette*, December 2, 1893; *North American* (Philadelphia, PA), December
     4, 1893; Redkey, *Black Exodus*, 189.

89   **"Canada and Mexico":** *Galveston Daily News*, November 11, 1893. See also
     Galveston Daily News, October 15, 1893.

90   **"quite wealthy":** *Dallas Morning News*, October 10, 1893; see also *Dallas
     Morning News*, October 11, 1893.

4: THE LAND OF GOD AND LIBERTY

91   **Should they go?:** US Census Office, *Report on Population of the United
     States at the Eleventh Census: 1890* (Washington, DC: GPO, 1895), 59.

92   **"colored people":** "Failure of the Scheme for the Colonization of Negroes
     in Mexico," House of Representatives, 54th Congress, 1st Session, Docu-
     ment No. 169, 59; *Sioux City Journal*, February 23, 1896. For more on "Peg-
     Leg" Williams, see William F. Holmes, "Labor Agents and the Georgia
     Exodus," *South Atlantic Quarterly* 79, no. 4 (Autumn 1980): 436–449.

92   **"United States":** "Failure of the Scheme for the Colonization of Negroes
     in Mexico," 59.

92   **"such treatment":** *Daily Picayune* (New Orleans, LA), February 4, 1895;
     San Antonio Daily Light, August 11, 1895; *Birmingham Age-Herald*, Septem-
     ber 21, 1895; *Tuskaloosa Gazette*, September 26, 1895; *Sioux City Journal*,
     August 1, 1895.

93   **several centuries:** *Sioux City Journal*, February 23, 1896; *Daily Register*
     (Mobile, AL), March 10, 1895; *San Antonio Daily Light*, August 11, 1895;
     San Antonio Express, July 30, 1895.

93 **"whole scheme":** *News and Observer* (Raleigh, NC), January 7, 1899; *Birmingham News*, January 18, 1895; *Times-Picayune* (New Orleans, LA), January 8, 1895.

94 **"race problem":** Ellis's presence in Tuscaloosa only emerged in later interviews with returning colonists. *Tuskaloosa Gazette*, June 13, January 31, 1895; *St. Louis Republic*, February 3, 1895. Undated clipping from Anderson Ruffin Abbott Papers, Toronto Reference Library, Scrapbook 2, 314.

94 **and captives:** Pekka Hämäläinen, *The Comanche Empire* (New Haven: Yale University Press, 2008), 224–225.

95 **into production:** For Mexico-US cross-border cooperation versus Native Americans, see María de Jesús Duarte Espinosa, *Frontera y diplomacia: Las relaciones México–Estados Unidos durante el porfiriato* (México: Secretaría de relaciones exteriores, 2001), 65–67; C. P. Mackie, "Canal Irrigation in Modern Mexico," *Engineering Magazine* 13, no. 2 (May 1897): 182; *Morning Oregonian* (Portland, OR), December 7, 1897.

95 **imported cotton goods:** William K. Meyers, *Forge of Progress, Crucible of Revolt: The Origins of the Mexican Revolution in La Comarca Lagunera, 1880–1911* (Albuquerque: University of New Mexico Press, 1994), 21; US Bureau of Statistics, *Money and Prices in Foreign Countries, Being a Series of Reports upon the Currency Systems of Various Nations in Their Relation to Prices of Commodities and Wages of Labor* (Washington, DC: GPO, 1896), 115–116; R. de Zayas Enríquez, *Los Estados Unidos Mexicanos: Sus condiciones naturales y sus elementos de prosperidad* (México: Oficina tip. de la Secretaría de Fomento, 1893), 454–455; Ramón Prida, *¡De la dictadura a la anarquia!* (El Paso, TX: El Paso del Norte, 1914), 113.

95 **scarce water:** Clifton B. Kroeber, "La cuestión del Nazas hasta 1913," *Historia Mexicana* 20, no. 3 (January–March, 1971): 432; C. Reginald Enock, *Mexico: Its Ancient and Modern Civilisation, History and Political Conditions, Topography and Natural Resources, Industries and General Development* (New York: Charles Scribner's Sons, 1909), 286; Bessie H. Steele, "A Visit to a Mexican Cotton Plantation," *American Journal of Nursing* 3, no. 12 (September 1903): 923. Pacheco was also a supporter of irrigation in the Comarca Lagunera, presiding over the opening of one of the region's canals. *Brooklyn Eagle*, July 13, 1890.

96 **"cultivating machines":** Casey Walsh, *Building the Borderlands: A Transnational History of Irrigated Cotton Along the Mexico-Texas Border* (College Station: Texas A&M University Press, 2008), 33; Mackie, "Canal Irrigation in Modern Mexico," 183–188, 197; *Two Republics* (Mexico City), August 7, 1895. For more on the Tlahualilo region, see *Escritura y Estatutos de la Compañía Agrícola Limitada del Tlahaulilo* (México: Imprenta de Francisco Díaz de Leon, 1889); *New York Evening Post*, July 25, 1895; Juan Ballesteros Porta, *Explotación individual o colectiva? El caso de los ejidos de Tlahualilo* (México: Instituto Mexicano de Investigaciones Económicas, 1964), 21–25.

96 **"civilized man":** Steele, "A Visit to a Mexican Cotton Plantation," 923;

Hunter Morrison, "Canal Irrigation in Mexico," *Yale Scientific Monthly* 4, no. 8 (May 1898): 382–3; Mackie, "Canal Irrigation in Modern Mexico," 181; Walter Meade O'Dwyer, "The Prospects of Mexico," *North American Review* 159, no. 452 (July 1894): 123; José Juan Tablada, *La defensa social: Historia de la campaña de le division del norte* (México: Imprenta de Gobierno Federal, 1913), 23. For Mexican ideas of progress during the Porfiriato, see Mauricio Tenorio-Trillo, *Mexico at the World's Fairs: Crafting a Modern Nation* (Berkeley: University of California Press, 1996), 28–35.

97 **"the old":** Katz, "The Liberal Republic and the Porfiriato," 88–90; Meyer, *Forge of Progress,* 34; Esteban L. Portillo, *Catecismo geográfico, politico e histórico del estado de Coahuila de Zaragoza* (Saltillo: Tipografia del Gobierno en Palacio, 1897), 128; "Where Cotton Is King," *Modern Mexico* 17, no. 1 (April 1904): 37; C. Amado Prado, *Prontuario de la municipalidad del Torreón* (Saltillo: Tipografia del Gobierno en Palacio, 1899), 6; [Ferrocarriles nacionales de México], *Mexico from Border to Capital.*

97 **natural resources:** Morrison, "Canal Irrigation in Mexico," 385; Manuel Plana, *El reino del algodón en México: La estructura agraria de la Laguna (1855–1910)* (Mexico: Patronato del Teatro Isauro Martínez, 1991), 194; Steele, "A Visit to a Mexican Cotton Plantation," 922; *Two Republics* (Mexico City), August 7, 1895; Mackie, "Canal Irrigation in Modern Mexico," 191.

98 **the hacienda:** Carlos Javier Castañón Cuadros, "Breve historia de la compañía," 2 (manuscript in author's possession); *New York Evening Post,* July 25, 1895; Testimonio de la escritura de colonización celebrado entre Guillermo Ellis y la Cía. de Tlahualilo, caja 18, expediente 12, Archivo Municipal de Torreón Eduardo Guerra. I am indebted to Carlos Castañón Cuadros for bringing this last document to my attention.

99 **the republic:** *Baltimore Sun,* July 25, 1904; *Mexican Herald* (Mexico City), August 13, 1896.

100 **a *cantina*:** Katherine Unterman, "Boodle over the Border: Embezzlement and the Crisis of International Mobility, 1880–1890," *Journal of the Gilded Age and Progressive Era* 11, no. 2 (April 2012): 151–189; *Papers Relating to the Foreign Relations of the United States, with the Annual Message of the President, Transmitted to Congress December 2, 1895* (Washington, DC: GPO, 1895), 997; *New York Times,* July 30, 1895, January 12, 1904; *San Antonio Daily Express,* July 26, 1895; *San Francisco Call,* December 27, 1903; Daniel S. Margolies, *Spaces of Law in American Foreign Relations: Extradition and Extraterritoriality in the Borderlands and Beyond, 1877–1898* (Athens: University of Georgia Press, 2011), 264.

101 **as his own:** Pablo Piccato, *City of Suspects: Crime in Mexico City, 1900–1931* (Durham: Duke University Press, 2001), 21; Mauricio Tenorio-Trillo, "1910 Mexico City: Space and Nation in the City of the Centenario," *Journal of Latin American Studies* 28, no. 1 (February 1996): 82–85; Johns, *The City of Mexico in the Age of Díaz,* 16–19, 30; Claudio Lomnitz, *The Return of Comrade Ricardo Flores Magón* (New York: Zone Books, 2014), 70; Serge

Gruzinski, *La ciudad de México: Una historia*, trans. Paula López Caballero (México: Fondo de Cultura Económica, 2004), 485–486.

101 **"public conveyances":** Clarence Pullen, "The City of Mexico," *Journal of the American Geographical Society of New York* 20 (1888): 159; Lomnitz, *The Return of Comrade Ricardo Flores Magón*, 70; *Daily Picayune* (New Orleans, LA), May 12, 1895.

102 **"at all":** Hotel Gillow, <http://www.hotelgillow.com/Epages/hotel_gillow _history.php> (accessed 8/26/12); Leone B. Moats, *Thunder in Their Veins: A Memoir of Mexico* (New York: Century, 1932), 30–31. For information on the American Hospital, see *Two Republics* (Mexico City), August 18, 1898.

102 **African Americans:** Moats, *Thunder in Their Veins*, 140; Delia Salazar Anaya, "Extraños en la ciudad: Un acercamiento a la inmigración internacional a la ciudad de México, en los censos de 1890, 1895, 1900 y 1910," in *Imágenes de los imigrantes en la ciudad de México, 1753–1910*, edited by Delia Salazar Anaya (México: Instituto Nacional de Antropologia e Historia, 2002), 227, 243–244; William Schell Jr., *Integral Outsiders: The American Colony in Mexico City, 1876–1911* (Wilmington, DE: Scholarly Resources, 2001), 25; Janice Lee Jayes, *The Illusion of Ignorance: Constructing the American Encounter with Mexico, 1877–1920* (Lanham, MD: University Press of America, 2011), 89–92; *Mexican Herald* (Mexico City), August 26, 1900.

102 **their drinks:** See the entries for W. Allen, G. D. Ballard, W. H. Braham, and B. F. Cleveland in *The Massey-Gilbert Blue Book of Mexico: A Directory in English of the City of Mexico* (Mexico City: Massey-Gilbert, 1901), 116, 122, 123, 127. These are just a few of the Pullman porters living in Mexico City, most by the train station. *El Tiempo* (Mexico City), June 23, July 5, 1895; Moisés González Navarro, *Los extranjeros en México y los Mexicanos en el extranjero, 1821–1970* (México: Colegio de México, 1994), 189. For more on the Iturbide Hotel, see Margati, *A Trip to the City of Mexico*, 46–47.

103 **cotton fields:** *Mexican Herald* (Mexico City), September 10, 1896; *El Tiempo* (Mexico City), January 8, 1895.

103 **"powerless nation!":** *El Tiempo* (Mexico City), January 8, February 14, March 1, March 10, 1895; *La Voz de México* (Mexico City), March 6, 1895. *El Monitor, Economista Mexicano, La Voz de México, El Heraldo, El Tiempo,* and Guadalajara's *La Linterna* all opposed black colonization; see *El Tiempo*, March 13, 1895.

104 **"located there":** W. E. B. Du Bois, "The Study of the Negro Problems," *Annals of the American Academy of Political and Social Science* 11, no. 1 (January 1898): 1–23; *Atlanta Constitution*, December 31, 1894; *Times-Picayune* (New Orleans, LA), January 8, 1895; Holmes, "Georgia Exodus," 439.

105 **"flora and fauna":** *Oakland Tribune*, August 8, 1895; "The Future of the Negro," *Gentleman's Magazine* 259 (December 1885): 612–614; *La Voz de México* (Mexico City), January 24, 1899; Sanchez-Guillermo, "Nacionalismo y racism en el México decimonónico"; *Monitor Republicano* (Mexico City), November 19, 1889; W. H. Nelson, "Should the Negro go to

238 · *Notes*

Africa?" in *Southwestern Christian Advocate* (New Orleans, LA), November
16, 1893. See also Turner's speech as reported in the *Galveston Daily News*,
August 20, 1893. For more on the linkage between the tropics and Latin
America, see Shawn William Miller, *An Environmental History of Latin
America* (New York: Cambridge University Press, 2007), 108–112.

105 **North America:** *Atlanta Constitution*, March 9, 1895. See also *Daily Inter
Ocean* (Chicago), January 19, 1895; *Denver Evening Post*, January 19, 1895;
West Alabama Breeze (Northport, AL), February 14, March 21, 1895.

106 **race unmentioned:** *Atlanta Constitution*, March 16, 1895; for an example
of Williams being emphasized over Ellis, see *Daily Picayune* (New Orleans,
LA), February 16, 1895.

106 **"the negro":** *Daily Picayune* (New Orleans, LA), February 4, 1895.

107 **cotton crop:** Muñoz Mata, "Presencia afrocaribeña en Veracruz," 77;
Atlanta Constitution, March 9, March 16, 1895; *Daily Picayune* (New
Orleans, LA), May 12, 1895; *Freeman* (Indianapolis, IN), May 4, 1895; *St.
Louis Republic*, February 3, 1895; *New York Evening Post*, July 25, 1895.

107 **hacienda to 816:** *Daily Picayune* (New Orleans, LA), February 16, 1895;
Atlanta Constitution, March 10, March 16, 1895; Rippy, "A Negro Colonization Project in Mexico, 1895," 68. See also the interview with Dan Hallaron
of the Southern Pacific Railway in *Daily Picayune* (New Orleans, LA), March
9, 1895.

108 **"God and Liberty":** *San Antonio Express*, October 14, 1895.

108 **"local affairs":** *Freeman* (Indianapolis, IN), May 4, 1895; *Tuskaloosa Journal*,
May 15, 1895. Note that A. A. Adams later made a plea to the governor of Alabama requesting help to come home. *Tuskaloosa Gazette*, September 26, 1895.

109 **economic advantages:** *Freeman* (Indianapolis, IN), May 4, 1895; *Atlanta
Constitution*, March 10, 1895; Andrew Wender Cohen, "Smuggling, Glo-
balization, and America's Outward State, 1870–1909," *Journal of American
History* 97, no. 2 (September 2010): 371–398.

109 **hacienda at night:** *New York Evening Post*, July 25, 1895.

110 **and Georgia:** Claudio Lomnitz offers an extended discussion of plantation slavery during the Porfiriato in *The Return of Comrade Ricardo Flores
Magón*, 112–125. *Daily Register* (Mobile, AL), March 6, 1895; *Philadelphia
Inquirer*, May 25, 1895; *Macon Telegraph* (Macon, GA), March 6, 1895; *Tuskaloosa Gazette*, March 21, 1895; *Atlanta Constitution*, March 9, March 10,
1895; *Denver Post*, April 20, 1895.

110 **brother-in-law:** John McKiernan-González, *Fevered Measures: Public
Health and Race at the Texas-Mexico Border, 1848–1942* (Durham: Duke
University Press, 2012), 86; *New York Times*, August 12, 1895; *San Antonio
Express*, August 11, July 28, 1895.

111 **Torreón:** *Brownsville Daily Herald*, July 13, 1895. *St. Louis Globe Democrat*,
July 8, 1895; *La Voz de México* (Mexico City), October 10, 1895; *Atchison
Daily Globe* (Atchison, KS), July 25, 1895.

111 **different enterprises:** Poston to McCaughan, July 19, 1895, in "Failure

of the Scheme for the Colonization of Negroes in Mexico," 16; Dispatches from United States Consuls in Durango, 1886–1906, RG 59, M290, Reel 1, Entry 52.

112   **for disease:** Alexandra Minna Stern, *Eugenic Nation: Faults and Frontiers of Better Breeding in Modern America* (Berkeley: University of California Press, 2005), 59; *Weekly Abstract of Sanitary Reports Issued by the Supervising Surgeon-General, Marine Hospital Service* (Washington, DC: GPO, 1895), 9:84–85; August Schachner, "Midwinter Travels in Mexico," *Mid-Continent Magazine* 4, no. 2 (June 1895): 99–100; *Macon Telegraph* (Macon, GA), July 25, 1895.

112   **American-owned enterprise:** *Fort Worth Gazette*, July 27, 1895; *New York Evening Post*, July 29, 1895.

113   **"United States":** *Galveston Daily News*, July 31, October 16, 1895; *Charlotte Observer*, July 31, 1895; *Daily Picayune* (New Orleans, LA), August 2, 1895; *Annual Report of the Supervising Surgeon-General of the Marine-Hospital Service of the United States, 1895* (Washington, DC: GPO, 1896), 371–372, 455.

113   **outside of town:** *Annual Report of the Supervising Surgeon-General of the Marine-Hospital Service of the United States, 1895*, 371–372.

114   **variola virus:** *Annual Report of the Supervising Surgeon-General of the Marine-Hospital Service of the United States, 1895*, 370; Jerrold M. Michael and Thomas R. Bender, "Fighting Smallpox on the Texas Border: An Episode from PHS's Proud Past," *Public Health Reports* 99, no. 6 (November–December 1984): 581–582; *Galveston Daily News*, October 30, 1895; *Fort Worth Gazette*, August 20, 1895. The most thorough discussion of the public health dimensions of Camp Jenner—and the questionable medical ethics around the testing of the serum—can be found in McKiernon-Gonzalez, *Fevered Measures*, 100–114.

114   **border region:** *Annual Report of the Supervising Surgeon-General of the Marine-Hospital Service of the United States, 1896* (Washington, DC: GPO, 1896), 237–238; *Annual Report of the Supervising Surgeon-General of the Marine-Hospital Service of the United States, 1895*, 376–377; J. R. Laine, "Reports of the State Board of Health," *Pacific Medical Journal* 38, no. 10 (October 1895): 669; *Galveston Daily News*, October 16, 1895; *La Voz de México* (Mexico City), November 20, 1895; *El Tiempo* (Mexico City), November 19, 1895; Felipe Suárez to Governor of Coahuila, September 30, 1895 <http://ahc.sfpcoahuila.gob.mx/admin/uploads/Documentos/modulo11/C24F4E3.pdf> (accessed 2/9/15).

115   **"American negro":** *Galveston Daily News*, August 7, 1895; *Daily Herald* (Brownsville, TX), October 3, 1895; *San Antonio Express*, October 14, 1895; "Failure of the Scheme for the Colonization of Negroes in Mexico," 29.

116   **into Mexico:** *Galveston Daily News*, October 25, 1895; "Failure of the Scheme for the Colonization of Negroes in Mexico," 32; *Tuskaloosa Gazette*, September 26, 1895; *Tuskaloosa Times*, October 16, 1895.

116   **"useful citizen":** *Chicago Herald*, August 17, 1891; *Victoria Advocate*, June 1, 1895; *Morning Oregonian* (Portland, OR), July 25, 1895; *Galveston Daily*

News, October 30, 1895; local newspapers quoted in Reynolds, "The Alabama Negro Colony in Mexico, 1894–1896, Part 2," 50.

116 **"and happy"**: *Sioux City Journal*, August 1, 1895; *Oakland Tribune*, August 8, 1895; *Philadelphia Inquirer*, September 21, 1895; *Freeman* (Indianapolis, IN), December 14, 1895; *Dallas Morning News*, October 31, 1895.

117 **the border**: *La Voz de México* (Mexico City), October 10, 1895. *Omaha World Herald*, August 12, 1895; *Tuskaloosa Times*, September 4, 1895; *El Tiempo* (Mexico City), May 8, July 12, October 16, 1895; Castañon Cuadros, "Breve historia de la compañía," 2.

118 **Mexican peon**: *San Antonio Daily Light*, August 11, 1895.

118 **Ellis had promised**: *Two Republics* (Mexico City), October 11, 1895; *New York Times*, August 12, 1895; personal communication with Juan Antonio Padilla Compean, January 9, 2012. Llamedo refers to these remaining colonists in an interview with the Mexico City press, reprinted in the *Austin Weekly Statesman*, August 29, 1895.

119 **US South**: Rose Ella Warner and C. Earle Smith Jr., "Boll Weevil Found in Pre-Columbian Cotton from Mexico," *Science* 162 (November 1968): 911–912; Frederick W. Mally, *The Mexican Cotton-Boll Weevil*, US Department of Agriculture, Farmers' Bulletin No. 130 (Washington, DC: GPO, 1901), 21–22; Eugene Clyde Brooks, *The Story of Cotton and the Development of the Cotton States* (Chicago: Rand McNally, 1911), 325.

120 **the trickster**: Jackson quoted in Levine, *Black Culture and Black Consciousness*, 241; Leon F. Litwack, *Trouble in Mind: Black Southerners in the Age of Jim Crow* (New York: Alfred A. Knopf, 1998), 175–178; Theodore Rosengarten, *All God's Dangers: The Life of Nate Shaw* (New York: Vintage Books, 1989), 221–224; Ayana Smith, "Blues, Criticism, and the Signifying Trickster," *Popular Music* 24, no. 2 (May 2005): 179–182.

120 **"*my home*"**: James C. Giesen, *Boll Weevil Blues: Cotton, Myth, and Power in the American South* (Chicago: University of Chicago Press, 2011), 40–41.

120 **prominent roles**: Ellis's colony likely also influenced the African-Americanist novelist Sutton E. Griggs, author of *Imperium in Imperio*. See Caroline Levander, "Sutton Griggs and the Borderlands of Empire," in *Jim Crow, Literature, and the Legacy of Sutton E. Griggs*, edited by Tess Chakkalakal and Kenneth W. Warren (Athens: University of Georgia Press, 2013), 36.

121 **on purpose**: "Cotton States and International Exposition," *Monthly Bulletin of the Bureau of American Republics* 2, no. 1 (July 1894): 40–43; Tenorio-Trillo, *Mexico at the World's Fairs*, 185–186; Jesse Sparks to Edwin F. Uhl, September 13, 1895, *Despatches from United States Consuls in Piedras Negras (Ciudad Porfirio Díaz)*, RG 59, M299, NARA–Microfilm Publication; *Hutchinson Daily News* (Hutchinson, KS), November 6, 1895; Theda Perdue, *Race and the Atlanta Cotton States Exposition of 1895* (Athens: University of Georgia Press, 2010), 125.

122 **"negro commissioners"**: *The Official Catalogue of the Cotton States and International Exposition* (Atlanta: Claflin and Mellichamp, 1895), 134, 145,

194–196; "Atlanta Exposition Speech" <http://memory.loc.gov/cgibin /ampage?collId=ody_mssmisc&fileName=ody/ody0605/ody0605page .db&recNum=0&it> (accessed 11/19/12); Henry McNeal Turner, "The American Negro and the Fatherland," in *Africa and the American Negro: Addresses and Proceedings of the Congress on Africa Held Under the Auspices of the Stewart Missionary Foundation for Africa of Gammon Theological Seminary in Connection with the Cotton States and International Exposition, December 13–15, 1895,* edited by J. W. E. Bowen (Atlanta: Gammon Theological Seminary, 1896), 195.

122 **for "colored":** *El Regidor* (San Antonio), April 2, 1896; *Jules A. Appler's General Directory of the City of San Antonio, 1895–96* (San Antonio: Jules A. Appler, 1895), 253–254.

122 **once again:** White, *Lost Boundaries,* 91.

5: A PICTURESQUE FIGURE

125 **deluxe suites:** *Denver Evening Post,* April 6, 1897. See also the description of Ellis's appearance in the *New York Herald,* June 25, 1904.

125 **"money-maker":** *Denver Evening Post,* April 6, 1897; *Rocky Mountain News* (Denver), April 7, 1897.

126 **Puerto Rican Company:** *Kansas City Star,* June 30, 1905; *Baltimore American,* July 25, 1904; *Pawtucket Times* (Pawtucket, RI), July 26, 1901; *Trow General Directory of New York City Embracing the Boroughs of Manhattan and the Bronx, 1920–1921* (New York: R. L. Polk, 1920), 634, 1269.

126 **"almost illimitable":** Marie Robinson Wright, *Picturesque Mexico* (Philadelphia: J. B. Lippincott, 1897), 444.

127 **"tropical products":** Samuel Truett, *Fugitive Landscapes: The Forgotten History of the U.S.-Mexico Borderlands* (New Haven: Yale University Press, 2006), 1–5; Jayes, *The Illusion of Ignorance,* 104–105; Romero, "Mexico," 329.

127 **"extreme South":** "The Conquest of the Tropics," *Modern Mexico* 17, no. 1 (April 1904): 38.

128 **"the tropics":** Lomnitz, *The Return of Comrade Ricardo Flores Magón,* 121; Michael Redclift, *Chewing Gum: The Fortunes of Taste* (New York: Routledge, 2004); Benjamin Kidd, *The Control of the Tropics* (New York: Macmillan, 1898), 5. See also *Fitzgerrell's Guide to Mexico: The Tropics and Highlands: New Homes in a Land of Great Opportunities* (Mexico: Imprenta y fototipia de la secretaria de fomento, 1906).

128 **its exports:** Elliott Young, *Catarino Garza's Revolution on the Texas-Mexico Border* (Durham: Duke University Press, 2004), 58; Jayes, *The Illusion of Ignorance,* 88; William Schell Jr., "American Investment in Tropical Mexico: Rubber Plantations, Fraud, and Dollar Diplomacy, 1897–1913," *Business History Review* 64, no. 2 (Summer 1990): 222; R. de Zayas Enríquez, *Los Estados Unidos Mexicanos: Sus condiciones naturales y sus elementos de prosperidad* (México: Oficina tip. de la Secretaría de Fomento, 1893), 416.

128 **Tlahualilo's director:** Sven Beckert, *The Monied Metropolis: New York City and the Consolidation of the American Bourgeoisie, 1850–1896* (New York: Cambridge University Press, 2001), 2–4; B. Olney Hough, ed., *American Exporter Export Trade Directory, 1921–1922* (New York: American Exporter, 1921), 893–894; US Bureau of Statistics, *Money and Prices in Foreign Countries*, 115–116; J. Fred Rippy, "The United States and Mexico, 1910–27," in *American Policies Abroad: Mexico* (Chicago: University of Chicago Press, 1928), 92; Kroeber, "La cuestión del Nazas hasta 1913," 438–439; Clifton B. Kroeber, *Man, Land, and Water: Mexico's Farmlands Irrigation Policies, 1885–1911* (Berkeley: University of California Press, 1983), 205; Meyers, *Forge of Progress, Crucible of Revolt*, 51.

129 **tropical mirage:** Schell, "American Investment in Tropical Mexico," 223–225; *Modern Mexico* 12, no. 3 (December 1901): 9; *Modern Mexico* 13, no. 3 (June 1902): 14; *Modern Mexico* 13, no. 4 (July 1902): 8.

130 **"and credit":** *New York Herald*, June 27, 1904; *New York World*, July 25, 1901.

130 **did as well:** Pletcher, *Rails, Mines, and Progress*, 297–309.

130 **next few years:** *Mexican Herald* (Mexico City), September 10, 1896, and January 31, 1899.

131 **1880s and 1890s:** *Mexican Herald* (Mexico City), September 30, 1895, and August 2, 1901; *New York Herald*, June 27, 1904; Shawn Lewis England, "The Curse of Huitzilopochtli: The Origins, Process, and Legacy of Mexico's Military Reforms, 1920–1946" (Ph.D. dissertation, Arizona State University, 2008), 91.

132 **its moniker:** *Trow's General Directory of the Boroughs of Manhattan and the Bronx, 1900* (New York: Trow, 1900), 372, 374; George Edmund Haynes, *The Negro at Work in New York City: A Study in Economic Progress* (New York: Longmans, Green for Columbia University, 1912), 48–53; Baldwin, *From Negro to Caucasian*, 31–32; James Weldon Johnson, *Black Manhattan* (New York: Alfred A. Knopf, 1930), 119; Marcy S. Sacks, *Before Harlem: The Black Experience in New York City Before World War I* (Philadelphia: University of Pennsylvania Press, 2006), 42, 65; *New York Times*, June 30, 1895.

132 **sought to play:** US Census, *Twelfth Census of the United States, Taken in the Year 1900*, vol. 1, *Population* (Washington, DC: United States Census Office, 1901), 800–803.

133 **natural resources:** *Washington Times* (Washington, DC), November 23, 1904; Bruce to Cromwell, November 20, 1905, in Adelaide M. Cromwell, *Unveiled Voices, Unvarnished Memories: The Cromwell Family in Slavery and Segregation, 1692–1972* (Columbia: University of Missouri Press, 2007), 268; *Cleveland Gazette*, July 2, 1904; *Kansas City Star*, June 30, 1905.

134 **to the United States:** "Elihu Root on the Negro Problem," *Harper's Weekly* 47, no. 2409 (February 21, 1903): 306–307.

134 **"last revolution":** Personal communication Jesse Hoffnung-Garskof, December 11, 2012; *New York Sun*, May 29, 1897; *Daily Herald* (Brownsville, TX), June 4, 1897; *Denver Evening Post*, April 6, 1897; *New York Herald*,

June 25, 1904; *New York Herald*, June 26, 1904. See also the account of an African American passing as Cuban in Sandweiss, *Passing Strange*, 142.

135 **"Spanish stock":** *Dictionary of Races or Peoples*, 61st Congress, 3rd Session, Senate Document No. 662 (Washington, DC: GPO, 1911), 49; Aline Helg, *Our Rightful Share: The Afro-Cuban Struggle for Equality, 1886–1912* (Chapel Hill: University of North Carolina Press, 1995), 3; Horne, *Race to Revolution*, 258.

135 **at Cubanness:** *Kansas City Star*, June 30, 1905; *Baltimore American*, July 25, 1904; *Dictionary of Races or Peoples*, 96.

136 **its legal privileges:** Natalia Molina, "'In a Race All Their Own': The Quest to Make Mexicans Ineligible for U.S. Citizenship," *Pacific Historical Review* 79, no. 2 (May 2010): 170; Gross, *What Blood Won't Tell*, 257–260; *In re Rodriguez*, 81 F. 337 (W.D. Tex. 1897), 338, 349; Arnoldo De León, *The Tejano Community, 1836–1900* (Dallas: Southern Methodist University Press, 1997 [1982]), 33.

136 **racial status:** Report of Special Agent Higgins, January 27, 1919, Case File 000-751, in *Federal Surveillance of Afro-Americans (1917–1925): The First World War, the Red Scare, and the Garvey Movement*, edited by Theodore Kornweibel, Jr. (Frederick, MD: University Publications of America, 1985). For Americans' responses to Maceo, see Horne, *Race to Revolution*, 134, 154. Intriguingly, some US whites failed to remark upon Maceo's African ancestry.

137 **the team:** *San Francisco Call*, December 23, 1898; *Ogden Standard* (Ogden, UT), August 9, 1919; *New York Evening Telegram*, July 25, 1901; *New York World*, February 26, 1899; *Milwaukee Journal*, May 9, 1902.

138 **the scandal:** *New York Times*, December 22, 1898; *Topeka State Journal*, October 20, 1909; *Evening Statesman* (Walla Walla, WA), October 25, 1909; *New York Herald*, December 2, 1898; *New York Sun*, December 11, 1908; *Denver Evening Post*, January 22, 1899; *Baltimore American*, July 25, 1904.

138 **and beyond:** Charles Lummis, *The Awakening of a Nation: Mexico of To-Day* (Honolulu: University Press of the Pacific, 2004 [1898]), 55; *New York Times*, July 13, 1903; *Cleveland Gazette*, October 13, 1923; *New York Herald*, June 27, 1904; *New York Tribune*, April 16, 1902; undated clipping in *New York Journal American* morgue, W. H. Ellis file, Center for American History, University of Texas at Austin; "Central Trust Company of New York v. New York and Westchester Water Company and Others," *Reports of Cases Heard and Determined in the Appellate Division of the Supreme Court of the State of New York* 68 (1902): 640–642.

139 **the passer?:** Baldwin, *From Negro to Caucasian*, 17. Kevin K. Gaines reminds us that the term passing was also an African-American expression for death in *Uplifting the Race: Black Leadership, Politics, and Culture in the Twentieth Century* (Chapel Hill: University of North Carolina Press, 1996), 229; Kennedy, "Passing," 9.

139 **San Antonio:** W. H. Ellis to Charles Ellis, September 11, 1903, and December 31, 1904, family letters shared with author; Langston Hughes,

"Passing," in *The Ways of White Folks* (New York: Alfred A. Knopf, 1933), 55; *Chicago Record*, September 15, 1902; *Chicago Journal*, September 15, 1902; *Inter Ocean* (Chicago), September 15, 1902; *Chicago Daily Tribune*, September 16, 1902; Susie Williams, interview by author, March 12, 2012.

140 **summer camps:** *Sacramento Daily Record-Union*, September 24, 1897; *Richmond Planet*, August 21, 1897; *Saint Paul Globe*, September 5, 1897; *World* quoted in Jillian A. Sim, "Fading to White," *American Heritage* 50, no. 1 (February/March 1999); Olivia Mancini, "Passing as White: Anita Hemmings," *Vassar Quarterly* 98, no. 1 (Winter 2001).

141 **"establish it":** *Mexican Herald* (Mexico City), August 2, 1901; "Battle, George Gordon" <http://ncpedia.org/biography/battle-george-gordon> (accessed 5/29/2014); *Pawtucket Times* (Pawtucket, RI), July 26, 1901; *New York Evening Telegram*, July 25, 1901; *Saint Paul Globe*, July 10, 1904; Undated clipping in *New York Journal American* morgue files, Center for American History, University of Texas at Austin. See also Arthur Train, *Courts and Criminals* (New York: Charles Scribner's Sons, 1912), 192.

141 **as possible:** Martha Hodes, *White Women, Black Men: Illicit Sex in the Nineteenth-Century South* (New Haven: Yale University Press, 1997), 165–175.

142 **work setting:** *New York Sun*, October 4, 1903; 1880 US Federal Census, Jersey City, New Jersey, T9, NARA–Microfilm Publications, 343; *Gopsill's Jersey City and Hoboken City Directory for the Year Ending May 1, 1880* (1879), 352; *Gopsill's Jersey City and Hoboken City Directory for the Year Ending May 1, 1887* (1886), 598; 1900 US Federal Census, Manhattan, New York, T623, NARA–Microfilm Publications, 17A. According to the *Baltimore American*, July 25, 1904, Sherwood had once been Ellis's "confidential secretary."

142 **"negro or black race":** Peggy Pascoe, *What Comes Naturally: Miscegenation Law and the Making of Race in America* (New York: Oxford University Press, 2009), 163–173; James Bryce, "Thoughts on the Negro Problem," *North American Review* 153, no. 421 (December 1891): 651; McAdoo quoted in Sacks, *Before Harlem*, 63; Gilbert Osofsky, "Race Riot, 1900: A Study of Ethnic Violence," *Journal of Negro Education* 32, no. 1 (Winter 1963): 21; Martha Hodes, "Knowledge and Indifference in the New York City Race Riot of 1900: An Argument in Search of a Story," *Rethinking History* 15, no. 1 (2011): 61–89; legislature quoted in Gilbert Osofsky, *Harlem: The Making of a Ghetto* (New York: Harper and Row, 1963), 42.

142 **"laugh over it":** *New York Sun*, October 4, 1903; Marriage Certificate 10242, May 27, 1903, New York City Municipal Archives. Ellis describes his religion as Catholic in Knox, *Who's Who in New York, 1917–1918*, 336.

143 **late 1880s:** Maude Ellis to Fannie Starnes, January 9, 1924, family letter shared with author; Susie Williams, interview by author, March 12, 2012; *Washington Times*, June 27, 1904; Book 218, Deed Records, 39, February 23, 1903; and Book 226, Deed Records, 501, March 7, 1904, Bexar County Clerk's Office.

144 **"town somewhere":** Joseph Golden, "Patterns of Negro-White Inter-

marriage," *American Sociological Review* 19, no. 2 (April 1954): 144–147; Internment Orders, Deed 12955, Woodlawn Cemetery Archives; *New York Sun*, October 4, 1903.

144 **"Anglo-Saxon":** Esther Romeyn, *Street Scenes: Staging the Self in Immigrant New York, 1880–1924* (Minneapolis: University of Minnesota Press, 1998); Jannath, "America's Changing Color Line," 62.

145 **"is supposed":** US Census, *Twelfth Census . . . 1900*, 1:631, 704–705, 800–803; Jannath, "America's Changing Color Line," 62.

145 **"they chose":** Walter White, "The Paradox of Color," in Alain Locke, ed., *The New Negro: An Interpretation* (New York: Albert and Charles Boni, 1925), 364; Karen Sotiropoulos, *Staging Race: Black Performers in Turn of the Century America* (Cambridge: Harvard University Press, 2006), 132–133; Horne, *Race to Revolution*, 161; Ann Douglas, *Terrible Honesty: Mongrel Manhattan in the 1920s* (New York: Farrar, Straus and Giroux, 1995), 98–99.

146 **social equal:** *Fort Worth Telegram*, July 1, 1905; *Victoria Advocate*, August 11, December 8, 1877, October 19, 1878, and April 3, 1880. The pain of passing is one of the central themes of Hobbs, *A Chosen Exile*.

147 **distant locale:** *Daily Express* (London), June 23, June 24, 1902; James Quirin, "W.E.B. Du Bois, Ethiopianism and Ethiopia, 1890–1955," *International Journal of Ethiopian Studies* 5, no. 2 (Fall/Winter 2010–2011): 1–26; William Scott, "The Ethiopian Ethos in African American Thought," *International Journal of Ethiopian Studies* 1, no. 2 (Winter/Spring 2004): 40–57; Herbert Vivian, *Abyssinia: Through the Lion-Land to the Court of the Lion of Judah* (New York: Negro Universities Press, 1969 [1901]), 126; "An American Promoter in Abyssinia"; *Mexican Herald* (Mexico City), February 27, 1903; *Los Angeles Herald*, July 10, 1904; *New York Times*, January 1, 1904; undated clipping in *New York Journal American* morgue, W. H. Ellis File, Center for American History, University of Texas at Austin.

148 **"large quantities":** *New York Times*, January 1, 1904; "An American Promoter in Abyssinia," *World's Work* 7, no. 5 (March 1904): 99–100; undated clipping from *New York Sun* in *New York Journal American* morgue, W. H. Ellis File, Center for American History, University of Texas at Austin.

148 **"negro race":** Hussein Ahmed, "The Chronicle of Menilek II of Ethiopia: A Brief Assessment of Its Versions," *Journal of Ethiopian Studies* 16 (July 1983): 77; W. H. Ellis to Dudley Carter, August 23, 1904, reprinted in Ulf J. Lindahl, "An Historic Letter from the United States' Mission to Menelik," *Menelik's Journal* 12, no. 3 (July–September 1996): 925; Pankhurst, "William H. Ellis," 95.

148 **ethnically distinct:** Robert P. Skinner, *The 1903 Skinner Mission to Ethiopia and a Century of American-Ethiopian Relations* (Hollywood, CA: Tsehai Publishers, 2003 [1906]), 84–85. Fikru Negash Gebrekidan discusses Ethiopians' complicated response to African Americans in the early twentieth century in *Bond Without Blood: A History of Ethiopian and New World*

> *Black Relations, 1896–1991* (Trenton, NJ: Africa World Press, 2005), 41–46; Bahru Zewde, *A History of Modern Ethiopia, 1855–1974* (London: James Currey, 1991), 92–94.

149 **"of mankind":** David Levering Lewis, *W. E. B. Du Bois: Biography of a Race, 1868–1919* (New York: Henry Holt, 1993), 248–251.

149 **Black Folk:** J. R. Hooker, "The Pan-African Conference 1900," *Transition* 46 (1974): 20–24; Marika Sherwood, "Pan-African Conferences, 1900–1953: What Did 'Pan-Africanism' Mean?" *Journal of Pan African Studies* 4, no. 10 (January 2012): 107; Alexander Waters, *My Life and Work* (New York: Fleming H. Revell, 1917), 257–258; *Colored American* (Washington, DC), August 25, 1900; *Appeal* (St. Paul, MN), August 18, 1900.

150 **Monterrey, Mexico:** *New York Times*, January 1, 1904; Book 3705, Deed Records, 275, June 24, 1955, Bexar County Clerk's Office; 1900 U.S. Federal Census, San Antonio, Texas, T623, NARA–Microfilm Publication, 3B; "World War II Draft Registration Cards, 1942," online database (Provo, UT: Ancestry.com Operations, 2010).

150 **"the country":** Pankhurst, "William H. Ellis," 92, 93; M. S. Wellby, *'Twixt Sirdar and Menelik: An Account of a Year's Expedition from Zeila to Cairo Through Unknown Abyssinia* (New York: Negro Universities Press, 1969 [1901]), 65; "An American Promoter in Abyssinia," *World's Work* 7, no. 5 (March 1904): 99–100; Skinner, *The 1903 Skinner Mission to Ethiopia*, 77–79, 85; Vivian, *Abyssinia*, 202; *New York Times*, January 1, 1904.

151 **encounter to come:** Francis Loomis to W.H. Ellis, June 19, 1903; Francis Loomis to Eno Littman, June 17, 1903; Francis Loomis to W. H. Ellis, August 29, 1903, all Roll 3, Book 1, Francis Loomis Papers, Special Collections, Stanford University Library. For more on Loomis, see Schoultz, *Beneath the United States*, 181–182; Amanda Kay McVety, "The 1903 Skinner Mission: Images of Ethiopia in the Progressive Era," *Journal of the Gilded Age and Progressive Era* 10, no. 2 (April 2011): 187–212.

151 **US business:** Skinner, *The 1903 Skinner Mission to Ethiopia*, 164; *New York Sun*, September 21, 1903; undated clippings in *New York Journal American* morgue, W. H. Ellis File, Center for American History, University of Texas at Austin.

152 **"King Menelik":** W. H. Ellis to John Hay, January 13, 1904 in Dispatches from United States Consuls in Marseille, France, 1790–1906, T220, RG 59; *Cleveland Gazette*, January 9, 1904. I am grateful to Amanda McVety for sharing Ellis's letter to Hay with me; Bruce to Cromwell, November 20, 1905 in Cromwell, *Unveiled Voices, Unvarnished Memories*, 268.

153 **the empire:** Undated clipping from *New York Sun* in *New York Journal American* morgue, W. H. Ellis File, Center for American History, University of Texas at Austin; *New York Sun*, October 30, 1904; "A Mysterious Disappearance."

153 **but relaxing:** Undated clipping in *New York Journal American* morgue files, W. H. Ellis File, Center for American History, University of Texas at Austin.

154 **upper decks:** *Poverty Bay Herald* (New Zealand), August 18, 1904; "A Mys-

terious Disappearance"; *Fulton County Republican* (Johnstown, NY), July 21, 1904.

154 **before death:** *Fulton County Republican* (Johnstown, NY), July 21, 1904; John Elfreth Watkins, *Famous Mysteries: Curious and Fantastic Riddles of Human Life That Have Never Been Solved* (Philadelphia: John C. Winston, 1919), 126–128.

154 **Addis Ababa:** *Syracuse Herald*, June 28, 1904; *Mexican Herald* (Mexico City), June 25, 1904.

155 **trans-Atlantic voyage:** "Disappearance of Loomis," *Pacific Monthly: A Magazine of Education and Progress* 12, no. 3 (September 1904): 183; "The Strange Death of H. Kent Loomis," *American Carpet and Upholstery Journal* 22, no. 8 (August 1904): 85; *New York Daily Tribune*, June 26, 1904; *Victoria Advocate*, November 10, 1904.

155 **"about him":** Undated clipping in *New York Journal American* morgue, W. H. Ellis file, Center for American History, University of Texas at Austin; *New York Daily Tribune*, June 25, 1904; Francis Loomis to Henry H. Childers, July 12, 1904, Francis Loomis Papers, Roll 3, Book 2, Special Collections, Stanford University Library.

155 **"his associate":** Francis Loomis to Baron von Sternburg, September 20, 1904, Francis Loomis Papers, Roll 4, Book 3, Special Collections, Stanford University Library.

156 **"his race":** *Fort Worth Telegram*, July 1, 1905.

156 **"'he got his'":** Nella Larsen, *Passing* (New York: Alfred A. Knopf, 1929), 97–98; *Freeman* (Indianapolis, IN), December 26, 1908; *Appeal* (St. Paul, MN), July 9, 1904.

157 **"Negro blood":** *Appeal* (St. Paul, MN), July 9, 1904; W. E. B. DuBois, "Passing," in *Passing: Authoritative Text, Backgrounds and Contexts, Criticism,* edited by Carla Kaplan (New York: W. W. Norton, 2007), 97–98.

158 **"*must* succeed":** Ellis to State Department, August 6, 1904, Series 1, Reel 46, Theodore Roosevelt Papers, Library of Congress; *New York Tribune*, November 22, November 23, 1904; W. H. Ellis to Fannie Starnes, August 9, 1904, family letter shared with author.

158 **being unmasked:** W. H. Ellis to Robert E. Peary, September 11, 1903, Letters and Telegrams Received, Entry 4, Box 21, Folder E-F, Peary Papers, RG XP, National Archives and Records Administration—College Park; W. H. Ellis to Andrew Carnegie, March 9, May 9, 1904, Andrew Carnegie Birthplace Museum; Pankhurst, "William H. Ellis," 95–97.

159 **island's ruler:** Ronald L. Jackson II, *Scripting the Black Masculine Body: Identity, Discourse, and Racial Politics in Popular Media* (Albany: State University of New York Press, 2006), 28–29; Robert M. Zecker, *Race and America's Immigrant Press: How the Slovaks Were Taught to Think like White People* (New York: Bloomsbury, 2011), 181; Marilyn Kern-Foxworth, *Aunt Jemima, Uncle Ben, and Rastus: Blacks in Advertising, Yesterday, Today, and Tomorrow* (Westport, CT: Greenwood Press, 1994), 45–46; Jan Nederveen

Pieterse, *White on Black: Images of Africa and Blacks in Western Popular Culture* (New Haven: Yale University Press, 1992), 152–156; Sotiropoulos, *Staging Race*, 144–146; *New York Dramatic Mirror*, December 7, 1907.

160 **two groups:** Sotiropoulos, *Staging Race*, 148–158.

160 **stereotyped role:** Yuval Taylor and Jake Austen, *Darkest America: Black Minstrelsy from Slavery to Hip-Hop* (New York: W. W. Norton, 2012), 109–133; Louis Chude-Sokei, *The Last "Darky": Bert Williams, Black-on-Black Minstrelsy, and the African Diaspora* (Durham: Duke University Press, 2006), 27–45; Daphne A. Brooks, *Bodies in Dissent: Spectacular Performances of Race and Freedom, 1850–1910* (Durham: Duke University Press, 2007), 253–256.

161 **all their own:** Sotiropoulos, *Staging Race*, 63–71, 152–153; Romeyn, *Street Scenes*, 258 n.53.

6: THE CITY OF HAPPY HOMES

162 **infant Guillermo:** 1905 New York State Census, Assembly District 21, Election District 4, 22; *New York Evening Telegram*, July 25, 1901; *Trow's General Directory of the Boroughs of Manhattan and the Bronx, 1902* (New York: Trow, 1902), 392; *Trow's General Directory of the Boroughs of Manhattan and the Bronx, 1905* (New York: Trow, 1905), 400; New York State Census, 1905.

163 **malicious intent?:** Karen Halttunen, *Confidence Men and Painted Women: A Study of Middle-Class Culture in America, 1830–1870* (New Haven: Yale University Press, 1982), 1–32.

163 **record keeping:** The 1890 federal census was destroyed in a fire, and Ellis does not appear in the 1900 federal census, presumably because he was in Mexico at the time it was taken. Thus, the salient comparison here is between the 1880 federal census and the 1905 New York census and 1910 federal census.

164 **variation thereof:** Knox, *Who's Who in New York, 1917–1918*, 336; Guillermo Enrique Eliseo Jr. Birth Certificate 5861, February 5, 1904, New York City Department of Records and Information Services, Municipal Archives; Porfirio Ellis Birth Certificate and Sherwood Ellis Birth Certificate, May 25, 1912, Mount Vernon Town Records.

165 **"given him":** "William H. Ellis," *Successful American* 2, no. 2 (August 1900): 62; W. H. Ellis to Fannie Starnes, August 9, 1904, family letter shared with author.

165 **twentieth century:** Larry H. Spruill, *Mount Vernon* (Charleston, SC: Arcadia Publishing, 2009), 55; personal communication with Larry Spruill, June 19, 2013. *Daily Argus* (Mount Vernon, NY), July 9, 1909, lists Ellis as newly connected to the town's telephone service. It is thus possible that he moved to Mount Vernon around this date.

166 **Sherwood:** Maude Ellis to Fannie Starnes, January 9, 1924, family letter shared with author. *Daily Argus* (Mount Vernon, NY), January 13, 1908;

March 9, July 6, 1916; March 3, March 4, 1919; November 9, 1920; September 23, 1921. Note the contrast in the 1910 Mount Vernon directory between William H. Ellis and the African American cook Gertrude Ellis on the same page. *Turner's Annual Directory of Mount Vernon, Pelham and Sherwood Park, 1910* (Yonkers, NY: W. L. Richmond, 1910), 130.

166 **closer to home:** Zewde, *A History of Modern Ethiopia, 1855–1974*, 111.

166 **for some time:** W. H. Ellis to Fannie Starnes, April 4, 1914, family letter shared with author; "H. de Blake Elena y Lisette de Blackmore Florencia contra Ellis W.E.," *Diario de jurisprudencia del distrito y territories federales* 7, no. 4 (January 4, 1906): 25–30.

167 **$145,169.75:** "Niquet Alberto, Ellis Guillermo H. y Araoz Manuel," *Diario de jurisprudencia del distrito y territories federales* 13, no. 56 (March 6, 1908): 441–47; Elias Delafond v. William H. Ellis, Caurto de lo Civil, 24 septiembre 1907, TSJDF Folio 102995, Tribunal Superior de Justicia del Distrito Federal, Siglo XX, Archivo Histórico, 1907, Caja 0582, Archivo General de la Nación; Bernardo Gracia Medrano y Iadislao Demandado Morales v. W.E. Ellis, 26 septiembre 1907, TSJDF Folio 114152, Tribunal Superior de Justicia del Distrito Federal, Siglo XX, Archivo Histórico, 1907, Caja 0647, Archivo General de la Nación; Ellis to Limantour, August 15 and August 24, 1907; Limantour to Ellis, August 21 and August 27, 1907 <http://www.archivo.cehmcarso.com.mx/janium-bin/janium_zui.pl?jzd=/janium/JZD/CDLIV/Copiadores/Ministro-III/7/Libro18/251/CDLIV.Copiadores.Ministro-III.7.Libro18.251.jzd&fn=266031> (accessed 8/5/15); *Diario oficial: Organo del gobierno constitucional de los Estados Unidos Mexicanos* 93, no. 32 (December 7, 1907): 506; *Diario oficial: Organo del gobierno constitucional de los Estados Unidos Mexicanos* 93, no. 39 (December 16, 1907): 620.

167 **fragile finances:** *New York Times*, May 29, 1921; *New York Tribune*, May 29, 1921.

168 **"to Mexicans":** *Nuevo Mundo* quoted in MacLachlan and Beezley, *El Gran Pueblo*, 224.

168 **"demand it":** Gilbert G. Gonzalez, "Mexican Labor Migration, 1876–1924," in *Beyond La Frontera: The History of Mexico-U.S. Migration*, edited by Mark Overmyer-Velázquez (New York: Oxford University Press, 2011), 33–40; Luis Aboites Aguilar, *Norte precario: Poblamiento y colonización en México (1760–1940)* (Mexico City: Colegio de México, Centro de Estudios Históricos, 1995), 95–104; Greg Grandin, *Empire's Workshop: Latin America, the United States, and the Rise of the New Imperialism* (New York: Metropolitan Books, 2006), 29; strikers quoted in W. Dirk Raat, *Revoltosos: Mexico's Rebels in the United States, 1903–1923* (College Station: Texas A&M University Press, 1981), 81.

169 **occupation of Mexico:** Kroeber, *Man, Land, and Water*, 29, 46–47, 203, 226; Ramón Eduardo Ruíz, *The Great Rebellion: Mexico, 1905–1924* (New York: W. W. Norton, 1982), 142; Robert McCaa, "Missing Millions: The Demographic Costs of the Mexican Revolution," *Mexican Studies/Estudios*

Mexicanos 19, no. 2 (Summer 2003): 367–400. Not all the casualties were from armed combat. Others died from the disease and starvation that the revolution brought in its wake.

169 **strange new Mexico:** Carlo de Fornaro, *Diaz, Czar of Mexico: An Arraignment* (N.p.: International Publishing, 1909), 51, 82, 95; John Womack Jr., *Zapata and the Mexican Revolution* (New York: Vintage Books, 1968), 15–16; *Mercury News* (San Jose, CA), August 24, 1913; *El Paso Herald*, April 14, 1911; *Leprelette Sweet v. William H. Ellis*, Supreme Court, New York State, 1912, New York Municipal Archives, 192–197.

170 **Latin American entrepreneur:** For more on Ellis's other business schemes at this time, see John Mason Hart, *Empire and Revolution: The Americans in Mexico Since the Civil War* (Berkeley: University of California Press, 2002), 213.

170 **his quest:** Mark R. Finlay, *Growing American Rubber: Strategic Plants and the Politics of National Security* (New Brunswick: Rutgers University Press, 2009), 3, 13; *Mexican Herald* (Mexico City), August 2, 1906, and September 21, 1908.

170 **foreign capitalists:** Otto Stapf, "A New Rubber Tree: Palo Amarillo," *Bulletin of Miscellaneous Information (Royal Botanic Gardens, Kew)* 1907, no. 7 (1907): 294–296; " 'Palo Amarillo' Rubber Bottled Up," *India Rubber World* 43, no. 1 (October 1, 1910): 4; *Boston Evening Transcript*, October 7, 1910; *El Paso Herald*, April 14, 1911; *New York Tribune*, February 7, 1909; *Arizona Republican*, September 4, 1907; *Mexican Herald* (Mexico City), August 2, 1906; *Directory of Directors in the City of New York, 1915–1916* (New York: Directory of Directors, 1915), 200; "Encouragement of the Rubber Industry," *Bulletin of the International Bureau of the American Republics* 28, no. 2 (April 1909): 732.

171 **foreign hands:** Ellis to Payne, July 17, 1923, and Ellis to Bryan, November 1, 1913, Folder 812.6461M57/10, Central Decimal File 1910–1929, RG 59, NARA–College Park.

171 **"as significant":** Great Britain, Foreign Office, *Correspondence Respecting the Renewal of Diplomatic Relations with Mexico, 1880–83* (N.p., 1884), 154; *New York Times*, September 7, September 14, September 30, October 8, 1912.

172 **collective portrait:** Passenger List of SS *Esperanza*, February 18, 1910, "Passenger Lists of Vessels Arriving at New York, New York, 1820–1957, " online database (Provo, UT: Ancestry.com Operations, 2010).

173 **revolution had begun:** Kroeber, *Man, Land, and Water*, 28–29; Martin R. Ansell, *Oil Baron of the Southwest: Edward L. Doheny and the Development of the Petroleum Industry in California and Mexico* (Columbus: Ohio State University Press, 1998), 81–82; Jonathan C. Brown, "Why Foreign Oil Companies Shifted Their Production from Mexico to Venezuela During the 1920s," *American Historical Review* 90, no. 2 (April 1985): 362–385; Michael J. Gonzales, "Imagining Mexico in 1910: Visions of the *Patria* in the Centennial Celebration in Mexico City," *Journal of Latin American Studies* 39, no. 3 (August 2007): 495–533.

174 **"iron hand":** W. H. Ellis to Fannie Starnes, April 4, 1914, family letter

shared with author; *New York Times*, September 21, 1912; W. H. Ellis to Felix Díaz, February 21, 1913 <http://community.fortunecity.ws/meltingpot/redruth/95/Pagina_Principal/Obregon/W__H__Ellis__Banquero_ Neoyorqu/w__h__ellis__banquero_neoyorqu.html> (accessed 7/11/13); *Aberdeen Daily News* (Aberdeen, SD), April 24, 1914; *New York Times*, March 24, April 25, 1914.

174 **"any alarm":** W. H. Ellis to Venustiano Carranza, January 19, 1916 <http:// www.archivo.cehmcarso.com.mx/janium-bin/janium_zui.pl?jzd=/ janium/JZD/XXI/84/9440/1/XXI.84.9440.1.jzd&fn=26163> (accessed 8/5/15); Frederich Katz, *The Life and Times of Pancho Villa* (Stanford: Stanford University Press, 1998), 557–560.

175 **"if necessary":** Katz, *Life and Times of Pancho Villa*, 560–569; W. Dirk Raat, *Mexico and the United States: Ambivalent Vistas*, 3rd ed. (Athens: University of Georgia Press, 2004), 122; Fall quoted in Donald Carl Baldridge, "Mexican Petroleum and United States–Mexican Relations, 1919–1923" (Ph.D. dissertation, University of Arizona, 1971), 25.

175 **agrarian reform:** Greg Grandin, "The Liberal Traditions in the Americas: Rights, Sovereignty, and the Origins of Liberal Multilateralism," *American Historical Review* 117, no. 1 (2012): 75–76; Alan Knight, *The Mexican Revolution*, 2 vols. (New York: Cambridge University Press, 1986), 2:470–471; N. Stephen Kane, "American Businessmen and Foreign Policy: The Recognition of Mexico, 1920–1923," *Political Science Quarterly* 90, no. 2 (Summer 1975): 296–297.

175 **to escape:** *New York Times*, July 4, 1920; *Winston-Salem Journal* (Winston-Salem, NC), July 9, 1920; Moats, *Thunder in Their Veins*, 233–235.

176 **"Carranza money":** Ellis to Bryan, July 22, 1914, Folder 812.512/369, and Ellis to Bryan, January 5, 1915, Folder 812.512/535, Central Decimal File 1910–1929, RG 59, NARA–College Park.

176 **government's decision:** Ellis to Bryan, November 1, 1913, Folder 812.6461M57/10, Central Decimal File 1910–1929, RG 59, NARA–College Park.

177 **neutrality acts:** US Senate, *Investigation of Mexican Affairs: Hearing Before a Subcommittee of the Committee on Foreign Relations, Part 12* (Washington, DC: GPO, 1920), 3301; Helen Delpar, "Exiliados y expatriados estadounidenses en México (1920–1940)," in *México, país refugio: La experiencia de los exilios en el siglo XX*, edited by Pablo Yankelevich (Mexico City: Instituto Nacional de Antropología e Historia, 2002), 142–144; Young, *Catarino Garza's Revolution on the Texas-Mexico Border*, 58–59; Raat, *Revoltosos*, 32–33, 37–38; Duarte Espinosa, *Frontera y diplomacia*, 111–118.

177 **Mexico City:** Offrey to Bielaski, November 10, 1916, Investigative Reports of the Bureau of Investigation 1908–1922, Mexican Files, 1909–21, Case Number: 678, Suspect Name: William H. Ellis, M1085, RG65, NARA–Microfilm Publications.

177 **"in Texas":** Sharp to Nye, March 20, 1919, Case File 000-751, in Kornweibel, *Federal Surveillance of Afro-Americans.*

177 **pressing business:** Report of Harry Berliner, October 28, 1916, Case File 000-751, in Kornweibel, *Federal Surveillance of Afro-Americans.*

178 **"I left him":** Lincoln G. Valentine, *The Case of Costa Rica* (New York: M. B. Brown, 1919), 73.

178 **the plotters:** Valentine, *The Case of Costa Rica*, 73–75, 81.

179 **petroleum fields:** Mavis Hiltunen Biesanz, Richard Biesanz, and Karen Zubris Biesanz, *The Ticos: Culture and Social Change in Costa Rica* (Boulder, CO: Lynne Rienner, 1999), 27–28.

179 **war-shattered economy:** Womack, *Zapata and the Mexican Revolution*, 325–327; Katz, *The Life and Times of Pancho Villa*, 765–766; Kane, "American Businessmen and Foreign Policy," 297–298; Linda B. Hall, *Oil, Banks, and Politics: The United States and Postrevolutionary Mexico, 1917–1924* (Austin: University of Texas Press, 1995), 2.

180 **"the Government":** *New York Times*, July 6, 1920 (a Spanish-language version of this article can be found in *La Prensa* [San Antonio, TX], July 8, 1920); Ellis to Fall, December 16, 1921, Fall to Ellis, December 4, 1921, and Ellis to Fall, December 16, 1921, Albert Fall Papers (FA Box 90 [19]), Huntington Library.

180 **non-Mexican:** *El Universal* (Mexico City), July 6, 1920; *Excélsior* (Mexico City), July 16, 1920, and July 25, 1921; *New York Times*, July 31, 1923, and July 22, 1924; Justin Castro, "Modesto C. Rolland, the Mexican Revolution, and Development of the Isthmus of Tehuantepec" (manuscript in author's possession); Ellis to Warren, July 13, 1923, Folder 812.1561/10, Central Decimal File 1910–1929, RG 59, NARA–College Park.

181 **and Mexico:** Modesto C. Rolland, *Los puertos libres Mexicanos y la zona libre en la frontera norte de la Republica Mexicana* (México: Empresa Editorial de Ingenieria y Arquitectura, 1924), 81; *New York Times*, July 31, 1923.

181 **take a toll:** John F. Kasson, *Rudeness and Civility: Manners in Nineteenth-Century Urban America* (New York: Hill and Wang, 1990), 195–200.

182 **"several hours":** *Leprelette Sweet v. William H. Ellis*, Supreme Court, New York State, 1912, New York Municipal Archives, 156–157. The stress of relocation and separation from family on African Americans is discussed in Dan A. Black, Seth G. Sanders, Evan J. Taylor, and Lowell J. Taylor, "The Impact of the Great Migration on Mortality of African Americans: Evidence from the Deep South," *American Economic Review* 105, no. 2 (February 2015): 477–503.

182 **"doing the same":** W. H. Ellis to Fannie Starnes, August 11, 1923, family letter shared with author.

182 **fifty-nine:** *Leprelette Sweet v. William H. Ellis*, Supreme Court, New York State, 152, New York Municipal Archives; Report of the Death of William Henry Ellis, American Consular Service, Mexico City, October 25, 1923, "Reports of Deaths of American Citizens Abroad, 1835–1974," online database (Provo, UT: Ancestry.com Operations, 2010).

183 **father's affairs:** "Inventory of the Personal Effects of William H. Ellis, deceased," Ellis, Guillermo Enrique, 312.113, Central Decimal File 1910–1929, RG 59, NARA–College Park.

183 **now in death:** *Mount Vernon Argus*, September 29, 1923.

184 **"colony failed":** *New York Times*, September 30, 1923; *New York World*, September 30, 1923.

184 **"'Guillermo Enrique Eliseo'":** *New York Age*, December 17, 1908, October 6, November 24, 1923.

185 **"was of us":** *Dallas Express*, October 13, 1923.

185 **"the ledger":** *Broad Axe* (Chicago), October 6, 1923; *Chicago Defender*, October 6, 1923.

186 **to cooperate:** W. E. B. Du Bois to W. H. Ellis, July 8, 1919, W. H. Ellis to W. E. B. Du Bois, July 10, 1919 <http://oubliette.library.umass.edu/view/full/mums312-b014-i071>, <http://oubliette.library.umass.edu/view/full/mums312-b014-i072> (accessed 1/26/15); W. E. B. Du Bois to J. D. Wetmore, October 5, 1923 <http://credo.library.umass.edu/view/full/mums312-b023-i532> (accessed 6/14/13); J. D. Wetmore to W. E. B. Du Bois, October 6, 1923 <http://credo.library.umass.edu/view/full/mums312-b023-i513> (accessed 6/14/13); Noelle Morrissette, *James Weldon Johnson's Modern Soundscapes* (Iowa City: University of Iowa Press, 2013), 86–87. One of the few traces of Ellis's ties to Wetmore can be found in Charles William Anderson to Booker T. Washington, October 3, 1912, in Louis R. Harlan and Raymond W. Smock, eds., *The Booker T. Washington Papers*, 14 vols. (Urbana: University of Illinois Press, 1972–89), 12:31.

186 **"Guillermo Enrique Eliseo":** "Who Would Be King," *Time* 2, no. 6 (October 8, 1923, 4; *Milwaukee Sentinel*, December 9, 1923. To illustrate reach of the AP obituary, it appeared in *Times-Picayune* (New Orleans, LA), October 1, 1923; *Atlanta Constitution*, October 1, 1923; and *Boston Daily Globe*, September 30, 1923, among other publications.

187 **"realty holdings":** *Mount Vernon Argus*, September 29, 1923; Report of the Death of William Henry Ellis, American Consular Service, Mexico City, October 25, 1923; *Cleveland Gazette*, October 13, 1923; *New York Tribune*, November 14, 1923; *Chicago Defender*, December 1, 1923; *New York Age*, November 24, 1923.

187 **"business through":** Maude Ellis to Fannie Starnes, January 9, 1924, family letter shared with author.

188 **"conduct and character":** Adee to Ellis, February 27, 1924. Folder 611.8431/3, Central Decimal File 1910–29, RG 59, NARA–College Park; Delpar, "Exiliados y expatriados estadounidenses en México (1920–1940)," 141; *Daily Argus* (Mt. Vernon, NY), December 21, 1923; Maude Ellis to Fannie Starnes, January 9, 1924, family letter shared with author.)

188 **rest of eternity:** *Daily Argus* (Mount Vernon, NY), May 3, 1924; *New York Times*, May 11, 1924; Report of the Death of Guillermo Enrique Ellis, American Consular Service, Mexico City, June 14, 1924, "Reports of

Deaths of American Citizens Abroad, 1835–1974," online database (Provo, UT: Ancestry.com Operations, 2010).

189 **names unknown:** Book 3527, Deed Records, 216, July 23, 1954 and Book 3705, Deed Records, 275–276, June 24, 1955, Bexar County Clerk's Office; 1930 U.S. Census, North Arlington, New Jersey, 26A, T626, NARA–Microfilm Publication; Susie Williams, interview by author, July 21, 2013; Vermont Death Records, 1909–2003,Vermont State Archives and Records Administration, Montpelier.

189 **Mexicans as well:** Douglas Flamming, *Bound for Freedom: Black Los Angeles in Jim Crow America* (Berkeley: University of California Press, 2005), 93; Berlin, *The Making of African America*, 152–153.

190 **post office:** Flamming, *Bound for Freedom*, 60, 82–83; B. Gordon Wheeler, *Black California: The History of African-Americans in the Golden State* (New York: Hippocrene Books, 1993), 199; Susie Williams, interview by author, November 18, 2013.

191 **Mexican dance:** *The Official Hotel Red Book and Directory, 1920* (New York: Official Hotel Red Book and Directory, 1920), 813; T. Philip Terry, *Terry's Guide to Mexico* (Boston: Houghton Mifflin, 1922), 235; *Evening Journal* (Jersey City, NJ), April 29, 1887, April 18, May 13, November 18, 1893; Patricia Aulestia de Alba, "Victoria (Vicky) Ellis," *Cuadernos del CID-Danza* 16 (1987): 3.

191 **outside Veracruz:** David E. Wilt, *The Mexican Filmography, 1916 Through 2001* (Jefferson, NC: McFarland, 2004), 32.

191 **existence of Afro-Mexicans:** Emilio García Riera, *Historia documental del cine mexicano: Época sonora, 1926–1940* (Mexico: Ediciones Era, 1969), 155; Roberto Ortiz Escobar, "El cine mexicano filmado en Veracruz," in *Microhistorias del cine en México*, edited by Eduardo de la Vega Alfaro (Guadalajara: Universidad de Guadalajara, 2001), 297, 310; Micaela Díaz-Sánchez and Alexandro D. Hernández, "The Son Jarocho as Afro-Mexican Resistance Music," *Journal of Pan African Studies* 6, no. 1 (July 2013): 187–209; *A la orilla de un palmar*, publicity brochure in author's possession; Alan Knight, "Racism, Revolution, and *Indigenismo*: Mexico, 1910–1940," in *The Idea of Race in Latin America, 1870–1940*, edited by Richard Graham (Austin: University of Texas Press, 1990), 77–102.

192 **marginalization of Afro-Mexicans:** Ellis, Victoria, May 6, 1930, and Ellis Sherwood, William Fernando, April 3, 1935, Departamento de Migración, Estadounidenses, Caja 48, Archivo General de la Nación; Gabriela Pulido Llano discusses how ideas of blackness were associated with Cuba in Mexico during this time in *Mulatas y negros cubanos en la escena mexicana, 1920–1950* (Mexico City: Instituto Nacional de Antropología e Historia, 2010).

193 **"black person":** Aulestia de Alba, "Victoria (Vicky) Ellis," 3; Peter Ellis, interview by author, February 18, 2015.

EPILOGUE: TRICKSTER MAKES THIS WORLD

195 **simply black:** Fear of white negroes quoted in Hobbs, *A Chosen Exile*, 128–129; Census Bureau quoted in Christine B. Hickman, "The Devil and the One Drop Rule: Racial Categories, African Americans, and the U.S. Census," *Michigan Law Review* 95, no. 5 (March 1997): 1187; Martha Hodes, "Fractions and Fictions in the United States Census of 1890," in, *Haunted by Empire: Geographies of Intimacy in North American History*, edited by Ann Laura Stoler (Durham: Duke University Press, 2006), 240–270.

195 **"just alike":** Amy Jacques Garvey, ed., *The Philosophy and Opinions of Marcus Garvey; or, Africa for the Africans* (Dover, MA: Majority Press, 1986 [1923]), 55; Hahn, *The Political Worlds of Slavery and Freedom*, 117–129.

195 **"the Whites":** José Vasconcelos, *The Cosmic Race/La raza cósmica*, trans. Didier T. Jaén (Baltimore: Johns Hopkins University Press, 1997 [1925]), 18–19, 39, 58.

196 **unwanted migrants:** Mae M. Ngai, *Impossible Subjects: Illegal Aliens and the Making of Modern America* (Princeton: Princeton University Press, 2004), 21–29; Kelly Lytle Hernández, *Migra! A History of the U.S. Border Patrol* (Berkeley: University of California Press, 2010), 28–32; Marilyn Lake and Henry Reynolds, *Drawing the Global Colour Line: White Men's Countries and the International Challenge of Racial Equality* (Cambridge: Cambridge University Press, 2008), 310–314.

196 **entry of African Americans:** Gustavo Durón González, *Problemas migratorios de México: Apuntamientos para su resolución* (Mexico City: Talleres de la Cámara de Diputados, 1925), 100; Lawrence Douglas Taylor Hansen, "La migraciones menonitas al norte de México entre 1922 y 1940," *Migraciones Internacionales* 3, no. 1 (January–June 2005): 17; Juan de Dios González Ibarra, *La negritude, tercera raíz mexicana* (Mexico City: Universidad Autónoma del Estado de Morelos, 2007), 123; and Grace Peña Delgado, *Making the Chinese Mexican: Global Migration, Localism, and Exclusion in the U.S.–Mexico Borderlands* (Stanford: Stanford University Press, 2012), 157–189.

197 **as "white":** Marta María Saade Granados, "Una raza prohibida: afroestadounidenses en México," in *Nación y extranjería: La exclusion racial en las políticas migratorias de Argentina, Brasil, Cuba y México*, edited by Pablo Yankelvich (México: Universidad Nacional Autónoma de México, 2009), 231–276; W. E. B. Du Bois to the President of the Republic of Mexico, November 16, 1926 <http://credo.library.umass.edu/view/full/mums312-b034-i346> (accessed 6/14/13). For more on the changing Mexican response to African-American immigration at this time, see Delores Nason McBroome, "Harvests of Gold: African American Boosterism, Agriculture, and Investment in Allensworth and Little Liberia," in *Seeking El Dorado: African Americans in California*, edited by Lawrence B. de Graaf, Kevin Mulroy, and Quintard Taylor (Seattle: University of

Washington Press, 2001), 162–169; Josh Kun, "Tijuana and the Borders of Race," in *A Companion to Los Angeles*, edited by William Deverell and Greg Hise (Malden, MA: Wiley-Blackwell, 2010), 314–324; and *Los Angeles Times*, February 8, 1923. For restrictions on Chinese immigrants, see Robert Chao Romero, *The Chinese in Mexico, 1882–1940* (Tucson: University of Arizona Press, 2010), 156–166; José Jorge Gómez Izquierdo, *El movimiento antichino en México (1871–1934): Problemas del racism y del nacionalismo durante la Revolución Mexicana* (Mexico: Instituto Nacional de Antropología e Historia, 1991), 99–108; and Gerardo Rénique, "Race, Mestizaje and Nationalism: Sonora's Anti-Chinese Movement and State Formation in Post-revolutionary México," *Political Power and Social Theory* 14 (2000): 91–140.

198 **one another?:** W. H. Ellis to Fannie Starnes, August 9, 1904, and W. H. Ellis to Charles Ellis, September 11, 1903, family letters shared with author.

199 **"nothing else?":** *New York Age*, July 5, 1917; Ellis to Theodore Roosevelt, July 7, 1917, Series 1, Reel 239, Theodore Roosevelt Papers, Library of Congress; Ellis quoted in E. R. Bills, *The 1910 Slocum Massacre: An Act of Genocide in East Texas* (Charleston, SC: History Press, 2014), 63. For more on Ellis's ties to Booker T. Washington's inner circle, see Harlan and Smock, *The Booker T. Washington Papers* 8:461–462, 12:31.

199 **by others:** Stetson quoted in Sollors, *Neither Black nor White*, 248; W. E. B. Du Bois, *The Souls of Black Folk* (New York: New American Library, 1969 [1903]), 45.

200 **complex self:** Hughes, "Fooling Our White Folks," 39; I am indebted to Matt Guterl for encouraging me to consider the implications of passing as Mexican instead of passing as white.

201 **"comida Hispana":** Claude Bataillon, *Las regiones geográficas en México*, 10th ed. (Mexico City: Siglo veintiuno editores, 1993), 172–173; US Census Bureau, "Total Hispanic Population by Selected Subgroups, New York City and Boroughs, 2010" <http://www.nyc.gov/html/dcp/pdf/census/census2010/t_sf1_p8_nyc.pdf> (accessed 7/29/13).

BIBLIOGRAPHY

ARCHIVAL MATERIALS

Andrew Carnegie Birthplace Museum, Dunfermline, Scotland
  Records

Archivo de la Secretaría de Relaciones Exteriores, Mexico City
  Records

Archivo General de la Nación, Mexico City
  Tribunal Superior de Justicia del Distrito Federal, Archivo Histórico

Archivo Municipal de Torreón Eduardo Guerra, Torreón, Coahuila
  Testimonio de la escritura de colonización celebrado entre Guillermo Ellis
    y la Compañía de Tlahualilo

Bexar County Clerk's Office, San Antonio, Texas
  Deed Records

California State Archives, Sacramento, California
  Records

Center for American History, University of Texas, Austin, Texas
  New York Journal American Morgue

Duke University Library, Durham, North Carolina
  Records of the Bureau of the Census, Seventh Census of the United States,
    1850, Agricultural Schedules, M1528

Huntington Library, San Marino, California
  Albert Fall Papers

Library of Congress, Washington, DC
  Theodore Roosevelt Papers

Missouri History Museum, St. Louis, Missouri
  AF-Mexico

Mount Vernon Town Records, Mount Vernon, New York
  Birth Records

Municipal Archives, New York City Department of Records and Information
    Services, New York, New York
  Birth Records
  Marriage Records
  Supreme Court Records

National Archives and Records Administration—College Park, Maryland
  Records of the Department of State, Central Classified Files, RG 59
  Records of the Department of State, Central Decimal Files, RG 59
  Robert E. Peary Papers

National Archives and Records Administration—Microfilm Publications
  Records of the Bureau of the Census, Seventh Census of the United States,
    1850, M432, RG 29
  Records of the Bureau of the Census, Eighth Census of the United States,
    1860, M653, RG 29
  Records of the Bureau of the Census, Ninth Census of the United States,
    1870, M593, RG 29
  Records of the Bureau of the Census, Tenth Census of the United States,
    1880, T9, RG 29
  Records of the Bureau of the Census, Twelfth Census of the United States,
    1900, T623, RG 29
  Records of the Bureau of the Census, Fifteenth Census of the United
    States, 1930, T626, RG 29
  Records of the Department of State, Dispatches from United States
    Consuls in Durango, Mexico, 1886–1906, M290, RG 59
  Records of the Department of State, Dispatches from United States
    Consuls in Marseille, France, 1790–1906, T220, RG 59
  Records of the Department of State, Dispatches from United States
    Consuls in Piedras Negras (Ciudad Porfirio Díaz), Mexico, 1868–
    1906, M299, RG 59
  Records of the Federal Bureau of Investigation, Mexican Files, 1909–21,
    M1085, RG 65
  Records of the Immigration and Naturalization Service, Passenger and
    Crew Lists of Vessels Arriving at New York, NY, 1891–1957, T715,
    RG 85
  Records of the Selective Service System, World War I Draft Registration
    Cards, M1509, RG 163

New York State Archives, Albany, New York
New York State Census, 1905

Special Collections, Stanford University Library, Palo Alto, California
Francis Loomis Papers

Toronto Reference Library, Toronto, Canada
Anderson Ruffin Abbott Papers

Universidad Iberoamericana, Mexico City
Colección Porfirio Díaz

Vermont State Archives and Records Administration, Montpelier, Vermont
Death Records

Victoria Regional History Center, Victoria College/University of Houston–
Victoria, Victoria, Texas
Barry A. Crouch Collection
Sidney R. Weisiger Papers

Victoria Town Records, Victoria, Texas
Brand Book
Probate Records
Deed Records

Woodlawn Cemetery Archives, Bronx, New York
Interment Records

ONLINE SOURCES

American Memory, Library of Congress, http://memory.loc.gov/ammem/
index.html
Archivo General del Estado de Coahuila, http://ahc.sfpcoahuila.gob.mx
Avalon Project: Documents in Law, History and Diplomacy, http://avalon.law
.yale.edu/default.asp
Centro de Estudios de Historia de México, http://www.cehm.com.mx/ES/
archivo/Paginas/archivo_cehm.aspx
NCpedia, http://ncpedia.org
Texas Slavery Project, http://www.texasslaveryproject.org
W. E. B. Du Bois Papers, http://credo.library.umass.edu/view/collection/
mums312

ORAL INTERVIEWS BY AUTHOR

Peter Ellis, February 18, 2015
Susie Williams, March 12, 2012; July 21, 2013; November 18, 2013
Susie Williams and Joan Williams, October 2011

NEWSPAPERS

Aberdeen Daily News (Aberdeen, SD)
Appeal (St. Paul, MN)
Arizona Republican (Phoenix)
Atchison Daily Globe
Atlanta Constitution
Austin Weekly Statesman
Baltimore American
Baltimore Sun
Birmingham Age-Herald
Birmingham News
Boston Daily Globe
Boston Evening Transcript
Brenham Weekly Banner (Brenham, TX)
Broad Axe (Chicago)
Brooklyn Eagle
Brownsville Daily Herald
Charlotte Observer
Chicago Daily Tribune
Chicago Defender
Chicago Herald
Chicago Record
Christian Recorder (Philadelphia, PA)
Civilian and Gazette (Galveston, TX)
Cleveland Gazette
Colorado Citizen (Columbus, TX)
Colored American (Washington, DC)
Daily Argus (Mount Vernon, NY)
Daily Express (London)
Daily Herald (Brownsville, TX)
Daily Inter Ocean (Chicago)
Daily Picayune (New Orleans)
Daily Register (Mobile, AL)
Dallas Express
Dallas Morning News
Denver Evening Post

Denver Post
El Monitor (Mexico City)
El Monitor Republicano (Mexico City)
El Paso Herald
El Regidor (San Antonio, TX)
El Siglo Diez y Nueve (Mexico City)
El Tiempo (Mexico City)
El Universal (Mexico City)
Evening Journal (Jersey City, NJ)
Evening Statesman (Walla Walla, WA)
Evening Telegram (New York)
Excélsior (Mexico City)
Flake's Bulletin (Galveston, TX)
Fort Worth Daily Gazette
Fort Worth Gazette
Fort Worth Telegram
Freeman (Indianapolis, IN)
Fulton County Republican (Johnstown, NY)
Gaceta de México (Mexico City)
Galveston Daily News
Galveston Weekly News
Houston Telegraph
Hutchinson Daily News (Hutchinson, KS)
Indianola Weekly Bulletin
Inter Ocean (Chicago)
Kansas City Star
La Libertad (Mexico City)
La Patria (Mexico City)
La Prensa (San Antonio, TX)
La Voz de México (Mexico City)
Ledger and Texan (San Antonio, TX)
Lethbridge News (Lethbridge, Canada)
Liberator (Boston, MA)
Los Angeles Herald
Los Angeles Times
Macon Telegraph
Mercury News (San Jose, CA)
Mexican Herald (Mexico City)
Milwaukee Journal
Milwaukee Sentinel
Morning Oregonian (Portland, OR)
Mount Vernon Argus (Mount Vernon, NY)
National Vindicator (Washington, TX)
Navarro Express (Corsicana, TX)

New York Age
New York Daily Tribune
New York Evening Post
New York Herald
New York Sun
New York Times
New York Tribune
New York World
News and Observer (Raleigh, NC)
North American (Philadelphia, PA)
Nueces Valley (Corpus Christi, TX)
Oakland Tribune
Ogden Standard (Ogden, UT)
Omaha World Herald
Pawtucket Times (Pawtucket, RI)
Philadelphia Inquirer
Pittsburgh Press
Poverty Bay Herald (New Zealand)
Richmond Planet
Rocky Mountain News (Denver)
Sacramento Daily Record-Union
Saint Paul Globe
San Antonio Daily Express
San Antonio Daily Light
San Antonio Express
San Francisco Call
Semana Mercantil (Mexico City)
Sioux City Journal
Southern Intelligencer (Austin, TX)
Southern Mercury (Dallas, TX)
Southwestern Christian Advocate (New Orleans, LA)
St. Louis Globe Democrat
St. Louis Republic
St. Paul Daily News
St. Paul Globe
Standard (San Antonio, TX)
Syracuse Herald
Texas Almanac (Austin)
Texas Countryman (Belville)
Texas Planter (Brazoria)
Texas Presbyterian (Victoria)
Texas State Gazette (Austin)
Times-Picayune (New Orleans, LA)
Toronto Daily Mail

Tuskaloosa Gazette
Tuskaloosa Journal
Tuskaloosa Times
Two Republics (Mexico City)
Victoria Advocate (Victoria, TX)
Waco Evening News
Washington Times (Washington, DC)
Weekly Herald (New York, NY)
Weekly Times Herald (Dallas, TX)
West Alabama Breeze (Northport, AL)
White Republican (San Antonio, TX)
Winston-Salem Journal

PUBLIC DOCUMENTS

Great Britain
Great Britain Foreign Office. *Correspondence Respecting the Renewal of Diplomatic Relations with Mexico, 1880–83.* 1884.

Mexico
de Zayas Enríquez, R. *Los Estados Unidos Mexicanos: Sus condiciones naturales y sus elementos de prosperidad.* México: Oficina tip. de la Secretaría de Fomento, 1893.
Diario de los debates de la Cámara de Senadores, Decimocuarto Congreso Constitucional: Tercero y cuatro períodos. México: Imprenta de gobierno federal, 1890.
Diario oficial: Organo del gobierno constitucional de los Estados Unidos Mexicanos 93, no. 32 (December 7, 1907); 93, no. 99 (December 16, 1907).
Durón González, Gustavo. *Problemas migratorios de México: Apuntamientos para su resolución.* Mexico City: Talleres de la Cámara de Diputados, 1925.
Prado, C. Amado. *Prontuario de la municipalidad del Torreón.* Saltillo: Tipografia del Gobierno en Palacio, 1899.
Tablada, José Juan. *La defensa social: Historia de la campaña de la division del norte.* Mexico City: Imprenta de gobierno federal, 1913.

Texas
The Constitution, as Amended, and Ordinances of the Convention of 1866. Austin: Joseph Walker, 1866.
A Report and Treatise on Slavery and the Slavery Agitation: Printed by Order of the House of Representatives of Texas. Austin: John Marshall, 1857.
Spaight, A. W., Commissioner of Insurance, Statistics, and History. *The Resources, Soil, and Climate of Texas.* Galveston: A. H. Belo, 1882.

United States

The Congressional Globe: Containing Speeches, Reports, and the Laws of the Second Session, Forty-Second Congress. Washington, DC: Congressional Globe, 1872.

Dictionary of Races or Peoples. 61st Congress, 3rd Session, Senate Document No. 662.

"Difficulties on Southwestern Frontier." 36th Congress, 1st Session, House Ex. Doc. No. 52.

Emigration and Immigration: Reports of the Consular Officers of the United States. Washington, DC: GPO, 1887.

"Failure of the Scheme for the Colonization of Negroes in Mexico." 54th Congress, 1st Session, House Document No. 169.

Hergesheimer, Edwin. Map Showing the Distribution of the Slave Population of the Southern States of the United States, Compiled from the Census of 1860. Engraved by Thomas Leonhardt. Washington, DC: GPO, 1861.

"Letter from the Secretary of War, Communicating his Views in Relation to the Bill (S. 165) to Reimburse the State of Texas for Expenses Incurred in Repelling Invasions of Indians and Mexicans." 45th Congress, 2nd Session, Senate Ex. Doc. 19.

Mally, Frederick W. The Mexican Cotton-Boll Weevil. U.S. Department of Agriculture, Farmers' Bulletin No. 130. Washington, DC: GPO, 1901.

"Papers Relating to the Foreign Relations of the United States, 1877." 45th Congress, 2nd Session, House Ex. Doc. 1.

"Papers Relating to the Foreign Relations of the United States, 1879." 46th Congress, 2nd Session, House Ex. Doc. 1.

Papers Relating to the Foreign Relations of the United States, with the Annual Message of the President, Transmitted to Congress December 2, 1895. Washington, DC: GPO, 1896.

Quartermaster General's Office. Roll of Honor: Names of Soldiers Who Died in Defense of the American Union, Interred in the Eastern District of Texas; Central District of Texas; Rio Grande District, Department of Texas; Camp Ford, Tyler Texas; and Corpus Christi, Texas. Washington, DC: GPO, 1866.

Report of the Joint Committee on Reconstruction, at the First Session of the Thirty-Ninth Congress. Washington, DC: GPO, 1866.

US Bureau of Immigration and Naturalization. Annual Report of the Commissioner-General of Immigration for the Fiscal Year Ended June 30, 1907. Washington, DC: GPO, 1907.

US Bureau of Statistics. Money and Prices in Foreign Countries, Being a Series of Reports upon the Currency Systems of Various Nations in Their Relation to Prices of Commodities and Wages of Labor. Washington, DC: Government Printing Office, 1896.

US Census Office. Report on Population of the United States at the Eleventh Census: 1890. Washington, DC: GPO, 1895.

———. *Twelfth Census of the United States, Taken in the Year 1900*, vol. 1, *Population*. Washington, DC: United States Census Office, 1901.

US Department of Commerce and Labor. *Immigration Laws and Regulations of July 1, 1907*. Washington, DC: GPO, 1908.

US Public Health Service. *Annual Report of the Supervising Surgeon-General of the Marine-Hospital Service of the United States, 1895*. Washington, DC: GPO, 1896.

———. *Annual Report of the Supervising Surgeon-General of the Marine-Hospital Service of the United States, 1896*. Washington, DC: GPO, 1896.

US Senate. *Investigation of Mexican Affairs: Hearing Before a Subcommittee of the Committee on Foreign Relations, Part 12*. Washington, DC: GPO, 1920.

Weekly Abstract of Sanitary Reports Issued by the Supervising Surgeon-General, Marine Hospital Service. Washington, DC: GPO, 1895.

COURT RECORDS

Central Trust Company of New York v. New York and Westchester Water Company and Others. In *Reports of Cases Heard and Determined in the Appellate Division of the Supreme Court of the State of New York* 68 (1902): 640–642.

H. de Blake Elena y Lisette de Blackmore Florencia contra Ellis W. E. In *Diario de jurisprudencia del distrito y territorios federales* 7, no. 4 (January 4, 1906): 25–30.

H. H. Childers v. The State, 30 Tex. Ct. App. 160; 16 S.W. 903; 1891 Tex. Crim. App. LEXIS 68.

Houck v. Southern Pacific Railway. In *Federal Reporter: Cases Argued and Determined in the Circuit and District Courts of the United States* (May–July 1889) 38: 226–230.

In re Rodriguez, 81 F. 337 (W.D. Tex. 1897).

Niquet Alberto, Ellis Guillermo H. y Araoz Manuel. In *Diario de jurisprudencia del distrito y territorios federales* 13, no. 56 (March 6, 1908): 441–447.

Leprelette Sweet v. William H. Ellis, Supreme Court, New York State, 1912, New York Municipal Archives.

DATABASES

Carter, Susan B., Scott Sigmund Gartner, Michael R. Haines, Alan L. Olmstead, Richard Sutch, and Gavin Wright, eds. *Historical Statistics of the United States: Millennial Edition Online*. New York: Cambridge University Press, 2006.

"Passenger Lists of Vessels Arriving at New York, New York, 1820–1957." Provo, UT: Ancestry.com Operations, 2010.

"Reports of Deaths of American Citizens Abroad, 1835–1974." Provo, UT: Ancestry.com Operations, 2010.

Ruggles, Steven, J. Trent Alexander, Katie Genadek, Ronald Goeken, Matthew B. Schroeder, and Matthew Sobek. *Integrated Public Use Microdata Series: Version 5.0.* Minneapolis: Minnesota Population Center, 2010.

"Selected U.S. Federal Census Non-Population Schedules, 1850–1880." Provo, UT: Ancestry.com Operations, 2010.

"U.S. World War II Draft Registration Cards, 1942." Provo, UT: Ancestry. com Operations, 2010.

MICROFILM PUBLICATIONS

Kornweibel, Theodore, Jr., ed. *Federal Surveillance of Afro-Americans (1917–1925): The First World War, the Red Scare, and the Garvey Movement.* Frederick, MD: University Publications of America, 1985.

BOOKS AND ARTICLES

A la orilla de un palmar. Publicity brochure for film, in author's possession.

Adams, Rachel. *Continental Divides: Remapping the Cultures of North America.* Chicago: University of Chicago Press, 2009.

Addington, Wendell G. "Slave Insurrections in Texas." *Journal of Negro History* 35, no. 4 (October 1950): 408–434.

Aguilar, Luis Aboites. *Norte precario: Poblamiento y colonización en México (1760–1940).* Mexico City: Colegio de México, Centro de Estudios Históricos, 1995.

Aguirre Beltrán, Gonzalo. *La poblacíon negra de México.* Mexico: Fondo de Cultura Economica, 1972.

Ahmed, Hussein. "The Chronicle of Menilek II of Ethiopia: A Brief Assessment of Its Versions." *Journal of Ethiopian Studies* 16 (July 1983): 77.

Ali, Omar H. *In the Lion's Mouth: Black Populism in the New South, 1886–1900.* Jackson: University Press of Mississippi, 2010.

"An American Promoter in Abyssinia." *The World's Work* 7, no. 5 (March 1904): 99–100.

Andreas, Peter. *Smuggler Nation: How Illicit Trade Made America.* New York: Oxford University Press, 2013.

Angell, Stephen Ward. *Bishop Henry McNeal Turner and African-American Religion in the South.* Knoxville: University of Tennesse Press, 1992.

Ansell, Martin R. *Oil Baron of the Southwest: Edward L. Doheny and the Development of the Petroleum Industry in California and Mexico.* Columbus: Ohio State University Press, 1998.

Aptheker, Herbert. *Essays in the History of the American Negro*. New York: International Publishers, 1945.

Anthony, Arthé A. "'Lost Boundaries': Racial Passing and Poverty in Segregated New Orleans." *Louisiana History* 36, no. 3 (Summer 1995): 291–312.

Ashbaugh, Carolyn. *Lucy Parsons: An American Revolutionary*. Chicago: Haymarket Books, 2012 [1976].

Aulestia de Alba, Patricia. "Victoria (Vicky) Ellis." *Cuadernos del CID-Danza* 16 (1987): 3–6.

Baker, Ray Stannard. *Following the Color Line: An Account of Negro Citizenship in the American Democracy*. New York: Doubleday, Page, 1908.

Baldwin, Louis Fremont. *From Negro to Caucasian; or, How the Ethiopian Is Changing His Skin*. San Francisco: International Publishing, 1929.

Ballesteros Porta, Juan. *Explotación individual o colectiva? El caso de los ejidos de Tlahualilo*. México: Instituto Mexicano de Investigaciones Económicas, 1964.

Baptist, Edward E. *The Half Has Never Been Told: Slavery and the Making of American Capitalism*. New York: Basic Books, 2014.

Barnes, Kenneth C. *Journey of Hope: The Back-to-Africa Movement in Arkansas in the Late 1800s*. Chapel Hill: University of North Carolina Press, 2004.

Barr, Alwyn. *Black Texans: A History of African Americans in Texas, 1528–1995*, 2nd ed. Norman: University of Oklahoma Press, 1996.

———. *Black Texans: A History of Negroes in Texas, 1528–1971*. Austin, TX: Jenkins Publishing, 1973.

———. *Reconstruction to Reform: Texas Politics, 1876–1906*. Dallas: Southern Methodist University Press, 2000 [1971].

———. "The Texas 'Black Uprising' Scare of 1883." *Phylon* 41, no. 2 (1980): 179–186.

Basave Benítez, Agustín F. *México mestizo: Análisis del nacionalismo mexicano en torno a la mestizofilia de Andrés Molina Enríquez*. Mexico: Fondo de Cultura Económica, 1992.

Bataillon, Claude. *Las regiones geográficas en México*. 10th ed. Mexico City: Siglo veintiuno editores, 1993.

Bates Brown, Harry. *Cotton: History, Species, Varieties, Morphology, Breeding, Culture, Diseases, Marketing, and Uses*. 2nd ed. New York: McGraw-Hill, 1938.

Bazant, Jan. "From Independence to the Liberal Republic, 1821–1867." In *Mexico Since Independence*, edited by Leslie Bethell. Cambridge: Cambridge University Press, 1991.

Beckert, Sven. *The Monied Metropolis: New York City and the Consolidation of the American Bourgeoisie, 1850–1896*. New York: Cambridge University Press, 2001.

Behnken, Brian. *Fighting Their Own Battles: Mexican Americans, African Americans, and the Struggle for Civil Rights in Texas*. Chapel Hill: University of North Carolina Press, 2011.

———, ed. *The Struggle in Black and Brown: African American and Mexican*

American Relations During the Civil Rights Era. Lincoln: University of Nebraska Press, 2011.

Bell, Gregory S. *In the Black: A History of African Americans on Wall Street*. New York: John Wiley & Sons, 2002.

Bennett, Herman L. *Africans in Colonial Mexico: Absolutism, Christianity, and Afro-Creole Consciousness, 1570–1640*. Bloomington: Indiana University Press, 2005.

Berlin, Ira. *The Making of African America: The Four Great Migrations*. New York: Viking, 2010.

Biesanz, Mavis Hiltunen, Richard Biesanz, and Karen Zubris Biesanz. *The Ticos: Culture and Social Change in Costa Rica*. Boulder, CO: Lynne Rienner, 1999.

Bills, E. R. *The 1910 Slocum Massacre: An Act of Genocide in East Texas*. Charleston, SC: History Press, 2014.

Black, Dan A., Seth G. Sanders, Evan J. Taylor, and Lowell J. Taylor. "The Impact of the Great Migration on Mortality of African Americans: Evidence from the Deep South." *American Economic Review* 105, no. 2 (February 2015): 477–503.

Brooks, Daphne A. *Bodies in Dissent: Spectacular Performances of Race and Freedom, 1850–1910*. Durham: Duke University Press, 2007.

Brooks, Eugene Clyde. *The Story of Cotton and the Development of the Cotton States*. Chicago: Rand McNally, 1911.

Brotz, Howard, ed. *African-American Social and Political Thought, 1850–1920*. Rev. ed. New Brunswick, NJ: Transaction Publishers, 1992 [1966].

Brown, Jonathan C. "Why Foreign Oil Companies Shifted Their Production from Mexico to Venezuela During the 1920s." *American Historical Review* 90, no. 2 (April 1985): 362–385.

Browne, Peter Arrell. *Trichologia Mammalium; or, a Treatise on the Organization, Properties and Uses of Hair and Wool*. Philadelphia: J. H. Jones, 1853.

Bryce, James. "Thoughts on the Negro Problem." *North American Review* 153, no. 421 (December 1891): 641–60.

Buchenau, Jürgen. "Small Numbers, Great Impact: Mexico and Its Immigrants, 1821–1973." *Journal of American Ethnic History* 20, no. 3 (Spring 2001): 23–49.

Burden, David K. "Reform Before *La Reforma*: Liberals, Conservatives and the Debate over Immigration, 1846–1855." *Mexican Studies/Estudios Mexicanos* 23, no. 2 (Summer 2007): 283–316.

Burma, John H. "The Measurement of Negro 'Passing.'" *American Journal of Sociology* 52, no. 1 (July 1946): 18–22.

Campbell, Randolph B. *An Empire for Slavery: The Peculiar Institution in Texas, 1821–1865*. Baton Rouge: Louisiana State University Press, 1989.

———. "The End of Slavery in Texas: A Research Note." *Southwestern Historical Quarterly* 88, no. 1 (July 1984): 71–80.

———. *Gone to Texas: A History of the Lone Star State.* New York: Oxford University Press, 2003.

———. *Grass-roots Reconstruction in Texas, 1865–1880.* Baton Rouge: Louisiana State University Press, 1998.

Carrigan, William D. *The Making of a Lynching Culture: Violence and Vigilantism in Central Texas, 1836–1916.* Urbana: University of Illinois Press, 2004.

Carroll, Patrick J. *Blacks in Colonial Veracruz: Race, Ethnicity, and Regional Development.* Rev. ed. Austin: University of Texas Press, 2001.

Carter, William T., and C. S. Simmons. *Soil Survey of Victoria County, Texas.* Washington, DC: US Department of Agriculture, 1931.

Cazneau, Mrs. William [Cora Montgomery]. *Eagle Pass; or, Life on the Border.* Austin: Pemberton Press, 1966 [1852].

Cerutti, Mario, and Miguel González Quiroga. "Guerra y comercio en torno al Río Bravo (1855–1867). Línea fronteriza, espacio económico común." *Historia Mexicana* 40, no. 2 (October–December 1990): 217–297.

Chambers, William, and Robert Chambers, eds. *Information for the People.* Vol. 2. London: W. R. Chambers, 1856.

Chude-Sokei, Louis. *The Last "Darky": Bert Williams, Black-on-Black Minstrelsy, and the African Diaspora.* Durham: Duke University Press, 2006.

Clampitt, Brad R. "The Breakup: The Collapse of the Confederate Trans-Mississippi Army in Texas, 1865." *Southwestern Historical Quarterly* 108, no. 4 (2005): 498–534.

Cleven, N. Andrew N. "Some Plans for Colonizing Liberated Negro Slaves in Hispanic America." *Journal of Negro History* 11, no. 1 (January 1926): 35–49.

Clowes, William Laird. *Black America: A Study of the Ex-Slave and His Late Master.* London: Cassell, 1891.

Coatsworth, John H. *Growth Against Development: The Economic Impact of Railroads in Porfirian Mexico.* Dekalb: Northern Illinois University Press, 1981.

Cohen, Andrew Wender. "Smuggling, Globalization, and America's Outward State, 1870–1909." *Journal of American History* 97, no. 2 (September 2010): 371–398.

"Colonization of Lower California." *Science* 13, no. 322 (April 5, 1889): 256.

"The Conquest of the Tropics." *Modern Mexico* 17, no. 1 (April 1904): 38.

Cornell, Sarah E. "Citizens of Nowhere: Fugitive Slaves and Free African Americans in Mexico, 1833–1857." *Journal of American History* 100, no. 2 (September 2013): 351–374.

"Cotton States and International Exposition." *Monthly Bulletin of the Bureau of American Republics* 2, no. 1 (July 1894): 40–43.

Crimm, Ana Carolina Castillo. *De León: A Tejano Family History.* Austin: University of Texas Press, 2003.

———. "Finding Their Way." In *Tejano Journey, 1770–1850,* edited by Gerald E. Poyo. Austin: University of Texas Press, 1996.

Cromwell, Adelaide M. *Unveiled Voices, Unvarnished Memories: The Cromwell Family in Slavery and Segregation, 1692–1972.* Columbia: University of Missouri Press, 2007.

Cronon, William. *Nature's Metropolis: Chicago and the Great West.* New York: W. W. Norton, 1991.

Crouch, Barry A. "'All the Vile Passions': The Texas Black Code of 1866." *Southwestern Historical Quarterly* 97, no. 1 (July 1993): 34.

———, ed. *The Dance of Freedom: Texas African Americans During Reconstruction.* Austin: University of Texas Press, 2007.

Cuney-Hare, Maud. *Norris Wright Cuney: A Tribune of the Black People.* New York: G. K. Hall, 1995 [1913].

Davis, David Brion. *The Problem of Slavery in the Age of Emancipation.* New York: Alfred A. Knopf, 2014.

Davis, Graham. *Land! Irish Pioneers in Mexican and Revolutionary Texas.* College Station: Texas A&M University Press, 2002.

de Fornaro, Carlo. *Diaz, Czar of Mexico: An Arraignment.* N.p.: International Publishing, 1909.

Delaney, Robert W. "Matamoros, Port for Texas During the Civil War." *Southwestern Historical Quarterly* 58, no. 4 (April 1955): 473–487.

De León, Arnoldo. *The Tejano Community, 1836–1900.* Dallas: Southern Methodist University Press, 1997 [1982].

———. *They Called Them Greasers: Anglo Attitudes Toward Mexicans in Texas, 1821–1900.* Austin: University of Texas Press, 1983.

del Moral, Paulina. "Mascogos de Coahuila: Una cultura transfronteriza." In *Desierto y fronteras: El norte de México y otros contextos culturales*, edited by Hernán Salas Quintanal and Rafael Pérez-Taylor. Mexico: Playa y Valdés, 2004.

Delgado, Grace Peña. *Making the Chinese Mexican: Global Migration, Localism, and Exclusion in the U.S.-Mexico Borderlands.* Stanford: Stanford University Press, 2012.

Delpar, Helen. "Exiliados y expatriados estadounidenses en México (1920–1940)." In *México, país refugio: La experiencia de los exilios en el siglo XX*, edited by Pablo Yankelevich. Mexico: Instituto Nacional de Antropología e Historia, 2002.

Denning, Michael. *Mechanic Accents: Dime Novels and Working-Class Culture in America.* New York: Verso, 1987.

de Vos, Jan. "Una legislación de graves consecuencias: El acaparamiento de tierras baldías en México, con el pretexto de colonización, 1821–1910." *Historia Mexicana* 34, no. 1 (July–September 1984): 76–113.

Díaz, George T. *Border Contraband: A History of Smuggling Across the Rio Grande.* Austin: University of Texas Press, 2015.

Díaz-Sánchez, Micaela, and Alexandro D. Hernández. "The Son Jarocho as Afro-Mexican Resistance Music." *Journal of Pan African Studies* 6, no. 1 (July 2013): 187–209.

Diouf, Sylviane A. *Slavery's Exiles: The Story of the American Maroons*. New York: New York University Press, 2014.

"Disappearance of Loomis." *Pacific Monthly: A Magazine of Education and Progress* 12, no. 3 (September 1904): 183.

Dollar, Susan E. "Ethnicity and Jim Crow: The Americanization of Louisiana's Creoles." In *Louisiana Beyond Black and White: New Interpretations of Twentieth-Century Race and Race Relations*, edited by Michael S. Martin. Lafayette: University of Louisiana at Lafayette Press, 2011.

Douglas, Ann. *Terrible Honesty: Mongrel Manhattan in the 1920s*. New York: Farrar, Straus and Giroux, 1995.

Downs, Gregory P. *After Appomattox: Military Occupation and the Ends of War*. Cambridge: Harvard University Press, 2015.

———. "The Mexicanization of American Politics: The United States' Transnational Path from Civil War to Stabilization." *American Historical Review* 117, no. 2 (April 2012): 387–409.

Duarte Espinosa, María de Jesús. *Frontera y diplomacia: Las relaciones México–Estados Unidos durante el porfiriato*. Mexico: Secretaría de relaciones exteriores, 2001.

Du Bois, W. E. B. "The Study of the Negro Problems." *Annals of the American Academy of Political and Social Science* 11, no. 1 (1898): 1–23.

———. *The Souls of Black Folk*. New York: New American Library, 1969 [1903].

Dyer, Brainerd. "The Persistence of the Idea of Negro Colonization." *Pacific Historical Review* 12, no. 1 (March 1943): 53–65.

Eckard, E. W. "How Many Negroes 'Pass'?" *American Journal of Sociology* 52, no. 6 (May 1947): 498–500.

"Elihu Root on the Negro Problem." *Harper's Weekly* 47, no. 2409 (February 21, 1903): 306–307.

"Encouragement of the Rubber Industry." *Bulletin of the International Bureau of the American Republics* 28, no. 2 (April 1909): 732–733.

Engerrand, Steven W. "Black and Mulatto Mobility and Stability in Dallas, Texas, 1880–1910." *Phylon* 39, no. 3 (1978): 203–215.

Enock, C. Reginald. *Mexico: Its Ancient and Modern Civilisation, History and Political Conditions, Topography and Natural Resources, Industries and General Development*. New York: Charles Scribner's Sons, 1909.

[Ferrocarriles Nacionales de México]. *Mexico from Border to Capital: A Brief Description of the Many Interesting Places to Be Seen en Route to Mexico City via the Laredo, the Eagle Pass and the El Paso Gateways*. Chicago: Corbitt Railway Printing, n.d.

Fiege, Mark. *The Republic of Nature: An Environmental History of the United States*. Seattle: University of Washington Press, 2012.

Finlay, Mark R. *Growing American Rubber: Strategic Plants and the Politics of National Security*. New Brunswick: Rutgers University Press, 2009.

Fitzgerrell's Guide to Mexico: The Tropics and Highlands: New Homes in a Land of Great Opportunities. Mexico: Imprenta y fototipia de la secretaria de fomento, 1906.

Flamming, Douglas. *Bound for Freedom: Black Los Angeles in Jim Crow America.* Berkeley: University of California Press, 2005.

Foley, Neil. *Quest for Equality: The Failed Promise of Black-Brown Solidarity.* Cambridge: Harvard University Press, 2010.

———. *White Scourge: Mexicans, Blacks, and Poor Whites in Texas Cotton Culture.* Berkeley: University of California Press, 1997.

Foner, Eric. *Fiery Trial: Abraham Lincoln and American Slavery.* New York: W. W. Norton, 2010.

———. *Gateway to Freedom: The Hidden History of the Underground Railroad.* New York: W.W. Norton, 2015.

———. *Reconstruction: America's Unfinished Revolution, 1863–1877.* New York: Harper and Row, 1988.

Fremantle, Arthur James Lyon. *Three Months in the Southern States: April–June 1863.* New York: John Bradburn, 1864.

"The Future of the Negro." *Gentleman's Magazine* 259 (December 1885): 612–614.

Gaines, Kevin K. *Uplifting the Race: Black Leadership, Politics, and Culture in the Twentieth Century.* Chapel Hill: University of North Carolina Press, 1996.

Garvey, Amy Jacques, ed. *The Philosophy and Opinions of Marcus Garvey; or, Africa for the Africans.* Dover, MA: Majority Press, 1986 [1923].

Gates, Henry Louis. *The Signifying Monkey: A Theory of Afro-American Literary Criticism.* New York: Oxford University Press, 1988.

Gatewood, Willard B. *Aristocrats of Color: The Black Elite, 1880–1920.* Bloomington: Indiana University Press, 1991.

Gebrekidan, Fikru Negash. *Bond Without Blood: A History of Ethiopian and New World Black Relations, 1896–1991.* Trenton, NJ: Africa World Press, 2005.

Giesen, James C. *Boll Weevil Blues: Cotton, Myth, and Power in the American South.* Chicago: University of Chicago Press, 2011.

Glenn, Nettie Henry. *Early Frankfort, Kentucky, 1786–1861.* Frankfort, KY: N. H. Glenn, 1986.

Golden, Joseph. "Patterns of Negro-White Intermarriage." *American Sociological Review* 19, no. 2 (April 1954): 144–147.

Gómez Izquierdo, José Jorge. *El movimiento antichino en México (1871–1934): Problemas del racismo y del nacionalismo durante la Revolución Mexicana.* Mexico: Instituto Nacional de Antropología e Historia, 1991.

Gonzales, Michael J. "Imagining Mexico in 1910: Visions of the *Patria* in the Centennial Celebration in Mexico City." *Journal of Latin American Studies* 39, no. 3 (August 2007): 495–533.

Gonzalez, Gilbert G. "Mexican Labor Migration, 1876–1924." In *Beyond La Frontera: The History of Mexico-U.S. Migration,* edited by Mark Overmyer-Velázquez. New York: Oxford University Press, 2011.

González Ibarra, Juan de Dios. *La negritud, tercera raíz mexicana*. Mexico: Universidad Autónoma del Estado de Morelos, 2007.

González Navarro, Moisés. *La colonización en México, 1877–1910*. Mexico: Talleres de Impresión de Estampillas y Valores, 1960.

———. *Los extranjeros en México Y los mexicanos en el extranjero, 1821–1970*. Mexico: Colegio de México, 1994.

———. "Las ideas raciales de los científicos, 1890–1910." *Historia Mexicana* 37, no. 4 (April–June 1988): 565–583.

González Quiroga, Miguel A. "Mexicanos in Texas During the Civil War." In *Mexican Americans in Texas History*, edited by Emilio Zamora, Cynthia Orozco, and Rodolfo Rocha. Austin: Texas State Historical Association, 2000.

———. "La puerta de México: Los comerciantes texanos y el noreste mexicano, 1850–1880." *Estudios Sociológicos* 11, no. 31 (January–April 1993): 209–236.

Grandin, Greg. *Empire's Workshop: Latin America, the United States, and the Rise of the New Imperialism*. New York: Metropolitan Books, 2006.

———. "The Liberal Traditions in the Americas: Rights, Sovereignty, and the Origins of Liberal Multilateralism." *American Historical Review* 117, no. 1 (2012): 68–91.

[A Gringo]. *Through the Land of the Aztecs; or, Life and Travel in Mexico*. London: Sampson Low, Marston, 1892.

Gross, Ariela J. *What Blood Won't Tell: A History of Race on Trial in America*. Cambridge: Harvard University Press, 2008.

Gruzinski, Serge. *La ciudad de México: Una historia*. Translated by Paula López Caballero. Mexico: Fondo de Cultura Económica, 2004.

Guterl, Matthew. *American Mediterranean: Southern Slaveholders in the Age of Emancipation*. Cambridge: Harvard University Press, 2008.

Gutman, Herbert G. *The Black Family in Slavery and Freedom, 1750–1925*. New York: Vintage Books, 1976.

Hackett, Charles W. "The Recognition of the Díaz Government by the United States." *Southwestern Historical Quarterly* 28, no. 1 (July 1924): 34–55.

Hahn, Steven. *A Nation Under Our Feet: Black Political Struggles in the Rural South from Slavery to the Great Migration*. Cambridge: Harvard University Press, 2003.

———. *The Political Worlds of Slavery and Freedom*. Cambridge: Harvard University Press, 2009.

Hale, Grace Elizabeth. *Making Whiteness: The Culture of Segregation in the South, 1890–1940*. New York: Pantheon Books, 1998.

Hales, Douglas. *A Southern Family in White and Black: The Cuneys of Texas*. College Station: Texas A&M University Press, 2003.

Hall, Linda B. *Oil, Banks, and Politics: The United States and Postrevolutionary Mexico, 1917–1924*. Austin: University of Texas Press, 1995.

Hall, Raymond A. *An Ethnographic Study of Afro-Mexicans in Mexico's Gulf Coast: Fishing, Festivals, and Foodways.* Lewiston, NY: Edwin Mellen Press, 2008.

Halttunen, Karen. *Confidence Men and Painted Women: A Study of Middle-Class Culture in America, 1830–1870.* New Haven: Yale University Press, 1982.

Hämäläinen, Pekka. *The Comanche Empire.* New Haven: Yale University Press, 2008.

Hammonds, Terry. *Historic Victoria: An Illustrated History.* San Antonio: Historical Publishing Network, 1999.

Hansen, Lawrence Douglas Taylor. "La migraciones Menonitas al norte de México entre 1922 y 1940." *Migraciones Internacionales* 3, no. 1 (January–June 2005): 5–31.

Harlan, Louis R., and Raymond W. Smock, eds. *The Booker T. Washington Papers.* 14 vols. Urbana: University of Illinois Press, 1972–1989.

Harmon, George D. "Confederate Migration to Mexico." *Hispanic American Historical Review* 17, no. 4 (November 1937): 458–487.

Harris, Cheryl I. "Whiteness as Property." *Harvard Law Review* 106, no. 8 (June 1993): 1707–1791.

Hart, John Mason. *Empire and Revolution: The Americans in Mexico Since the Civil War.* Berkeley: University of California Press, 2002.

Haynes, George Edmund. *The Negro at Work in New York City: A Study in Economic Progress.* New York: Longmans, Green for Columbia University, 1912.

Helg, Aline. *Our Rightful Share: The Afro-Cuban Struggle for Equality, 1886–1912.* Chapel Hill: University of North Carolina Press, 1995.

Hernández, Kelly Lytle. *Migra! A History of the U.S. Border Patrol.* Berkeley: University of California Press, 2010.

Herringshaw, Thomas William, ed. *Herringshaw's American Blue-Book of Biography: Prominent Americans of 1919.* Chicago: American Blue Book Publishers, 1919.

Hickman, Christine B. "The Devil and the One Drop Rule: Racial Categories, African Americans, and the U.S. Census." *Michigan Law Review* 95, no. 5 (March 1997): 1161–1265.

Hobbs, Allyson. *A Chosen Exile: A History of Racial Passing in American Life.* Cambridge: Harvard University Press, 2014.

Hodes, Martha. "Fractions and Fictions in the United States Census of 1890." In *Haunted by Empire: Geographies of Intimacy in North American History,* edited by Ann Laura Stoler. Durham: Duke University Press, 2006.

———. "Knowledge and Indifference in the New York City Race Riot of 1900: An Argument in Search of a Story." *Rethinking History* 15, no. 1 (2011): 61–89.

———. *White Women, Black Men: Illicit Sex in the Nineteenth-Century South.* New Haven: Yale University Press, 1997.

Holmes, William F. "Labor Agents and the Georgia Exodus." *South Atlantic Quarterly* 79, no. 4 (Autumn 1980): 436–449.

Hooker, J. R. "The Pan-African Conference 1900." *Transition* 46 (1974): 20–24.

Horne, Gerald. *Black and Brown: African Americans and the Mexican Revolution, 1910–1920.* New York: New York University Press, 2005.

———. *Race to Revolution: The United States and Cuba During Slavery and Jim Crow.* New York: Monthly Review Press, 2014.

Hughes, Langston. *The Big Sea: An Autobiography.* New York: Hill and Wang, 1993 [1940].

———. "Fooling Our White Folks." *Negro Digest* 8, no. 6 (1950): 38–41.

———. *I Wonder as I Wander: An Autobiographical Journey.* Columbia: University of Missouri Press, 2003.

———. "Jokes on Our White Folks." In *Langston Hughes and the* Chicago Defender: *Essays on Race, Politics, and Culture, 1942–62,* edited by Christopher C. DeSantis. Urbana: University of Illinois Press, 1995.

———. "Passing." In *The Ways of White Folks.* New York: Alfred A. Knopf, 1933.

Hunt, Jeffrey William. *The Last Battle of the Civil War: Palmetto Ranch.* Austin: University of Texas Press, 2002.

Hyde, Lewis. *Trickster Makes This World: Mischief, Myth, and Art.* New York: Farrar, Straus and Giroux, 1998.

Jackson, Ronald L., II. *Scripting the Black Masculine Body: Identity, Discourse, and Racial Politics in Popular Media.* Albany: State University of New York Press, 2006.

Jacoby, Karl. "Between North and South: The Alternative Borderlands of William H. Ellis and the African American Colony of 1895." In *Continental Crossroads: Remapping U.S.-Mexico Borderlands History,* edited by Samuel Treutt and Elliott Young. Durham: Duke University Press, 2004.

Jannath, Heba. "America's Changing Color Line." In *Negro: An Anthology,* edited by Nancy Cunard. New York: Continuum Publishing, 1996 [1934].

Jayes, Janice Lee. *The Illusion of Ignorance: Constructing the American Encounter with Mexico, 1877–1920.* Lanham, MD: University Press of America, 2011.

Johns, Michael. *The City of Mexico in the Age of Díaz.* Austin: University of Texas Press, 1997.

Johnson, Benjamin Heber. *Bordertown: The Odyssey of an American Place.* New Haven: Yale University Press, 2008.

———. *Revolution in Texas: How a Forgotten Rebellion and Its Bloody Suppression Turned Mexicans into Americans.* New Haven: Yale University Press, 2003.

———. "The Cosmic Race in Texas: Racial Fusion, White Supremacy, and Civil Rights Politics." *Journal of American History* 98, no. 2 (September 2011): 404–419.

Johnson, James Weldon. *Along This Way: The Autobiography of James Weldon Johnson.* New York: Viking Press, 1933.

———. *The Autobiography of an Ex-Colored Man*. New York: Hill and Wang, 1960 [1912].

———. *Black Manhattan*. New York: Alfred A. Knopf, 1930.

Johnson, Walter. *River of Dark Dreams: Slavery and Empire in the Cotton Kingdom*. Cambridge: Harvard University Press, 2013.

———. "The Slave Trader, the White Slave, and the Politics of Racial Determination in the 1850s." *Journal of American History* 87, no. 1 (June 2000): 13–38.

Johnson, W. H. *Cotton and Its Production*. London: Macmillan, 1926.

Jones, C. Allan. *Texas Roots: Agriculture and Rural Life Before the Civil War*. College Station: Texas A&M University Press, 2005.

Kane, N. Stephen. "American Businessmen and Foreign Policy: The Recognition of Mexico, 1920–1923." *Political Science Quarterly* 90, no. 2 (Summer 1975): 293–313.

Kantrowitz, Stephen. *More than Freedom: Fighting for Black Citizenship in a White Republic, 1829–1889*. New York: Penguin Press, 2012.

Kaplan, Carla. *Miss Anne in Harlem: The White Women of the Black Renaissance*. New York: HarperCollins, 2013.

Kasson, John F. *Rudeness and Civility: Manners in Nineteenth-Century Urban America*. New York: Hill and Wang, 1990.

Katz, Friedrich. "The Liberal Republic and the Porfiriato, 1867–1910." In *Mexico Since Independence*, edited by Leslie Bethell. Cambridge: Cambridge University Press, 1998.

———. *The Life and Times of Pancho Villa*. Stanford: Stanford University Press, 1998.

———. *The Secret War in Mexico: Europe, the United States, and the Mexican Revolution*. Chicago: University of Chicago Press, 1981.

Keith, Verna M., and Cedric Herring. "Skin Tone and Stratification in the Black Community." *American Journal of Sociology* 97, no. 3 (November 1991): 760–778.

Kelley, Blair L. M. *Right to Ride: Streetcar Boycotts and African American Citizenship in the Era of Plessy v. Ferguson*. Chapel Hill: University of North Carolina Press, 2010.

Kelley, Sean M. *Los Brazos de Dios: A Plantation Society in the Texas Borderlands, 1821–1865*. Baton Rouge: Louisiana State University Press, 2010.

———. " 'Mexico in His Head': Slavery and the Texas-Mexico Border." *Journal of Social History* 37, no. 3 (Spring 2004): 709–723.

Kennedy, Randall. "Racial Passing." 62 *Ohio State Law Journal* 1145 (2001).

Kephart, William M. "The 'Passing' Question." *Phylon* 9, no. 4 (1948): 336–340.

Kern-Foxworth, Marilyn. *Aunt Jemima, Uncle Ben, and Rastus: Blacks in Advertising, Yesterday, Today, and Tomorrow*. Westport, CT: Greenwood Press, 1994.

Kidd, Benjamin. *The Control of the Tropics*. New York: Macmillian, 1898.

Klein, Marcus. *Easterns, Westerns, and Private Eyes: American Matters, 1870–1900.* Madison: University of Wisconsin Press, 1994.

Knight, Alan. *The Mexican Revolution.* 2 vols. New York: Cambridge University Press, 1986.

———. "Racism, Revolution, and *Indigenismo*: Mexico, 1910–1940." In *The Idea of Race in Latin America, 1870–1940,* edited by Richard Graham. Austin: University of Texas Press, 1990.

Knox, Herman W., ed. *Who's Who in New York: A Biographical Dictionary of Prominent Citizens of New York City and State, 1917–1918.* New York: Who's Who Publications, 1918.

Kosary, Rebecca A. " 'Wantonly Maltreated and Slain, Simply Because They Are Free': Racial Violence During Reconstruction in South Texas." In *African Americans in South Texas History,* edited by Bruce A. Glasrud. College Station: Texas A&M Press, 2011.

Kroeber, Clifton B. "La cuestión del Nazas hasta 1913." *Historia Mexicana* 20, no. 3 (January–March 1971): 428–456.

———. *Man, Land, and Water: Mexico's Farmlands Irrigation Policies, 1885–1911.* Berkeley: University of California Press, 1983.

Kun, Josh. "Tijuana and the Borders of Race." In *A Companion to Los Angeles,* edited by William Deverell and Greg Hise. Malden, MA: Wiley-Blackwell, 2010.

Lack, Paul D. "Slavery and Vigilantism in Austin, Texas, 1840–1860." *Southwestern Historical Quarterly* 85, no. 1 (July 1981): 1–20.

Laine, J. R . "Reports of the State Board of Health." *Pacific Medical Journal* 38, no. 10 (October 1895): 669.

Lake, Marilyn, and Henry Reynolds. *Drawing the Global Colour Line: White Men's Countries and the International Challenge of Racial Equality.* Cambridge: Cambridge University Press, 2008.

Larsen, Nella. *Passing.* New York: Alfred A. Knopf, 1929.

Lee, Erika. *At America's Gates: Chinese Immigration During the Exclusion Era, 1882–1943.* Chapel Hill: University of North Carolina Press, 2003.

Leiker, James N. *Racial Borders: Black Soldiers Along the Rio Grande.* College Station: Texas A&M University Press, 2002.

Levander, Caroline. "Sutton Griggs and the Borderlands of Empire." In *Jim Crow, Literature, and the Legacy of Sutton E. Griggs,* edited by Tess Chakkalakal and Kenneth W. Warren. Athens: University of Georgia Press, 2013.

Levine, Lawrence W. *Black Culture and Black Consciousness: Afro-American Folk Thought from Slavery to Freedom.* New York: Oxford University Press, 1977.

Lewis, David Levering. *W. E. B. Du Bois: Biography of a Race, 1868–1919.* New York: Henry Holt, 1993.

Lewis, Earl, and Heidi Ardizzone. *Love on Trial: An American Scandal in Black and White.* New York: W. W. Norton, 2001.

Lindahl, Ulf J. "An Historic Letter from the United States' Mission to Menelik." *Menelik's Journal* 12, no. 3 (July–September 1996): 924–935.

Litwack, Leon F. *Trouble in Mind: Black Southerners in the Age of Jim Crow.* New York: Alfred A. Knopf, 1998.

Lomnitz, Claudio. *The Return of Comrade Ricardo Flores Magón.* New York: Zone Books, 2014.

Lummis, Charles. *The Awakening of a Nation: Mexico of To-Day.* Honolulu: University Press of the Pacific, 2004 [1898].

Mackie, C. P. "Canal Irrigation in Modern Mexico." *Engineering Magazine* 13, no. 2 (May 1897): 181–198.

MacLachlan, Colin M., and William H. Beezley. *El Gran Pueblo: A History of Greater Mexico.* Upper Saddle River, NJ: Prentice Hall, 2004.

Mancini, Olivia. "Passing as White: Anita Hemmings." *Vassar Quarterly* 98, no. 1 (Winter 2001).

Margati, José. *A Trip to the City of Mexico.* Boston: Putnam, Messervy, 1885.

Margolies, Daniel S. *Spaces of Law in American Foreign Relations: Extradition and Extraterritoriality in the Borderlands and Beyond, 1877–1898.* Athens: University of Georgia Press, 2011.

Massey, Sara R. "After Emancipation: Cologne, Texas." In *African Americans in South Texas History,* edited by Bruce A. Glasrud. College Station: Texas A&M Press, 2011.

Matthews, Michael. *The Civilizing Machine: A Cultural History of Mexican Railroads, 1876–1910.* Lincoln: University of Nebraska Press, 2013.

May, Robert E. *The Southern Dream of a Caribbean Empire, 1854–1861.* Gainesville: University Press of Florida, 2002 [1973].

McBroome, Delores Nason. "Harvests of Gold: African American Boosterism, Agriculture, and Investment in Allensworth and Little Liberia." In *Seeking El Dorado: African Americans in California,* edited by Lawrence B. de Graaf, Kevin Mulroy, and Quintard Taylor. Seattle: University of Washington Press, 2001.

McCaa, Robert. "Missing Millions: The Demographic Costs of the Mexican Revolution." *Mexican Studies/Estudios Mexicanos* 19, no. 2 (Summer 2003): 367–400.

McKiernan-González, John. *Fevered Measures: Public Health and Race at the Texas-Mexico Border, 1848–1942.* Durham: Duke University Press, 2012.

McKinley, Carlyle. *An Appeal to Pharoah: The Negro Problem, and Its Radical Solution.* New York: Fords, Howard and Hulbert, 1890.

McVety, Amanda Kay. "The 1903 Skinner Mission: Images of Ethiopia in the Progressive Era." *Journal of the Gilded Age and Progressive Era* 10, no. 2 (April 2011): 187–212.

Meyers, William K. *Forge of Progress, Crucible of Revolt: Origins of the Mexican Revolution in La Comarca Lagunera, 1880–1911.* Albuquerque: University of New Mexico Press, 1994.

Michael, Jerrold M., and Thomas R. Bender. "Fighting Smallpox on the Texas

Border: An Episode from PHS's Proud Past." *Public Health Reports* 99, no. 6 (November–December 1984): 579–582.

Mignolo, Walter D. *The Idea of Latin America*. Malden, MA: Blackwell Publishing, 2005.

Miller, Robert Ryal. "Arms Across the Border: United States Aid to Juárez During the French Intervention in Mexico." *Transactions of the American Philosophical Society* 63, no. 6 (December 1973): 1–68.

Miller, Shawn William. *An Environmental History of Latin America*. New York: Cambridge University Press, 2007.

Mitchell, Michele. *Righteous Propagation: African Americans and the Politics of Racial Destiny After Reconstruction*. Chapel Hill: University of North Carolina Press, 2004.

Moats, Leone B. *Thunder in Their Veins: A Memoir of Mexico*. New York: Century, 1932.

"Modern Mexicans." *Chambers's Journal of Popular Literature, Science, and Arts* 389 (June 15, 1861): 380.

Molina, Natalia. "'In a Race All Their Own': The Quest to Make Mexicans Ineligible for U.S. Citizenship." *Pacific Historical Review* 79, no. 2 (2010): 167–201.

———. "The Long Arc of Dispossession: Racial Capitalism and Contested Notions of Citizenship in the U.S.-Mexico Borderlands in the Early Twentieth Century." *Western Historical Quarterly* 45, no. 4 (Winter (2014): 431–447.

Moneyhon, Carl H. *Texas After the Civil War: The Struggle of Reconstruction*. College Station: Texas A&M University Press, 2004.

Montejano, David. *Anglos and Mexicans in the Making of Texas, 1836–1986*. Austin: University of Texas Press, 1987.

———. "Mexican Merchants and Teamsters on the Texas Cotton Road, 1862–1865." In *Mexico and Mexicans in the Making of the United States*, edited by John Tutino. Austin: University of Texas Press, 2012.

Mora-Torres, Juan. "'Los de casa se van, los de fuera no vienen': The First Mexican Immigrants, 1848–1900." In *Beyond La Frontera: The History of Mexico-U.S. Migration*, edited by Mark Overmyer-Velázquez. New York: Oxford University Press, 2011.

———. *The Making of the Mexican Border: The State, Capitalism, and Society in Nuevo León, 1848–1910*. Austin: University of Texas Press, 2001.

Morrison, Hunter. "Canal Irrigation in Mexico." *Yale Scientific Monthly* 4, no. 8 (May 1898): 382–386.

Morrissette, Noelle. *James Weldon Johnson's Modern Soundscapes*. Iowa City: University of Iowa Press, 2013.

Mozingo, Joe. *The Fiddler on Pantico Run: An African Warrior, His White Descendants, a Search for Family*. New York: Free Press, 2012.

Muñoz Mata, Laura. "La migración afroantillana a México: Una historia olvidada." *Del Caribe* 24 (1994): 124–130.

————. "Presencia afrocaribeña en Veracruz: La inmigración jamaicana en las postrimerías del siglo XIX." *Sotavento* 3 (1997–1998): 73–88.

"A Mysterious Disappearance." *Week's Progress* 24, no. 400 (July 9, 1904): 24.

Nackenoff, Carol. *The Fictional Republic: Horatio Alger and American Political Discourse.* New York: Oxford University Press, 1994.

Neal, Diane, and Thomas W. Kremm. "What Shall We Do with the Negro? The Freedman's Bureau in Texas." *East Texas Historical Journal* 27, no. 2 (1989): 23–34.

Ngai, Mae M. *Impossible Subjects: Illegal Aliens and the Making of Modern America.* Princeton: Princeton University Press, 2004.

Nichols, James. "The Line of Liberty: Runaway Slaves and Fugitive Peons in the Texas-Mexico Borderlands." *Western Historical Quarterly* 44, no. 4 (Winter 2013): 413–433.

Obadele-Starks, Ernest. "Black Labor, the Black Middle Class, and Organized Protest Along the Upper Texas Gulf Coast, 1883–1945." *Southwestern Historical Quarterly* 103, no. 1 (July 1999): 52–65.

O'Dwyer, Walter Meade. "The Prospects of Mexico." *North American Review* 159, no. 452 (July 1894): 123.

The Official Catalogue of the Cotton States and International Exposition. Atlanta: Claflin and Mellichamp, 1895.

Olmsted, Frederick Law. *A Journey Through Texas; or, a Saddle-Trip on the Southwestern Frontier.* New York: Dix, Edwards, 1857.

One Thousand American Men of Mark of To-Day. Chicago: American Men of Mark, 1916.

Ortiz Escobar, Roberto. "El cine mexicano filmado en Veracruz." In *Microhistorias del cine en México,* edited by Eduardo de la Vega Alfaro. Guadalajara: Universidad de Guadalajara, 2001.

Osofsky, Gilbert. *Harlem: The Making of a Ghetto.* New York: Harper and Row, 1963.

————. "Race Riot, 1900: A Study of Ethnic Violence." *Journal of Negro Education* 32, no. 1 (Winter 1963): 16–24.

Palmer, Colin A. *Slaves of the White God: Blacks in Mexico, 1570–1650.* Cambridge: Harvard University Press, 1976.

"'Palo Amarillo' Rubber Bottled Up." *India Rubber World* 43, no. 1 (October 1, 1910): 4.

Pankhurst, Richard. "William H. Ellis—Guillaume Enriques Elleseo: The First Black American Ethiopianist?" *Ethiopia Observer* 15 (1972): 89–121.

Pascoe, Peggy. *What Comes Naturally: Miscegenation Law and the Making of Race in America.* New York: Oxford University Press, 2009.

Passarelli, James J. "Italy in Mexico." *Italica* 23, no. 1 (March 1, 1946): 40–45.

Pegler-Gordon, Anna. *In Sight of America: Photography and the Development of U.S. Immigration Policy.* Berkeley: University of California Press, 2009.

Perdue, Theda. *Race and the Atlanta Cotton States Exposition of 1895.* Athens: University of Georgia Press, 2010.

Petty, J. W., Jr., ed. *A Republishing of the Book Most Often Known as Victor Rose's History of Victoria.* Victoria, TX: Book Mart, 1961.

Pfeiffer, Kathleen. *Race Passing and American Individualism.* Amherst: University of Massachusetts Press, 2003.

Piccato, Pablo. *City of Suspects: Crime in Mexico City, 1900–1931.* Durham: Duke University Press.

Pimentel, Francisco. "La colonización negra." In *Obras completas.* Mexico: Tipografía Económica, 1904.

Plana, Manuel. *El reino del algodón en México: La estructura agraria de La Laguna (1855–1910).* Mexico: Patronato del Teatro Isauro Martínez, 1991.

Pletcher, David M. *Rails, Mines, and Progress: Seven American Promoters in Mexico, 1867–1911.* Ithaca: Cornell University Press, 1958.

Ponton, M. M. *Life and Times of Henry M. Turner.* New York: Negro Universities Press, 1970 [1917].

Porter, Kenneth Wiggins. *The Negro on the American Frontier.* New York: Arno Press, 1971.

Portillo, Esteban L. *Catecismo geográfico, politico e histórico del estado de Coahuila de Zaragoza.* Saltillo: Tipografia del Gobierno en Palacio, 1897.

Prida, Ramón. *¡De la dictadura a la anarquia!* El Paso, TX: El Paso del Norte, 1914.

Pridgen, H. M'Bride. *Address to the People of Texas, on the Protection of Slave Property.* Austin: John Marshall, 1859.

Pubols, Louise. *The Father of All: The de la Guerra Family, Power, and Patriarchy in Mexican California.* Berkeley: University of California Press, 2009.

Pulido Llano, Gabriela. *Mulatas y negros cubanos en la escena mexicana, 1920–1950.* Mexico City: Instituto Nacional de Antropología e Historia, 2010.

Pullen, Clarence. "The City of Mexico." *Journal of the American Geographical Society of New York* 20 (1888): 153–182.

Quirin, James. "W.E.B. Du Bois, Ethiopianism and Ethiopia, 1890–1955." *International Journal of Ethiopian Studies* 5, no. 2 (Fall/Winter 2010–2011): 1–26.

Raat, W. Dirk. *Mexico and the United States: Ambivalent Vistas.* 3rd ed. Athens: University of Georgia Press, 2004.

———. *Revoltosos: Mexico's Rebels in the United States, 1903–1923.* College Station: Texas A&M University Press, 1981.

Randall, Robert W. "Mexico's Pre-Revolutionary Reckoning with Railroads." *Americas* 42, no. 1 (1985): 1–28.

Rawick, George P., ed. *The American Slave: A Composite Autobiography*, vols. 4 and 5, *Texas Narratives.* Westport, CT: Greenwood Publishing, 1972 [1941].

Reagan, John Henninger. *Memoirs, with Special Reference to Secession and the Civil War.* New York and Chicago: Neale Publishing, 1906.

Redclift, Michael. *Chewing Gum: The Fortunes of Taste.* New York: Routledge, 2004.

Redkey, Edwin. *Black Exodus: Black Nationalist and Back-to-Africa Movements,* *1890–1910.* New Haven: Yale University Press, 1969.

Reed, S. G. *A History of the Texas Railroads and of Transportation Conditions* *under Spain and Mexico and the Republic and the State.* Houston: St. Clair, 1941.

Rénique, Gerardo. "Race, Mestizaje and Nationalism: Sonora's Anti-Chinese Movement and State Formation in Post-revolutionary México." *Political* *Power and Social Theory* 14 (2000): 91–140.

Remy, Caroline. "Hispanic-Mexican San Antonio: 1836–1861." *Southwestern* *Historical Quarterly* 71, no. 4 (April 1968): 564–582.

Reports of the Committee of Investigation Sent in 1873 by the Mexican Government *to the Frontier of Texas.* Baker and Goodwin, 1875.

"Restoration of Self-Government in the South." *Old Guard* 4 (July 1866): 424–428.

Reynolds, Alfred W. "The Alabama Negro Colony in Mexico, 1894–1896, Parts 1 and 2." *Alabama Review* 5 (October 1952): 243–268 and 6 (January 1953): 31–58.

Rice, Lawrence D. *The Negro in Texas, 1874–1900.* Baton Rouge: Louisiana State University Press, 1971.

Richter, William L. *The Army in Texas During Reconstruction, 1865–1870.* College Station: Texas A&M University Press, 1987.

Riera, Emilio García. *Historia documental del cine mexicano: Época sonora, 1926–* *1940.* Mexico: Ediciones Era, 1969.

Rippy, J. Fred. "A Negro Colonization Project in Mexico, 1895." *Journal of* *Negro History* 6, no. 1 (January 1921): 66–73.

———. "The United States and Mexico, 1910–27." In *American Policies Abroad:* *Mexico.* Chicago: University of Chicago Press, 1928.

Rister, Carl Coke. "Carlota, a Confederate Colony in Mexico." *Journal of* *Southern History* 11, no. 1 (February 1945): 33–50.

Roberts, John W. *From Trickster to Badman: The Black Folk Hero in Slavery and* *Freedom.* Philadelphia: University of Pennsylvania Press, 1989.

Robertson, Craig. *The Passport in America: The History of a Document.* New York: Oxford University Press, 2010.

Robinson, Charles F., II. "Legislated Love in the Lone Star State: Texas and Miscegenation." *Southwestern Historical Quarterly* 108, no. 1 (July 2004): 65–87.

Rolland, Modesto C. *Los puertos libres mexicanos y la zona libre en la frontera* *norte de la republica mexicana.* Mexico: Empresa Editorial de Ingenieria y Arquitectura, 1924.

Rolle, Andrew. *The Lost Cause: The Confederate Exodus to Mexico.* Norman: University of Oklahoma Press, 1965.

Romero, Matías. "Mexico." *Journal of the American Geographical Society of New* *York* 28, no. 4 (1896): 327–386.

Romero, Robert Chao. *The Chinese in Mexico, 1882–1940.* Tucson: University of Arizona Press, 2010.

Romeyn, Esther. *Street Scenes: Staging the Self in Immigrant New York, 1880–1924.* Minneapolis: University of Minnesota Press, 1998.

Rosengarten, Theodore. *All God's Dangers: The Life of Nate Shaw.* New York: Vintage Books, 1989.

Rothman, Adam. *Slave Country: American Expansion and the Origins of the Deep South.* Cambridge: Harvard University Press, 2005.

Rothman, Joshua D. *Notorious in the Neighborhood: Sex and Families Across the Color Line in Virginia, 1787–1861.* Chapel Hill: University of North Carolina Press, 2003.

Ruíz, Ramón Eduardo. *The Great Rebellion: Mexico, 1905–1924.* New York: W. W. Norton, 1982.

Saade Granados, Marta María. "Una raza prohibida: Afroestadounidenses en México." In *Nación y extranjería: La exclusion racial en las políticas migratorias de Argentina, Brasil, Cuba y México*, edited by Pablo Yankelvich. Mexico: Universidad Nacional Autónoma de México, 2009.

Sacks, Marcy S. *Before Harlem: The Black Experience in New York City Before World War I.* Philadelphia: University of Pennsylvania Press, 2006.

Salazar Anaya, Delia, ed. "Extraños en la ciudad: Un acercamiento a la inmigración internacional a la Ciudad de México, en los censos de 1890, 1895, 1900 y 1910." In *Imágenes de los imigrantes en la ciudad de México, 1753–1910*, edited by Delia Salazar (México: Instituto Nacional de Antropologia e Historia, 2002).

Salvucci, Richard J. "The Origins and Progress of U.S.-Mexican Trade, 1825–1884: 'Hoc Opus, Hic Labor Est.'" *Hispanic American Historical Review* 71, no. 4 (November 1991): 697–735.

Sanchez-Guillermo, Evelyne. "Nacionalismo y racismo en el México decimonónico: Nuevos enfoques, nuevos resultados." *Nuevo Mundo/Mundos Nuevos* (2007).

Sandweiss, Martha. *Passing Strange: A Gilded Age Tale of Love and Deception Across the Color Line.* New York: Penguin Press, 2009.

Schachner, August. "Midwinter Travels in Mexico." *Mid-Continent Magazine* 4, no. 2 (June 1895): 99–114.

Schell, William, Jr. "American Investment in Tropical Mexico: Rubber Plantations, Fraud, and Dollar Diplomacy, 1897–1913." *Business History Review* 64, no. 2 (Summer 1990): 217–54.

———. *Integral Outsiders: The American Colony in Mexico City, 1876–1911.* Wilmington, DE: Scholarly Resources, 2001.

Schoonover, Thomas David. *Dollars over Dominion: The Triumph of Liberalism in Mexican–United States Relations, 1861–1867.* Baton Rouge: Louisiana State University Press, 1978.

———. "Misconstrued Mission: Expansionism and Black Colonization in

Mexico and Central America During the Civil War." *Pacific Historical Review* 49, no. 4 (November 1980): 607–620.

Schoultz, Lars. *Beneath the United States: A History of U.S. Policy Toward Latin America.* Cambridge: Harvard University Press, 1998.

Schwartz, Rosalie. *Across the Rio to Freedom: U.S. Negroes in Mexico.* El Paso: Texas Western Press, 1975.

Scott, James C. *Weapons of the Weak: Everyday Forms of Peasant Resistance.* New Haven: Yale University Press, 1987.

Scott, Rebecca J., and Jean M. Hébard. *Freedom Papers: An Atlantic Odyssey in the Age of Emancipation.* Cambridge: Harvard University Press, 2012.

Scott, William. "The Ethiopian Ethos in African American Thought." *International Journal of Ethiopian Studies* 1, no. 2 (2004): 40–57.

Shankman, Arnold. *Ambivalent Friends: Afro-Americans View the Immigrant.* Westport, CT: Greenwood Press, 1982.

Shapiro, Herbert. *White Violence and Black Response: From Reconstruction to Montgomery.* Amherst: University of Massachusetts Press, 1988.

Sharfstein, Daniel J. *The Invisible Line: Three American Families and the Secret Journey from Black to White.* New York: Penguin Press, 2011.

Sheridan, Philip. *Personal Memoirs.* Vol. 2. New York: D. Appleton, 1902.

Sherwood, Marika. "Pan-African Conferences, 1900–1953: What Did 'Pan-Africanism' Mean?" *Journal of Pan African Studies* 4, no. 10 (January 2012): 106–126.

Shook, Robert W. *Caminos y Entradas: Spanish Legacy of Victoria County and the Coastal Bend, 1689–1890.* Victoria, TX: Victoria County Heritage Department, 2007.

Shook, Robert W., and Charles D. Spurlin. *Victoria: A Pictorial History.* Norfolk, VA: Donning, 1985.

Silverthorne, Elizabeth. *Plantation Life in Texas.* College Station: Texas A&M University Press, 1986.

Sim, Jillian A. "Fading to White." *American Heritage* 50, no. 1 (February/March 1999).

Skinner, Robert P. *The 1903 Skinner Mission to Ethiopia and a Century of American-Ethiopian Relations.* Hollywood, CA: Tsehai Publishers, 2003 [1906].

"Slavery Extension." *DeBow's Review* 15, no. 1 (July 1853): 1–14.

Smallwood, James M. *The Feud That Wasn't: The Taylor Ring, Bill Sutton, John Wesley Hardin, and Violence in Texas.* College Station: Texas A&M University Press, 2008.

———. *Time of Hope, Time of Despair: Black Texans During Reconstruction.* Port Washington, NY: Kennikat Press, 1981.

Smith, Ayana. "Blues, Criticism, and the Signifying Trickster." *Popular Music* 24, no. 2 (May 2005): 179–191.

Smith, Charles Spencer. *A History of the African Methodist Episcopal Church.* New York: Johnson Reprint, 1968 [1922].

Sollors, Werner. *Neither Black nor White yet Both: Thematic Explorations of Interracial Literature*. Cambridge: Harvard University Press, 1997.

Sotiropoulos, Karen. *Staging Race: Black Performers in Turn of the Century America*. Cambridge: Harvard University Press, 2006.

Spruill, Larry H. *Mount Vernon*. Charlestown, SC: Arcadia Publishing, 2009.

Spurlin, Charles D. "The World Turned Upside Down? The Military Occupation of Victoria and Calhoun Counties, 1865–1867." In *Still the Arena of Civil War: Violence and Turmoil in Reconstruction Texas, 1865–1874*, edited by Kenneth W. Howell. Denton: University of North Texas Press, 2012.

Stapf, Otto. "A New Rubber Tree: Palo Amarillo." *Bulletin of Miscellaneous Information (Royal Botanic Gardens, Kew)* 1907, no. 7 (1907): 294–296.

Steele, Bessie H. "A Visit to a Mexican Cotton Plantation." *American Journal of Nursing* 3, no. 12 (September 1903): 922–927.

Stern, Alexandra Minna. *Eugenic Nation: Faults and Frontiers of Better Breeding in Modern America*. Berkeley: University of California Press, 2005.

St. John, Rachel. *Line in the Sand: A History of the Western U.S.-Mexico Border*. Princeton: Princeton University Press, 2011.

Stout, Joseph A., Jr. *Schemers and Dreamers: Filibustering in Mexico, 1848–1921*. Fort Worth: Texas Christian University Press, 2002.

"The Strange Death of H. Kent Loomis." *American Carpet and Upholstery Journal* 22, no. 8 (August 1904): 85.

Sumler-Edmond, Janice L. "Lola and Leon Houck Versus the Southern Pacific Railway Company." In *African Americans in South Texas History*, edited by Bruce A. Glasrud. College Station: Texas A&M University Press, 2011.

Tafolla, Santiago. *A Life Crossing Borders: Memoir of a Mexican-American Confederate*, translated by Fidel L. Tafolla. Houston: Arte Público, 2010.

Taylor, Alan. *The Internal Enemy: Slavery and War in Virginia, 1772–1832*. New York: W. W. Norton, 2013.

Taylor, Quintard. *In Search of the Racial Frontier: African Americans in the American West, 1528–1990*. New York: W. W. Norton, 1998.

Taylor, Yuval, and Jake Austen. *Darkest America: Black Minstrelsy from Slavery to Hip-Hop*. New York: W. W. Norton, 2012.

Telles, Edward. *Pigmentocracies: Ethnicity, Race, and Color in Latin America*. Chapel Hill: University of North Carolina Press, 2014.

Tenorio-Trillo, Mauricio. *Mexico at the World's Fairs: Crafting a Modern Nation*. Berkeley: University of California Press, 1996.

———. "1910 Mexico City: Space and Nation in the City of the Centenario." *Journal of Latin American Studies* 28, no. 1 (February 1996): 82–85.

Terry, T. Philip. *Terry's Guide to Mexico*. Boston: Houghton Mifflin, 1922.

Thompson, Jerry. *Cortina: Defending the Mexican Name in Texas*. College Station: Texas A&M University Press, 2007.

Train, Arthur. *Courts and Criminals*. New York: Charles Scribner's Sons, 1912.

Travelers' Official Guide of the Railway and Steam Navigation Lines in the United States, Canada and Mexico. New York: National Railway Publication Company, 1897.

Truett, Samuel. *Fugitive Landscapes: The Forgotten History of the U.S.-Mexico Borderlands*. New Haven: Yale University Press, 2006.

Tucker, Phillip Thomas. *The Final Fury: Palmito Ranch, the Last Battle of the Civil War*. Mechanicsburg, PA: Stackpole Books, 2001.

Turner, Henry McNeal. "The American Negro and the Fatherland." In *Africa and the American Negro: Addresses and Proceedings of the Congress on Africa Held Under the Auspices of the Stewart Missionary Foundation for Africa of Gammon Theological Seminary in Connection with the Cotton States and International Exposition, December 13–15, 1895*, edited by J. W. E. Bowen. Atlanta: Gammon Theological Seminary, 1896.

———. *Civil Rights: The Outrage of the Supreme Court of the United States upon the Black Man*. Philadelphia: AME Church, 1889.

———. *A Speech on the Present Duties and Future Destiny of the Negro Race*. N.p.: Published by the Lyceum, 1872.

Twentieth-Century Successful Americans: Local and National. N.p.: United Press Service Bureau, 1917(?).

Tyler, Ronnie C. "Cotton on the Border, 1861–1865." *Southwestern Historical Quarterly* 73, no. 4 (April 1970): 456–477.

———. "Fugitive Slaves in Mexico." *Journal of Negro History* 57 (January 1972): 1–12.

Tyndale, Troilus Hilgard. *Don Cosme: A Romance of the South*. New York: G. W. Dillingham, 1899.

Unterman, Katherine. "Boodle over the Border: Embezzlement and the Crisis of International Mobility, 1880–1890." *Journal of the Gilded Age and Progressive Era* 11, no. 2 (April 2012): 151–189.

Valdés, Carlos Manuel, and Ildefonso Dávila. *Esclavos negros en Saltillo, siglos XVII–XIX*. Saltillo: Universidad Autónoma de Coahuila, 1989.

Valdés, Dennis N. "The Decline of Slavery in Mexico." *Americas* 44, no. 2 (October 1987): 167–194.

Valentine, Lincoln G. *The Case of Costa Rica*. New York: M. B. Brown, 1919.

Van Young, Eric. *The Other Rebellion: Popular Violence, Ideology, and the Mexican Struggle for Independence, 1810–1821*. Stanford: Stanford University Press, 2001.

Vasconcelos, José. *The Cosmic Race/La raza cósmica*. Translated by Didier T. Jaén. Baltimore: Johns Hopkins University Press, 1997 [1925].

Vinson, Ben, III. "Fading from Memory: Historiographical Reflections on the Afro-Mexican Presence." *Review of Black Political Economy* 33, no. 1 (Summer 2005): 59–72.

Vivian, Herbert. *Abyssinia: Through the Lion-Land to the Court of the Lion of Judah*. New York: Negro Universities Press, 1969 [1901].

Volanto, Keith J. "James E. Youngblood: Race, Family, and Farm Ownership in Jim Crow Texas." In *Beyond Forty Acres and a Mule: African American Landowning Families Since Reconstruction*, edited by Debra A. Reid and Evan P. Bennett. Gainesville: University Press of Florida, 2012.

Vorenberg, Michael. "Abraham Lincoln and the Politics of Black Colonization." *Journal of the Abraham Lincoln Association* 14, no. 2 (Summer 1993): 22–45.

Wahlstrom, Todd W. *The Southern Exodus to Mexico: Migration Across the Borderlands After the American Civil War.* Lincoln: University of Nebraska Press, 2015.

Wallace, Ernest, ed. *Documents of Texas History*. Austin: Steck, 1963.

Walsh, Casey. *Building the Borderlands: A Transnational History of Irrigated Cotton Along the Mexico-Texas Border*. College Station: Texas A&M University Press, 2008.

Warner, Rose Ella, and C. Earle Smith, Jr. "Boll Weevil Found in Pre-Columbian Cotton from Mexico." *Science* 162 (November 1968): 911–912.

Waters, Alexander. *My Life and Work*. New York: Fleming H. Revell, 1917.

Waters, Andrew, ed. *I Was Born in Slavery: Personal Accounts of Slavery in Texas*. Winston-Salem, NC: John F. Blair, 2003.

Watkins, John Elfreth. *Famous Mysteries: Curious and Fantastic Riddles of Human Life That Have Never Been Solved*. Philadelphia: John C. Winston, 1919.

Webster, Michael G. "Intrigue on the Rio Grande: The Rio Bravo Affair, 1875." *Southwestern Historical Quarterly* 74, no. 2 (October 1970): 149–164.

Weisiger, Benjamin Boisseau, III. *The Weisiger Family: An Account of Daniel Weisiger, the Immigrant, of Henrico and Chesterfield Counties, Virginia, and His Descendants*. Richmond, VA: B. B. Weisiger, 1984.

Welke, Barbara Young. *Recasting American Liberty: Gender, Race, Law, and the Railroad Revolution, 1865–1920*. New York: Cambridge University Press, 2001.

Wellby, M. S. *Twixt Sirdar and Menelik: An Account of a Year's Expedition from Zeila to Cairo Through Unknown Abyssinia*. New York: Negro Universities Press, 1969 [1901].

Wells, David Ames. *The Year-Book of Agriculture; or, The Annual of Agricultural Progress and Discovery for 1855 and 1856*. Philadelphia: Childs and Peterson, 1856.

Wheeler, B. Gordon. *Black California: The History of African-Americans in the Golden State*. New York: Hippocrene Books, 1993.

"Where Cotton Is King." *Modern Mexico* 17, no. 1 (1904): 37.

White, Richard. *Railroaded: The Transcontinentals and the Making of Modern America*. New York: W. W. Norton, 2011.

White, Walter. *A Man Called White: The Autobiography of Walter White*. New York: Viking Press, 1948.

———. "The Paradox of Color." In *The New Negro: An Interpretation*, edited by Alain Locke. New York: Albert and Charles Boni, 1925.

White, William L. *Lost Boundaries*. New York: Harcourt, Brace, 1947.

"Who Would Be King." *Time* 2, no. 6 (October 8, 1923): 4.

"William H. Ellis." *Successful American* 2, no. 2 (August 1900): 62.

Williams, Docia Schultz. *The History and Mystery of the Menger Hotel*. Plano, TX: Republic of Texas Press, 2000.

Wilt, David E. *The Mexican Filmography, 1916 Through 2001*. Jefferson, NC: McFarland, 2004.

Womack, John, Jr. *Zapata and the Mexican Revolution*. New York: Vintage Books, 1968.

Wooster, Robert. "The Army and the Politics of Expansion: Texas and the Southwestern Borderlands, 1870–1886." *Southwestern Historical Quarterly* 93, no. 2 (1989): 151–167.

Work, David. "United States Colored Troops in Texas During Reconstruction, 1865–1867." *Southwestern Historical Quarterly* 109, no. 3 (January 2006): 337–358.

Wright, Marie Robinson. *Picturesque Mexico*. Philadelphia: J. B. Lippincott, 1897.

Young, Elliott. *Catarino Garza's Revolution on the Texas-Mexico Border*. Durham: Duke University Press, 2004.

Young, Kevin. *The Grey Album: On the Blackness of Blackness*. Minneapolis: Grey Wolf Press, 2012.

Zecker, Robert M. *Race and America's Immigrant Press: How the Slovaks Were Taught to Think like White People*. New York: Bloomsbury, 2011.

Zewde, Bahru. *A History of Modern Ethiopia, 1855–1974*. London: James Currey, 1991.

Zimmerman, Andrew. *Alabama in Africa: Booker T. Washington, the German Empire, and the Globalization of the New South*. Princeton: Princeton University Press, 2010.

UNPUBLISHED MATERIALS

Baldridge, Donald Carl. "Mexican Petroleum and United States–Mexican Relations, 1919–1923." University of Arizona, 1971. Ph.D. dissertation.

Castañón Cuadros, Carlos Javier. "Breve historia de la Compañía." Manuscript.

Castro, Justin. "Modesto C. Rolland, the Mexican Revolution, and Development of the Isthmus of Tehuantepec." Manuscript.

England, Shawn Lewis. "The Curse of Huitzilopochtli: The Origins, Process, and Legacy of Mexico's Military Reforms, 1920–1946." Arizona State University, 2008. Ph.D. dissertation.

Ramos, Marisela Jiménez. "Black Mexico: Nineteenth-Century Discourses of Race and Nation." Brown University, 2009. Ph.D. dissertation.

Smith, Sharon H. "Victoria County, Texas, 1824–1870." Southwest Texas State University, 1998. Master's thesis.

ILLUSTRATION CREDITS

Abandoned sharecropper shack: Author photo
Ellis ad in San Antonio Directory: Courtesy of Ancestry.com
San Antonio's military plaza in the 1890s: DeGolyer Library, Southern
    Methodist University, Dallas, Texas: Photographs, Manuscripts, and
    Imprints
Norris Wright Cuney: Negative #068-0939, General Photograph Collection,
    UTSA Special Collections—Institute of Texan Cultures, University of
    Texas at San Antonio
Henry McNeal Turner: Manuscripts, Archives and Rare Books Division,
    Schomburg Center for Research in Black Culture, the New York Public
    Library, Astor, Lenox and Tilden Foundations
Hotel Gillow: Author's collection
Tlahualilo hacienda: Author's collection
Mexican overseers: Author's collection
Former colonists from Tlahualilo: Author's collection
Ellis as Guillermo Enrique Eliseo: Courtesy of Fanny Johnson-Griffin
Drawing of Ellis from the 1901 New York World: Library of Congress
Maude Sherwood: Courtesy of Peter Ellis
Ellis's Wall Street office: Courtesy of Fanny Johnson-Griffin
Emperor Menelik II and his court: Image from Robert Peet Skinner's Scrapbook,
    1903, Gift of Mrs. Horatio Wales, Massillon Museum, Massillon, Ohio
Charles Starnes: Courtesy of Fanny Johnson-Griffin
Ellis in Mexico City with his father and sons: Courtesy of Fanny Johnson-Griffin
Maude and children in Mount Vernon: Courtesy of Fanny Johnson-Griffin
Victoria Ellis in Irma la mala: Agrasánchez Film Archive

INDEX

Note: Page numbers beyond 210 refer to notes.